Six
Silent
Killers

Management's
Greatest Challenge

Six Silent Killers

Management's Greatest Challenge

James R. Fisher, Jr., Ph.D.

S^t_L

St. Lucie Press
Boca Raton, Florida

Library of Congress Cataloging-in-Publication Data

Catalog information may be obtained from the Library of Congress

This book contains information obtained from authentic and highly regarded sources. Reprinted material is quoted with permission, and sources are indicated. A wide variety of references are listed. Reasonable efforts have been made to publish reliable data and information, but the author and the publisher cannot assume responsibility for the validity of all materials or for the consequences of their use.

Neither this book nor any part may be reproduced or transmitted in any form or by any means, electronic or mechanical, including photocopying, microfilming, and recording, or by any information storage or retrieval system, without prior permission in writing from the publisher.

The consent of CRC Press LLC does not extend to copying for general distribution, for promotion, for creating new works, or for resale. Specific permission must be obtained in writing from CRC Press LLC for such copying.

Direct all inquiries to CRC Press LLC, 2000 Corporate Blvd., N.W., Boca Raton, Florida 33431.

No claim to original U.S. Government works
International Standard Book Number 1-57444-152-3
Printed in the United States of America 1 2 3 4 5 6 7 8 9 0
Printed on acid-free paper

For my wife, Betty, always,
and for Jorge Fernandez

Table of Contents

Foreword

Today's workplace is experiencing change at a breathtaking pace. Before our eyes, opportunities are growing exponentially. What's less obvious is that the road ahead is booby-trapped. If we're going to move forward, the biggest change of all will have to be in the maps we draw for ourselves—in how our culture chooses to define value and contribution.

In my 40 years of work experience, I've held jobs in every type of organization and came away with viscerally etched memories of the trials and tribulations of trendy management. I've had countless front-line adventures amid the rants and ravings of management gurus, from classical management theory to the new age. I've heard the old songs of company loyalty, have sung a few of my own, and have listened to incantations about soul from people who champion "value added" gratuitously, until you ask them what it means. Even guru Michael Hammer, whose *Re-Engineering the Corporation* is credited with starting an avalanche of corporate layoffs, is not exempt from rethinking his position. In the aftermath of his book's success, Hammer (sometimes called the father of downsizing) reportedly suggested he wasn't smart enough in his advice about the people equation, that his book overreflected his engineering background. Great. Imagine an engineer suffering the overinfluence of his discipline. The people who constitute the human equation are the ones who felt the brunt of it.

Scott Adams' cartoon character Dilbert reminds us daily of the importance of the human equation, but corporations continue handing out pink slips, even when doing so cuts into the muscle of their organizations. They don't know what else to do to positively affect their quarter's profits, even when the knowledge in the heads of workers is their most valuable asset. Because the bottom line and the human equation have never been parallel considerations, the results now seem out of kilter.

One thing is certain: the time for well-intentioned fads is over. And a short-term-profit mentality at the expense of longer term strategies for survival is assurance that a business will not endure. We have one foot on the front step of a global marketplace which promises more change in the next decade than we have experienced in the past half century in terms of how we earn our living. Our other foot is tiptoeing reluctantly toward the new millennium—a time of exaggerated flux which exacerbates human anxiety by design, an era when pessimists pronounce the end of everything and optimists the reverse. In times like these, organizations and political groups attempt to leverage insecurity by scapegoating easy targets. Such times call not for gurus, but for people who see clearly. We need keen observers like James R. Fisher, Jr.

In a style reminiscent of Ralph Waldo Emerson, Fisher's vibrant prose packs more purpose into a paragraph than most writers achieve in a whole chapter. Emerson was the architect who laid the groundwork for the contemporary thesis "what goes around comes around." In his essay titled "Compensation," he said, "Every excess causes a defect; every defect an excess...For every grain of wit there is a grain of folly...Every advantage has its tax." In similar fashion, Fisher shows how every action taken in the modern business world has consequences, both good and bad. He portrays today's organizational reality with striking precision and clarity. It's a reality you will recognize immediately if you have a long work record, and one you dare not ignore if you lack experience.

James Fisher shares with self-taught social critic Eric Hoffer a talent for making provocative observations that burst the bubbles of popular opinion. The silent killers he writes about here represent the residue of an obsolete job culture. They harken back to a mechanical era that served its purpose well, but one which Fisher makes obvious cannot be sustained. The velocity of change we are experiencing renders current knowledge increasingly obsolete exactly at a time when we are witnessing the unraveling of the expert. The lock on knowledge customarily held by institutions and "experts" is giving way to individual initiative. What you know is rapidly becoming more important than who you know.

My own prescription is to think of an education not as something you get but something you take. Fisher asserts that all real education is self-education, that disaster awaits those who leave it to others to define value. Those who hope to latch their "destiny to another's rainbow" will find nothing solid to grasp and a total absence of reward at the end.

In *Six Silent Killers: Management's Greatest Challenge*, James R. Fisher, Jr. offers compelling insights into how we can move from a culture of comfort and complacency to a culture of contribution. This is not a simple task. There are no easy exits or off ramps. The road to genuine contribution is steep, crooked, pot-holed and sometimes full of land mines. Visibility is obscured; the greatest danger might occur when the road appears smooth and straight. It's a sign of the times that no one can mark your map for you, whether you are a CEO, a middle manager, or a line worker. But James R. Fisher, Jr. is a guide whose acute observations from the trenches of international corporate life offer a kind of wisdom seldom found in books about management. If you pay the price of attention, he will help you chart your own path to the future.

Charles D. Hayes
Author of *Proving You're Qualified,*
Beyond the American Dream (in press)

Preface

> The microchip has extended the reach of the human brain the way machines, beginning nearly two centuries ago, extended the reach of human muscle.
>
> Steve Forbes
> *Foreign Affairs* (July/August 1996)

Over the past 30 years, my laboratory has been the workplace. Here, I have witnessed everything changing and nothing changing. What we call work has changed. The majority of people we call workers have changed. Steve Forbes writes sagely when he traces this change to the microchip. Knowledge has replaced brute force, finesse, naked energy. Yet what we call the workplace remains essentially an anachronism—a formal, regulated, highly controlled environment where the few dominate the many. Stated otherwise, the workplace culture has changed little in my three decades of work, while there has been more technological change in that period than in the previous 300 years.

My first exposure to the industrial workplace was as a student laborer for five summers in a chemical plant while attending university. I did everything from unloading raw materials to stocking 100-pound bags of finished product in railroad box cars. Upon graduation, I first became a bench chemist in a food processing plant, working in research and development, then on to a chemical sales engineering career with a specialty chemical company, and up the executive ladder of line management to an international corporate executive. The range of my career put me in touch with workers from the shop floor and mail room to board rooms across four continents.

Then in 1968, in my thirties, I chose to take a time out from the rat race to assess my life. My assignment in South Africa was coming to a close at a time when the world seemed to be coming apart at the seams. In America, Martin Luther King was assassinated, with riots breaking out in 126 cities. Columbia University's administrative buildings were occupied by students protesting the Vietnam War. Robert Kennedy was assassinated. Nearly 550,000 troops were in Vietnam, only to be rendered impotent by the Viet Cong Tet Offensive. At the Olympic Games in Mexico City, African American medalists raised black-gloved fists defiantly above their heads as the National Anthem played, while riots broke out at the Democratic Convention in Chicago.

Elsewhere, Soviet troops and tanks invaded Czechoslovakia, Prague was fermenting, Warsaw students were rioting, 300 Mexican students were massacred by the police and Mexican army, half of the universities in Italy were occupied by hostile students, and violence had broken out in the streets of West Berlin. In Johannesburg, one of our servants was murdered on my estate—he was handled by the police as though he were a dog. My disenchantment was further advanced by having to travel to meaningless meetings back to the states and to London at the expense of my work in South Africa.

Much later it would occur to me why I left the corporation so young. Work was killing my spirit, destroying my creativity. More to the point, I was allowing what was called work to do a number on me. I was earning a good living—several times what my laboring father had earned—but with little satisfaction. Moreover, I was in a cage of my own making with a wife and four small children to support. Somehow this failed to hold my feet to the fire. I became a dropout, a novel idea in 1968.

Once separated from the corporation, I retired to the west coast of Florida to read, think, and write. Two years later, when I was broke, I went back to the university for four years as a full-time student, consulting on the side to support my family. My practical desire was to become credentialed, while my passion was to acquire some tools to better understand my life. The deck, I decided, was stacked against me, not by some mysterious sinister force, but by the benevolence of my benign cultural conditioning. I was programmed to be passively responsive to my life, not to be the active creator of its form and substance. In my idealism, I expected the university to free me from that triviality and to create a climate for all-embracing intellectual expression. Instead, I found that the same factory mentality existed there as elsewhere. The university was an assembly line producing a product, *programmed education.*

Most professors didn't teach while most students seemed disinclined to learn. Professors had discovered a way to avoid confrontation with the real world, while students sought to gain credentials as quickly and painlessly as possible. Thus, I found *non-teaching teachers* were complemented by *non-learning student.* Even so, professors complained that publish or perish was their scourge and prevented them from being student-centered. Students protested the cruel and inhuman demands of professors who required them to read more than ten pages of text or to complete a research paper of more than 500 words between class periods. Authentic teaching and genuine learning were preempted by *crucial contact* hours for professors and by the gradepoint for students, both wuantitative, not qualitative stsandards.

Alas, I discovered it wasn't only the workplace *with such a restrictive agenda,* but the classroom as well. Society, I decided, expected to play *dominant parent* to my *submissive child.* This gave me pause. The more I thought about it, the more convinced I became that I was programmed to simulate a microchip, a thing. Students were as averse to challenging their unproductive curriculum as were workers their inept work schedules. The best way to get along was to go along.

After earning my Ph.D., consulting, which I had been doing part-time, was now my next venture. *Consulting!* There is a word which describes our times! Consultants strive to make *non-thinking thinking* and *non-work work.* They aspire to fill the vacuum left by a society bent on form at the expense of substance. Consultants seek to sell a proactive strategy to a reactive client. Little if any attempt is made to disengage the client from its predominantly passive orientation. Not surprising, most consultants prefer to see their role as the quick fix embellisher, not the pesky disturber of the status quo. This reduces most interventions to "smoke and mirrors," which provoke little change, however arcane or entertaining. It was for this reason that I re-entered the corporation, not in a line capacity as I had in the past, but as a staff person. I wanted to see if I could make a difference.

The year was 1980. I had been consulting for ten years and now joined the human resources department of a high-tech (NASA and a defense contractor) company. This was at the peak of the touchy-feely human growth movement, where the delicate psyches of employees were being massaged with high priest solemnity. The high-tech workplace was perfect for this set of circumstances. It formed a cozy liaison with sensitivity gurus and quick fix social engineers. Money was no problem, as President Reagan's supply-side economics poured billions of high-tech dollars into Star Wars, NASA space programs, and defense spending, exceeding the military budget of World War II by several billion dollars. Optimism, not patience, combined with paranoia to rule the day.

American industry and commerce were waking up to the economic reality of Japan, Europe, and the Pacific Rim countries. The essentially reactive mode of industry was now displayed in panic and crisis management. In this atmosphere, fads grew to epic proportions, while tactics were celebrated as strategies. Everything was done to and for workers to make them more productive without understanding them or bringing them on board. Seldom, if ever, were workers involved in the creation of workplace improvement designs. More importantly, little note was taken that workers had changed the color of their collars from essentially blue to predominantly white.

Once back in the corporation, I used the workplace as a laboratory. I started by taking an inventory of the meetings, reports, presentations, performance criteria, job requirements, and impact of my work on my function as an organizational development psychologist. It was nil. I concluded that most of my work amounted to *non-doing doing of non-thing things*, which were defined as work. I looked around and saw my colleagues were similarly employed. Why? Because that is the way it had always been done before. Most of the training I was required to complete was generic. Seldom did it challenge me to think differently or improve my skills and performance. It made me more complacent and my existence more inert. Yet training was essential to fill the boxes to be eligible for promotion. Consequently, nobody objected, nor were they inclined to ask for more appropriate skill-building.

Granted, none of this would register as disturbing were the rate of productivity against the Gross Domestic Product what it had been in the past or from the Civil War until 1973. During the past 20 years, this rate has wavered around 2.3 percent versus 3.4 percent for the previous 100 years. This amounts to a loss in the production of goods and services of $12 trillion, or a personal loss to every man, woman, and child (over that 20-year period) of nearly $50,000 in income, enough for a down payment on a home or a college education. Jeffrey Madrick writes in *The End of Affluence* (1995), "if this trend continues during the next 20 years, each American will lose $75,000 over that period, and the loss to the nation in production will be $25 trillion." He argues that if we had sustained the previous rate of productivity (3.4 percent) until the present, the debate over the national debt, welfare benefits, and national healthcare coverage would all be academic.

My hypothesis: We don't know how to manage, motivate, or mobilize our brilliant workforce. Perhaps this is because we haven't taken the time to understand our workers, nor, indeed, ourselves in this new world of work. In frustration, we attempt to impose an anachronistic workplace culture. This spawns and proliferates *six silent killers*, which are destroying our will not only to survive, but to prevail. These silent killers are social termites, which burrow into the inner recesses of our workplace infrastructure. They are essentially unconscious and, therefore, passive responses to a spirit-killing culture. This is management's greatest challenge, not only in the United States, but in every advanced society. The answers are unlikely to come from breakthrough paradigms, but rather through the willingness of management to be learners, not knowers, in the conduct of work and to recognize that change comes in dribbles, one person at a time, and requires overcoming the enormous psychological inertia of our reactive cultural programming.

Acknowledgments

Novelist George V. Higgins in his book *On Writing* (1990) has a simple formula to help people decide if they can write, and after writing, publish. If there's a lot of writing in your files, "then the chances are you have the talent to write more. If you haven't written anything, you do not have the talent because you don't want to write." Higgins has published more than a dozen novels but spent many years in partial or full obscurity. I know the feeling. I have been writing since I was eight years old, and you might say, this being my sixth book, I still exist in partial obscurity, albeit I've written more than a million words, most of them unpublished, and some 200 articles. Reading this book, I sense you will feel my passion, my concern, and my belief in our ability to cope with a changing world and to go forward.

In 1990, I left the corporate world to devote my full time to writing. It has been a difficult but rewarding experience. Struggle, as I address in this book, is an essential ingredient to growth. I thank God for giving me the health and energy to persevere. I thank my wife, Betty, for her love and support and for editing this book several times, along with doing all the illustrations, charts, and schematics. But most of all, I thank her for loving a man whose mistress is the printed word. I would also like to thank Jorge Fernandez, my agent and publicist, who compensates for my preference for sanctuary—that is, he bangs on literary doors until somebody answers and through that effort introduces my writing to you. An uncommon appreciation goes to Carrie Livingston. Carrie read this work in its original form, then with wit and sage design, made it more reader-friendly. Neither of us knew, at the time, that it would one day be this book. A special thanks goes to the state of Iowa, where I was born and reared, for providing me with a nourishing climate for growing up, along with a solid, fundamental education at St. Patrick's Grammar School, Clinton High School, and the University of Iowa. I come from working-class parents—my father was an Irish Roman Catholic brakeman on the Chicago & NorthWestern Railroad, my mother a homemaker of inestimable persuasion—who gave me room to find my own way and an Irish home where mirth, storytelling, mischief, and religion were a concoction only God could appreciate. I would also like to thank Dennis McClellan and St. Lucie Press for giving me this opportunity to address a larger audience. Finally, I would like to thank my late mother and father, who gave me the self-sustaining values of industry, perseverance, commitment, belief in myself, and a passion for ideas and enlightenment.

James R. Fisher, Jr.
Tampa, Florida

About the Author

Dr. Fisher's view of the plight of the complex organization, its management, and the professional worker is based on an exceptionally diverse background of over more than three decades of working and living on four continents at all levels of organization, from blue-collar laborer to the board rooms of America's *Fortune* 500 companies. While attending the University of Iowa, he worked as a laborer for five summers at the Clinton Corn Processing Company, Division of Standard Brands, Inc., Clinton, Iowa; subsequently, after graduating, he worked in this company as a chemist in research and technical service. This was followed by working as a chemical sales engineer, field manager, and corporate executive for Nalco Chemical Company. His work with Nalco found him working throughout the continental United States, South America, Europe, and South Africa. In South Africa, he facilitated the formation of a new chemical entity. Still in his early thirties, he retired to the west coast of Florida to read, write, and think, consulting on the side to support his wife and four children, forming Psyche-ology, Inc., an organizational development company. Prentice-Hall published his first book, *Confident Selling* (1971), during this period. At the same time, he went back to school, full time, consulting on the side, to earn his M.A. in social psychology at the University of South Florida and a Ph.D. in social and organizational psychology at Walden University. This was followed by a ten-year stint with Honeywell, Inc., first as an organizational development psychologist, then as Director of Human Resources, Planning & Development for Honeywell Europe, Ltd., living and working in Brussels, Belgium. Dr. Fisher left Honeywell in 1990 and has since devoted his full time to writing and consulting. He now lives with his wife, Betty, in Tampa, Florida. This is his sixth book and first book with St. Lucie Press. Other books by the author include *Work Without Managers: A View from the Trenches* (1991), *Confident Selling for the 90s* (1992), *The Worker, Alone! Going Against the Grain* (1995), and *The Taboo Against Being Your Own Best Friend* (1996).

Introduction

Give up the feeling of responsibility, let go your hold, resign the care of your destiny to higher powers, be genuinely indifferent as to what becomes of it all, and you will find that you gain a perfect inward relief, but often also, in addition, the particular goods you sincerely thought you were renouncing.[1]

William James

This book is about the *new workforce* that the post-industrial society has created. This workforce is brilliant, gifted, well educated, and also greatly frustrated by its inability to make meaningful connection with its *work* because of an inappropriate *workplace culture*. It is also about management, which appears willing but unable to manage, motivate, and mobilize this workforce to sustained productivity. It now seems apparent that the key to economic revitalization resides in these workers. Regrettably, management has been unable to inspire them to sustained productive effort mainly because it has treated these professionals as workers in the past. This fresh, intelligent, decision-making talent has been essentially force-fitted into a management system designed for an industrial society, where smokestacks, not microchips, were the symbols of productive work. This book is written for these modern professional workers, who seem to have little sense of their *real* power or their ability to enact change. It is also written for management, which desperately wants to know what workers are thinking and feeling about work, management, their company, and themselves.

Since World War II, the world has exploded with this totally new class of workers, generated by more technological change in that period than the previous 300 years. Five transformations have reshaped the working world:

(1) Up until 1973, the blue-collar worker represented more than 60 percent of all workers. As we approach the end of the century, these workers constitute little more than 10 percent of all workers.[2]

1

(2) The majority (80 percent) of all workers are minorities and women, with the white male now in the minority (20 percent).[3]

(3) Mind and spirit have become the cutting edge over the machine and matter. The ability to think and the passion to grow have far more impact on economic outcomes than the willingness to take orders and to drift toward retirement.

(4) Symbolic interaction lies at the core of all positive performance, while hard work, as we know it, is mainly irrelevant.

(5) The symbolic economy now drives the real economy, driven by the flow of information and capital. The industrial economy is anachronistic and has become uncoupled from production, while trade has become uncoupled from capital movement.[4]

On balance, nothing is as it was half a century ago, yet the conduct of business stubbornly holds to that tradition. Meanwhile, American workers have watched traditional support systems disappear. They can no longer count on the company, nor can the government ensure their safety and security. Nothing is certain anymore, and rumors carry the day. This is a chilling ordeal for a workforce heretofore protected from the reality of the working world. Now the world is a global village, and global competition shrinks economic advantage. Once all American workers had to do was show up for work, do what they were told, abide by the rules, and their standard of living became progressively better over time. Now, they must take charge of their lives and expect no institutional guarantees, or they could literally lose the clothes on their backs.

Wake-Up Call to a New Day

What is happening in the workplace is currently confusing to workers and managers alike. They all know that the workplace is not working as it should, but they are hard-pressed to know what would be better. The new professional worker is being asked to take more command of his work without knowing clearly how that should be accomplished. The result is that his performance lags appreciably behind that of his blue-collar brother. In sheer numbers, the professional class—those workers who invest years in formal education to acquire specific skills and abilities—is quickly becoming the dominant group in American society. What's more, their numbers have been growing in Europe, Japan, and the Pacific Rim countries for some time and are now starting to increase in South America and Africa as well. The legitimacy to their influence is founded in knowledge, not in connections or in pluck and luck. Yet professional workers remain apprehensive as to their identity and tentative as to their role. This is not helped by the fact that they are selected, trained, measured, and rewarded as though they were no different from blue-collar workers. They are different and respond to a different set of stimuli. This is not meant as a put-down to blue-collar workers but to underscore the palpable difference that exists. Blue-collar workers are themselves no longer responding to traditional stimuli as they have in the past. They, too, are becoming professional. [5]

Professional workers have accepted antiquated management practices begrudgingly until now. Downsizing, rightsizing, streamlining, restructuring, and re-engineering have made them anxious. Is this meant to imply they have become suddenly confrontational? No, not at all. Instead, they have hidden their angst in *six silent killing behaviors*, behaviors which equally penalize employer and employee.

If it is true that the workplace is in the midst of a radical revolution, then professional workers are the critical mass of that revolution. They spell the difference between success and failure. Management, as we know it, belongs to another era. In that era, it led the way to the magnificent triumph of World War II, a war which could be called "Management's War." Yet, management is another key to future success, for it needs to be integral to and partner with professional workers. Professional workers and modern managers belong to the same post-industrial guild, similar in many ways to the guilds of old. They are indispensable to each other, like the heart and lungs are requisites to life. The organization sinks or swims on workers and managers functioning as a team.

Organization of This Book

Six themes are presented here in nine chapters. Chapter 2 is a presentation of the punishing dilemma that has spawned the *six silent killers* and discusses why this phenomenon is the newest and greatest challenge to management. Chapter 3 discusses why the present structure and infrastructure of organization is not working, despite many valiant attempts to reactivate it to its former greatness. Workers and managers are pointing fingers at each other, when they should be pulling together. This situation is explored in terms most readers will recognize from their own experience. We don't usually think of the problems of organization in terms more appropriate to describing earthquakes, but such a comparison is made in Chapter 4 for a reason. Continuity, discontinuity, and catastrophe are present in the subterranean space of organizations the same as they are present under the earth's crust. Using René Thom's model of "Catastrophe Theory," the remarkable and inevitable shift in organizational power and influence is depicted as following a much ignored fault line. Time is running out on things as they are, and it is time to "fish or cut bait." The choice seems apparent—panic and let events dictate the future, or embrace reality and predict the future by creating it. Chapter 5 discusses why business, as invented by American enterprise, is now being duplicated by others and used against America's interests. Europeans and non-Occidentals are eating our lunch while playing the American game, and there appears to be little evidence that Americans know what to do about it other than to panic. Corporate calm, which is profiled in business journals and in board rooms, is replaced operationally by a merry madhouse.

Chapter 6 describes the *six silent killers*, which have evolved in organizations as a reaction to and frustration with the growing breach between the role demands of modern workers and the self-demands of those in charge to preserve an anachronistic workplace culture. This newest challenge to management will not go away with fads, liberal employee policies, or attempts to bring harmony to the workplace. What is required is so different from traditional demands and so obverse to conventional wisdom that management seems too paralyzed to act. Chapter 7 presents the concept of the "Culture of Comfort." In a simpler time, workers functioned with a considerable degree of effectiveness by reacting to demands of management. Management functioned as a surrogate *parent* to the worker's *child*. Behavior was reactive and loyal to the wishes of management. For this conformity, workers enjoyed security and, in most cases, lifetime employment. The emotional maturity required of workers was that of a 12-year-old obedient child.

As Chapter 8 shows, the result was a "Culture of Complacency." A philosophy of management surfaced that considered the more an employer did for employees, the more workers would do in appreciation for the company. What happened instead is that workers became complacent and dependent, not only on management, but on the company itself to control their lives and direct their destinies. Unwittingly, management protected workers from the full impact of the challenges of foreign competition, feeling that such knowledge would destabilize productive effort. Workers were believed not mature enough to deal with the big picture. This isolated them from reality and created a codependency that became an albatross around the neck of enterprise. Workers became obsessed with what they could get, not give, seeing company problems as belonging exclusively to management. Meanwhile, entitlement and benefit programs, which skyrocketed in cost, meant little to workers because these programs were not taxable income. Moreover, management, unable to corral workers into a defensive posture, abdicated responsible leadership for fear they might offend. A series of misdirected and hapless interventions sponsored by well-meaning consultants and human resource professionals only made matters worse.

Chapter 9 discusses the "Culture of Contribution." In desperation and only sporadically at first, management commenced to see through the fog to the new world of work. Here workers are on equal footing with management, where self-directed work teams, skunk works, team work cells, and individual contractors rule the day. Position power has been replaced by the power of knowledge, where decisions are made at the level of consequence and on a timely basis. Harmony was the most sought-after characteristic of the old regime; chaos is now accepted as having value. Conflict is common, but it is managed conflict. Workers and managers may frequently differ, but do so politely rather than infrequently and violently. The focus is on the work at hand, not on hostility. Moreover, it is on performance, not personality; on meeting the objective of the operation, not on looking good. Workers in this culture can easily outperform their predecessors by a factor of three or more. Chapter 10 brings the discussion to its conclusion. Even at this overdue stage, the situation obviously can be turned around. What is essential, however, is the will, the understanding, and the courage to make it happen. No challenge has ever been greater for management and workers than the one facing them now, but at no time in history have workers and managers been better equipped to meet this challenge.

In Chapter 11, we see that we need to get back to the basics and recognize that the "ship-of-state" is a single vessel and that we are all passengers on it, heading either for the open seas or troubled waters. The choice is ours to make.

Shock as Therapy

Never underestimate the power of shock. When America's survival was threatened in World War II and its pride bruised by Russia's launching of Sputnik, America mobilized its resources to regain its former advantage. Both instances were reactions of an essentially passive, complacent people to external threats. The shock woke America up, if only too briefly, to its obvious challenges. America won World War II because of its capacity to work. It placed the first man on the moon because of its capacity to husband its resources to a discernible goal. Now that its economic foundation and standard of living are in peril, it doesn't sense the threat, and thus the challenge remains a phantom. Each chapter of this book attempts to get inside this phantom challenge and reveal the apparent nature of it and America's options for dealing with it. Other advanced societies will no doubt see similarities to their own situations in these revelations. This phantom challenge is seen as having a cultural base, which has grown out of a desire to solve a problem (worker productivity) without recognizing that the problem-solving may be the incorrect framework.

The **Culture of Comfort** grew out of a splendid opportunity—unlimited world markets for American products as a result of the destruction of the industrial capacity of many nations during World War II. When Western Europe and Japan, with their miraculous economic recoveries, came to challenge America's dominance in the 1960s, ill-conceived attempts were launched to meet that challenge, which drove America deeper into isolation or the **Culture of Complacency**. Now America is struggling, as are many other post-industrial nations, to rediscover the **Culture of Contribution**. Such a return calls for patience with, as well as radical thinking about, workers, work, workplace culture, management, and the requirements of organizations in a post-industrial society.

Karl Marx once said, "We know who we are by what we do." That is less obvious today. Identity is more likely defined in terms of our economic status than our actual work. We have also moved from a society of revered institutions (home, family, church, school) to a psychedelic collage of formal and informal connections. We are not happy campers, and we seem to have misplaced our moral compass.

Endnotes

1. William James, *The Varieties of Religious Experience* (New York: Macmillan, 1961), p. 101, cited by Garry Wills in *Reagan's America* (New York: Doubleday, 1985), pp. 384–385. Wills goes on to say, "James is describing, in religious terms, the free lunch. The very preachers who deplore certain modern developments are celebrators of the greatness of

America, its way of life, its capitalistic system, its moral claims on the world. A happy Jeremiah is not a convincing scourge of sin. Optimism accepts; it blesses what is; it transmutes initiative into acquiescence—one rides the process and thinks one is guiding it."

2. U.S. Department of Labor, *Study of White-Collar Employment Growth—1987*, Section One.

3. Ibid.

4. Peter F. Drucker, "The Changed World Economy," *Foreign Affairs,* Spring 1986, 768–791.

5. Rick Suarez, Roger C. Mills, and Darlene Stewart, *Sanity, Insanity, and Common Sense* (New York: Fawcett Columbine, 1987), pp. 32–38. The authors argue convincingly that each individual experiences a *separate reality*, which dictates how he or she will perceive and behave towards others.

The Dominant Cultures of the Workplace, or Why We Can't Get There from Here

> It is the fact that man does not experience himself as the active bearer of his powers and richness, but as an impoverished "thing," dependent on powers outside of himself, unto whom he has projected his living substance.[1]
>
> Erich Fromm

In the world of business, "culture" is a word that is often tossed about with the cavalier glee of a carnival barker. Workplace culture is a critical facet of work that is neither fully understood nor used to its best advantage. Indeed, the success of a new strategic intervention or the adoption of a new technology depends on workplace culture. If the cultural landscape is not appropriate, the workplace will reject the intervention or misapply the technology.

Workplace culture pertains to what process is used to get things done over time in a company and how that company responds to internal stress and strain and accelerating external demands. It represents an integration of the predominant patterns of conduct in the human work group. This includes, but is not limited to, the significant thoughts, actions, beliefs, values, and prevailing jargon, rites, and rituals associated with purposeful performance. Workplace culture depends on the capacity of the company for learning and transmitting new information and knowledge from one generation of workers to the next. Like an individual, workplace culture can deny or resist change, ignore or downplay internal stress and strain, and stubbornly refuse to admit or deal with normal decline to its ultimate peril. For far too long, workplace culture has adhered to outdated, wrong, or inappropriate paradigms.

Many of the workplace cultural indicators are subtle, historic, thematic, and mythic. They are buried in the soul of the company. Therefore, sophisticated psychometrics, or even consultants with impeccable credentials, are unlikely to resolve the inscrutable mystery. For example, what workers score on survey instruments or reveal in lengthy personal interviews during such interventions seldom exposes more than the tip of the iceberg. Thus, the company fails to uncover *root causes* and, instead, focuses on a medley of symptoms. Workers are strongly influenced by the structure of the questions in such surveys and by their personal frame of reference at the time. Senior management needs to be involved in every step of workplace cultural change, for it needs to grasp the subtle meanings of worker behavior along with what inspires workers to top performance. Turmoil always emanates from the base of the company, where workers may display dissatisfaction with what they have or are, but yet be unable to indicate what they want or need. Workplace cultural change, however, can only be instituted and managed from the top.

The Changing Cultural Landscape of Work

For the past quarter century, the word "productivity" has been etched into the American psyche, reminding us of the upsurge of Japan, the Pacific Rim countries, and Europe into markets once dominated by the United States. Yet, the American blue-collar worker was and is still the most productive worker in the world. The problem is not productivity in the normal sense of the word, but the changing nature of work and the changing makeup of the workforce. Direct labor costs are not the problem. Indirect labor, the domain of white-collar or professional workers, is killing profits and causing abortive company bailouts.

After World War II, the workforce was dominated by blue-collar workers, or direct labor, which made up nearly 90 percent of all workers. Today, their numbers are closer to 10 percent, with 90 percent of the workers being white-collar service employees or college-trained professionals. The things that motivate a blue-collar worker to be productive and those that motivate a college-trained professional are worlds apart. Workers have changed because the nature of work has changed. Now, brain power and the handling of information, not brawn and the handling of things, are the essential components of most work. Moreover, knowledge or information carries the decision-making weight, not the pecking order.[2]

This has created a paradoxical dilemma: traditional management no longer has the power, but still retains the responsibility. Power has passed to professional workers at the level of consequence, where decision-making must take place on a timely basis. These professional workers are not managed, motivated, or mobilized to constructively take hold of power as a responsibility or to execute decisions effectively. They are programmed as though they were blue-collar workers. Responsible behavior falls in the breach between the call for a decision and its execution, as form takes precedence over substance, ritual over reality, impression over making a difference, and personality over performance. Meanwhile, the inclination is for senior people to grasp for the latest fad to deal with this perturbation (see Figure 2.1). What they really need is to educate themselves on what is happening and why.

This ignorance became palpable with the 1980 NBC television program "Japan Can, Why Can't We?" It dealt with the Japanese use of American workplace technology in capturing a shocking share of the American market in automobiles, televisions, and electronics. The technology was "quality control circles (QCC)," the

The Present Dilemma

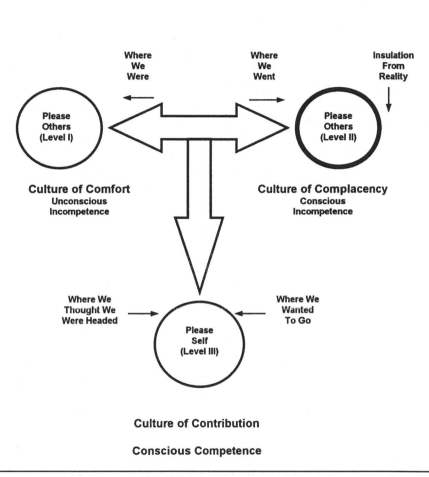

Culture of Contribution

Conscious Competence

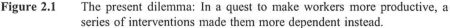

Figure 2.1   The present dilemma: In a quest to make workers more productive, a series of interventions made them more dependent instead.

creative work of W. Edwards Deming, J.M. Juran, and Peter Drucker. Since the early 1960s, Japan's major industries had their workers meeting regularly in work teams to solve work-related problems. The results were astounding, and there was a mad frenzy in America to have every American worker imitate their successful practices.

What was left out in the hysteria was the fact that these teams were essentially composed of blue-collar workers who focused on the "trivial many" problems they encountered. If they were 100 percent successful, 80 percent of the "vital few" problems relating to management issues would remain untouched.[3] Moreover, the Japanese culture and the American culture are the antithesis of each other. Japanese workers are conditioned to respond with differential reverence to its management, and to be disciplined, reactive, obedient, polite, and conforming.

The workplace culture in Japan was ideal for this intervention. Feudal lords of traditional Japanese society were, after World War II, Japan's top executives. Japanese industry had a sweetheart deal with its government, giving rise to the expression "Japan, Inc." Workers, conditioned in the customs of feudalism, responded to edicts of management without fanfare. Nearly 90 percent of Japanese workers were blue-collar workers in 1962. Although that number is closer to 70 percent today, the American workplace has always had higher indirect labor costs or a greater number of engineers, administrators, and other types of professionals per project. It is important to note that Japanese industry has experienced a growing disenchantment with its labor practices as its professional class of workers has grown.[4]

Authority has shifted as power now rests in knowledge that resides essentially with professional workers. Failure to acknowledge this and to develop a workplace culture conducive to these workers is an important contribution to erratic performance. Redundancy exercises, rightsizing, downsizing, merging, re-engineering, and streamlining can be traced to companies attempting to cope with this frustration. These tactics have been necessary, but they are not the answer, nor are attempts to imitate successful companies. Many companies in desperation looked to their Human Resources Department (HRD) professionals, only to discover that the cure in most cases was worse than the disease. HRD could argue, with some justification, that it became the corporate scapegoat.

To understand what workplace culture involves, it is useful to examine the three cultures that have dominated the workplace over the past 30 years: the Culture of Comfort, the Culture of Complacency, and the Culture of Contribution.

None of these evolved by design, but all appear as a function of circumstances. For example, the Culture of Comfort evolved without apparent notice between 1945 and 1970 or during the halcyon days when the rest of the world was rebuilding from the devastation of World War II and America controlled the marketplace. To combat the panic of 1979–80, when American markets were consciously feeling the challenge of Japan and Western Europe, and to establish a more competitive posture, worker-centered interventions became the powerful bromide. The writings of Douglas McGregor, Robert Blake and Jane Mouton, Rensis Likert, Deming-Juran-Drucker, Paul Hersey and Kenneth Blanchard, William Ouchi, Robert Mager, and George Odiorne were translated into instant therapies. Their common intent was to establish a Culture of Contribution in the workplace, but instead they produced a Culture of Complacency.

The Culture of Comfort

In the 1950s and 1960s, demand exceeded supply by a good margin. Jobs were plentiful. The opportunity for advancement was nearly unlimited. In this climate, advancement usually meant into management, no matter what the discipline or function. Managers could look back with nostalgic pride to their crisis management performance in World War II and look forward to promising careers as *organization men.*

Everything revolved around management. It set the tempo, the agenda, and the climate. The workplace culture, like society in general, was totally management-dependent. A management elite evolved out of the war, with many military types running industry and commerce as though they were the owners. Technically, managers-as-stockholders could make such a claim, as no single individual owned more than one percent of most major companies.

In those years, society conditioned its citizens to a series of small steps from the womb of home to the womb of school to the womb of work. Each climate was paternalistic, authoritarian, and absolute. As long as the individual was punctual, obedient, polite, loyal, disciplined, orderly, and conforming to operating policies and procedures, he was revered at home, applauded at school, and promoted on the job. In *Fortune* 500 companies, such as General Motors, General Electric, and U.S. Steel, the prospects were good for lifetime employment.

Workers were essentially treated as dependent children (Figure 2.2). The emotional maturity required of the average worker was that of a compliant 12-year-old child. A worker could be 50 years old, for example, but he wouldn't be expected to take the initiative if his life depended on it. He was programmed to be reactive, to be responsive to directives on cue, and to do no more than asked. Workers told managers what they wanted to hear, while on the sly they behaved like mischievous children, sneaking a smoke in no-smoking areas, purloining company property, such as small tools, pens, stamps, and other easily concealed items, or resorting to counterproductive practices, such as goldbricking and featherbedding.

Management was the parent to this worker-as-dependent-child, a worker inclined to see what he could get away with, not what he could do. Passive or reactive behaviors came to dominate. When this worker was perturbed, he might come in late and leave early (passive aggression); do only what he was told, then stand around (passive responsive); have a ready excuse for why a job wasn't done or wasn't done on time (passive defensive); accept assignments but seldom or rarely complete them on time (approach avoidance); spread malicious gossip about co-workers, his manager, or the company; do what he was told even when he knew it was wrong; fail to present key information needed for success (malicious obedience); or display a false sense of his own worth, with the grass always greener on the other side of the fence, while wanting to be what he wasn't and to have what he didn't (obsessive compulsive).

These six behaviors, or *silent killers*, were born in the Culture of Comfort, but may now invade any workplace culture at any level at any time when a worker is miffed. They are silent killers because they are the equivalent of social termites, invading the infrastructure of a company, unseen and unnoticed. When they are noticed, it is often too late for damage control. When most workers were confined to handling the trivial many problems rather than the vital few, the consequences

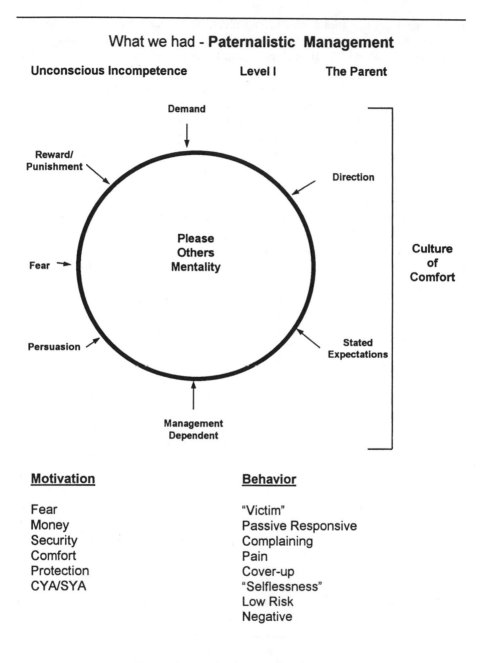

What we had - **Paternalistic Management**

Unconscious Incompetence   **Level I**   **The Parent**

Demand

Reward/
Punishment

Direction

**Please
Others
Mentality**

**Culture
of
Comfort**

Fear

Persuasion

Stated
Expectations

Management
Dependent

Motivation	**Behavior**
Fear	"Victim"
Money	Passive Responsive
Security	Complaining
Comfort	Pain
Protection	Cover-up
CYA/SYA	"Selflessness"
	Low Risk
	Negative

Note: All motivation is external to the individual

Figure 2.2   The Culture of Comfort: The surrogate parent dominates.

were seldom catastrophic. But today, as we have seen, a single individual can break a bank, as did Nick Leeson, a 28-year-old trader who caused the collapse of the 232-year-old Baring Bank of Great Britain by his reckless and greedy computer gambit.[5]

Motivation in the Culture of Comfort was and remains external to the individual. No attempt is made to establish an internal governor that might guide, direct, and monitor the worker's behavior. The total menu of controls and motivators represents a combination of rewards and punishment, demands and directives, stated expectations and persuasions, and fear. Security, comfort, protection, and money are the principal manipulative devices of this culture.

Because this worker is a spectator of his own destiny, it is not surprising that he often resorts to the "victim complex." Quite incredibly, however, he also is inclined to see himself as a selfless company man, who puts the company before his own interests. The combination of victim complex and company-man routine often confuses management and puts it on the defensive. This is how the child controls the parent to its own ends, and it is the principal reason why performance appraisal in the Culture of Comfort among professionals has never worked. Management in this climate finds it easier to give unearned raises and token promotions than to confront poor performance. Again, this situation was of little concern when demand exceeded supply. Workers could be preoccupied with the negative and avoid risk or pain to their hearts' content because their impact on the bottom line was nil.

This was the workplace culture and the prototype worker that materialized during unprecedented economic growth in the decades following World War II up to 1980 and NBC's pivotal "Japan Can, Why Can't We?" program. The United States was basking in a workplace culture of *unconscious incompetence*, unaware of its growing incompetence and, thus, unconscious of its diminishing competitive status. Work was conducted 1945-style, with managers unaware of the subtle global changes and the impact of technology that were shaping the workplace and the workers themselves. When wholesale action was finally taken, it was driven more by panic than prudent appraisal of the situation. The Culture of Complacency followed.

The Culture of Complacency

The concept of quality circles exploded in the American workplace. An aerospace facility in the South had more than 1,000 workers, primarily in blue-collar operations, and had more than 100 quality circles in place when this panic set in. Its greatest success was in terms of churn (reducing job changing) and absenteeism, not productivity per se. Yet paper gains were celebrated as though they represented great achievements.[6]

Across the American continent, companies were seeing their market share erode dramatically. HRD professionals traced this erosion to workplace issues: quality of work, quality of work life, quality of management, pay, fairness practices, job security, group feelings, and benefits and entitlement programs. Concentrate on these aspects, so the rationale went, and the ancillary benefit will be soaring productivity. The central theme was, "Do everything you can for your workers, and your workers will do everything they can for the company." Doubters were reminded of Japanese workers' lifetime employment and its incredible payback. Not commonly circulated, however, were the facts that only 20 percent of Japanese workers enjoyed these benefits and that more than 60 percent of Japanese industry was confined to primitive cottage-type industries of five to ten employees per company.

Between 1980 and 1984, this strategy created a country club atmosphere at this high-tech 4,000-employee facility. Many workers openly conducted parallel careers at their desks or work stations. They sold real estate, cosmetics, jewelry, stocks and bonds, Amway, Avon, NSA, and even vegetables beyond the security stations. No one seemed to notice or mind. The atmosphere was collegial, social, and agreeable, with little evidence of work. This nonchalant attitude was personified indirectly in soaring medical costs. With no significant increase in personnel, medical costs skyrocketed from $780,000 in 1978 to $8 million in 1982. Meanwhile, records indicate that most employees took their maximum sick leave as though it equaled vacation, not a standby benefit for an emergency, but a right. To be fair, skyrocketing physician charges, healthcare paranoia, and soaring insurance premiums also factored into the equation. Unfortunately, worker self-indulgence during this period proved the rule rather than the exception.

In their desire to create a more responsive workplace culture, managers had instead created an infantile monster (Figure 2.3). The workplace had gone from workers being "management-dependent" to being "counterdependent" on the company for their total well-being—a lose–lose proposition for all. A codependency bond had formed between employer and employee, which was killing the worker's spirit and strangulating the company. If workers are suspended from the consequences of their actions, if they are protected from the occasional pain of failure, they are unlikely to ever grow up, or appreciate the joys of mature adulthood. They will be forever suspended in terminal adolescence, holding the company back from soaring to its destiny.

These well-meaning HRD interventions, which unfortunately had an internal focus, insulated workers from the reality of the marketplace and the impact of their negative performance on the company's bottom line. Most critical of all, they insulated workers from customer requirements. Management, as parent, no longer had control, for control now fell to the worker as pampered child. What made this apparent was who got promoted and why—usually the ones who made the most noise. The whole atmosphere of work was like a Broadway play, where the best actors got the best parts. The majority of workers were now professionals who placed credentials ahead of experience and the management of their careers ahead of the work at hand. Nothing was as it seemed. Like enigmatic teenagers impossible to pigeonhole, these workers wavered between approach and avoidance. They wanted the perks, but not the pain. The emotional maturity required here was that of a 13-year-old child in arrested development, caught between a need for comfort and little capacity for anguish. One worker might put in eight hours and let management worry about "saving the company," for "it's not my problem," while another worker might utterly ignore management to access the company store—computers, faxes, toll-free

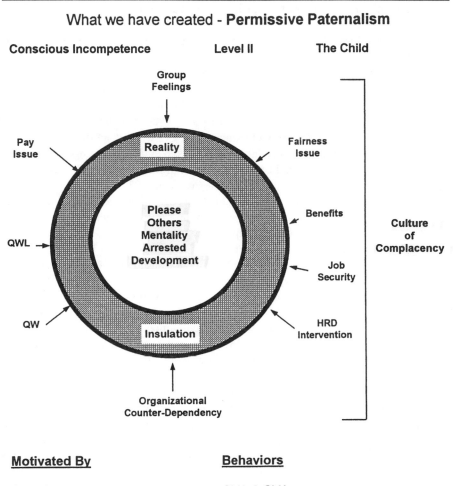

Figure 2.3   The Culture of Complacency: The propensities of the child are displayed in the worker.

lines, franking privileges—as though it belonged to him in promoting an entirely different career.[7]

With the Culture of Complacency, security ranks high as a motivator, but having a good time at work, getting along well with co-workers, having caring management, and having the right mix of perks are not far behind. Workers play Cover-Your-Ass (CYA) and Show-Your-Ass (SYA) games, are devotees of crisis management, are more non-responsible than irresponsible, resort to "learned helplessness" or "we/they" polarity when it suits them, and know how to "appear busy" to perfection.

Fortune 500 companies are well acquainted with the impact of the Culture of Complacency on operations, especially as it relates to entitlement programs. A 1988 study indicates that fringe benefit and entitlement programs will cost these companies, at the present rate of growth (1988 baseline), more than $3 trillion by the year 2000, a cost which is forcing them to be brutally objective concerning operations. This culture is obviously an important consideration when mounting a downsizing strategy.

In retrospect, the Culture of Complacency was easy to sell because it didn't threaten the status quo, was easy to implement, and promised to bring out the best in workers. But it didn't work, and it wouldn't have worked in 1945. The culture was worker-sensitive and generous, but it required little change in workers themselves. Workers today need to be proactive and to be risk-taking problem-solvers, bold decision-makers, self-responsible, accountable self-managers and self-initiators, not obedient, compliant, conforming company men/women. Yet, they remain conditioned and programmed to be precisely reactive pawns to a management elite, to a signatory authority that is itself anachronistic and essentially a barrier to productive work.

This puts senior management squarely in the frame. It can no longer plead ignorance of cultural issues and delegate the matter of workplace culture to knowledgeable staffers. A cardinal rule of delegation is to delegate what you know and understand A to Z and hold close to your person that which you don't know or understand. Failure to take ownership of workplace cultural issues contributed to the initial problem. Senior management must now school itself in the nuances of workplace culture, design a cultural climate best able to support the company's mission and the needs of its workers, and then implement and monitor this culture in a phasic unveiling with the scrutiny now devoted primarily to the bottom line. Do this and the bottom line will take care of itself.

Driven by the challenge of work itself, by control of what it does, by an opportunity to take risks, by the right to an opinion and the right to be wrong, and by the freedom to fail so that it might succeed, this new class of workers has a totally different attitude and appetite for what is called "trust." It expects to share in the spoils of its labor, for it claims parity and partnership with management and cannot be humored by slogans, baubles, and beads. The situation necessitates the Culture of Contribution, the land where skunk works, self-managed work teams, and team work-cells exist without a single manager, where on any given day 7 to 10 workers can easily outperform 100 workers from the Culture of Complacency.[8]

The Culture of Contribution

A workplace with a Culture of Contribution has many faces, forms, and styles. It is not a single paradigm, but a multiplicity of paradigms and subparadigms in the same company. Contribution is not frozen in a precise formula, but is unique to every group. The Culture of Contribution is a hero of a thousand faces with a singular aspect—the group is the job; the worker is the company.

Still, individual workers in this culture have a high need to please themselves, not management or the company. Their loyalty is first and foremost to themselves and then to what they do. They know the purpose of life is what they are doing now, and what they are doing now is all-consuming. Give them an objective, a time frame, and adequate resources, then leave them alone!

Cosmetic approaches and company rhetoric turn these workers off and make them tune out. Never passive, they are confrontational and challenging with a difference. They protest frequently but politely, not infrequently and violently as their colleagues did in the past. They have little patience with position power and show the greatest allegiance to those who know. They are responsible and accountable doers, not because it is the thing to do, but because it is the way to get things done. They are learners, not knowers; performers, not personalities; consummate problem-solvers, not solution fanciers.

The Culture of Contribution is recognizable by the climate of purposeful behavior, alive with chaos and conflict (Figure 2.4). Harmony and order are foreign to it. This is a climate of risk-taking, where workers are not afraid to fail; where they move with confidence but without arrogance; where there is always someone to listen, to help, or to advise; where disagreement is rife but where humor also pervades; where everyone is respected but not necessarily considered a buddy; where roles shift as requirements of work change; where conflict is managed and is the glue that holds them to their purpose. The supervisor–employee relationship does not exist. Self-managed work teams dominate activities. Management's role is to design, monitor, and maintain the culture for productive work and then to stay out of the way. Only one such manager is needed for every 200 workers, for workers supervise themselves. In this culture, peer pressure is much more effective than management-generated performance appraisal.

The "please-self" and self-management mentalities give rise to the emotional maturity of "the adult." The adult is guardian of the Culture of Contribution, as compared to "the parent" in the Culture of Comfort and "the child" in the Culture of Complacency. It follows logically that all motivators are internal to this worker. Motivation spans the range from an appreciation for having a job, the opportunity to do something constructive, the sense of worth that comes with satisfying work, the sensation of ownership that is derived from control, to the spiritual satisfaction for being effectively employed. Such a worker envisions himself as the victor. He is where he chooses to be, doing what he chooses to do. He is purposeful, confident, cooperative, positive, responsive, and, yes, selfish. It is his belief that it is impossible to

Where we want to be - **Interdependent Management**

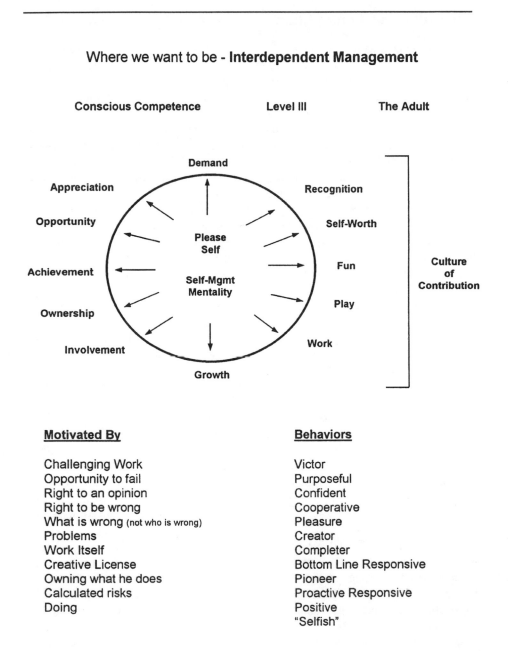

Conscious Competence   **Level III**   **The Adult**

Motivated By

Challenging Work
Opportunity to fail
Right to an opinion
Right to be wrong
What is wrong (not who is wrong)
Problems
Work Itself
Creative License
Owning what he does
Calculated risks
Doing

Behaviors

Victor
Purposeful
Confident
Cooperative
Pleasure
Creator
Completer
Bottom Line Responsive
Pioneer
Proactive Responsive
Positive
"Selfish"

Figure 2.4   The Culture of Contribution: The characteristics of the adult are displayed in the worker.

meet other people's needs before one's own. Once these needs are met, however, a sense of interdependency is created, which is synergistic, soaring to collective achievement.

From Complacency to Contribution

We have created a worker elite that we stubbornly insist on employing as common labor. These new workers have been in our midst for some time, but have been mainly ignored. They have tried vainly to fit into their existing workplace cultures. Management, on its part, finds them a riddle that is impossible to solve. It has thrown a series of tantalizing trinkets their way and promoted "empowerment" theories and other strategies that have failed to tap their spirit, while putting the company's coffers and confidence in jeopardy. The result is a stalemate. The actual productivity realized from these workers is about 20 percent of their capability. The irony is that they and their management, mainly consumed with busy work, couldn't be working harder. The focus of their efforts would seem to be on the 80 percent of work ("doing everything right" or quality management) that makes only 20 percent of the difference, instead of the 20 percent ("doing the right things" or strategic management) that makes 80 percent of the difference.

Still, the loss of familiar bearings that proves tragic to most workers has allowed a small contingent of these new professional workers to thrive. Workers who have been able to survive the company in transition, who have made it work for them, are doing great. For example, a chief financial officer in the Silicon Valley is not likely to be found in a three-piece suit, but more likely to come bounding out in sneakers, chinos, and a pullover shirt. These new workers may have all kinds of social problems or may not look you in the eye or remember to shake your hand, but do they know the computer! Computers sing for them in a language and rhythm the production assembly line worker never heard before. It is safe to say that 20 years ago, this worker wouldn't have been employable because this worker wouldn't have fit in anywhere. The corporate culture that was so familiar to most workers and managers a generation ago is gone. All those rules of that age have been thrown out as a new notion of loyalty and "the contract" between employer and employee is evolving.

The smokestack industry is gone, but its work ethic and theology prevail. Most workers get more work done at home, a day away from the office, than they get done in a week at work. Skunk works—small groups of seven to ten zealots off in a corner—can outperform ten times their number. This is common knowledge, but yet the old theology holds firm.

Admittedly, we don't have the management, the workplace culture, or the workers conditioned to take charge the way the Culture of Contribution demands. That is why senior management must become involved. Here are some preliminary considerations in creating a Culture of Contribution:

Performance Appraisal. *Soften and phase this out.* Making workers constantly look over their shoulders at how others judge what they are doing causes them to worry about their next raise and leads to inauthentic behavior and cheating. With workers under constant observation, the risk-taking, creative urge, and desire to learn go underground. Workers are more productive when concerned primarily with how satisfied they are with their accomplishments rather than with focusing on how they are being evaluated.

Reward and Recognition Programs. *Curtail these.* Excessive use of prizes, incentive programs, and cash rewards deprives workers of the intrinsic pleasure that comes from work itself. Far more effective is to treat workers with respect, support them when they fall short of the mark or fail, and make them feel as though they are an important part of the enterprise by giving them meaningful work and the appropriate tools to do it.

Individual and Interdepartmental Competition. *Suspend these programs.* Competition is the antithesis of creative exchange. The payback is minimal because competition embraces comparing, competing, imitating, and generating win–lose hysteria. Placing workers in a desperate win–lose work situation, where one worker or group of workers can come out on top (at the expense of others), promotes division, not collaboration. Individual workers, as with a group of workers on a project, should be allowed to progress at their own respective rates. If there is to be competition, make it positive competition. Challenge individual workers (or the group of workers) to exceed their previous best. Competing against oneself is healthy competition. The focus should always be on an integration of individual/team efforts toward overall company performance.

Micromanagement. *Cease and desist.* Overcontrol creates precisely what it attempts to avoid—chaos. It also promotes low morale, we/they polarity, counterfeit behavior, and poor performance. Telling workers exactly how to do the minute aspects of their jobs produces passive, reactive, and management-dependent workers. Paternalistic management spawns immature workers who are unlikely to take the initiative. When things go wrong, they chirp, "Not my problem!"

Ownership. *Create the sense of it.* If workers are not made to feel as though they are part of the problem, they will not feel as though they are part of the solution. Too much is done with workers, for workers, and to workers with surprisingly little involvement of them in the process. When decisions are made regarding what is "good" and "bad" for workers without their participation, they think like renters. A rented mind never thinks like that of a homeowner.

Faddism. *Refrain from it.* Grandiose schemes to turn the company around and to "make work fun" are just that—grandiose schemes. Nor are "hothouse" training programs or "cutting-edge" technologies likely to inspire confidence. There are no shortcuts to resolving the effects of decade-old neglects. Pain cannot be avoided; neither can failure. Ultimately, success will be realized if one simple idea permeates all activities—workers are allowed to wrestle with their problems and to fight their way (with senior management's leadership and direct involvement) to viable solutions.

There are many operations today with environments that resemble this workplace culture to varying degrees, but they are in the minority. On balance, the transformation required is in a holding pattern, for it means a total change in the relationship of workers and managers to work and to each other. This will take time, patience, and many failures before success will become common.

But do we have any choice? No fad, program, or perfect paradigm is likely to come down the pike to let senior management off the hook. It would be nice to take time to assess the situation. The problem is that those on the cutting edge of competition aren't taking any time-outs. Therefore, corporate management must become involved, and it must involve these new workers in creating a workable culture for maximum performance. Unfortunately, preventive measures seldom win over corrective ones. America remains the most dynamic economy of the Western world, and it is hard to generate concern when that is still the case. But what about tomorrow?

Endnotes

1. Erich Fromm, *The Sane Society* (Fawcett Premier, 1955), p. 114.
2. Elizabeth Whitney, "The Real Laggards: White-Collar Workers," *St. Petersburg Times*, January 17, 1988, Business Section, 1.
3. J. M. Juran, "International Significance of the QC Circle Movement." *Quality Progress*, November 1980, 18–22.
4. "Japan's Troubled Future," *Fortune* (special report), March 30, 1987, 21–49.
5. Howard G. Chua-Eoan, "Ego & Greed: The Inside Story of the 28-Year-Old Trader Who Blew a Billion Dollars, Broke a Bank and Stunned the World," *Time*, March 13, 1995, 40–47.
6. James R. Fisher, Jr., "Quality Control Circles: Motivation Through Participative Management." Paper presented at the National Conference of the Institute of Printed Circuits, Dallas, TX, October 1981. Unpublished.
7. James R. Fisher, Jr., "Participative Management: An Adversary Point of View." Paper presented at the Defense Contractors Administration System (DCAS) Forum, Caribbean Gulf Resort, Clearwater Beach, FL, March 30, 1984. Unpublished.
8. See William L. Livingston's *Have Fun at Work*, F.E.S., Ltd., 1988. Livingston and his group have found ways to increase company performance by multiples of ten times normal rates of production.

The Need for a New Set of Organizational Paradigms

It was the best of times, it was the worst of times, it was the age of wisdom, it was the age of foolishness, it was the epoch of belief, it was the epoch of incredulity, it was the season of Light, it was the season of Darkness, it was the spring of hope, it was the winter of despair, we had everything before us, we had nothing before us, we were all going direct to Heaven, we were all going direct the other way—in short, the period was so far like the present period....[1]

Charles Dickens

Dickens was writing about the French Revolution of 1789 and its impact on society, especially the societies of London and Paris. He goes beyond this to suggest that changing society begins with the individual's decision to change. *The world becomes a different place once the individual chooses to think differently on purpose.* In every period of history there has been a gulf between revolutionary ideas of a few and the stubborn resistance of the many to embrace them. This built-in caution is characteristic of humans. It delineates not only the American character, but citizens across the world who are wary, although swept into the future by the hurricane forces of change.

Dickens could have been writing about the persistent struggle today between workers and managers. The workplace culture is caught in the breach as it fails to meet either of their needs. This struggle is concealed in the disguises of thematic change—re-engineering, empowerment, total quality management—which mask forward inertia.

Make no mistake, the workplace is in the midst of a revolution. Yet the focus more often than not is exclusively on management, not workers. This is due to the faulty belief that if you fix management, you fix the problem. Social engineers have been fixing management for a quarter century with little success. Meanwhile, modern workers wait. This is not to suggest that it would be prudent to put the focus entirely on workers. Workers and managers are cut from the same cloth today and, therefore, have a mutual interdependence. Both are struggling with the same reality. More prudent would be to focus on their shifting roles and overlapping demands. The longer we ignore this tension between them, the more likely it is to intensify.

Power has shifted from being fashionably management's business to being a shared responsibility with workers. Newly acquired power appeals to workers, but not its responsibility. Workers would like to continue to strut their stuff and proclaim, "Not my problem!" when trouble comes. Consequently, many organizations waffle like a rag doll in the wind. Several factors contribute to this ambivalence:

- Values have changed and are changing across the globe in advanced societies of the East and West. This threatens the established order.
- These changes affect the way people relate to each other.
- The information explosion has made it impossible for the workplace to keep abreast of telecommunication breakthroughs. Information technology is creating a distinctly different worker with a unique style and perspective.
- Information is the critical mass of work, not conventional activity. All that is known for sure is that there is a discernible shift from *doing* to *thinking*, from primarily producing a product to symbolic interaction.
- The information edge no longer belongs to management, but is well distributed throughout the workforce. With beepers, cellular phones, faxes, E mail, laptops, the Internet, and soon video phones, there are no more secrets.
- Management is at the mercy of not only expert systems, but the experts who design, build, and control them.
- With the shift from doing to thinking, the debate heats up as to what constitutes *real work*. There is also the matter of who is in charge.

Because management is results-oriented and looks for meaning in the bottom line, and workers appear primarily process-driven, real work creates a puzzling dichotomy:

- If work is measured in terms of results only, management is likely to see workers as costs.
- Seldom are workers asked to come up with schemes to produce a cheaper widget, a more efficiently produced widget, or even to design a better widget.
- When workers are treated as a cost, they behave as a cost, dragging their feet and doing as little as possible to get by. When workers are treated as an asset, they behave as an asset, extending themselves to the limits of their potential.
- Cost-cutting practices aimed solely at reducing head count put into play the complementary forces of cheating, cover-up, finger-pointing, backstabbing, and the *six silent killers*, particularly malicious obedience.

- When the focus is on process rather than outcome, work is more strategically driven or centered around doing the right things. When the focus is on outcomes only, work is more tactically oriented or centered around doing everything right. Doing the right things fosters teamwork. Doing everything right promotes finger-pointing, polarity, and invariably results in dissension among the ranks.

What truly influences the outcome, whatever the focus, is more a matter of *collective values* or *workplace culture* than it is of management style. McGregor's *Theory X & Y*, Blake and Mouton's *Managerial Grid*, and Ouchi's *Theory Z* prevailed upon the conduct of management for nearly two generations. Obviously, style played a more significant role when management held the power.[2] Even so, when the passion for management style waned, attention was not focused on workplace culture. Instead, the focus shifted to *Total Quality Management* with the convincing refrain, "quality is the answer." But again, quality has proven as flawed as management style. Why?

The fallacy is in the *thinking*. Both strategies are driven by problem-solving. Conventional problem-solving creates boxes, which make the world easier to observe and classify. The organization went from emphasizing one box (management style) to another box (Total Quality Management) because it wanted to be able to predict outcomes:

> *If managers are both task-oriented and worker-oriented, workers will be happy and productive (management style). If we do a systematic process flow analysis and check quality at critical points along the way, we will produce a quality product (Total Quality Management).*

Some success has registered with both strategies, but neither has proven a panacea. Perhaps this is not the fault of the boxes, but the arrogance and absolute certainty with which advocates of these two strategies viewed their construction. Admittedly, workplace culture does not fit neatly into solution-driven problem-solving and, therefore, cannot be easily placed in a box or even a series of boxes. Consultants avoid workplace cultural issues like the plague—too ambiguous, ambivalent, and beyond the pale of the concrete. Workplace culture demands a whole new design, indeed, a set of paradigms which go against the grain of conventional thinking. These paradigms will never be discovered by "search and eliminate" problem-solving. Metaphorically, a workplace culture must be built from scratch, with a foundation, support beams, walls, sashes, windows and doors, and a roof. A house is not discovered, it is designed and built. Nor can a workplace culture be discovered. It must be designed and built out of an appropriate set of paradigms.

This is difficult to grasp because we are programmed to the problem-solving, where we define, evaluate, and separate the wrong from the right answer. There is no right answer for workplace culture, but simply a collection of values which support the purpose of a specific organization. Logic, we believe, gives us the best perception of the problem and, therefore, the correct solution. Not so with workplace culture. What we do, when we get beyond the problem-solving, is examine the nature of the workplace culture now; how does it meet the current needs of the mission? Then, we consider what can be, allowing our minds to travel beyond the restrictions of right and wrong, good and bad, true and false, cause and effect, to the possibilities for a more energized organization. We surrender the rational approach to embrace the arational. The rational approach is the legacy of Socrates and Plato, which is our heritage, now exalted to dogma. Human behavior is non-linear and arational and doesn't respond to conventional wisdom or to the problem-solving framework.[3]

This is not to suggest that the conduct of managers is not important or that quality is not a desirable goal. What it is meant to convey is that if the all-consuming idea that management style, quality, or any other litmus test is the answer, it is bound to disappoint, because each tends to be a stylistic overlay on a faulty foundation. The collective values of the workplace, otherwise known as culture, will reject or weaken the strategy if workers are not first programmed to be receptive. Quality management, refined to a fault, will fail if the organization has not thought through the quality problem with the people meant to affect quality. An important part of quality management is to transform crippling *cultural biases* to more desirable values. Typically what happens when a conflict develops between meeting schedule and maintaining quality standards is that schedule wins and quality loses. If quality permeates every system and subsystem of a workplace, both quality and schedule are likely to win because workers will find a way. Quality is a mind-set, not a program or process. It is the workplace culture. For this reason, the quick cosmetic fix will not suffice. *Attention must be paid to workplace culture because culture drives behavior.*

The cultural climate in America is not the same as in Europe, Japan, Korea, or Singapore. Nor is the workplace culture in a General Motors operation in Indiana the same as one in Kentucky or Tennessee; nor are GM's operations the same in Belgium, Germany, or India. Moreover, within a specific General Motors plant, the workplace culture in production is not the same as in engineering or in sales and marketing. Nor is it likely that a General Motors plant in another region can attest to production being the same as production elsewhere. All differ. All are unique to the prevailing cultural biases of groups within those respective operations. Yet, there is indeed a predominant American culture that differs from ones in Japan, China, and elsewhere, just as there is a predominant culture in General Motors that differs from ones at General Electric and other corporations. It is the combination of micro and macro cultures, within and between entities, which needs to be better understood, respected, dealt with, and utilized to attain the results desired.

Economic challenge is real, and no organization can manage to survive on its past laurels. It must remain vigilant and ready to meet the demands of constant change. We are at war, with commerce and industry as the new battleground. Economics is the successor to the military in terms of security and protection of national interests. The quest for markets and market share, not territory and the spoils of nations, is what drives modern warfare. America's dilemma is that it has little sense of this war. Economic threat to its survival is a phantom challenge and largely not felt.

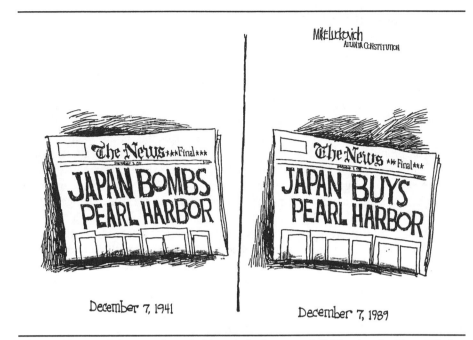

Figure 3.1   "When you don't feel it, you don't react to it." (Reprinted with permission of Creators Syndicate; cartoon by Mike Luckovich.)

When the Japanese bombed Pearl Harbor in 1941, Americans put aside their differences and mobilized as a nation because they felt threatened. Physical security and unspeakable dread held them to the task. When the U.S.S.R. launched Sputnik in 1957, Americans were shocked into action because their pride was on the line and their psychological security was threatened. Once again, Americans put aside their differences and consolidated their efforts in technology, placing a man on the moon in another decade. But today, when economic survival is at stake and the middle class is shrinking, placing their flaunted standard of living in jeopardy, they don't put aside their differences, but seem instead preoccupied with them, whining about political correctness, lost virtue, the decline of traditional values, and the woes of growing old. Economic survival is not experienced because it is not yet felt (Figure 3.1). Most Americans are financially comfortable and find only a remote connection with the more than 30 million homeless and hungry or the 50 million below the poverty line. They read in their morning newspapers these statistics at breakfast and say, "Honey, pass the sugar."

World War III has been raging for more than 30 years as an economic war, a war which has not touched the landscape of the American mind, despite the rumbling quakes of seismic proportions reverberating underfoot.

A New Look at Old Values

Not unlike Dickens' *A Tale of Two Cities*, subtle but massive changes in society and the individual have led to a cultural breakdown. Traditional institutions have been split down the middle, which has fractured the home, school, church, workplace, and government. Yet, while many causes are attributed to this breakdown, denial is perhaps the most consequential. What is happening, whatever the cause, is sending shock waves across the globe. America is going through what columnist Robert Wright calls "the false politics of values." But this is not exclusively an American problem. Age-old societies are succumbing to centrifugal forces, which are driving them away from their traditional values and beliefs. Meanwhile, centripetal forces are driving these same societies into a common global village or toward each other, whether they like it or not. So, it is unwise to see these changes simply in terms of good and bad. They are manifestations of a changing world. It is this conflicting combination of being at once pulled apart and forced together which strains the mind in its attempt to comprehend and deal with conflicting knowledge. The tension between free markets and strict morals, which economic progress and capitalism sponsor, tends to fracture families and communities. Crime, poverty, drugs, illegitimacy, illiteracy, and moral decay are pervasive across the globe but have found a home where capitalism thrives. A consumer-driven culture, like ours, fosters hedonism that weakens the work ethic and thwarts conservative values.

Another mechanism at play in this cultural breakdown, prominent at the moment, is the attempt to make traditional approaches to work in particular and to life in general submit to the rationale of old values—another example of boxamania. William Bennett's *Book of Virtues*, Ben Wattenberg's *Values Matter Most*, Gertrude Himmelfarb's *The De-Moralization of Society*, and Michael Sandel's *Democracy's Discontent*, to name a few, espoused the blessings of values. They all have very specific values in mind—the old values of the *common good*—as the ideal remedy for an anxious society. These advocates are a chorus trumpeting, "What is good for the family, school, church, company, and the government is good enough for me!" But the generation that survived Vietnam and the generation that followed are not buying this. They have seen their lives fractured by divorce, miseducation, and the secularization of the church; fractured, too, by the company that deserted their community and the government that lied to them; and fractured by the need to be their own parents. They are cynical, never having had a chance to be innocent, old before their time, tired beyond measure, escaping periodically into excess, while trying to deal with a world they didn't create but are forced to inherit.

This 30–40-something generation values *personhood*. If they can't rely upon themselves, they feel they can't rely on anyone. They are not awed by success or celebrity or committed to work as were their parents, and they are certainly not as gullible or as groveling to the powers that be. They think in terms of the right to know, the right to an opinion, the right to work or not work, the right to be wrong,

	Common Good	Personhood
Authority	Position power	Popularity/knowledge
Loyalty	To the orgainzation	To self/peers
Discipline	Reward/punishment	Caring/respect
Motivation	Fear	Challenge/contribution

Figure 3.2   Shifting American values.

the right to be confused or enlightened, the right to be heterosexual or homosexual or asexual, the right to believe or disbelieve, and the right to fail or succeed. They think in terms of controlling their destiny by not trying to control it (Figure 3.2).

Yet the myth persists if these people are managed and trained differently, and if work is defined differently, problems will dissolve, and workers will automatically change. Results demonstrate, however, that little changes when workers are left out of the design phase of the equation. Billions of dollars are being spent in the name of Total Quality Management and Total Employee Involvement. These programs are meant to redefine work and train workers and managers differently. It could be argued that this is a panic attempt to appear in control, when everything is running out of control. It gives the illusion of dealing with the problem without actually exploring it. Is quality a concern? Of course. Are passive employees a problem? Obviously. Yet both poor quality and submissive personnel are symptomatic of a greater problem: the failure of the workplace culture to support quality and initiative.

Creating a suitable culture in the workplace is a demanding project and often requires radical change in the conduct of business, change that must be carefully introduced and monitored by senior management. This is not a project that can be handed off to experts. If senior management wants its watch to feature high performance, it needs to create and cultivate the appropriate workplace culture. Cultural change requires a complete review of the values, beliefs, and expectations of workers and managers alike and a no-holds-barred attitude.

Senior management can gain a quick reading of the health of its workplace by paying attention. Dysfunction is openly displayed in the dominance of the rumor mill and the prominence of backstabbing, duplicity, chicanery, Cover-Your-Ass (CYA) and Show-Your-Ass (SYA) games, in such factors as turnover and churn figures, absenteeism, percentage of sick leave taken to that available, rate of injuries on the job, activity in Employee Assistance Programs (especially substance abuse), waste as a percentage of product, medical insurance benefit claims, customer complaints, and overtime as a percent of man-hours per project. Less obvious indicators are the *six silent killers*, which feast on the diseased climate and which will be covered in

Chapter 6. The behaviors described in that chapter are **passive aggression, passive responsive, passive defensive, malicious obedience, approach avoidance,** and **obsessive compulsive behaviors**. These behaviors signal to management the effect (not the cause) of organizational instability and fatigue. A company, like an individual, can become frustrated, overstressed, and feel impotent to deal with internal stress and strain and accelerating external demands. It is rare that an individual so possessed will admit as much and ask for help. More likely, the individual will project loyalty and affection for his employer, while becoming increasingly a liability. Still worse, the offending employee is usually unconscious of the negative impact of his acts until the behavior so dominates him that he is finally confronted. Damage control is too late to save the worker or to undo the damage done.

Workers of a Different Mind

Average workers, formerly tied to their jobs by fear, lack of skill, and ignorance, have become educated and mobile, discovering new horizons of opportunity. Many were reared in latchkey or single-parent homes and left mainly to their own devices. They grew up by default with little guidance in acquiring a supportive value system.

In the absence of external control and parental programming, they acquired their own internal self-monitoring system. Parental neglect denied them the security of traditional values, leaving many bruised or scarred by early life experiences, experiences for which they were not adequately prepared. Yet these conditions also produced individuals who, in an effort to survive, had to find their own *centers* and their own *moral compass*. They had to think for themselves. Karl Zinsmeister of the American Enterprise Institute puts this in perspective: "While only five percent of the children in Japan live in something other than an intact two-parent home, in the United States the figure is currently 27 percent and rising...about two-thirds of all American children will spend some time in a single-parent household before they leave their teens."[4]

Individuals of such experience respond quite differently than their parents did to external control or to conventional wisdom. They are more inclined to be influenced by intrinsic interests (what they would like to do) than by extrinsic interests (what they ought to do) and more stimulated by challenge than in pleasing others. A 1993 study conducted by John Cochran, a criminology professor at the University of Oklahoma, found 83 percent of the students surveyed admitted their willingness to lie, cheat, or steal for a grade.[5] Not only were they disinclined to respond positively to traditional rewards and punishment, they found them more amusing than germane, and shame seemed foreign to them. Consistent with this, the traditional punishment of giving a worker a few days off for violation of company policy or a monetary bonus as reward for outstanding effort has far less impact on behavior than management would like to believe. Approval at work is not the center of this worker's life. So, time off is neither an embarrassment nor a particular concern. As for money, this worker will take it, "thank you very much," and go on behaving as he would anyway. Indeed, attempts to stimulate a sense of the *common good* only seem to enliven self-interest.

Control is now shifting to the center, where workers and managers need to learn how to share power (authority) and responsibility (accountability). There is a reluctance of managers to share power and an equal reluctance of workers to assume responsibility. This flags a difficult but inevitable period of frustration. Most workers are not conscious of their new powers, which is apparent as they naively challenge the role of management and the requirements of work as if they were a third party. It is perplexing for workers to see themselves as both the controller and the controlled. "Empowerment, "a word that has become a modern cliché, gained legitimacy with the *Women's Rights Movement*. When women insisted on being treated as persons and not as chattel, they made a breakthrough. Women realized that if they didn't surrender their power to men, as they had traditionally, power would continue to reside with them. By this simple observation, women came to understand that no one could have power over them unless they surrendered their power to them, either voluntarily or by force. The idea that management can *empower* workers is to look at the issue of power backwards. Once power is given up, it is lost, unlikely to be recovered. This makes the empowerment movement a little ironic. Management is bent on giving back to workers what has always belonged to them. It is very doubtful that traditional workers, who gave up their power decades ago, will ever reclaim it. These workers abdicated their power for safety and security. Modern professional workers come along displaying a reluctance to separate themselves from their power but, at the same time, show little understanding of how to utilize it. This is management's challenge. Modern professionals are looking for opportunity, emotional freedom, and psychological (not only economic) security in terms of meaningful work. Provide this, and these workers will find their way to empowerment.

The ambiguity of empowerment is well known but rarely gets much attention. This is not totally the fault of management. Well-meaning executives have turned to social engineers for help. What they too often have received is psychobabble. The 30-something crowd has found its own answer. Currently, Deepak Chopra, a psychiatrist, is very popular with them. His entertaining message has an Eastern flavor and relates to heightened consciousness. "The new intelligence is a female intelligence," he insists, "which is nonlinear, holistic, intuitive, creative, nourishing, and wise. It is nonpredatory, not about winning or losing, and needs to be embraced in society by both men and women. Half the U.S. Congress has prostate cancer," he advises, "because they express their male energy only through predatory intelligence."[6]

Imagine a worker going into his boss with that kind of message. What Chopra is saying has merit. In an isolated context, however, it is certainly open to misinterpretation. Werner Erhard and his Erhard Seminar Training (EST) filled a similar need in the 1970s.[7] Anxious people were looking for neat little boxes with answers.[8] EST proved it was a need impossible to fill.[9] It remains to be seen how Chopra will fare. It isn't wise to get caught up too quickly in the latest craze. HRD has too often taken half-baked ideas and sold them to management as finished goods. These fads, once disseminated, go through a phasic chain from excitement, euphoria, acclaim, critical review, confusion, and disappointment to termination. Cultural change is not witchcraft.

Management is receptive to new ideas as long as it doesn't involve too much of its time. Unfortunately, if management doesn't have a substantial role in the process, it is a waste of everybody's time. There are no miracles or magic formulas—only hard work and persistent effort. Thanks largely to Isaac Newton, management sees the organization as a fine-tuned clock. Management, then, as a machine mind, breaks everything down and then applies experts to the care of the parts. This is a masculine mind, a linear mind, a mind that can never get enough detail. Its obsession with data predisposes it to distort reality—*if it can't be measured, it doesn't exist!* More energy can be spent in dysfunctional quantification than is appropriate. Chopra calls this "predatory intelligence," while writer Alan Valentine advises, "Whatever else may be made mechanical, human values cannot."[10] So that is the intrigue. Executives are known for their no-nonsense *quantitative thinking*, for their ability to "stay in the kitchen and take the heat," as President Harry S. Truman put it, while being disinclined to invest much time in what they see as frivolous *qualitative thinking*. "Give me the facts and get on with it," they cry, the implication being "my powers of reasoning will do the rest." This makes them vulnerable to the *tyranny of judgment.* They are, much like their traditional workers, more inclined to be reactive than proactive, finding it easier to criticize ideas than create them. The pattern of their thinking is usually confined to *thesis, antithesis,* and *synthesis,* which represents only a fraction of their creative potential. This inductive thinking is little more than a shorthand summary of past experience. Consequently, they are completely unprepared when an adviser comes in with an off-the-wall idea, an idea which might just be what the doctor ordered. Instead, they buy into a rehash of dated schemes: incentive plans, pay-for-performance, empowerment, or project skills training. *Experience is fossilized into a roster of the familiar.* Executives seldom escape cultural biases any better than anyone else. Faced with a problem, our programming commits us to judge, categorize, analyze, and dissect the problem to death. Few of us are inclined to explore it qualitatively. This involves considering several possibilities, generating a series of options, outlandish and otherwise, and then arriving at some experimental methodology to test its relevance to our requirements. We prefer to test an individual's thinking ability, and place his I.Q. score in a neat little box, rather than to design a climate in which he might increase his thinking ability.

Most CEOs of American *Fortune* 500 companies were educated in finance, science, or engineering. With rare exception does a CEO of a major corporation have a liberal arts background, which might be the best education of all for the twenty-first century executive. Their predominant educational programming is on what things can do rather than what they can make people be. The arrogance of this education is in the belief that if you have knowledge, then action is easy. Well, it isn't. Being susceptible to thinking in boxes is painfully illustrated in such programs as Quality of Work (QW), Quality of Work Life (QWL), Quality of Management (QM), Total Quality Management (TQM), Total Employee Involvement (TEI), Participative Management (PM), Performance Management Systems (PMS), Shared Management Programs (SMP), and Empowerment Initiatives (EI).

With so much time, energy, and expense spent on packaging, few resources remain for action. Take the venerated Malcolm Baldrige Award for Quality. Florida Power Corporation pulled out all stops to attain this award, only to have the award become an all-consuming end in itself, not the intended means to a cultural change. It couldn't have been otherwise because the award was a test instrument, a judgmental device to measure quality, not a creative design to establish a quality culture. The same thing happens in education. A problem is identified, and a new curriculum is generated; another problem spins off this curriculum, with still another curriculum generated, ad infinitum. So, each of the initiatives listed above, with few exceptions, has sputtered to death, only to be replaced by yet another. These imperfect practices indicate our preference for interpretation to exploration, analysis to design. There isn't a CEO in industry, commerce, education, the church, government, or the military whose staff cannot produce an impressive analytical slide show to document the organization's commitment to change. Yet seldom is there a perceptible departure from the familiar. Such a departure could be career-limiting. There seems a passion for information, but an aversion to ideas; a need to discover, but a reluctance to create. We are more apt to describe a problem than take action on it. Cleverness has a higher value than wisdom. The clever person is often an adept problem-solver; the wise person more apt to be insightful as to why the problem exists. Cleverness is like a sharp-focus lens. Wisdom is like a wide-angle lens. We seem more comfortable with the extroverted thinker than with the person who displays introspection. Yet, in the end, advises Edward de Bono, "it is the inner world which makes life worth living. The real purpose of the outer world is to keep us alive and to feed the dreams (visions and objectives) of the inner world."[11]

Unfortunately, the only workers who respond to the mechanistic by-the-numbers agenda are the fast-disappearing blue-collar workers. They were regimentally conditioned to take orders. We can no longer afford this type of worker. Society in general and the workplace in particular require *mature adult workers,* not conforming children who become uninspired, unimaginative, complying adults. The *Hawthorne Effect* is a benchmark of note. In that famous study at Western Electric (1927–32) in Chicago, no matter how conditions were altered, workers responded positively.[12] Professional workers are less responsive to manipulation. Since manipulation still goes on, professionals play their own sly game of "what you see is not necessarily what you get." In essence, the dichotomy between professional and blue-collar workers is as real as that between the *common good* and *personhood*. Patriotism is obvious among rank and file workers, less so among professionals. Management, despite this, insists on interpreting worker motivation along familiar lines as though there were a homogeneous workforce. It frequently magnifies its effectiveness by saluting the achievements of blue-collar workers, while overlooking the relative underachievement of professionals. Perhaps there is a disconnect between management and professionals because they view the world through similar eyes. Blue-collar workers, for instance, see themselves as soldiers and their managers as officers. Insubordination seldom enters their minds, whereas it plagues professionals. Blue-collar workers may be the last bastion of the *common good*, and they are a shrinking army.

Blue-collar workers are not the problem. Thanks to a good assist from automation, robotics, computer-aided design and manufacturing, and laser technology, hands-on labor costs continue to drop. American blue-collar workers are among the most productive in the world. But hands-on labor represents only 10 to 15 percent of the cost of a product or service. True cost savings and operating efficiency are found in indirect labor costs—the costs associated with the services of managers and professionals. This explains why cost-cutting redundancy exercises have become common. What it doesn't explain is why the first tier of layoffs is invariably directed at blue-collar workers, unless it is because of the ease of implementation. Blue-collar workers have had a history of displacement. Managers and professionals have not. This is a new and quite wrenching experience for them. These workers considered themselves safe. Pruning the organizational tree by cutting at the roots conveys the wrong message. To management's credit, it is correcting this error and is conducting sensible downsizing across most organizations. This is a hopeful sign.

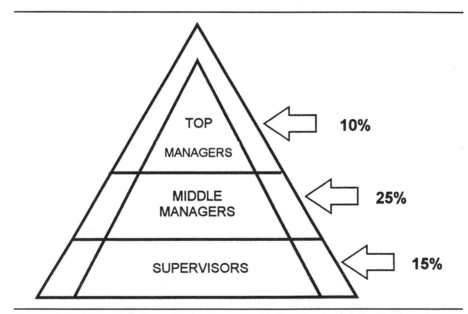

Figure 3.3   Pruning the management pyramid for organizational effectiveness.

Judicious and timely pruning of the management pyramid is a noble mission. There is an obvious glut of management, the accumulative effects of 50 years of neglect. Were any organization to summarily reduce its top management by 10 percent, middle management by 25 percent, and first-line supervision by 15 percent and not cut a single blue-collar worker, productivity would undoubtedly double in six months (Figure 3.3). The easiest way to implement such a process might be through attrition and retirement.

Management's Union

While organizations are reducing their raw numbers of people, the pesky problem of *management creep* still persists. Staff engineers, administrators, and service professionals know how to work this phenomenon. In 1980 I saw management creep up close and personal. A *Fortune* 500 facility had 4,200 employees and a complement of 250 managers, supervisors, and staff engineers. In 1989, after several iterative reductions in personnel, the facility had 3,200 employees and 400 managers, supervisors, and staff engineers. Over the same period, the operation doubled in sales. In 1980, for example, HRD had 65 employees and 7 managers. In 1989 the HRD staff had been reduced to 34 employees, but still retained its 7 managers. Meanwhile, most workers were asked to do the work of two or more people. HRD, the assumed advocate of workers, was in a position to educate management on the cultural shadings to the issue of the *common good* and *personhood*, particularly as it related to the changing nature of work. It was also in a position to create a psychological climate conducive to open exchange between managers, professionals, and other workers on the changing nature of the work relationship. Instead, HRD literally became part of the problem. This was accomplished by unwittingly becoming management's union rather than the employee's advocate. By telling management what it wanted to hear instead of what it needed to know, by failing to report the arrogant way many professionals went about their jobs, and by creating innocuous but costly and time-consuming cosmetic interventions, which challenged none of management's pet biases, HRD failed management and tuned out professionals and most workers. What's worse, chances are HRD will never again be trusted with so much influence.

The function of HRD is that of an inside-outsider. It is never that of the "yes man." To discharge its function effectively, HRD is a provocateur—the role of the consultant—which is the antithesis of the consoler, the role of the sycophant. HRD gravitated to what the organization didn't need, a union for management. As a result, it put many organizations in jeopardy, not by design, but certainly by default. This happened at a time when the organization most urgently needed leadership and healing. By being reactive, HRD compounded an already tenuous situation—the need for senior management to become totally involved and committed to change and the failure of this management to accept this role, choosing instead to unwisely delegate it to HRD.

Individual Success and Organizational Values

An organization has values. An individual has values. If the values of the organization and the individual are congruent, there is synergy, and nothing is impossible. If the values are in conflict, much energy is dissipated, and both the organization and the individual are put at risk. Work does not take place in a vacuum, nor is it likely that a collision in values can be completely avoided. What is important is that workers and managers learn to accept value differences as a condition to mutual understanding. The collision of values can be illustrated by what success means to one modern professional versus what it means to a traditional manager. Take this case study:

Dirk Edwards is a corporate executive for an American multinational living in Brussels, Belgium. He accepted the assignment primarily because he wanted to see the European Economic Community up close. He also felt he could make a contribution, given his expertise in organizational development. Neither money nor career enhancement was considered in his decision to accept the assignment.

Dirk sees himself as an enabler. He has been successful in creating self-management work teams and watched unreliable workers become responsible in an encouraging work climate. To him, achievement means contributing to the success of others. "If we can serve our first customers well, our peers and the users of our services," he says, "we will be successful, and so will they." This finds him inclined to pay more attention to what those below him think than what those above him demand. Obviously, Dirk is not into politically correct behavior. Nor is he inclined to having his people perform to standards other than their own. Everyone likes to be measured, he believes, but only if he or she has some input into the design.

Dirk is a student of servant leadership, believing it is his role to provide people with the tools, training, and freedom to do the job. "Once everyone is on the same page as to what needs to be done," he says, "my job is to get out of the way." This supportive behavior makes Dirk popular with his people. Within the company, he has gained a reputation for doing the impossible. That is why he was selected for the European assignment. Given these circumstances, he thought, perhaps naively, that this would be yet another opportunity to serve. Six months into the assignment, the following conversation took place between Dirk and his boss during a three-hour train trip from Brussels to Amsterdam:

Boss: "I get the feeling I want you to be more successful than you want to be."

Dirk: "Define success."

Boss: "Well, making an impression on the European affiliate general managers, keeping our corporate fathers happy in the United States and keeping me out of trouble."

Dirk: "What about operations?"

Boss: "What about them?"

Dirk: "What if doing something significant requires making some people uncomfortable or making you unhappy? What then?"

Boss: "You don't do it. You're only over here for a few years. Don't try to be a hero. Remember, all I want is to make you successful. That's my point."

Dirk: "What do you think motivates me?"

Boss: "What motivates you? What motivates all of us: pleasing the boss, promotions, belonging to the club, making the bucks, getting the perks, being able to provide comfort for the family...how am I doing?"

Dirk: "What motivates me is challenging work, the freedom and control of what I do, your trust, respect, and support when I fall short of the mark. Money has little to do with my motivation; nor do the perks, status, or promotions."

Boss: "Bullshit!"

This exchange illustrates not only a considerable strain between the two men, but a deep breach in values. The boss, a vice president, clearly expected Dirk, a director, to think, feel, and behave as he did. No surprises! Yet both men operated in *separate realities*.[13] This doesn't make one right and the other wrong. It only points out that they are different, and this difference prevents them from communicating meaningfully with each other. There is little trust and less compassion of either man for the other's point of view. Where the men are alike is that they both think they are right.

Curiously, because Dirk did not respond as expected, he intimidated his boss. Where the two men actually differ is that Dirk's authority comes from within, whereas his boss's authority does not. Dirk has a high need to please himself; his boss has a high need to please his superiors. The boss is a product of the company, where the *common good* remains still in place. Dirk is a product of *personhood*, where the company is valued as long as it supports his self-interests. He is the new professional. The boss is the old traditional manager who expects Dirk's loyalty as his number one priority. Implicitly, the boss seeks Dirk to be beholden to him and dependent upon him for his success. This offends Dirk, who is inclined to be his own man. Dependency is a way to control. It will not lead to interdependence. Nor is Dirk's independence likely to lead to teamwork. Thus, we have a standoff. Dirk is disinclined to humor his boss, while his boss is exasperated with his attitude. This clash in values led to Dirk's being sent home early.

The Need to Please Others

To the traditional manager, success is commonly measured in terms of status, money, promotions, and perks. These incentives are meant to motivate the recipient in a predictable manner. Such incentives count heavily on the cultural conditioning of the recipient having a high *need to please others*. Incentives are the cultural currency of the *common good*. This currency promotes the paternalistic authority of the benefactor and the accompanying dependence of the recipient. The role relationship here is one clearly of dominance (giver) and submission (taker). It leads to the

recipient of the exchange looking outside himself for authority, answers, and justification. It is a dependent relationship in which the *parent* of the exchange (benefactor) controls the *child* of the exchange (benefitted) to its purpose. No matter what the
level of success of the recipient, as long as this relationship exists, the currency of
the incentive creates a dependent situation, which is the equivalent of being suspended in adolescence, never to experience what might be called mature adulthood
(see Iacocca, Chapter 6, p. 123).

A high need to please others should not be confused with the need to *serve
others*. These are worlds apart. The high need to please others is actually self-serving
and reactive. The person doesn't develop a point of view, but tries to perceive the
most valued point of view and then attempts to echo this sentiment. It is the reason
polls are so popular. This person wants to be where it counts, with the majority. For
the same reason, this person reads books that are listed as best-sellers, attends films
with three or more stars, consults a tourist guide for what places to visit on vacation,
and seldom ventures beyond the acceptable. Mega-industries have developed to
anticipate and satisfy this person's every anxiety.

It is a myth that once a person reaches a certain level of success, psychic
dependence vanishes. If anything, it intensifies. This dependency can go all the way
to the board room. Such a person doesn't cast a corporate vote until he is sure which
side will prevail. He thrives in the land of the tentative and the home of the indecisive.
A high need to please others also exhibits a curious preoccupation with *position
power, personal wealth, and presence* at the expense of *purposeful performance*.
Appearances mean everything to him who has a high need to please others. Even
information cannot be handled straightforwardly. It must be massaged to put the right
spin on it before passing it on. Consequently, CEOs, surrounded by those so inclined,
are the last to know what is truly going on. Information passed through several layers,
each layer tailoring the message to satisfy the assumed needs of the person above
before passing it on, cannot help but distort and dilute. Relevant information seldom
gets beyond the functional group without contamination.

Organizational climbers are lifetime members of the "High Need to Please
Others Association." They are much more adept at serving those above them than
serving the organization. To the climber, those above are the organization. Climbers
display an ability to anticipate a superior's needs before he knows them. This skill
is essential in the traditional organization, but represents a handicap which goes
beyond the disingenuous in today's mainstream organization. It demands fresh ideas
to survive and requires unfiltered information to act in a timely fashion, neither of
which are part of the organizational climber's arsenal. He is still around, but he is
going nowhere. He has been schooled to react and displays little talent for being
creative.

A profile of the organizational climber provides a clue as to the type of organization which best suits him. A climbers shows an amazing facility for reacting to
paper generated by others, red-penciling it, and making astute comments. Yet he is
terrified of the blank page. He thinks in terms of the part (department, discipline,

position, person) rather than the whole (system, function) and always in linear, never non-linear, terms. He is an aficionado of nostalgia, enamored of what was, not what can be; a guardian of stability, while intimidated by chaos. He prefers to defend the status quo rather than challenge it. Others find him clever, never wise. He thinks in terms of the singular, not the plural, and can wax humble if it serves him. Consultants materialize out of the high need to please. Climbers and consultants are cut from the same cloth. No one is a better customer of these providers than the climber, who understands them implicitly. Climbers translate their superiors' needs into a complement of experts, programs, and assorted confections. Climbers are beholden to these providers because they have little sense of what is needed. The fact that we have more fad solutions than identified problems is a tribute to the liaison between consultants and climbers. On a more positive note, climbers render stability, predictability, and continuity to a maintenance-type organization. They perform well in a stable market where a tolerance for excess is high, but much less effectively where soaring growth or precipitous decline is the problem.

The Need to Please Self—A Different Path

We seem determined to drive the round peg into the square hole. Throughout the ages, the *discovery of truth* has been the idiom of philosophers, religious thinkers, and scientists. This idiom is proving inadequate when the need today is to design, construct, build, and change paradigms to move us forward. Notice that when the drive is to *search for truth*, it leads to dogma, arrogance, righteousness, and defensiveness. Edward de Bono writes, "If you are seeking the truth, then you are not interested in creating truths."[14] The way we view truth could be construed as a fundamental problem of our time. Is truth a static thing or dynamic process? Why can't we create truths? Why do we insist on seeing truth as a wheel that we keep reinventing—a more and more sophisticated wheel, to be sure, but still a wheel? Could it be because a complacent arrogance prevents us from seeing the absurdity of our ways? I wonder. Our Western thinking is clearly failing because it is not designed to deal with a changing world. It loves a static, stable, predictable, nostalgic world, a world which can be classified and cemented into boxes. If you need evidence, look no further than the central themes of popular non-fiction. Typical is the famed Harvard University entomologist Edward O. Wilson's book *In Search of Nature* (1996), in which he attempts to unravel the mystery of the finite world of insects. Other books enthusiastically search for our origins, lost continents, life in outer space, God, and the source of the soul. There is even, at this moment, a valiant search for Jesus, as though it is conditional for Christians to prove the historic Jesus consistent with all His myths in order for them to believe.[15] We keep building our knowledge base in our searching, yet no one even knows what general intelligence is. The point is that none of this brings us closer to dealing adequately with change.

The truth of the Gospels, Joseph Campbell tells us in *The Hero with a Thousand Faces* (1968), is not in the literal truth of the Bible, but in its mythic wonder, which guides us to living better lives.[16] Campbell shows how ancient societies have designed their lives around the mythic oral histories of their people. These myths and mysteries sustain them. Similarly, we need to design and construct paradigms to manage change more successfully. We cannot discover paradigms. There is not a lost continent of paradigms anywhere.

This is offered as preamble to the following hypothesis: *the creative verve to design and construct paradigms for change is only possible in a mind that has a high need to please itself.* Such a mind is a discriminating mind, a mind that does not take its programming at face value, a mind that questions protocol and authority, education and religious doctrine, customs and mores. There is evidence, perhaps faint-hearted at this stage, of a new breed of professional workers bent on asking themselves the hard questions and meeting the challenges of change. They are willing to take the risks to do something significant, to embrace the freedom necessary to achieve this, to accept ostracism if need be, and to assume the responsibility of taking control of what they do. Most organizations are not structured to accommodate these workers. Many find it necessary to struggle on their own, but they are out there. To think differently on purpose, they must deprogram themselves from conventional thinking. Quietly, imperceptibly, they move away from the *common good* and into the "no man's land" of *personhood*. They move away from the bureaucratic constraints that sponsor *non-thinking thinking* and the *non-doing doing of non-thing things*. The society of the *common good* was and is a different society than the society of today. What's more, we cannot go back to the way it was. We must move forward. Yesterday, a family meant a man, woman, and child, not two members of the same sex in an intimate and monogamous relationship. Yesterday, religion meant faith in a god or gods of choice, not a Church of Scientology. Yesterday, school meant a place dedicated to education, not a satellite dish beaming television lectures into a room, or a Web site on a computer monitor. Yesterday, government meant a national entity, not an international marketplace. And yesterday, work meant making a product, not creating information. Work also involved a place outside the home; now it is more likely to be inside the home. Early in the next century, one out of every two families will be self-employed. The structure and infrastructure of the society of the common good were designed to maintain a paternalistic relationship between parent and child, teacher and student, priest and parishioner, employer and worker, politician and citizen. This construct is not working any longer. Yet there is a nostalgic longing for the order, stability, and harmony of this society, as chaos, instability, and disharmony play havoc with our lives.

The irony is that the present conditions are ideal for invention and creative pursuit. Out of World War II and subsequent wars, we have evolved into a smaller, more heterogenetic world community. Engineers in India are working on a common project with American engineers while their colleagues are sleeping, and vice versa. In this way work goes on 24 hours a day. These workers are part of the new breed that has come into prominence across the globe. They differ radically from workers of the past in terms of education, experience, attitude and values, motivation, perspective, discipline, and outlook. Spiritually and materially, they are more authentic because they reflect the conflicts and contradictions of their times. Americans may cringe when they hear of the authoritarian policies in Singapore, where punishment is harsh for breaking simple rules, as in the 1994 case of 18-year-old Michael Fay, son of an American executive based in this Asian nation. After the young man was convicted of spray-painting graffiti on some cars, he was sentenced to four months in prison and six strokes of the lash across his bare bottom. Even the most strict "spare the rod and spoil the child" defenders were aghast. The U.S. Embassy got involved, and Lee Kuan Yew's government, which had been celebrated as part of the Asian miracle of economic recovery, was put on notice that it had stepped over the line.[17] This is but a small indication of how the world is shrinking and power is shifting.

In America, this new breed of professional will soon represent nearly 90 percent of all workers. Yet, most organizations behave as if it were 1950, when four out of five workers were blue-collar. Regardless, today's professionals are set on choosing a different path, even though the organization may give them little room to maneuver. Wherever they look, they see a preoccupation with comfort, where caution is sponsored at the expense of courage, dependency at the expense of initiative, the status quo at the expense of growth, and mediocrity at the expense of greatness. Greatness, which Walt Whitman celebrated without embarrassment, is throbbing in their hearts. But to reach for greatness is threatening to a maintenance-driven culture. Perhaps the best indicator of today's aversion to greatness is the venality of our times. Greatness is reflected in the quality of sinners as well as saints. Periods of history are punctuated by extremes in human behavior. Great saints are commonly accompanied by great sinners because both are a part of each other. Most sins today are venial, unimaginative, petty, and blasé. Granted, they are brutal, malicious, ugly, and horrendous, but they are not diabolical. There are no Fausts, no mortal sinners in sight.

Perhaps we are too preoccupied with the external world. This finds us questioning everything, believing in little. Beliefs of the inner world are not easily altered by reference to the outer world. The inner world is selective, subjective, and fallible; the outer world is objective and certain. The inner world has its own truth, its own logic, and tends to be fluid rather than fixed. Thinking is the laboratory of the inner world, while experiments are the laboratory of the outer world. Values, metaphors, objectives, and paradigms all exist first in the inner world. That is why it is to our advantage to pay more attention to this world. People with a high need to please themselves are motivated primarily by this inner world. Their pleasure comes from being involved in and committed to something of consequence. By the same token, they are appalled by busy work, people without an opinion, people who have a high need to be liked, people who are secretive, people who are terrified of losing control, people who are afraid to disobey, people who are afraid to show affection or disappointment, people who are afraid to fail, people who avoid those who tell them what they think.

Traditionalists might read this motivation as selfish and callous. What motivates people with a high need to please themselves is the mind-set of *enlightened self-*

interest, with the principal drive being to serve and to be useful in the service of others. Robert Greenleaf captures this essence in his book *Servant Leadership* (1977): "A new moral principle is emerging which holds that the only authority deserving one's allegiance is that which is freely and knowingly granted by the led to the leader in response to, and in proportion to, the clearly evident servant stature of the leader."[18] Greenleaf goes on to say that those who choose to follow this principle will not casually accept the authority of existing organizations. Indeed, professionals will only respond to those chosen as leaders who are trusted servants. Greenleaf concludes that in the future, the only viable organization will be that which is servant-led. This is consistent with the common drive of professionals. *They desire to serve, to be useful, to enhance the interests of others, to influence without resorting to the use of their power, and to discover their own greatness in the achievements of those that they support and serve.*

Fortunately for all of us, professionals flourish in an atmosphere of chaos, conflict, confrontation, and contention. What is different about them is that they manage this environment rather than be mangled by it. This creative climate is alive with the excitement of possibility. Here diverse control emanates, and surprise is routine fare. Role identity is fluid, while authority and responsibility respond to circumstances. The group has a role identity, and members of the group have the skills required for the work at hand. This is a customer-friendly environment with the first customer being colleagues. Final customer requirements are identified, validated and checked, and updated in order to bring about customer satisfaction. In short, professionals focus on their customer, the people with whom they work, and the user community. What is perhaps surprising about these professionals, no matter their discipline, is that they have more the mind of the artist than the analyst, more the heart of the creator than the discoverer, more the soul of the rebel than the patriot. A small contingent of professionals are in the process of designing new paradigms with no clear vision as to their parameters. They are flying blindly but boldly. They have chosen to confront their limits. Beyond that, they embrace the challenge to create dangerously and to surpass the limits of pleasing others to the joy in pleasing self.

Endnotes

1.   Charles Dickens, *A Tale of Two Cities* (London: Penguin Classics, 1970), (first published 1859), p. 35.
2.   Douglas McGregor, *The Human Side of Enterprise* (New York: McGraw-Hill, 1960); Robert Blake and Jane Mouton, *The Managerial Grid* (Houston: Gulf Publishing, 1964); William Ouchi, *Theory Z* (Reading, MA: Addison-Wesley, 1981); Kaoru Ishikawa, *What Is Total Quality Control?* (Englewood Cliffs, NJ: Prentice-Hall, 1985); Masaaki Imai, *Kaizen: The Key to Japan's Competitive Success* (New York: Random House, 1986); Frederick Herzberg, *Work and the Nature of Man* (New York: World Publishing Co., 1967); W. Edwards Deming, *Out of the Crisis* (Cambridge, MA: MIT Center for Advanced Study, 1986). Note: Few of these authors acknowledge, much less give credence to, the impact of *workplace culture* on performance.

3. Edward de Bono, *Parallel Thinking: From Socratic to de Bono Thinking* (London: Penguin Books, 1995).
4. Karl Zinsmeister (American Enterprise Institute), *The Tampa Tribune*, April 10, 1990, opposite editorial page.
5. Cathy Cummins, "College Survey Aims at Cheating," *The Tampa Tribune*, September 7, 1996, University section, 1, 3.
6. Deepak Chopra, "The New Intelligence." *The Tampa Tribune,* September 4, 1996, Baylife, 2.
7. W. W. Bartley, III, *Werner Erhard: The Transformation of a Man* (New York: Clarkson N. Potter Inc., 1978).
8. Bartley's book is a hagiography of Erhard, the founder of EST, whom he sees as having answers for all these anxious people.
9. Kathy Hacker (Knight-Ridder Newspapers), "EST's Werner Erhard Creates a New Forum to Sell Ideas," *The Tampa Tribune*, August 22, 1988, 5-D. Hacker writes, "Getting in touch with your feelings is out. Making money is in. So Werner Erhard has switched from pushing EST to offering money-making forums."
10. Alan Valentine, *Age of Conformity* (Chicago: Henry Regnery Company, 1954), p. 93.
11. de Bono, op. cit., p. 132.
12. Randall Collins and Michael Makowsky, *The Discovery of Society* (New York: Random House, 1972), pp. 165–167.
13. Rick Suarez, Roger C. Miles, and Darlene Stewart, *Sanity, Insanity, and Common Sense,* (New York: Fawcett Columbine, 1987), pp. 59–71.
14. de Bono, op. cit., p. 222.
15. David Van Biema, "The Search for Jesus: The Gospel Truth?" *Time*, April 8, 1996, 52–60.
16. Joseph Campbell, *The Hero with a Thousand Faces* (Princeton, NJ: Princeton University Press, 1973).
17. Freed Zakaria, "Culture Is Destiny: A Conversation with Lee Kuan Yew," *Foreign Affairs*, March/April 1994, 109–126.
18. Robert K. Greenleaf, *Servant Leadership: A Journey into the Nature of Legitimate Power and Greatness* (New York: Paulist Press, 1977), p. 10.

4 Incipient Catastrophe

Traditionally, one party identifies itself with the establishment's power structure, while the other is the people's advocate. Prosperous times, when the political pie is big enough to satisfy everyone, favour the establishment because popular involvement declines into sentiments such as "you never had it so good" and "don't rock the boat." Hard times, on the other hand, lead people to adopt more militant political stances, and the dominant slogan is "it's time for a change."[1]

Alexander Woodcock and Monte Davis

I have noticed when visiting the West, a certain illness, and I call this the illness of stabilization.

Lech Walesa, founder of Poland's Solidarity Union,
on visiting the United States in November 1989

War belongs to the province of business competition, which is also the conflict of human interests.[2]

Karl Von Clausewitz

To fully appreciate the explicit ideas that are to follow, it seems advisable to establish a theoretical foundation. The workplace is experiencing an unfolding of continuous, oftentimes imperceptible change that could—at any moment—bring about an abrupt, discontinuous change in the behavior of masses of people. Already a half century old and gaining momentum, this phenomenon strains the economic and the emotional and intellectual fabric of Western society. A rational ordering society such as ours has great difficulty admitting, much less grasping, what is not readily apparent, for this possible calamity is unresponsive to quantitative methodologies.

René Thom, a theoretical mathematician, accepts the limitations of conventional wisdom, developing what he refers to as "catastrophe theory." This theory is an attempt to understand the subtleties of the *change process* and to deal with them

45

accordingly. Catastrophe theory is a predictive concept. In mapping such trends, Thom uses differential mathematical topology, a sophisticated form of geometry, to avoid the restrictions of linear curves and regular solids of Greek geometry. My intention here is to use the model for descriptive purposes in an explanatory framework.

Due to its foundation in topology, *catastrophe theory is qualitative, not quantitative.* This is an important distinction. Being qualitative, it describes and predicts the shapes of processes like maps without scales. What it does not do is indicate how far away these processes are from occurring, how large, or even when they might occur. It is rather a consciousness-enlightening mechanism to alert us to impending change so that we can deal with it appropriately. Change can be of such proportions as to set off a chain reaction of catastrophes, leaving nothing but chaos and confusion in its wake. Adequately forewarned, measures can be taken to minimize its impact.

According to Thom, all phenomena continuously seek and then struggle to maintain a *stable state*. Stable states, in terms of topology, represent sets of points, lines, or surfaces in a behavioral space. Catastrophe, then, is *any discontinuous transition that occurs when a system can have more than one stable state.* The catastrophe occurs when one stable state surges to the other stable state.

That could be, in an organizational sense, moving from the stable state of the *management-centered* organization to the adaptable state of the *professional worker-centered* organization. Because there exists no intervening states between these two stable states, the transition here becomes *discontinuous*. The ultimate passage from the initial state of management control to the final state of *professional worker control* is likely to be precipitously brief in comparison to the time spent in the previous stable states. Indeed, one day very soon, in the blinking of an eye, the organization may well be transformed from paternalistic control to egalitarian consensus.

The stable state of organization is resisting this change. Picturing an organization without managers is a radical idea. The fact that many experts do not buy into this possibility reflects the reason catastrophe theory is such a valid concept. Either the majority would preserve the stable state of management control or deny the radical transformation of organization suggested here. Most would agree that there is continuous change in the landscape of an organization on the surface, what with computers, robotics, laser technology, telecommunications, and global networking of around-the-clock production. These are essentially quantitative changes that might be disturbing in one sense, but in another are seen as the price of progress. What might be challenged is the idea that accompanying these quantitative changes are much more significant qualitative changes. Quantitative continuous change on the surface is also fostering qualitative discontinuous change below the surface. A change from the stable state of management control to the stable state of professional worker control is unlikely to happen without widespread disruption and unwholesome hostility.[3]

What further confuses this scenario are the surface histrionics gaining all the attention. An epic battle is taking place between two dazzling opponents, Microsoft and Netscape, for dominance of the Internet—with the battle cry "Winner take all!"

Bill Gates of Microsoft operates like General Patton, while James Barksdale, CEO of Netscape, counterattacks like General Grant. It is total warfare—ugly, personal, ruthless, but in the open. Workers in both camps have no voice in the matter and endure humiliation, subjugation, and deprivation (psychological) because the electronic stock ticker tells them every day they are getting richer (or poorer) by the minute. Warp-speed reinvention is a given in the information industry, which makes conventional warfare look like child's play. Just as few can survive for long in a blitzkrieg before madness intervenes as relief; the casualties here promise to be great, for these generals take no prisoners. Catastrophe theory applies here as well, but with a difference—the phantom, extinction, can always be on the next stock ticker. This industry is essentially one-dimensional. It is controlling the agenda but is only a sideshow to what is happening across society or a distraction or entertainment, not the main event. Professionals and managers provide that.[4]

It is difficult to see things differently. The most complex system imaginable is the human mind, which must be one degree more complex than whatever it chooses to imagine. Catastrophe theory proposes that qualitative stability is a necessary characteristic of thought. We think on the basis of how we are trained to think. We deal with our problems on the basis of what we already know. We see what we expect to see. Without *qualitative stability*, recognition and memory would be impossible. This ability finds us never venturing too far from the safety net of the expected.

Thom holds the evolutionary view that just as our bodies are adapted for crawling, walking, and running and just as our hands are adapted for grasping objects and shaping tools, so our minds are adapted for topologically modeling the world. Everywhere—in thought, language, and perception—discontinuity and qualitative change occur continuously. It so happens our inclination is to be more comfortable with quantitative change. Yet the transition from one way of seeing something to another is qualitatively discontinuous. You cannot stop the process halfway. Catastrophe theory, then, offers an alternative way of looking at the world, perhaps not more correct, but certainly more complete and surely radically different than what our cultural conditioning and our cultural biases have afforded.

Consider Figure 4.1. When you look at this optical illusion steadily, the transition from seeing the little circle in the center of one face to seeing it in the corner of the other is qualitatively discontinuous. Some may see it in the corner first and in the center second. There is no way of predicting which way one will see it. Whatever the perceptual mechanism at work, the change itself is stable. Both visual interpretations are coherent. Both make sense of the pattern.

We obviously see what we want to see. Yet perhaps one reason the concept of incipient organizational catastrophe is difficult to grasp is because stable discontinuity (professional worker control) does not depend on the specific potential for the change involved (high, medium, low), but merely on the existence of this discontinuity. Remember, management's dominance was unchallenged before the rise of the professional class of workers, a working class that now represents nearly 90 percent of all workers, that is better educated across the board than its management, and that

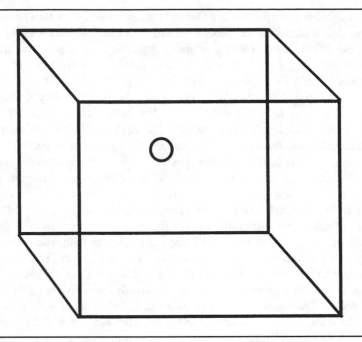

Figure 4.1   Where is the circle in the cube?

is a resource which controls the intellectual assets of organization. Management was unchallenged before because it was the elite with no one of comparable authority or competence in its world. This is no longer true.

Thom is correct in seeing this in evolutionary terms. At the turn of the century, most businesses were small and run by their owners. World War I gave many of these businesses a jump-start. Then there was also the explosion in technology—the automobile, airplane, radio, and transcontinental cable. Business owners now confined themselves to keeping the books and hiring supervisors to run the day-to-day operations. Shops merged into larger job shops, eventually becoming a General Motors or a General Electric. It was found necessary to acquire cash for expansion, so these fledgling businesses sold stock. To manage the expansion and grow the business, a new class of workers evolved—managers. Having sold hundreds of thousands of shares of stock, ownership became a misnomer as the chief stockholders of most major corporations owned less than one percent of a company. This gave management an opportunity to run operations as surrogate owners. A board of directors set the policy, while managers operated the business with little interference. The primary focus of these managers was on profits and dividends for stockholders. As long as profits were up and the stock price appreciated, management was unchallenged. Rank and file workers gradually came to feel exploited beyond their tolerance. Enter labor unions. The fight between labor and management during the 1920s and 1930s, all but forgotten today, was bloody and ruthless. Many lost their lives in this agonizing struggle. At the height of this disruption, the Great Depression sent shock waves of poverty across America. With one-third of the workforce unemployed (16 million), it turned the United States into a bleak continent. By 1933, the Gross Domestic Product (GDP) plummeted to little more than half of what it had been in 1929. The wild prosperity of the 1920s was unevenly distributed among various parts of the American economy. Notably, farmers and unskilled workers failed to participate, with the result that the nation's productive capacity was greater than its capacity to consume. With the election of President Franklin Delano Roosevelt in 1932, an ardent supporter of labor, order was restored, and labor peace was realized. Yet the Depression was to hang over America like a grim reaper.[5]

Not until the government started to spend heavily for defense in the early 1940s did the Depression fade and the tide start to turn. Labor and management put aside their differences to create the miracle of military mobilization. David Halberstam writes in *The Next Century* (1991), "With our great assembly lines and our ever-expanding industrial core…we became the industrial arsenal for the mightiest of war efforts. In 1942 and 1943 America alone produced almost twice as many planes as the entire Axis Powers (Germany, Italy and Japan). In 1943 and 1944 we were producing one ship a day and an airplane every five minutes."[6] World War II was management's finest hour. The war was a triumph as much for management as for the military. After the war, with many of the world's great industrial nations leveled, American management became opportunistic. Its know-how led the way to fulfill the world's appetite for American products. A *management elite* evolved naturally out of the war, with many military leaders becoming CEOs. Everyone, it seemed, wanted to be a manager. It wasn't enough to be an engineer, accountant, or technician. Success did not ring true unless "manager" followed your name. The management career track was open-ended. Managers soon realized the route to power was through "empire building." Compensation and title were based on the number of people reporting to a manager. So it wasn't long before managers found ways to have more people reporting to them with much less work to do.

Early in the 1960s, the economic recovery in Europe and Japan came to challenge a bloated corporate America. It hit the American automotive industry first and then expanded to appliances, clothing, glass, light fixtures, televisions, and motorcycles. Foreign products were of better quality, more durable, and cheaper. Panic set in. Mergers and hostile takeovers became common fare. Extreme tactics were used to fend off the onslaught, but to no avail. Meanwhile, Third World countries started to produce on their own—previously a guaranteed market for American raw materials and farm goods. In the mid-1960s, President Lyndon Baines "guns and butter" Johnson attempted to escalate the war in Vietnam and promote his "Great Society" at home. Subsequently, inflation reached double digits, as did unemployment on President Carter's watch. Then, in 1980, President Reagan set out to outspend the "Evil Empire" (Russia) in military hardware. Supply-side economics borrowed on the future to re-establish a controlled economy. An army of MBAs poured out of

American universities to monitor this recovery. MBAs were the newest iteration of the management elite. Their expertise was in symbolic economics—exchange rates and currency values—not in the production of goods and services. MBAs were a harbinger of things to come. Then in the early 1990s, the U.S.S.R., while giving every appearance of vigor, stability, and continuity, suddenly and abruptly collapsed and died before a disbelieving world—catastrophe theory manifested.

Today, sophisticated technology is changing the way we live. The creators of this technology have watched their world become increasingly mismanaged, misapplied, and misdirected. It is no mere coincidence that Steven Jobs of Apple fame, Bill Gates of Microsoft, and Marc Andreessen of Netscape, to name a few, are college dropouts. The answers for them were not confined to books warehoused in academia.[7]

This exploding new class of professional workers, for the most part docile and compliant, have seen their wages frozen, their career ladders vanish, their spendable incomes decline, and their predicament increasingly volatile, through no fault of their own. Looking around, they see management putting the business in the toilet and their futures in jeopardy. Yet they do nothing. Incipient catastrophe is at hand. Despite this somber note, professional workers have become increasingly the voice of influence through the exercise of *knowledge power*. Qualitative discontinuity has been gaining momentum. To ignore this qualitative change or to suggest that it is of little consequence does not reverse the pattern.

Incipient organizational catastrophe does not depend on a specific set of conditions that regulate organizational behavior, such as policies and procedures, formal structures, and the chain of command. What it does depend on is the *frequency and complexity of these restricting indices*. As a rule, the greater the chaos, the more the inclination is to increase these to re-establish order. As restricting policies increase, however, the conflicts they generate are likely to multiply and to become more complex and consequential. Stated otherwise, the greater the intensity with which restrictive policies are pursued, the less effective they become, and the sooner they lead to catastrophe. Nor is there much benefit to the strategy of *find the cause* (of the chaos) and effect order by dealing with it specifically. Cause is not relevant here. Catastrophe does not depend on the relationship of existing conditions and the resultant behaviors, but on the fact that they exist. Indeed, catastrophe does not lend itself to problem-solving. Cause and effect relationships cannot be easily isolated from events at hand. People are not wind-up dolls. Behavioral situations are not, as a rule, neat and clean—*this is the cause, that is the effect!* To define them so only provides answers without significance. To deal with catastrophe effectively requires putting problem-solving aside, perhaps even accepting that the problem is not solvable. That requires a mental leap for the Western mind, as does tabling the inclination to judge principals. What is better is to develop a conceptual framework which furthers the interests of all and involves some action which is neither disciplinarian nor punitive to any.

Even the most hardened citizens, as wardens in penitentiaries have discovered, respond to humane treatment. A near-riot situation developed in Indianapolis during the volatile 1970s as Vietnam protesters readied themselves to take on the police at

Monument Circle Park. They had successfully done so in many other major American cities, effecting much negative publicity for the war. Instead of riot gear, flak vests, clubs, shields, and smoke bombs, Mayor Richard G. Lugar (now U.S. Senator) had the police distribute ice cream cones to the potential rioters. This neutralized and humanized the crowd and avoided a potential catastrophe.

The situation in corporate organizations across the globe is less obvious. On the surface, corporations give the distinct appearance of harmony, industry, collegial regard, and purposefulness. What about under the surface? What about the so-called anxious class of corporate workers who wonder if today is to be their last? What about managers who believed in a management elite and worked hard to deserve membership? What about workers who grumble through the day about having no power, only to discover they have it, but haven't a clue as to what to do with it? Workers take comfort in playing the victim and wait to be rescued by management. *The irony is that workers are the system; only they can rescue themselves.* Management attempts to still play the rescuer, a role for which it is no longer suited. Frustration mounts, for workers and managers alike, as their physical and psychological health is put at risk. All of this impacts negatively on performance as the *six silent killers* lurk in the shadows. Experience tells us "something's gotta give!" The time for circular logic is gone. The thinking that created the problem is not sufficient to solve it. There appears to be little choice but to view organizations differently. This is no time for halfway measures. Encroaching discontinuity signals imminent catastrophe.

When Great Dreams Implode

The course of organization has, over time, been charted in terms of challenge and response. An external threat consistently enhances identity. An internal threat (which is often denied) consistently diminishes identity. Tangible threats alert the organization, yet obscure threats seal its destiny. The early growth of the American organization was accelerated by World War II. America materialized from that war with a sense of invincibility. It could do whatever it wanted with impunity. Whereas World War I found America's fighting men referred to as "doughboys" and being accused of arriving in Europe just in time to join the Armistice parade, World War II was different. The years 1942–45 demonstrated to dubious Allies that Americans were willing to fight for what they believed in. This war brought the United States out of isolation and into geopolitics. On the home front, it radically changed the fabric of society, threatening its moral, social, and psychological standards. The war years pried many women away from the home into large, impersonal defense factories, and it pried many young men away from farms and quaint towns into military uniform. Women met and worked with others who were like foreigners to them, so different from their own kind—more worldly, amoral, and unruffled. Men traveled to places they had never heard of before and found themselves thinking like philosophers as they danced with death. When the war ended in August 1945, many women stayed on as factory workers, while few soldiers returned to the farm. The war had given women a taste of freedom, independence, and economic power. Women found they could hold their own as mechanics, riveters, sheet metal workers, electricians, blueprint readers, and lathe and machine operators.[8] Soldiers came home less sure of themselves, more aware of a larger world, with an appetite to learn, understand, and experience. Provincial society was left behind as corporate society replaced it.

"Corpocracy," society functioning as a bureaucratic organization, made the simple complex and the familiar nostalgic.[9] The nuclear family—from taking meals together to sharing common interests—became self-consciously remote. Corporate farms replaced ancestral farms, with machines replacing farm hands. The identity of the farmer with the land became a memory. Semi-automated, mass production factories, perfected during the war, droned around the clock. Factory hands were further separated from the end product. Words such as "alienation" and "anomie" were invented to explain loss of pride and growing disenchantment. Protests were faint. Workers took home more money. Renters could be homeowners. Families could have two cars. Women could buy a dress a week, rather than every Easter. Parents who had not finished grammar school saw sons and daughters finish high school, and many go on to college. A new middle class of hard-working factory hands emerged. It was the best and worst of times.

Families saw their most cherished wishes fulfilled, but not as they envisioned. Children were given every advantage. They appeared to find little happiness and projected less joy. Spoiled and resentful, they refused to work for what they achieved or to struggle for what they wanted. It was difficult for them to establish trust with parents, peers, and themselves. Somehow they had managed to have everything and nothing at all. They were full of themselves, but empty of fulfillment. Greed became their creed—the more they had, the more they wanted—a case of being materially gorged but spiritually famished. As the song goes, "they were laughing on the outside, and crying on the inside," the legacy of too much, too many, too soon.

For a remarkable 20-year period (1945–65), this indulgence received scant attention. Children became their own parents. Parents escaped into work. Business couldn't be better. American enterprise could do no wrong. The dream as nightmare was ignored. Whatever America made, there was a market for it somewhere. "Buy American" was a cry that resonated around the globe. American power and prestige expanded as the American dream imploded into quiet desperation—first homes fell apart, then schools, then churches, then communities, then cities, and then the environment. The game of *making things well and thinking for the long haul*, never America's strong suit, rode herd on America's forte—*making things fast and living for today*. It became a zero-sum game, with *quantity* the winner at the expense of *quality*.

What made this expedience ironic is that the world's most gifted teachers on quality management, quality control, and corporate planning were Americans—W. Edwards Deming, J.M. Juran, and Peter Drucker. Deming created a science of quality around statistical process control, Juran developed foolproof quality management systems to detect and resolve chronic problems, and Drucker invented the tools to track management performance. These men were considered intrusive, their methodologies too complex and their ideas too academic. Cash registers were ringing too loud for their message to be heard. Yet it was heard elsewhere. This trio is credited with Japan's economic recovery and for the subsequent international focus on quality standards.

Success put blinders on America. The United States did not join the League of Nations after World War I, even though President Woodrow Wilson was one of its chief architects. He couldn't cut through the power of the isolationists. In the post–World War II period, America assumed the role of policeman to the world. Police invariably project their cultural bias on the policed. The *ethnocentrism* of the United States is epitomized by the belief that everyone wants to be an American. Moreover, this policing was devoid of any clear purpose save "making the world safe for democracy." This found Americans in Korea in the 1950s and in Vietnam in the 1960s and 1970s. The cost of these ill-advised incursions, in terms of loss of life and pride, remains vivid. What's more, the legacy of these misadventures will remain with taxpayers for generations to come as they wrestle with the national debt.

The agony of defeat in Korea was mollified by calling it a police action. For Americans who took pride in the United States never having lost a war, Vietnam was a humiliation. Dreams die hard even in the face of the nightmares they implode. Parents full of patriotism and the spirit of the *common good* were impotent to deal with their children of *personhood*. It wasn't until the "me" generation—the baby boomers born after World War II—came of age that this *continuity* set in motion a new qualitative *discontinuity*. Contentious of established precedence, no longer enamored of conspicuous materialism, disenchanted with the lies of government and presidents of questionable character, baby boomers distanced themselves first from their parents and then the establishment. They were impervious to the sentimentality of folklore and the belief that it was an honor to die for one's country. So they burned their draft cards or fled to Canada to avoid the draft. Bored with school, they either flunked out purposely, were thrown out, or simply dropped out. They quit or were fired from their jobs. They formed communes in open relationships as the idea of family and monogamy was found repugnant. They sought solace in ancient religions and mixed them liberally with whatever came to mind. They got in trouble with the law, called police "pigs," and tried to neutralize their ethnicity and class by dressing and looking alike. Shocking parents, who never had as much as a parking ticket, was not what they were about. They were about shedding their stultifying culture. They accepted the tags of "flower children," "hippies," "yuppies," and "not trusting anyone over 30." They saw war for what it was—the poor fighting the battles of the rich. They became the first disenfranchised generation in American history to stop a war without the vote. They chose not to be part of something that their values of *personhood* did not support. In a curious way, they upheld values that went back to their Puritan forbearers.

Now middle aged, two-thirds of them as parents expect their children to experiment with drugs, as they did, according to a Columbia University study (1996).[10] This confession made prominent newspaper headlines across America as drug usage, especially among teenagers, is a real problem to the establishment. To baby-boomer parents, it is seen as part of growing up. What if they are right? These baby boomers were witness to the United States' fall from grace. These sons and daughters of staunch American patriots did not exalt themselves for being right about the Vietnam War. They turned away from that war and inward against established authority and a schizophrenic society. America had developed a highly individualized logic to justify everything from the Vietnam War to the "War on Drugs." *Group think* centered around ludicrous daily reports of Viet Cong body counts as a measure of that war's progress, while shock statistics carried the message for teenage drug usage— "The government reports (August 1996) drug use among 12- to 17-year-olds rose from 5.3 percent of those surveyed in 1992 to 10.9 percent last year." Notice that it didn't say 94.7 percent of those surveyed in 1992 and 89.1 percent of those surveyed in 1996 were drug free. Group think rarely puts us more in contact with the world of our own reality.

The Vietnam "fall from grace" set in motion a generation of *self-directed* baby boomers. This frame of reference differed dramatically from their *other-directed* parents. These baby boomers had a high need to *please self*, whereas their parents had a high need to *please others*. Baby boomers could no longer comply with an American society that was veering dangerously off course and out of control. Hardly anarchists, they saw themselves as patriots in a new sense of American tradition. Indeed, they deemed the continuity of letting the establishment do their thinking and exercise carte blanche authority over their destiny as pure madness. Survival demanded the discontinuity of thinking for themselves and controlling their own destiny. Against this background, the favored economic status, which the United States had enjoyed since World War II, started to wane. The disregard of the industrial resurgence of Europe and Asia proved costly. Plant renovations lagged, equipment was not replaced, quality issues were not addressed, obsolescent skills of the workforce were not upgraded, competitive marketing analysis was ignored, and long-range planning was, at best, hasty and inconsequential. Sometimes this arrogance became somewhat comical, such as appliance manufacturers trying to sell huge American refrigerators to tiny Japanese kitchens, which were not much bigger than broom closets. The same was true of automobile manufacturers, who attempted to sell American cars to Europe and Asia. These resembled cumbersome boats trying to negotiate narrow channels. I once was held up for 20 minutes in Brussels when a Belle Air Chevrolet tried to make a U-turn and blocked both lanes. The car was literally impaled between two trees and a hedge like a bizarre sculpture.

Then oil nationalism became the shock of the 1970s. Detroit stubbornly continued to make gas-guzzlers, while the world market turned to the compact. Gasoline prices in Europe and Asia have always been several times those of the United States. When the Organization of Petroleum Exporting Countries (OPEC) raised the price of a barrel of oil from $2.50 to $10.00 in 1973, it sent the global economy into a downturn. Then, at the end of the 1970s, revolution disrupted supplies from Iran, creating a panic that drove prices from $13 to $33 a barrel, finally waking Detroit up to the inevitable compact.[11] The next decade saw Detroit striving to play "catch up," with compacts finally pouring out of its assembly plants. The point is that encroaching qualitative discontinuity was ignored. Impertinent industrialists were not alone. America's pristine universities, where scholarship is expected to register some detachment from passing events, came up with such grand strategies as the *competitive edge* and *competitive advantage* long after it was lost. *A society that is programmed to be reactive to events can seldom muster anything other than catch-up strategies, which are not strategies at all, but are declarations of panic and behavior suggestive of incipient catastrophe.*

The absence of American product quality (1970–85) and the counterbalancing consumption hysteria of the American people combined to make a nightmare of the great American dream—a house in the country, two cars in every garage, a secure income, and a promising retirement. Culture-watcher Christopher Lasch traces conspicuous consumption to its becoming the primary therapy for anxious Americans.[12] Chances are that what is consumed today is a product made somewhere other than in the United States. Foreign manufacturers have gotten rich on the appetite of Americans for more…of everything. With their foreign exchange, some speculators have bought large blocks of American metropolitan real estate, while others have purchased American companies. Many of these purchases have backfired, forcing these foreign investors to sell their interests at a considerable loss. They were willing to invest in a sick America. Obviously, they believed their acumen at home would translate into success in America. Once again, the arrogance of culture is to believe what is possible at home is probable elsewhere. Not always true.

The prescriptions designed to turn America around had one thing in common— none would radically restructure the organization. Managerial dominance was seen as the legitimate means of organizational renewal. America's economic woes were traced not to itself but to Japan, Inc. and European nationals. These competitors enjoyed advantages, according to this argument, that American firms didn't have, especially as these advantages related to government support and protective tariffs. The shifting of responsibility for America's woes to its competition, along with the failure to think through its problems to what it might be doing wrong, are what Christopher Lasch refers to as the "legacy of America's self-indulgence." We would have the world change towards us, but would find it absurd to suggest that we might change towards the world. Nothing must disturb the illusion of stability.

Few books are written about atavistic management or the robocratic organization. *Workplace culture drives behavior.* A corollary: *Individual behavior follows the organizational structure.* No one survives in an organization too long who insists on defying the structure. Most organizations are failing because they are not organized to succeed. What worked in 1950 will not work today. When an organization is born, it has one kind of culture and structure. Once it gains a little age and settles into a maintenance routine, the organization requires a different culture and structure. Then, it finds itself with a solid bank of customers, a firm place in the market, and a retinue of loyal but ill-fated employees, who started coasting long ago. In the last phase, the company is dying and doesn't know it. IBM, the giant that everyone thought was beyond danger, nearly went under. A series of computer nerds started snipping at its ankles. Big Blue ignored them and their interests: personal computers (PC) and software development. This nearly left IBM in the wake of the great telecommunication renaissance. Xerox, which essentially invented the PC, was so encumbered by its own inertia that it ignored its own engineers' constant appeal for modest funds to develop the PC's commercial potential. So Steven Jobs and Steven Wozniak literally stole it out of Xerox's laboratories, with the cooperation of its engineers. The lessons of workplace culture and organizational structure don't end here. Later, Steven Jobs was curtly kicked out of the company he co-founded by the man he personally recruited to give Apple stability, John Sculley of Pepsi fame. Jobs was brutal, brash, and brilliant and treated co-workers as part of his intellectual harem.[13] This was okay for a newborn company, but not for one when it found its own legs. The hubris that technology will save us from ourselves is encountering some uncertainty. Technology has changed us. It has made the organization, as we know it, anachronistic and management irrelevant. It has changed the nature of work and created a professional class of workers, but the workplace culture and the organizational structure remain essentially unchanged. So the dream still implodes, causing nightmares for nearly everyone.

Precedence or Prophecy?

Looking backward sometimes helps. When World War 1 was followed by the "Roaring Twenties," the common man was not invited to the party. He was there for exploitation. Conditions were so bad in industry that workers of his circumstance had little recourse but to organize into labor unions. Today, we think of the American labor union movement as if it has always been. It is essentially a phenomenon of the twentieth century, which reached its apogee in the 1950s and has been declining ever since. The labor union movement won early support (1933) from President Roosevelt. FDR, at the height of the Great Depression, declared war on the instability of the American economic system. With the cooperation of the unions, he constructed a government protective umbrella over the common man. What Roosevelt saw was wholesale physical deprivation (poor working conditions, unsafe equipment, inhuman treatment, dangers to health and safety, and enslaving wages) for the common man. Labor rode on FDR's coattails for his four successful runs for the presidency. He became known as the "Patron Saint of the Downtrodden." Not until this president's commitment to labor, however, did corporate America pay attention to the common worker. But was Roosevelt's compassion the right medicine for America? Patrician Roosevelt, who came from one of America's first families, moved the common man from experiencing the ordeal of his life to a strained dependency. This was not intended. What Roosevelt intended was to furnish immediate relief of a cruel inequity. His biographers admit that the New Deal was not a carefully thought out strategy, but that it snowballed. This was unpropitious. During the previous 15 years, the common man had come to rely on himself. Now, without experiencing obvious struggle, the American character started a surprising emotional decline. Over a 60-year period (1933–93), the worker went from the protective clime of the Culture of Comfort (management dependence) to the Culture of Complacency (organizational dependence), thus avoiding, for the most part, the most necessary Culture of Contribution (interdependence) to meaningful work. Unfortunately, unions contributed to this decline by sacrificing the control of work by workers for money and benefits. With each contract settlement, workers improved their economic status, but lost more control of what they did. This growing dependence on management for emotional and psychological sustenance, as well as economic security and, subsequently, counterdependence on the organization, found the majority of workers trapped in extended, suspended, and terminal adolescence. Workers found it easier to be taken care of than to take hold, easier to adapt to a dysfunctional system than to challenge it, and easier to vegetate than think for themselves.

When these workers were experiencing the post–World War II bonanza, Europe and Asia were in the midst of a historic clean-up after a crushing defeat. These people had no choice but to confront the reality of their situation, accept their past failures, disappointments, and sorrows, and get on with their lives. The Marshall Plan and Truman Doctrine helped. This wise foreign policy aided considerably in this recovery and demonstrated America's natural humanity. But these vanquished people were responsible for their recovery, not America. The miracle of Japan and Western Europe is due to their acceptance of defeat and their ability to embrace their worst fears and nightmares, not run from them. Devastated by war beyond imagining, these people could have rationalized their plight, could have hated their enemies, and sunk even lower in despair. Instead, they admitted that the only enemy they had to overcome was self-contempt. They had a choice—see themselves as permanent victims of the cruelties of war or find their way back to victorious celebration. They chose the latter.

Roosevelt's New Deal, Truman's Fair Deal, Kennedy's New Frontier, and Johnson's Great Society all rose out of a common soil designed to liberate the common man. The baby-boomer President William Jefferson Clinton is moving away from this *common good* and more toward *personhood*. Born in 1946, President Clinton is the first president born after World War II. At this writing, he is starting his second term, sounding more like a Republican than a Democrat. Moreover, the labor union movement, which rose to prominence with the values of the *common good*, is now fighting for its life as workers are finding their own voice. Somewhere there is a balance between doing too much and too little for workers, a balance which we have yet to discover.

Today professional workers find themselves in a situation similar to that of blue-collar workers decades ago. Whereas blue-collar workers were mainly concerned with physical deprivation, professionals are more concerned with psychological deprivation. Economically, professionals have fared relatively well in comparison, but psychological deprivation is more subtle and less definable. That does not make it any less painful. Modern workers are better prepared, however, to deal with physical than psychological abuse. Psychological deprivation is frequently expressed in such subtle ways as the:

- Constant threat of being made redundant or the constant rumor of downsizing.
- Freezes on promotions and wages.
- Reduction in entitlements and benefits or the taxing of these as real income.
- Requirement to complete inane projects.
- Failure to be given challenging work.
- Job realignment without assigning sufficient support.
- Monotonous and constant reorganization and rumor of discontinuing functions.
- Competition between husband and wife for who has the economic clout.
- Desire to have children and the fear that it might jeopardize the job and marriage.
- Failure of children in school due to parents' commitment to work rather than family.
- Climate of panic that pervades the workplace like sweat.
- Requirements to attend company events, which prevent having much time with family.
- Frustrating realization that more can be done in an hour at home than a day at work.
- Failure to know where you stand with your boss.
- Sense of powerlessness to change any of this.

What is truly unfortunate is that psychological deprivation is beyond management's moral center and moral compass. It is not considered part of the job. Managers are trained to think concretely in terms of things, not abstractly in terms of people and the ambivalent needs of people. In the eyes of most managers, these concerns do not exist if data regarding them cannot be quantified or reduced to logical interpretation. Yet it is the psychological climate that can either kill the spirit of organization bit by bit, day by day, or catch the spirit and bring the organization to new levels of achievement. Many managers don't know the difference. This ignorance extends to not knowing what constitutes real work for professionals, not recognizing how power has shifted, or not acknowledging the wisdom of sharing power with workers. Granted, professional workers don't make it any easier. They feel a kinship with management, but would prefer that management remain account-able for what goes wrong. Erroneous as this might be, self-delusion is a common way of dealing with anxiety. Moreover, blue-collar workers are not seen by professionals as having the same sense of psychological deprivation. After all, they make widgets, which are real. What professionals have to sell is information, which may eventually become something concrete, but when, if, and how are another matter. Then, too, how can you separate *your* contribution from umpteen others? Consequently, professionals see packaging perceptions as nearly a full-time activity. For survival's sake, making an impression has far more clout, from their perspective, than making a difference. Career development becomes, out of necessity, a marketing design in which personality is more carefully engineered than performance. The only way to get ahead, this line of thinking goes, is to focus on the short-term, short-range payback to the energy expended. Nothing is done for future payoff to the organization. With this obviously cynical design, the professional comes to be in sync with the workplace culture and the structure of the organization—not as it professes to be, but as it actually is. Feelings gravitate to a mood and then are compounded into a method—*Never say what you think; say what you think is the prevailing belief of power. Never trust anyone with your most private thoughts; always talk as if your adversary is listening right over your shoulder. Never openly display your dissatisfaction to anyone; instead echo the current rhetoric with feeling. Conceal your contempt with faint praise and calculated good will and let the six silent killers meander with resolve.*

The Fall of Rome or The More Things Change...

Evidence of catastrophe theory is present as far back as in the fall of ancient Rome. It came about when loyal Roman subjects turned inward against their ruler. What precipitated the fall was the eroded integrity of Roman leadership and the growing disenchantment of Roman citizens at home, combined with the escalating and ignored challenges from abroad. From a technological perspective, military warfare was changing. Armored cavalry was overwhelming Roman infantry legions and their light cavalry. Rome denied this technological breakthrough. On the home front, Rome saw itself as a rural society, even in the face of sprawling urban growth. Complicating the picture further, Romans saw themselves as warriors, not farmers. So agriculture was ignored. This neglect had a direct effect on the efficiency of the military. It meant the army could not support the cavalry with the necessary fodder for its horses. At home, it could not feed its swollen urban population because years of warring had forced many peasant soldiers from their ancestral farmlands, which now remained fallow. The idle urban proletariat, which was drifting into Rome in ever increasing numbers, was contributing to urban sprawl. With little to do, this disenchanted citizenry sat around the public squares and argued. They blamed the emperor for their misdirected lives and the poverty of their will. Out of these commoners rose rabble-rousers who fomented political discontent into open rebellion. In this political and psychological climate, the Huns shook the empire, while the Visigoths and Germanic invaders shattered it. Rome was being attacked from all sides and from within as well. These Northern tribes came from the interior where the soil was heavy, rich, and well watered, providing abundant fodder for horses. Rome was on the Mediterranean fringe where the soil was sandy and infertile, better suited for vineyards. This allowed the Northern tribes to hold the technological edge of a heavy armored cavalry, which dispersed Rome's light cavalry and sacked its ground troops. Back in Rome, agitators were increasingly holding sway, leaving Roman citizens in psychological turmoil and political chaos. Catastrophe followed.[14]

Thom uses catastrophe theory to describe a society in turmoil (Figure 4.2). It could be Rome or the United States. What we have is social order versus disorder in times of danger. What is important to note is that it matters little whether the danger is perceived or not. It exists. Thom considers the control factors of this topology to be cohesiveness and perceived danger. *Cohesiveness is the tendency for individuals to identify with the group and its mission. Danger*, on the other hand, is based on the *perceived level of danger*, not the actual danger confronting the group. This is because rumor can be as detrimental as concrete fact. Note path A-B in Figure 4.2 indicates that soldiers are conditioned to regard the integrity of their unit as of paramount importance. Most managers are good soldiers (*organization men*). They will do nearly anything to sustain this integrity. From a historical perspective, Elbert Hubbard provides an interesting answer with his famous pamphlet, "A Message to Garcia" (1899). The pamphlet dealt with a soldier named Rowan who carried a message through enemy lines during the Spanish-American War to General Garcia. Hubbard ends the pamphlet with,

> The point I wish to make is this: McKinley gave Rowan a letter to be delivered to Garcia; Rowan took the letter and did not ask, "Where is he at?" By the Eternal! There is a man whose form should be cast in deathless bronze and the statue placed in every college of the land. It is not book-learning young men need, nor instruction about this and that, but a stiffening of the vertebrae which will cause them to be loyal to a trust, to act promptly, concentrate their energies; do the thing—"Carry a message to Garcia."[15]

Hubbard was applauding the man who values the *common good*—the man who asks no questions, just carries out orders, posthaste! Hundreds of thousands of copies of this pamphlet were made and distributed among employees across America at the turn of the century. And now, 100 years later, society calls for an entirely different man and woman, no longer an obsequious soldier motivated by blind obedience or an officer without a point of view. *Personhood* does not lend itself to such rapture, nor does it have such a passionate spokesman as Hubbard.

Cohesiveness increases as danger is perceived to be increasing, when the threat of competition is apparent. The danger could be the threat of physical survival as in the case of the Japanese bombing of Pearl Harbor. In a psychological sense, the danger could be the perceived threat to one's personal security (rumor of plant closing, cutback in personnel) or group pride (Russia edges the United States out in space with Sputnik). Cohesiveness decreases when soldiers see comrades flee. The breakdown of the army may be sudden (B-C-D) because panic has set in. Catastrophe follows. This is what happened with the stock market collapse in October 1987 and again in October 1989. The army of stockholders took to the hills, mainly on rumor (not fact) of wholesale market breakdown. A few months later the market absorbed

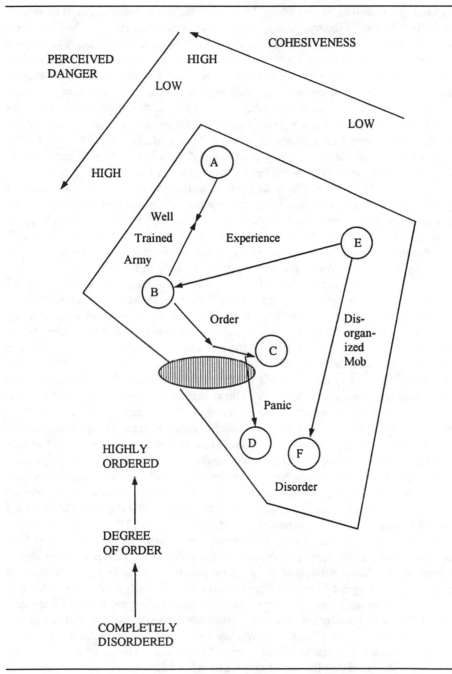

Figure 4.2   After Woodcock and Davis: Social order versus disorder in times of danger.

its lows and soared on to new highs. This makes the stock market an ideal enterprise to study catastrophe theory. At this writing, the market is a runaway bull market.

My son-in-law is a lawyer. He has on two occasions experienced his colleagues leaving the firm, sensing that it was headed for collapse. Key people, sensing impending danger (lack of clients), can leave and bring failure about by their behavior. With mob behavior, it gets a little more tricky. Mob behavior becomes less orderly as danger increases (E-F), but this can be misleading. If the mob's sense of cohesiveness increases steadily over time, while the danger is rising, an ill-organized group can become orderly, as did the Chinese Communist forces in the "Long March of 1935." It was that remarkable march which ultimately overwhelmed the Chinese Nationalists in 1949. China had never, in modern times, been organized under one political system.[16]

Closer to home, in the so-called skunk works of industry, the same kind of growing cohesiveness can find order growing out of chaos. Many companies, with reason, are proud of their skunk works. Usually they are a loose band of eight or ten zealots off in a corner, often outproducing product development groups which number in the hundreds. Skunk works are becoming common, but the application of this intensity and this drive to achieve is unpredictable in larger groups.

We have historical precedence for this unpredictability. Large groups at critical moments of stress may move toward or away from order. Take the French Revolution and the crowds that were storming the Bastille in 1789. French citizens, suffering through a horrible bread famine, were a contemptuous mob with little to lose. As the mob moved through the Paris streets, it became more coherent and purposeful. Come whatever, this hostile crowd was determined to release the prisoners from that dreaded place as a symbol of their contempt for the establishment. The military contingent guarding the Bastille could hear the crowd singing, like approaching thunder, before it came into the clearing. For a terrible moment, it seemed that there would be great bloodshed. Then the soldiers, under extreme duress, broke ranks, threw down their guns, and joined the crowd in its quest to liberate. What happens at such moments is evidence of the crowd mind as if the crowd moves as one person. Such a mind has immense unconscious energy. Obviously, each soldier and revolutionary varied quantitatively in terms of level of tension. But the qualitative behavior that became a single force—the storming of the Bastille and the capitulation of the military—was a group phenomenon.

Thom's model makes it easy to see how rumors can be so demoralizing or how failure to address real issues of concern to the group can foreshadow catastrophe. Learning the official version of events is purposely false can trigger a heightened awareness of danger (Watergate tapes), while diminishing group cohesiveness. A generation of young people are contemptuous of public life because of the Watergate Affair. Yet, had President Nixon gone before the American people after the break-in and told the country what he knew, when he knew it, and avoided the cover-up, he might have left office in triumph instead of shame. When leaders lie to their followers, it signals that the leader doesn't trust his followers to deal with the truth. Next, we will explore the implications of this in terms of "The Echoing Footsteps."

Endnotes

1. Alexander Woodcock and Monte Davis, *Catastrophe Theory: A Revolutionary New Way of Understanding How Things Change* (Middlesex, England: Penguin Books, 1978), pp. 140–141.
2. The Karl Von Clausewitz quote is from his book *On War* (1833) and is cited by Joshua Cooper Ramo in "Winner Take All," a piece on the war between Microsoft and Netscape, *Time*, September 16, 1996, 56–64.
3. Paul Krugman, "Competitiveness: A Dangerous Obsession" *Foreign Affairs*, March/April 1994, 28–44. He sees it skewing domestic policy to bad decisions from healthcare to trade.
4. Joshua Cooper Ramo, *Time*, September 16, 1996, 62–63.
5. Jeffrey Madrick, *The End of Affluence: The Causes and Consequences of America's Economic Dilemma* (New York: Random House, 1995), pp. 20, 21–22.
6. David Halberstam, *The Next Century* (New York: William Morrow & Company, 1991), p. 59.
7. Ramo, op. cit., pp. 59–63.
8. Rose Will Monroe was the poster girl, "Rosie the Riveter." Rose built B-29 and B-24 bombers in Ypsilanti, Michigan from 1942–1945. After the war, she stayed in the workforce and did a lot of different things, including being a hair dresser and forming a construction company called the "New Liberated Women." She died in 1997 at the age of 77.
9. Wirtschaft Woche, *Business Week*, January 16, 1987, 48–49. "Corpocracy," the "Amerikas Krankheit" (American Disease), has these symptoms (according to this German publication): (1) management is insensitive to its employees, (2) management supports company politics at the expense of productivity, (3) secretiveness is the measure of communication, (4) the principal product of work is paperwork, (5) endless meetings are the way, (6) an internal focus is maintained, so potential markets are ignored, (7) short-term planning and thinking is preferred to embracing challenges, (8) individual initiative is never supported, (9) management has isolated itself from employees, and (10) covert hostility to innovation is maintained while it is overtly praised.
10. "Boomers Expect Kids to Try Drugs" (Associated Press report), *The Tampa Tribune*, September 10, 1996, Nation/World section, 1, 5.
11. Joseph Stanislaw and Daniel Yergin, "Oil: Reopening the Door," *Foreign Affairs*, September/October 1993, 83.
12. Christopher Lasch, *The Culture of Narcissism: American Life in an Age of Diminishing Expectations* (New York: W.W. Norton & Co., 1979).
13. PBS television, *Front Line*: "Computer Industry." Also on the Learning Channel, October 3, 1996.
14. Woodcock and Davis, op. cit., 136–139.
15. Freeman Champney, *Art & Glory: The Story of Elbert Hubbard* (New York: Crown Publishers, 1968), p. 87.
16. Woodcock and Davis, op. cit., 135–146.

5 Echoing Footsteps

In modern-day business versions of Greek tragedy, executives are leading the charge on their companies. They carry out Wall Street's orders to restructure, often before learning that their company is a target. The increase in self-restructuring is an important ripple effect of...hostile takeovers. Most restructurings occur not because the firm lost a takeover battle...They occur because top executives pull the trigger on their own companies. A defensive strategy of Downsize, Dismantle and Debt, of "raid yourself first and be safe," has taken hold...When top executives put their own restructuring into motion to "save" the company...they usually bring on the same terror they hoped to prevent...Although the recent wave of corporate streamlining has greatly improved profit margins, it has so decimated executive ranks that America may never recover...By the end of 1990 a million managers will have lost their jobs.[1]

Paul Hirsch

What ever folly their kings commit, it is the Greeks themselves that suffer. Let Kings go mad and blunder as they may, the people in the end are sure to pay.[2]

Horace (65 B.C.–8 B.C.)

The corporate board room is under siege. Panic is in the air. The organization is going through a transforming, exchanging, and discarding phase as it attempts to cope with change. Although not recognized as such, this is *qualitative discontinuity*. As Paul Hirsch points out, this gives the appearance of *continuity* while the organization is wrenching with anxiety. Imminent catastrophe is in the air, and it will come without warning when the organization takes a quantum leap from the stable state of the status quo of management dependence to worker–manager interdependence. A codependency bond has formed between managers and workers. This strains management and stresses the workforce. It is making it impossible for the organization to devote all its energy to its mission. Many organizations are healthy on the outside and sick on the inside, vulnerable to the slightest acceleration in external demands. An organization's health is no longer a simple index of cash flow and stock earning ratios, but the spiritual currency of worker–manager synergy.

Energy is dissipated in transition from one stable state to another. Although the current discontinuity forewarns of this draining propensity, it continues to be ignored. A kind of madness grips many organizations, the madness of stability and control, waxing sane and painting a smile on depressive trends. Conventional tools for tracking and predicting these developments are proving inadequate. They fail to capture the social morphology of organization. Demographics, social psychometrics, and trend analyses cannot identify, much less capture, qualitative discontinuity. These tracking devices can quantify and label and, yes, create excitement, but they miss the mark. How do we know? We have been using them for 50 years, and our insight into where we are and where we are going remains, at best, primitive. These tracking tools are linear, quantitative exercises in rationalism, devices for which we are ably trained, but which conceal situations, misread behavioral dynamics, and are either too restrained or too optimistic. Our obsession with *discovering the right answer, right approach, or correct solution to "the problem"* often ignores people in the organization wholly capable of designing a better approach to the daily business of work than any social scientist. They need only to be let loose, not with problem-solving on their minds, but with a desire to design, construct, and build a better way of working together.

Well-intentioned executives are too frequently caught up in cosmetic cures— changes that experts tell them will solve their problems. Cosmetic cures won't because they can't. In any case, problems are not killing the organization. What workers think is killing it. And what workers think is tied to the workplace culture and the structure of the organization. It does not take precipitous action, such as radically downsizing, to save the day. A prominent surgeon once admitted that 90 percent of elective surgery was totally unnecessary. The same holds true in organizations. When panic sets in, companies have been known to risk market standing, technological advantage, and wealth-producing capacity to offset an immediate crisis. To an organization under siege, a slight negative stimulus can manifest a distress response. Forget the continuity it is struggling to maintain. Discontinuity, which is rumbling with psychic energy under the surface and gaining momentum, will not be denied. Given this scenario, an organization under siege can be suddenly demoralized or toppled by a single rumor—followed by mass hysteria and corporate paranoia. Goodwill built over years can be destroyed in a single moment by an irresponsible act.

Organizational stability is controlled by *awareness* and *acceptance of that awareness*. Awareness, otherwise known as *conscious competence*, compels the organization to be fully conscious of what it is (and what it is not), where it is (and where it is not), and how it got there, where it wants to go, and what it must do to get there. It sounds simple. Under siege, the simple becomes complex. The most difficult thing to do is to stay focused on mission because where the organization wants to go often gets short shrift, overwhelmed by the flood of psychic impulses to act compulsively. This is unfortunate, but all too human. The mind of an organization, which is seldom a quiet mind, cannot think clearly. Under siege, it is caught in the madness it would avoid. The problem is that corporations are trying to be problem-solvers with the same kind of thinking that got them into trouble in the first place. Solution-driven thinking is dominated by left-brain linear logic and labeling— classify everything and put it into neat separate little boxes. The left brain is the seat of logic, analysis, and rational problem-solving. It is also the seat of language. It is the basis of the Socratic Method, which is a truth-seeking methodology. What truth are we seeking? How do we know when we have found it? Why do we believe there is truth here to be found? The Socratic Method is the basis of the Western mind's approach to problem-solving and the foundation of scientific inquiry. We owe much regarding the advancement of mankind to this method, but we are now discovering it has limitations in the area of dealing with people's behavior. The Socratic Method uses induction as its basis of logic. The main business of induction is to lead from the particular to the general. Inductive logic is the logic of discovery. Searching for the truth or discovery is important in science. It is an evaluative approach. What we need when it comes to the behavior of people is, first, awareness of the behavior; second, understanding the behavior by accepting it without judgment; and, third, examining options to come up with creative designs that might be constructed to change behavior. At this point, it seems enough to say that discovery hasn't brought us any closer to resolving issues relating to people's behavior. We need to *design* a workplace culture, not discover one. If anything, this thinking has made us more complacent and content because the Socratic Method is treated with the vigor of a religious belief more than a conceptual framework. As a consequence, language is used against itself (psychobabble) to explain away the essence of the situation rather than create a new design. In order to soften the crush of reality, euphemisms are invented as the order of the day. Out of these come fads, quick and dirty solutions, and a mania for data.

LEFT HEMISPHERE	RIGHT HEMISPHERE
Verbal	Nonverbal, visuo-spatial
Sequential, temporal, digital	Simultaneous, spatial, analogic
Logical, analytical	Gestalt, synthetic
Rational	Intuitive
WESTERN THOUGHT	EASTERN THOUGHT

Figure 5.1   Two brains: Two cognitive styles.

The emergence of the MBA is symptomatic of this mania for quantification. A corps of nearly 100,000 new MBAs, epitomizing the quintessence of the verbal, analytical, and rational problem-solving skills of left-brain thinking, annually march out of American universities. Western Europe, by comparison, which has a population of 100 million more citizens than the United States, produces fewer than 10,000 MBAs. But MBAs are not to be faulted for their diligence. What is suspect are the tools such diligence brings to the party. The tools are concrete. Thinking about behavior is abstract. What is meant to bring relief often makes matters worse. MBAs epitomize the prison of the Western mind—its love of boxes: categories, labeling, and quantification. Missing is the realization that economics is as much qualitative and subjective as quantitative and objective. The problems of organizational behavior are subjective, not objective. Understanding behavior takes right-brain thinking, but thinking fully integrated with left-brain analysis. A holistic perspective gives us the bicameral mind with the visual, perceptual, and intuitive thought centered in the right hemisphere of the brain, acting in consort with the rational mode of the left hemisphere[3] (see Figure 5.1). The right brain sees a problem from the general to the particular (deductive thinking). Conversely, the left brain takes exclusive charge of a problem and moves hastily into its problem-solving mode, moving from the particular (defining the problem) to the general (inductive thinking). Once in the problem-solving mode, virtually everything must submit to the nightmarish labyrinth of the problem-solving. The tyranny of problem-solving, then, is evident when corporations, in desperation, start throwing "Hail Mary passes" at problems. We see this in merger bids of companies on the blocks, in the software world where products are hyped and released before they are ready, and where one competitor feels its only option is to wipe out the other to survive (see Chapter 4, pp. 46–47).

World economic forecasts into the next century are bright, although for the United States the long business expansion generated in the 1980s appears to be slowing. Wall Street, however, remains incredibly bullish. Still there is the sense of a deep economic worldwide slump looming over the horizon. Many American corporations that acquired large amounts of debt from leveraged buyouts and junk bonds are uneasy. The anxiety is not that things are so bad. The fear is that should things slow down, even a little, a tidal wave of panic may engulf the world, followed by a surge of bankruptcies. Notice how human a face is painted on enterprise when survival is at risk.

If a society's greatest resource is its young people, then their preparation determines society's future. In face of a shrinking planet, where it is necessary to understand as well as compete with different cultures, this has broad implications. The only way to truly understand another culture is through its language. If this is true, then, against Western Europe, Japan, and the Pacific Rim countries—America's prime competition—the United States is falling behind. As we prepare for the next century, we find that more than one million American young people drop out of school annually before they have fully matriculated. The estimated cost of this dropout is $240 billion in lost earnings and unearned taxes over their lifetime.[4] What is equally disturbing is that those who remain in school will most likely be deficient in language skills at a time when language skills are critical to success in a world economy. Moreover, in America, learning is viewed primarily as a formal necessity, like taking medicine to get well. The consensus justification for a good education is economic: to attain and hold a good job. This medicine is confined to the classroom, not lifelong learning. Many, once they have completed their formal education, put learning on the back burner. Learning is not associated with pleasure, while a free public education is taken for granted. Few students, while they are consigned to compulsory education, realize that education is the most liberating experience they will ever have. Elsewhere, the quest for an education finds German students going to school six days a week and in Japan and Singapore going one to three months longer than American students.

Another measure of a society's stability is its frugality. Americans have a disdain for saving. This thinking infects the corporate and public psyche alike. As U.S. trade deficits spiral, the Germans and Japanese create surpluses. The average Japanese worker earned half the income of the average American worker in 1973. Today, he earns 20–25 percent more. German workers, who in 1973 were making two-thirds as much as the average American worker, are now making 30–40 percent more. If this trend continues, American workers will awaken one day to having the lowest standard of living in the industrial world. Before you consider this an exaggeration, consider the U.S. trade deficit. If it continues at its present level, major borrowing from abroad will be required. This will result, in turn, in more buildup of foreign debt. The United States already has foreign obligations of nearly $1 trillion, which requires a debt service of some $10 billion per month. This is money that would otherwise be available to invest in such critical areas as schools, police forces, anti-drug campaigns, medical research, environmental cleanup, and repair of the infrastructure of American society.

An even more debilitating barrier, after taking into account quality, marketing savvy, and exchange rates, involves the social and cultural implications of declining personal performance on the job. The decline of the work ethic is less intentional than an act of frustration. This is most apparent among professionals. This predicament is discounted by optimists who point out the $210 billion spent annually by employers on training. These same optimists also remind us of our technological leadership and economic clout with, "The GDP is double that of Japan and four times that of Germany." True, but what will it be in another 20 years? As for training, the whole rationale for training is wrong for this workforce and these times. Training is mechanistic, quantitative, linear, and essentially programmed learning to indoctrinate workers into the "how to do," but not the "why to" of things. The original training model was designed for blue-collar widget-makers, not for professionals who must think conceptually to intelligently handle information. Moreover, the "how to" of things is not enough to keep professionals interested, much less involved. The mechanistic formula is quantitative, objective, and impersonal. A more appropriate creative model for professionals would be qualitative, subjective, and personal. The legacy of the mechanistic formula and its impersonal *cultural bias* resounds in the words of Frederick Winslow Taylor, the father of scientific management: "*...one of the very first requirements for man who is fit to handle pig iron as a regular occupation is that he shall be so stupid and so phlegmatic that he more nearly resembles an ox than any other type.*"[5]

This powerful bias toward workers still exists. It is reflected in the way in which they are being trained for their jobs. Many organizations, in this information age, are moving further into the labyrinth of the obscure. They devote most training to the viewing of computer monitors at the desks of workers with specific software programs. The personal facilitative trainer has been all but excised from the process, thus eliminating the primary benefit of group learning—the socialization aspects of the seminar. In this manner, a new way has been discovered to move forward by moving backward. Training is geared to instruct, not enlighten, with variations of the nitty-gritty operant conditioning advocated by psychologist B. F. Skinner.[6] The focus is on behavior modification—on doing something differently—not to think differently on purpose. The problem with this is that every time the situation changes, new software is designed. But once a person can think, he has a tool kit of choices beyond the range of any software.[7]

We don't need more instruction. We need greater enlightenment—clearer insight into the futility of our present thinking. No question, people are working hard, but are they working on the right things? Training fails to deal with cultural biases. If anything, it enhances them by omission. Cultural biases can be either positive or negative and are directly responsible for performance. For example, one organization may be obsessed with "doing everything right the first time." This is a tactical approach. Cover up is common because workers don't like to be caught making errors. Another organization may be committed to "doing the right things"—concentrating on the critical 20 percent of their problems that make 80 percent of the difference. "Doing the right things" encourages joint problem-solving, cooperation, and teamwork. This is a strategic approach to quality. These approaches are worlds apart in terms of the way workers are trained to think. Before there can be any success in changing behavior, unsuitable biases must be dealt with first. The capacity to change depends on the worker's mind-set, which depends heavily on previous learning and the stored biases. Giving uniform instruction to everyone without regard to these biases guarantees failure. Enlightened education is first awareness and acceptance of these biases and then an action plan to deal with them head on by acquiring the worker's active participation.

You may recall the excitement generated by the *One Minute Manager* (1982). It was the answer to management's prayer—simple, direct, and conclusive. No fuss. No muss. Catherine Tritsch observed, "Shamu the Whale may be better trained than most U.S. workers," because the "one minute manager" formula was already being used successfully at Sea World on killer whales in its aquatic shows. What Tritsch was referring to is no doubt true. Animals respond very well to training, but people respond better to education. This has never been more true than today. Professional workers have been educated to think and respond to stimulus designed for thinking, not mechanistic behavior modification. Consequently, conventional training, even with all its modems, monitors, software, Internet menus, and flashy visuals, has little capacity to improve performance. Training fails to deal with cultural bias. In fact, the mechanism of training introduces cultural biases. To change a cultural bias requires qualitative, exploratory, non-linear, and abstract thinking. Any chance of changing a firmly held bias must, of necessity, energize qualitative thinking. If the main problem of productivity in the modern organization is workplace culture, then billions of training dollars devoted to mechanistic, quantitative practices are like pouring money down a bottomless pit. Only qualitative education can deal with the organization's cultural resistance to change, because such education uses previous learning as a basis for building a bridge to new understanding and learning experiences. Notice, once again, that in this new thinking the emphasis is on *building a new workplace culture*, not on discovering one.

Education does this by assisting the individual in exploring his conduct in terms of these biases, not on evaluating whether they are good or bad, positive or negative. The latter leads to becoming defensive and, ultimately, to circular logic. With education, the worker enlightens himself as to what works and doesn't work for him. He can then choose to create new ways that do. It is a slow and patient process that is generated by the worker's own momentum, established by his will to change. Once the worker's momentum takes hold, a series of meaningful breakthroughs follow. Education is driven by psychological time (breakthroughs), whereas training is driven by chronological time (One Minute Manager). Training is too frequently a panic response to an ill-conceived problem (NBC TV's "Japan Can, Why Can't We?"). Education is a response to chronic problems that persist because of inappropriate thinking. Training is quantitative and concrete ("I took ten hours of computer training"). Education is qualitative and abstract ("I see work differently. I feel differently about work").

Will and spirit are intangibles. They personify the thrust of a successful organization's psyche. With will and spirit, no setback is overwhelming because the spirit to survive is combined with the will to prevail. Will and spirit are part of a common value system, otherwise known as a workplace culture. Workplace culture is an abstraction. You cannot touch it, see it, or feel it, yet it dominates. Workplace culture is energized by an organization's history, which is either a catalyst or impediment to the future. Should the twin narcotics of comfort and complacency invade the organization's psyche, then there is little sense of danger ahead, for few can hear the echoing footsteps. The gift of technology has deadened the sound of these footsteps. Man has survived on this essentially hostile planet for one reason—the human brain. The brain is a necessary apparatus, with the human mind as the software recording man's struggle. What is imprinted upon the mind dictates behavior. With the virtual community and the information highway and its ever-expanding Internet, technology has pushed back the veil of ignorance with a flood of information, while it has lost the coordinates of wisdom and humor. It would seem that science is replacing religion as the keeper of dogma and ritualistic consensus. Few question the motivation of scientists or the incentives of technologists who translate these findings into products. The Western mind seems bent on discovery, not on creation; on truth as if it were a commodity only to be discovered, not to be created. Awareness and acceptance of the limitations of this pursuit are buried in a flood of new discoveries. Yet, there is a strange and haunting connection between the *Information Age* of material light and spiritual darkness and the *Middle Ages* and its spiritual light and material darkness. Scientists were impeded at every turn by the dogma of Christendom (the unifying force of the Middle Ages) to shed light on the material world. Science succeeded, and the landscape of catastrophe saw the continuity of a God-centered Western culture give way to the discontinuity of a man-centered Renaissance. This led the nineteenth century philosopher Friedrich Nietzsche to declare "God is dead," meaning the stable state of secularism had replaced the stable state of ecclesiastical authority as the dominant culture of Western society. In this post-modern era, we are experiencing difficulty in allowing light to be shed on the spiritual world. There is a decided bias toward the empiricism of science and an unfavorable bias toward the mystical. This is apparent in the way we handle practical problems.

Organizations, across the globe, are now throwing impressive amounts of resources at their *cant nemesis*—poor quality. Salvation through quality is the new litany. "Improve the quality and the product will sell," others say. No one disagrees. Quality does sell. Quality is the answer. Still, these words are misleading. Quality is frequently a panic response to a strategic issue of "how do we get back on track?" Global competition made quality standards an issue. Global issues require global strategies. Does the workplace culture educate us to think strategically? The answer is "no." Global strategies require a conceptual framework and a theoretical perspective, both abstractions, neither submitting well to quantification. Global strategies, then, require a framework that entails qualitative modeling and subjective thinking. Most Western executives are extremely skeptical of this framework because it does not have empirical integrity, and so it is seldom considered, much less used. Despite this, perhaps the most jarring and revealing qualitative picture of where we are and why we are struggling with this reality is found in two works by futurist Alvin Toffler, *Future Shock* (1970) and *The Third Wave* (1980). What is preferred is a quantitative empirical framework with experiential data which reference how much, how many, and how soon. Pleasure is taken in the sense of being objective, value-free, and not contaminated by these data. We can be inductive, scientific, and smart. We can digest figures, schematics, projections, and complex technical minutiae and then agree on a "quick and dirty" solution. This "Prison of Panic Called 'NOW'" seems to provide escape and tranquilizing comfort. Executives of this inclination want more data; politicians want more polling results. It is not surprising that First Lady Hillary Rodham Clinton turned to a psychic with a desire to converse with former First Lady Eleanor Roosevelt. Former First Lady Nancy Reagan also had her favorite psychic. Why, you might wonder, would well-educated people be so inclined?

There is an inclination in American society to *seek answers* to perplexing problems, whatever their intellectual acumen, rather than to *create solutions*. This is a trivializing time, a world devoid of heroic proportions, but teeming with Seinfeldian proportions, a world defined not by a battle between good and evil, but a choice between skim or whole milk, caffeine or decaffeinated coffee, foam or no foam café au lait, carbonated or Perrier, and lemon or lime eau. We are a consumer culture of baby boomers—*More foie gras, por favor*—the most spoiled, overmarketed generation in history, accustomed to having products tailored to them. When someone feels something is missing, however well educated they might be, there is a tendency to "discover" the answer, as if hidden somewhere. The discovering mentality looks for shortcuts to difficult problems. The Western mind is predisposed to reduce data to quantitative mathematics, neat and tidy summaries, yes, even a clear channel to the hereafter.[8] Such a mind wants nothing messy, inconclusive, or speculative. This deludes some executives into thinking that everything can be reduced to a convenient syllogism: "If we do this (reduce cost) and that (improve quality), we're home free (product will sell)."

This infers that operating problems are more responsive to quantitative analysis than qualitative analysis, more objective than subjective, more operational than psychological, and more systemic than symbolic. Problems are never either–or, but are always connected by the conjunction "and." Generally speaking, cost-cutting and continuous quality improvement will improve the health and stability of the organization along with the quality of its products and services. But for how long? These data make for a convincing presentation, but in the long haul, how do they play? Experience has shown that if a bad system is designed and workers believe in it, for whatever reason, it will work. If a perfect system is designed and workers fail to buy into it, again, for whatever reason, that system will fail. The workplace culture in the first instance was receptive; in the second it was not. Quality is important, but to focus on quality and productivity as exclusive algorithms is never wise.

Western Europe, perhaps because its culture is so richly nurtured, varied, and maintained, has been responsive to almost every economic system ever attempted. Max Weber identifies this as *authoritarian bureaucracy*. Western Europe's cultural foundation is the basis for this phenomenon. Germans, in particular, are a resourceful people and respectful of their authoritarian tradition. This resourcefulness is not to be confused with being industrious. Germans work to live, whereas Americans live to work. When Germans are at work, they work. They don't treat the workplace as a second home, social center, or a shopping mall to visit. They find it strange that Americans like to hang out after work. Germans find it even stranger that most Americans have difficulty taking their earned leave. Perhaps this explains why many Americans carry vacation time over to the next year, while German workers seldom do.

The Japanese Mind or a Talent for Survival

What about the Japanese?[9] They are different than we think. Robert Christopher offers us an insight in his book *The Japanese Mind: The Goliath Explained* (1983).

Here are a few *enlightening* insights from Christopher's book:

- The men who manage the Japanese economy know that they must de-emphasize the traditional workplace culture and reorient the Japanese worker around sophisticated technologies in which Third World nations cannot hope to make themselves competitive. Managing the workplace culture is fundamental to success.[10]
- The Japanese are not inherently a mystical people. Confucianism dominates the value system of Japan, which is more an ethical system than a religious faith.[11]
- Survival is not a phantom, but very real to the Japanese. Consequently, in their hearts, they have only one absolutely immutable goal—the survival and maximum well-being of the Japanese tribe. Because of Japan's almost total dependence on imported energy and the fact that it possesses few natural resources required by modern industry, the Japanese never forget that any prolonged interruption of their imports would signal their doom.[12]
- The Japanese understand limits and accept them with stoic fanaticism. Japan is about the size of the state of Montana, but nearly three quarters of its land is mountainous. Because of a history of typhoons and earthquakes, the Japanese prefer living on the flatter parts of the country. Therefore, roughly 120 million are jammed into an area significantly smaller than the state of Connecticut.[13]
- Young people are into "now." A government poll found youngsters between 15 and 19 simply doing what they wanted to do (50%), as opposed to working toward future goals (28%). There is a hint of a cultural breakdown with Japanese tradition in that young people are attaching more importance than their elders to self-gratification and a privately centered value system.[14]
- The Japanese people are essentially law-abiding and disciplined because they choose to be. It is a case of automatic controls regulating behavior. In all of Japan in 1979, crimes involving handguns totaled only 179; the same impressive statistics are true of other crimes. Over the past two decades, crime has been on the decline in Japan. On the other hand, 99 percent of those people brought to trial for crimes are found guilty, but only 4 percent go to jail. The prime objective of Japanese justice is not to send an offender to jail, but to secure his confession, repentance, and reform.[15]
- Japan is not a litigious society. Civil lawsuits filed annually represent only about 5 percent of those filed in the United States, while the Japanese population is approximately one-half that of the United States.[16]
- The Japanese distaste for confrontation benefits them in their society, but frustrates them in dealing with foreigners. Generally speaking, if

you accommodate them in matters of style, they will usually do likewise in matters of substance.[17]

- Japanese youngsters appear literally smarter than American youngsters on the basis of I.Q. scores. In 1982 British psychologist Richard Lynn conducted a study of children between ages 6 and 16. The average I.Q. score of the Japanese youngsters was 111 compared to 100 for their American peers. Only 2 percent of all Americans had I.Q.s of 130 or more, but more than 10 percent of all Japanese did.[18]
- Thoughtful Japanese believe the "informatization process" will prove as much a turning point in human history as the Industrial Revolution. That is why it has become an information society.[19]
- World War II destroyed the Japanese feudal system, which dominated Japanese society. People in prewar days stuck to the community to which they were born. When Japan was reindustrialized, the company became the new community as people flocked to the central industrial complexes, and the old sense of geographic community largely disappeared. The new feudal lords of the manor are the executives of industry.[20]
- Japanese workers have not been brainwashed into docility by their bosses. Japanese executives manifest precisely the same attitudes, values, beliefs, and expectations as their assembly-line workers.[21]

The Great Separators

Executive Perks	Employee Eligibility
40 percent **Chauffeur Service**	One-tenth of 1 percent
63 percent **Company Plane**	Three-tenths of 1 percent
30 percent **Executive Dining Room**	Top executives only
55 percent **Country Club Membership**	One-half of 1 percent
62 percent **First Class Air Travel**	Seven-tenths of 1 percent
19 percent **Health Club Membership**	Top Executives only

Miscellaneous Perks

In addition to salaries, bonuses and stock options:

• **Car Telephone**	Free to top executives
• **Company Car**	Free to top executives
• **Legal Advice**	Free to top executives
• **Financial Planning**	Free to top executives
• **Interest Free Loans**	Free to top executives

Figure 5.2 American corporate executives take care of their own (*Wall Street Journal*, "Special Report of Executive Perks," April 18, 1990).

- Individual, corporate, and national survival are all woven from the same cloth. Cooperation between unions and management lies in the recognition of this fact.[22]
- Japanese executives find their American counterparts too aristocratic. They see everything in Americans organized to separate executives from the workers (see Figure 5.2). For Japanese executives to be effective, they find they must be a valued member of the working community, integral to and not separated from it.[23]
- The Japanese system, with its heavy emphasis on the survival of the institution, forces managers to think constantly about the long term. American managers are judged by their stockholders on the basis of quarterly profits, which forces them to focus on the short term.[24]
- The basic difference between Japan and the United States is not economic, but differing social systems. Americans are individualistic and pride themselves in being independent-minded, whereas the Japanese are conditioned from birth to be group-oriented. Group orientation sponsors long-term planning, which the Japanese concede is the primary reason for their business success. This planning is always conducted on the basis of a consensus model.[25]
- Japanese planning is a flexible rather than a rigid formal process—an eclectic, intuitive, and somewhat chaotic process driven by strong tribal consciousness to reach consensus. It is more qualitative than quantitative, more abstract than concrete, more understood as an adaptable design rather than a rigid document.[26]
- Japanese corporations are far more ready to mortgage the present in order to secure the future than most American firms. Exceptions to this in the United States are such high-profile firms as Microsoft and Netscape.[27]
- The productivity of American workers, as a whole, is more than one-and-one-half times that of Japanese workers. This is largely because of the dual economy of Japan. More than 70 percent of all Japanese industrial workers are employed by companies of fewer than 300 people, and more than half of all Japanese manufacturing enterprises employ only 5 to 10 people. Less than 30 percent of the Japanese workforce enjoys lifetime employment.[28]
- The Japanese receptivity to robotics is attributed to the influence of Buddhism, which, unlike Christianity, does not place man at the center of the universe. Buddhism makes no distinction between the animate and inanimate worlds. Japanese do not feel threatened by machines with human attributes, as Westerners tend to be.[29]
- The per capita GDP—the value of the goods and services produced by each citizen—which is one-half that of the United States, is expected to be 20 percent higher than that of the United States by the year 2000.[30]

- Japan once looked upon the United States as its teacher. Now Japan sees the United States and itself as peer students of economics, with the better marks going to the Japanese. Japan would like this equality to be recognized, and for Japan to be treated with the same respect that the United States accords France and Great Britain.[31]

Christopher concludes that Americans have little idea how the Japanese think and concedes that ignorance of our top economic competitor can be dangerous. If the Japanese have one advantage over the United States, he believes, it is their ability to fuse a sense of individual responsibility and achievement with the discipline and consciousness of the group. Ultimately, Christopher argues, every Japanese achievement is rooted in the dictates of a primitive tribe and is shaped by a *sense of impending catastrophe* and the overwhelming need to survive. These primordial urges explain the sometimes violent Japanese reaction to the outside world and their intense competition and desire for group consensus at any price.

"Just Say Noh"

A document surfaced in 1989 that gives credence to Christopher's warning. Two prominent Japanese executives penned an article, "The Japan That Can Say 'No': The Case for a New U.S./Japan Relationship," which alarmed many who thought relationships between the two countries couldn't be better. The article is xenophobic and written for a Japanese audience. It is clear the authors are nostalgic for the dominance of the Emperor and a return to the feudalistic consistency of that society: "Our honest and sincere emperor is the tribal symbol within our national polity and our culture; indeed, he is like the father of our family"—a variation of the culture of the common good.[32]

Europe is culturally an authoritarian society, whereas Japan is equally a feudalistic society. To an American working in Europe, the deference paid to people who have professional credentials and position power or who are senior in their years is a new experience. The courtesy encountered in modern Japan is feudalistic, reminiscent of that country's ancient society. Japan's bureaucracy is as feudalistic as Europe's is authoritarian. Both differ considerably with the American bureaucracy. These ancient social systems work surprisingly well, far better than their American counterpart. A possible reason is that, as gifted as the European and Japanese people are in science, technology, and industry, they continue to be dominated by the past, with an essentially submissive blue-collar constituency, whereas the United States is dominated by an egalitarian professional class of workers. Yet to be determined is how well the European and Japanese social systems will function in the post-modern era as professional workers become more dominant in all societies.

Culturally speaking, the United States has always been a renegade society. The Pilgrims deserted the oppressive authoritarian and feudalistic confines of Europe for America. Like a child rebelling against its parents, America, from its beginning, was an individualistic and violent society. In the New World, the right to bear arms was considered as much an inalienable right as the right to free speech. In more than 300 years of violence, turmoil, and abrasive individualism, America has not satisfied its anger against itself. Everything in America is treated as a war—marriage, work, sport, leisure, education, health, business, and religion. America is a dynamic, materialistic society with an appetite for more, but also with the soul of the Good Samaritan. No people are more generous, and compassionate, or more naive.

Philip Slater wrote perceptively about the American character in his book *The Pursuit of Loneliness* (1970). It was written during the Vietnam era, when America was at the cultural breaking point. Slater found three basic human desires uniquely frustrated by the American culture:[33]

- *The desire for community*—the wish to live in *trust* and *cooperation* with one's colleagues in a viable collective entity.
- *The desire for engagement*—the wish to come to grips with social and interpersonal problems and to confront an environment that is not composed of ego extensions.
- *The desire for dependence*—the wish to share responsibility and control of one's impulses and the direction of one's life.

When the Pilgrims broke away from the stable state of European society and from the continuity of an ancient cultural tradition and sought asylum in the New World, they embraced abrupt, discontinuous change and encountered many catastrophes. The stable state that the Pilgrims established, Slater observes, has always existed with an undercurrent of discontinuity. It is this inter/intrapsychic war that pervades every dimension of American society and that breathes fire into its most complacent soul. This produces its ambivalence: competition versus cooperation, non-involvement versus engagement, and dependence versus independence. It is always "either–or," never an integration of the two extremes. Were it so, an individual would compete with himself to bring out his best and cooperate with others, would savor his privacy but be an active participant in the community, and would sustain an independent point of view but recognize the need for interdependence in work and life.

While Americans struggle against themselves in psychic war games on every front, the economic war is seemingly being won by European and Oriental cultures. Community, engagement, and dependence permeate these cultures, whereas competition, non-involvement, and independence are the dominant constructs of the American character. The American character, in truth, remains that of the self-indulgent, spoiled child who must get its way. The focus of the American culture, from the beginning, has been on *becoming something* rather than *being someone*, on the competitive drive rather than the *spirit of cooperation*, on the role of *critical spectator* rather than *vulnerable participant*, on the *illusion of progress* rather than the *reality of regression*.

Professional workers as a group are coming to recognize these character flaws. They sense that the construction of the American organization is leveraged against full participation and the exercise of full potential. Increasingly, they see management in a caretaker posture—attempting to be all things to everyone—which frustrates it and prevents them from the pursuit of satisfaction. Yet, professional workers are not ready to take on the system. Indeed, before they come to grips with their frustrations, there is a good chance they will continue to display covert rebellion in the six silent killers.

Given this predicament, where foreign critics see Americans in less than idyllic terms, the United States was bound to come in for some hard economic bashing, primarily by the Japanese, but also by Europeans. From Europe, the bashing of the United States instructs us that "American business is not serious," while Akio Morita, chairman of Sony says, "Americans look ahead 10 minutes, while Japanese look ahead 10 years." This harsh assessment is because Europe and Japan are counterdependent on the American market for their products and on the American military for their security. Yet they both concede nothing in the world is comparable to the United States. This notwithstanding, there is some truth to their criticism. What it means is that the gloves are off. The bowing and polite smiles have turned to nervous grimaces. Europe and Japan are tired of playing second fiddle to the United States. There is daylight now between World War II and these former adversaries. They no longer want to be treated as economic apparitions, but to have a place at the head of the table. They are bent on taking the game away from the United States because it either cannot or will not lead.

Writing in 1989 about superconductivity as a key to the future of Japan, Shintaro Ishihara, Japanese Minister of Transportation states:

> *This type of technology does not exist anywhere in the Soviet Union or the United States. It exists only in Japan and West Germany. If the giants in the economic field and the politicians can join together around this type of technology, it would open up new possibilities for our advancement. Whether or not this can be achieved depends upon our large and small choices in the future; in sum, it is a question involving the sensibilities of our politicians.*[34]

When you take this statement and its implicit contention, along with the collapse of the Soviet Union, East Germany, and the Berlin Wall, the climactic breakdown of the Ceausescu Regime in Romania, and the civil war in Bosnia, you have manifestations of Thom's catastrophe theory in action. The discontinuity begins with words, which builds to a crescendo, then precipitously plunges to abrupt action. None of the world's writers could have predicted that the Soviet bloc of nations would respond so quickly and precipitously to *glastnost* and *perestroika*. It is clear that World War II has finally come to an end. Men of reason are putting military warfare behind them and are looking for diplomatic answers to their differences. Bosnia, Iraq, and other hot spots are perhaps exceptions, but the rule still prevails. What these foreign powers say about the United States can be easily refuted by the indispensable role America played in their miraculous recovery from World War II and their subsequent prominence. As Mike Royko writes: "I just wonder what the Japanese would have done for us if they had won World War II? Would the United States now be an open society run by Americans? Would Japan be letting us sell almost anything to them, while we turn away their products? Would Japan have let us—indeed, helped us—become an independent economic world power?"[35]

Beyond this obvious self-conscious defensiveness, what Europeans and Japanese are saying can be reduced to this reality: *Europeans and Japanese want to buy fewer things made in the United States, while Americans want to buy more things made in Europe and Japan.* Now this statement can be extended to Singapore, Korea, Taiwan, and points East. To be fair, this tide is turning as quality improvement has made American products more desirable, but it has not reversed the trend. The trade imbalance between the United States and the combined European/Japanese/Pacific Rim countries has widened, producing the thunder of echoing footsteps. Given this posture, these confederates know they need the United States. Yet they worry that America will never again be able to restore its effective productivity. This is not the concern of humanitarians. This is the concern of economic partners who feel that if America continues to sink into further lethargy, all of them may go down together. Meanwhile, Europe's consolidation into the European Economic Community (EEC) in 1992, a move meant to ensure European economic stability and to break away from the protectionism of the United States, has proven less than successful. With regard to Japan, there has been little demonstrable movement away from the United States, despite Ishihara's insistence that "Japan needs Asia more than America." It is a decade since he advocated revoking the U.S. Security Treaty and establishing a much greater deterrent capacity for Japan. American military installations remain on the Japanese islands. Little has been shut down, nor has there been any appreciable military withdrawal. Confidence in the United States is not yet lost, but the rhetoric in that direction has heated up. A growing concern is that due to America's economic self-indulgence, lack of discipline, and corporate greed, the United States is doomed as a super power. "The time will never again come when America will regain its strength in industry," says Morita. "We (Japan) are going to have a totally new configuration in the balance of power in the world." Ishihara is even more pessimistic regarding the United States, arguing, "There is no hope for the United States. Economic warfare is the basis for existence in the free world," he insists, "and America continues to fail in this warfare." At yet another point in "The Japan That Can Say 'No,'" Ishihara foresees "the end of the modern era as developed by white Westerners." History, he continues, is entering a new period of genesis. Indeed, he lectures America on its laziness, decadence, and racism. The revealing shock of these words is that they come through foreign eyes, like Alexis de Tocqueville's *Democracy in America* did more than 160 years ago. Americans learned much about themselves from Tocqueville.[36] But what about these words? Do they strip away the illusion, or are they merely polemical?

The United States is the greatest melting pot of nations in the world. America is truly a multiracial, multinational, multicreed, and pluralistic society. Only one percent of the Japanese population is not Japanese, and that tiny minority's involvement in that nation's charity is hardly visible. What is equally true is that as communism collapses, the world is moving toward free enterprise and democracy—

again, emulating American society. Has America been distracted from its course? The United States has never made its purpose too clear to itself, much less the world. It has been too busy growing, prospering, diversifying, and creatively exploding to direct much energy to purpose. Americans will admit readily to being self-indulgent, but not lazy. Even American criminals are industrious. Nor will most Americans challenge historian Arnold Toynbee's declaration that Western society is doomed. This is an interesting declaration, but what does it mean, given the fact that the world cannot seem to Westernize itself fast enough? America has problems, no question. Yet it could be argued that America's century is not yet here, but is just about to begin—the Americanization of the world. Whether the United States itself is at its peak or in serious decline is certain to be heard in the "echoing footsteps." The problem, however, is that these footsteps are muted by the *six silent killers*. There is little doubt that America's influence will continue into the next century. What is still open to question is whether the United States itself will have a prominent role in that dominance.

Endnotes

1. Paul Hirsch, "The Management Purges," *Business Month*, November 1988, 39.
2. C. O. Sylvester Mawson, *Dictionary of Foreign Terms* (New York: Bantam Books, 1961), p. 261.
3. Scientific development offers a radical new way to look at learning. We have known for years that learning occurs only in the brain. The brain controls all emotion and all goal-seeking behavior. Only in the last 35–40 years has the information developed that gives us a useful understanding of the brain. The adult brain weighs around three pounds, has a volume about equal to a quart bottle, and may be the most complex apparatus in the universe. This magnificent organ is unquestionably a form of computer, but despite its tiny size, it puts to shame the largest electronic systems. True, compared to the electronic digital types, the brain works at an ox-cart speed, but unlike them, it can operate along many thousands of channels simultaneously.
4. Ethan B. Kapstein, "Workers and the World Economy," *Foreign Affairs*, May/June 1996, 16–37.
5. Frederick Winslow Taylor, *The Principles of Scientific Management* (New York: W.W. Norton & Company, 1911), p. 59.
6. B. F. Skinner, *About Behaviorism* (New York: Alfred A. Knopf, 1974), pp. 39–41.
7. Daniel Goleman, "The Behaviorist Box of B. F. Skinner," *International Herald Tribune*, August 28, 1987. Goleman asks Skinner if he would rethink his views if he had the techniques available today. No, he wouldn't. "I would still call the mind a black box," he replied, which suggests he sees the mind as irrelevant to understanding why people behave as they do.
8. Jacques Servan-Schreiber, *Le Defi Americain* (The American Challenge), (New York: Athenaeum, 1968). See P. Lawrence, *Managers and Management in West Germany* (New York: St. Martin's Press, 1980).
9. See Robert E. Cole, *Work, Mobility & Participation: A Comparative Study of American and Japanese Industry* (Berkeley, CA: University of California Press, 1979); Robert E. Cole, *Japanese Blue Collar: The Changing Tradition*, (Berkeley, CA: University of

California Press, 1971); and Robert E. Cole, "The Japanese Lesson in Quality: More Than Skin Deep..." *Technology Review*, July 1981, 29–31.

10. Robert C. Christopher, *The Japanese Mind: The Goliath Explained* (New York: Simon & Schuster, 1983), p. 28.
11. Ibid., pp. 44, 46.
12. Ibid., pp. 55, 250.
13. Ibid., p. 119.
14. Ibid., pp. 136, 301.
15. Ibid., p. 148.
16. Ibid., pp. 163–164, 166.
17. Ibid., p. 174.
18. Ibid., p. 193.
19. Ibid., p. 207.
20. Ibid., p. 243.
21. Ibid., p. 245.
22. Ibid., p. 248.
23. Ibid., p. 249.
24. Ibid., pp. 250, 252, 254.
25. Ibid., p. 253.
26. Ibid., p. 255.
27. Ibid., p. 256.
28. Ibid., p. 267.
29. Ibid., p. 292.
30. Ibid., p. 298.
31. Ibid., pp. 313, 325.
32. Ian Buruma, "Just Say Noh," *New York Review*, December 7, 1989, 19.
33. Philip Slater, *The Pursuit of Loneliness* (Boston: Beacon Press, 1970) pp. 4–5.
34. Flora Lewis, "Japanese U.S. Bashing Is Instructive," *The Tampa Tribune*, November 17, 1989 (opposite editorial page).
35. Mike Royko, "Japanese...Why Are They Complaining?" *The Tampa Tribune*, November 17, 1989 (opposite editorial page).
36. Alexis de Tocqueville, *Democracy in America*, Vols. I, II (reprint of 1835 edition) (New York: Alfred A. Knopf, 1945). Politicians are fond of quoting Tocqueville, implying that he said, "America is great because America is good." What Tocqueville did write was, "I sought for the greatness and genius of America in her commodious harbors and her ample rivers, and it was not there."

Six Silent Killers: The Manic Monarchs of the Merry Madhouse

It's here, sir, that one is oneself with a vengeance;
Oneself, and nothing whatever besides.
We go, full sail, as our very selves.
Each one shuts himself up in the barrel of self,
In the self-fermentation he dives to the bottom,—
With the self-bung he seals it hermetically,
And seasons the staves in the well of self.
No one has tears for the other's woes;
No one has mind for the other's ideas.
We're our very selves, both in thought and tone,
Ourselves to the spring-board's uttermost verge—
And so, if a Kaiser's to fill the throne,
It is clear that you are the very man.[1]

Henrik Ibsen

The crippled genius of American workers contains many paradoxes. Contrast when workers are full of themselves with when they are not. In the case of the former, they are obsessed with *self*, preoccupied with *things*. With the latter, they are concerned with others and their well-being. Workers have an essential drive *to acquire*, but an equal need *to serve*. Their paradoxical nature takes on many forms. A few years ago, after a winter thaw, the Mississippi River at Waterloo, Iowa, threatened to flood the city. Faced with this crisis, the city mobilized its resources, and people of all ages filled sand bags, mounted them on trucks, and distributed them throughout the city to form man-made dikes. Hundreds of citizens worked around the clock beside neighbors and friends and, yes, beside strangers as well. The separate identities of age, race, religion, values, and profession dissolved into a faceless common challenge. For one brief moment, a *sense of community* possessed their consciousness.

After the crisis had passed, several volunteers were asked why they did it. The consensus was "because it had to be done. The city had to be saved!" Would they do it again? Without hesitation, they replied in unison, "Yes, of course." They would submit themselves to the demands of crisis management. Waterloo at that moment had no insiders or outsiders. It was a community with a common mission. This is but one event in the kaleidoscopic spectrum of self-forgetfulness in times of perceived crisis. As previously mentioned, whenever physical survival is at stake (World War II) or psychological survival is at issue (launching of Sputnik), whenever the threat comes from outside, the sense of belonging to a communal tribe is at its strongest. The key words are "perceived crisis." Throughout history, tension invariably produces tribal music, while relaxation typically generates tribal noise. If we don't feel it, can't see it, or it doesn't touch us, as with the current economic world instability, it doesn't exist. Yet tension is as natural to the spirit as joy is unnatural. We Americans are a tense and intense lot. We find it difficult dealing with ourselves when things are going well. We are always waiting, ever anxious, for the other shoe to fall. For some reason, we have to work very hard at not working at all. Leisure is intimidating. Work is our sanctuary.

The odyssey of American workers and their quest for satisfaction has not been a particularly joyous one. When you see joy on the faces of workers, it is likely a mask concealing the tension of struggle and fear within—struggle to become what they are not and fear of being found out for what they are. *Pretend* and *pretension*, derivatives of tension, are prominent features of the American character. Show me a youngster smiling easily in play. Instead, America has seven-year-olds playing football as if they were in the NFL. Parents-as-coaches can be heard yelling at these prepubescent youngsters, whose bones are not yet mature enough for such punishment. "Put your head down and take him out," parents cry. "Hey! Hey! Hey! What's your problem, fellah, where's your toughness?" Would that such energy and enthusiasm were directed at education and enlightenment. Young minds are quite nimble for such challenge if their bodies are not ready for such abuse.

This mania of forcing maturity on youngsters is programmed at a very early age. My grandson, Ryan James Carr, is two. He is a big boy for his age, about the size of many four-year-olds, but his mother is 6'1", so that is not too much of a surprise. He is attending a religious-sponsored preschool for two-year-olds, which is run like an army boot camp. These two-year-olds are expected to go to the bathroom precisely at 10 A.M., to play prescribed games without stepping out of line, to neither cry nor fuss with their peers, and to clean up their play area or be given demerits. God forbid, one of these little tykes should have an accident and go in their pants. First, they are scolded in front of the group, then asked to sit outside the group and, worst of all, to manage in soiled drawers until a parent comes along. The teacher sees nothing wrong with this. Listening to her, you would think she was talking about teenagers. What she is doing could not be more wrong. If a child is not allowed to have fun and spontaneity when he is young, the child will likely be a problem for society when he is older.

It doesn't stop here. Watch six-year-old baton twirlers, toothy grins barely covering absent teeth, displaying little joy in the exercise. How many of these little girls chose to be so regimented? How many of them are playing out their parents' fantasies? There is a greater pull in the American culture to *please others* than to *please self*. This programming is justified by "it is good for you." More often than not, pleasing others is simply *parental authority* over adolescent powerlessness and its *need to be pleased*. What this creates in a developing youngster is *self-doubt*, bordering on *self-contempt*—internal conflict when the child is starting to learn to be a friend to himself. Translated, this manufactures tension to replace natural nurturing. It is an American disease, orchestrated by well-meaning parents on the young. "Doing what is good for you" is inadvertently interpreted as "doing what is ex-pected." Disquieting at best, the whole process turns to viciousness when the aspect of *competition* is added. American workers assume that competition is as inherently good as breathing is natural. Competition is worn as though a badge, and workers swagger with a sense of what they think it means. Author W. W. Rostow believes that before Americans can compete, they must first learn how to cooperate.[2] Americans, he argues, must first discover their tribal capacity for communal action before they attempt, individually, to outdo each other. Rostow even goes further. He fears America might go the way of Great Britain which, between 1870 and 1971, went from 32 percent of the world's industrial production to generating only 4 percent. Rostow suggests that the only way to avoid this catastrophe is for the American workplace to develop an organizational infrastructure that champions cooperation over competition.

Toward the Fully Developed Human Being

Competition imitates initiative in a deceptive manner. Competitive people train to outperform others. If they are successful, we imagine they enjoy a sense of initiative. Not so. They are in a completely reactionary mode. They are becoming the other person, only better. The standard by which they judge themselves is not what they are capable of doing, but what other people can do. This develops the patina of skill and the appearance of competence.[3] Taken to the extreme, it can reflect what is hated, not loved; despised, not desired. Roger Bannister, the great British miler, typifies the innovative person with initiative. A medical doctor, Dr. Bannister was the first person to break the legendary barrier of the four-minute mile (1954). He did this not by being more competitive or imitative of the training of past great middle-distance runners, but by studying his own physiology. He then trained against this standard, expunging from his mind the psychological limitations imposed by com-petitive zeal 2,000 years ago in the Ancient Greek Olympiad. Thanks to Dr. Bannis-ter, today well over 100 individual milers have broken the four-minute-mile barrier.

Compare this to the *organizational climber*. Competitive? Yes. Competent? Probably not. With success comes the almost certain requirement to initiate policy and deal with situational ambiguities that demand original thinking. The climber is groomed to think imitatively and to adopt the party line (otherwise known as getting promoted), so functional imagination is out of the question. Resourcefulness has been trained out of the individual, as the climber only knows how to imitate existing patterns of thinking. Besides, the individual is a creature of safety. Given a challenge, such a person is in unchartered territory, with neither the freedom of mind nor the passion of heart to create new forms. When old forms fail, it is an invitation to become ruthless to survive, typical behavior of the climber under duress.

True organizational leadership requires the capacity to see and the ability to serve (Figure 6.1). The organizational climber is devoid of both. Vision seems to be a problem of many organizations today, and service is a confused priority. Too frequently, service is either self-aggrandizing or beholden to the power structure, not to the organization per se. The *ability to serve* is not meant to imply a relentless campaign for promotion or to anticipate and satisfy the needs of the hierarchy. On the contrary, it means to think in terms of how to keep the best interests of the organization at heart and how to always be customer-friendly to other members of the organization.

Henry Ford and Thomas Edison are good examples of organizational leadership in terms of the *capacity to see (vision) and the ability to serve*. Ford is credited with mass-producing automobiles and Thomas Edison with inventing the incandescent light bulb. Neither of these achievements compares with their visionary leadership. In 1914, when most industrial workers were earning less than a dollar a day, Ford created the five-dollar work day. This shrewd decision guaranteed a market for Ford automobiles. Beyond that, Ford created a $30 million profit-sharing plan (1914 dollars) and other incentives, which helped establish the working middle class. Western industrial nations followed his lead.

Edison, once he had invented the light bulb, did not sit on his reputation. He envisioned a city being eternally illuminated with 24 hours of daylight. To accomplish this, he created the Pearl Street Municipal Utility in New York City, the first central electric-light power plant in the world. The year was 1881.

Think of it. Ford never got beyond grammar school and was trained as a bicycle mechanic. Edison was essentially self-taught, dropping out of school at an early age due to a severe hearing disability. He spent his youth working on the railroad. Both men were considered odd, difficult, irascible, and eccentric, but their minds were alive with ideas. They were free-thinkers and dreamers, and they changed the world. Consider their genius against the obsession today with being credentialed, with legitimizing worth by the number of degrees behind a name and, even more importantly, the institution granting the degrees. Most of the men who have built society around the globe couldn't get an interview today, much less a job in their own companies. These men were *doers*, not takers; *performers*, not personalities. Erich Fromm writes, "Man himself, in each period of history, is formed in terms of the prevailing practice of life which, in turn, is determined by his mode of production."[4] Man's primary motivation is to contribute, not to consume. Capitalism makes the wish *to have and to use* the most dominant of human desires. A man so dominated, Karl Marx reasons, *is a crippled genius with the ambition to acquire overpowering his desire to accomplish.* Yet, neither private property nor profit is man's mission,

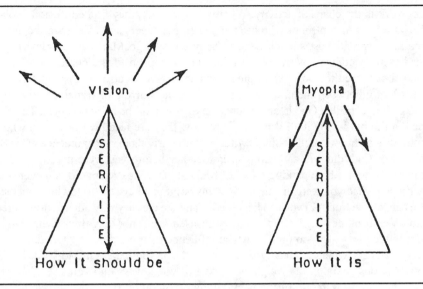

Figure 6.1   True leadership requires the capacity to see and the ability to serve.

which is actually the free unfolding of his human powers. Fromm captures the essence of this: "*Not the man who has much, but the man who is much is the fully developed, truly human being.*"[5] This appears to be the crux of the problem today. Materialism in Western society is out of control, and spiritualism has taken a holiday.

Since World War II, each succeeding generation has seemed to be more materialistic, and the current baby boomers (ages 30–50), otherwise known as the "spoiled-brat generation," are especially deceptive. Young professionals don't talk about greed. They practice it. Bruce Willis, 42, the film star, who has made as much as $75 million on a single film, expresses a common point of view: "It (film making) is all about money, nothing else." They don't flagrantly violate the Judaic-Christian ethic. They ignore it. Dick Morris, 49, the campaign strategist for President Clinton who was forced to resign because of a sex scandal, has indicated that winning elections is doing whatever is necessary to win, a completely amoral approach to politics. They strut their stuff. When things go awry, they don't get mad—they get even. They retreat into the *six silent killers* of an organization wearing mocking smiles that say, "Gotcha!" They have become custodians of the "Manic Monarchs of the Merry Madhouse," otherwise known as **passive aggression, passive responsive, passive defensive, malicious obedience, approach avoidance,** and **obsessive compulsive behaviors.**

These silent killers eat at the sinews of organization, and workers who display them have an amazing ability to appear as performers when they clearly are not. They are caught in the crunch between hypocrisy and hype, turning their frustrations into deceptive devices. They are looking for leadership in a leaderless society. They are looking for direction when nobody admits to being off course. They are looking for real work in the chaos of activity. Wherever they look, they find confusion. Nobody knows who is in control or who has the power. Managers and workers alike, equally frustrated, spread these silent killers. Nobody is in charge. Management plays the role but has little control. Workers are reluctant to step up to the challenge of taking control because they don't want the responsibility. So control and productive effort slip silently between them, covered by smoke and mirrors of frenzied activity.

Columnist Ellen Goodman captures the dilemma of the baby boomers. They have spent a life of "letting it all hang out," and now they are faced with children who ask embarrassing questions. Goodman writes: "You're driving to soccer practice when Sean asks, 'So, Dad, did you and Mom sleep together before you were married?' You're leaving the junior high parking lot when Melanie pipes up, 'Mom did you ever smoke marijuana when you were in college?' At this point you have the following options: (1) you can tell the truth, (2) you can lie, (3) you can take the easy way out and drive directly into an embankment....Parents who tried or used drugs not only think their own kids will, but are less likely to think they can influence their children..."[6] Goodman could have included, which is equally duplicitous, "Dad, you expect me to work hard, be conscientious, and pull my weight at work. Did you always pull yours?"

The parenting motto of the baby-boomer generation seems to be "Do as I say, not as I did." The same sense of deception is experienced by workers and managers alike. Those who have lived through these times of enormous change have had great difficulty clarifying their roles. How could workers and managers believe they could succeed at work when they were failing at home? The sins of permissiveness, abdication, omission, and commission all committed at home now play havoc at work. Those who have had trouble reconciling their experiences with their parental anxieties have put their children into a more at-risk position. Children who were not taught proper behavior or responsibility at home now refuse to behave responsibly at work.

Our root problem, suggests Karl Zinsmeister of the American Enterprise Institute, is a moral disorder traced to the destroyed family. American children, especially, are growing up in unstable homes without regular and consistent support from one or both parents. This is leading to demonstrable intellectual and moral scars. What makes this family disaster doubly dangerous, Zinsmeister insists, is that the trend pervades our society at a time when there is a significant decline in things material throughout the world. Clearly, there appears a counterbalancing upswing in the importance of the capacities of the mind and soul everywhere but in America. Zinsmeister puts it bluntly: "On a societal level, national riches are now toted in human aptitude and attitudes, not ounces of bullion. On a personal level, poverty is increasingly a function of character or personal behavior."[7] Zinsmeister sees the world losing its patience with America's self-indulgence as it moves away from the United States, spiritually and economically, to establish its own more enlightening identity.

Why Johnny Won't Work!

A better question than "Why won't Johnny work?" is "Why should he?" Princeton historian Daniel T. Rodgers writes, "We have exaggerated the death of the work ethic largely because its converts have so greatly exaggerated its existence."[8] The work ethic has always been a minority phenomenon. The idea that hard work is the greatest good in life never cut deeply into the American South. It was violated in scores of eighteenth century frontier settlements, in rich men's ballrooms, and in most of the nation's workshops and factories. Workers resented having to leave their ancestral farms to be forced to move to urban areas and work in cluttered, noisy, dirty plants, mills, and machine shops. From the beginning, the work ethic belonged to a fraction of the population, primarily the northern Protestant propertied classes popularly known as WASPs (white Anglo-Saxon Protestants). WASPs were an immensely influential minority who did their best to nationalize their intense faith in hard work. WASPs drilled its value into their school children, poor recipients of relief, freed slaves, immigrants, and industrial workers of all sorts. The lessons never fully took, so the story of the work ethic is one of conflict and commitment. Yet the dream of self-made success continued to win converts to the work ethic through the nineteenth and well into the twentieth century as thousands of Europeans and Asians sought the American promise. Once immigration was restricted, the ranks of the believers diminished quickly. Hard times took up the slack, as did economic relocation, and with these hardships, a renewed respect for work arose once again. In the 1930s, for instance, during the years of the Great Depression, when work was hard to find, respect for work grew appreciably. Since the late 1940s, however, the workplace has become a veritable war zone. The struggle first for the eight-hour day, then resistance to job changes and increased production quotas, followed by strikes and heated contract negotiations, especially in the automotive industry, broke repeatedly into public view. Even so, by comparison, American factories were much more turbulent in the nineteenth century, when turnover was double what it is today and absenteeism was better than 10 percent.

The dramatic change was primarily caused by *leisure*, not work. Before the twentieth century, there was little leisure for most Americans, and it wasn't a threatening occurrence. Work and struggle were all the average family ever experienced, generation after generation. After World War II, when leisure became a legitimate aspect of a working person's life, the majority of working-class Americans did not know how to handle it. To this day, many refuse to take their accrued vacation, and others are proud to voice their disdain for leisure—*an idle mind is a devil's workshop*. Leisure is not associated with constructive, creative, or recreational activity. Many would rather be paid the benefit than face the break. The conflict between work and leisure is real. Americans see themselves in terms of two speeds—all-out "go" or a complete "stop." Seeing work and leisure as part of the same whole is baffling. Leisure is grudgingly compartmentalized like a giant cavity to be filled, something necessary, but not comfortable to do. How is leisure filled? Frequently with frivolous goods and escapist entertainment, the opium of an impatient and not fully turned out people.

This was dramatically illustrated by the 1960s furlough program at such corporations as Bethlehem Steel and Aluminum Company of America (Alcoa). In *Crisis in Bethlehem* (1986), John Strohmeyer explains how such steel industry excesses actually crippled "the goose that laid the golden egg."[9] When the 13-week furlough program was inaugurated, metal workers in the 1960s already enjoyed practically every benefit and financial concession imaginable. This program allowed the senior half of the workforce to be given an additional 13 weeks of paid vacation every five years. The furlough program was designed to administer manpower requirements more effectively, to give the workforce the incentive to pursue self-enhancement interests (including educational pursuits), and to improve productivity. What the program produced instead was a nightmare of resentment. What do you imagine most furloughed workers did? Renovate their homes? Take European vacations? Spend time at the lake? Tour the great U.S. National Parks? Go back to school? Most furloughed workers did none of the above. They acquired a second job. When the time came to go back to work, many refused to give up their temporary jobs because they needed the extra income to maintain their new standard of living. Here is where the problems started. Attempts to balance the two jobs resulted in poor performance on both. So, for many, instead of the furlough program providing a broadening experience, it created conflict and compressed their spirits into anger and resentment, not at themselves and their stupidity, but at the company for its generosity. Were it not for the company's hair-brained idea, they wouldn't be in so much confusion! Work was what they knew, and work was what filled the 13-week void.

What's the Point of Working Anyhow?

The price of freedom, despite this ambivalence, is still work. Our mythology makes that quite clear. When Adam and Eve exercised their freedom by disobeying God, they were driven from the womb of nature into the world of work. A prejudice against work has existed ever since. Yet late twentieth century life has played a trick on this cultural mythology. Most work now is "make work" to occupy people to do something, which could just as well not be done at all. Take the tens of thousands involved in the media, frantically attempting to out-scoop each other and dramatize inane events 24 hours a day as if they were reporting Armageddon.[10] Then take the infomercials in which similar numbers are involved in promoting activities, products, information, and opinions that have little to do with anything or anybody. True, they take up time and give viewers an opportunity to consider buying things they don't need, don't want, and have little use for but which they may purchase to add clutter to empty spaces. These essentially useless products give jobs to people which they might not otherwise have. Then take the tens of thousands of government employees, elected, hired, or appointed, and you have another body of people doing essentially nothing to further the cause of humanity. Many of these people are important and are interviewed by reporters on television, who are equally important and who would otherwise not have jobs. Literally millions of people listen to these serious, concerned, and loquacious individuals, buying their books, ideas, or their products and then totally forgetting who was interviewed or what was said. Lest we forget, there are tens of thousands of academics in thousands of citadels of learning in which little learning interrupts the decorum and in which erudite journals are enriched with their research that seldom moves the current of humanity. Students hang out at universities until they are too old to be kids or until a job comes along that pays well but is not too demanding. Then there are tens of thousands of people working for airlines, ship lines, railroads, and bus lines who provide transportation for millions who are on the move going from nowhere to nowhere as quickly and frantically as they can. These travelers will congregate at resorts, spas, scenic and historic places, seminars, conventions, and remote corners of the earth to be able to feel they are doing something consequential with other notable people of consequence or to have something to brag about to the neighbors back home.[11] There is nothing wrong with any of this if people have a sense of humor about it, or if they choose to turn their backs on it and have a full, eventful life outside the mainstream, which is neither "main" nor "stream" to anything.

Most work is more playful, weightless, and spiritual than leisure, no matter how much people try to see or make it otherwise. In the words of poet Kahlil Gibran, "Work is love made visible." When work is love, and when it makes us feel more alive and complete and more in touch with ourselves, then we are in a kind of paradise. We have managed to find our way back into the Garden of Eden. Despite this, many still manage to treat work as though it were punishment. What would these people do with their time if they didn't work? Work is made into what it is not. Work is life, and life is work. It isn't how much you make, or how much you have accumulated, or even how high you manage to rise in the food chain that is important. What is important is what the work does for you as a human being. Does it make you kinder, more loving, more alive, more in touch with reality? If it doesn't, then you are in the wrong work. Studs Terkel, the prolific author on commonplace subjects, commits a cardinal error in his book *Working* (1974) with the opening line: "This book, being about work, is, by its nature, about violence…to the spirit as well as the body."[12] Nothing could be further from the truth. Work is about struggle, pain, success and failure, disappointment and exaltation, futility and competence, and limits and pushing the envelope. Work is about making connection between the body and the spirit. Terkel makes his living expressing his love of words, so why be patronizing? All work is ennobling. Does this mean that the Dickensian horrors of child labor, sweatshops, worker exploitation, and sterile robotics emporiums don't exist? Of course they do. But for the majority, the struggle has gone out of work, pain has taken a leave of absence, and the motivation to work is as confused as work itself. Work has gone from the toil of moving the great stone of mortality to moving the weightlessness of the human spirit. It is hard to measure work when we are mainly orphans to it.

As is man's inclination, work is avoided whenever possible. Now, when it is not necessary to avoid work and is no longer threatening, people appear obsessed with making *non-work work*. Their priorities are out of control. Madness has taken center stage and the lead in the play. The modern professional worker is ill-prepared for this development. His whole being is heaped in the cultural mythology of guilt that Terkel continues to compose, the guilt for work still not being laborious. Work is even fading for economic survival. Were it not for the frenetic race to spend money before it is earned, like greyhounds chasing the mechanical rabbit that is going nowhere around the race track, this would be more apparent. Actually, when work as struggle abates, the motive to work changes.

In our Western culture, parents have traditionally worked hard to provide a better life for their children, as if this were a divine obligation. It is not. This, too, is fading. Many parents, disillusioned by the insolence of their spoiled brats, are retreating from this *noblesse oblige*. In fact, many parents, after surrendering their homes and most cherished possessions to their thoughtless offspring, are too tired and burned out to complain. Baby boomers feed on themselves (the more they get, the more they want) and everybody else. Cynical, with little sense of purpose or vision, this generation now marches into middle age suspended in terminal adolescence.

For the baby boomers, leisure has been distracted by work, doubly so because work and leisure are interchangeable. Given this predicament, with so much time on their hands, they have had the insane desire to make the simple complex ("I don't need transportation. I need a Porsche!"), the banal profound (read Anthony Robbins or Stephen Covey), and the sacred profane (same-sex marriages). The baby boomers are custodians of *non-thinking thinking*, generating *non-doing doing* of *non-thing things*. Work is feeding on itself as the principal product of work today is the generation of more work, with no discernible outcome, other than work. Consequently, work has become essentially a counterfeit activity.

With the Great Depression of 1929, the Oklahoma Dust Bowl of the 1930s, and the 100-day bank holiday of President Roosevelt's first administration (1933), all of which have been nearly forgotten, there is little sense of pain in the American conscience. John Steinbeck captures this pain in his book *The Grapes of Wrath* (1939). When the banks foreclosed on their land, Oklahoma sharecroppers left the dust bowl of that region, caused by the terrible drought, for the promised land of California. Steinbeck's book is a bittersweet portrayal of an uprooted family that had been devastated by the Depression. Many Americans, at the time, could identify with this family. Shortly after being inaugurated in 1933, President Roosevelt declared a "bank holiday" by closing all the banks in the United States so that they could be reorganized. When they reopened, 100 days later, many Americans found they were wiped out financially. Today, recessions and inflation are hardly felt by most citizens. Elaborate financial buffers, including unemployment insurance, pension funds, union benefits, IRAs, welfare relief benefits, and food stamps, have taken the catastrophe out of unemployment or economic downturn. It would require a total economic collapse to get most people's attention. Meanwhile, nearly everyone is a prisoner of organization, going from a sense of individualism and independence to a sense of organizational counterdependence. This is as true in the private sector as in the public. The relationship between workers and the workplace is not healthy, nor is it mutually beneficial. Indeed, it is reciprocally detrimental. The structure of the workplace culture is killing the worker's spirit, while it is destroying the organization's ability to compete. This has precipitated a punishing dilemma that becomes worse as more attention is paid to it. Most organizations have been separated from the Culture of Contribution, where workers earn their keep and a reasonable balance exists between work expected and work completed. For the past quarter century, attempts to regain this culture have instead created either the Culture of Comfort or the Culture of Complacency (see Figure 2.1).

Most work today is more symbolic and abstract, much less tied to any concrete activity. Consequently, work is more geared toward making an impression than to producing definitive outcomes. Work is respected more for the identity it provides than the satisfaction it gives. So what is the point of working? What people call work is too often not tied to anything utilitarian other than satisfying a boss, who is satisfying a boss, who is...until someone stops and says, "Why, and what for?" *What gives a person satisfaction is being useful in the service of others.* Now, it is no longer a vague concept but a real possibility. Work has gone from punishment to pleasure, from something workers have to do to something they want to do, from a vocation to an avocation, from extrinsic interests (outside demands) to intrinsic interests (inside commands), and from work to play. Workers have choices they never had before. It is possible today to make a living and still have plenty of time left over for leisure or to do something worthwhile in the service of others. All that is necessary is that workers be in command of their own destiny by making choices rather than having them made for them and for having the gumption to do what pleases them rather than worrying about what pleases others. The fact that these words appear strange and incongruous with the reader's experience is indicative of how "work" has boondoggled the average worker.

At a time when workers around the world should be enjoying freedom as never before, the spiritual component of *giving* competes with the conscious pursuit of *getting*. Masses of people across advanced technological societies no longer must focus on work as their central concern. These workers have the luxury of harboring ideals and giving life to them. They may choose to work or ignore work in pursuit of other interests. When it comes to such choices, most workers allow their primitive instincts to command their attention. Work is what they know. Work is a safety net, a socially approved way to be a bully, to command attention, to be somebody, and to sublimate fear. To justify this mania for work, struggle is contrived as its essence.

Work, so defined, is the only thing they understand. Now that work is more ambiguous, workers hide their confusion in secretly esteeming the self-made media mogul, the professional sports owner, the fast-food franchise owner, the college professor, and the manager. As work needs less of a human driver, what we call work is not enough to keep body and soul together. The spiritual component of work is now more vital than ever. The next most vital aspect of work is self-direction. And the final integer is the triangular component of trust-control-freedom—the trust to give the worker control of work and the freedom to do the job (Figure 6.2).

One effect of post-industrial society is that economic struggle has been essentially taken out of work. No longer is there the same sense of economic deprivation

Figure 6.2   Purposeful performance motivation triangle.

as there was a century ago. Unemployment for high-technology Western nations is less than 10 percent and in many nations, including the United States, only around 5 percent. There are literally more jobs available than people to fill them, and the jobs referred to here are well-paying jobs—jobs as technicians, technologists, academics, teachers, researchers, psychologists, medical health professionals, architects, and engineers. The problem is that there is a worldwide shortage of qualified people. Yet cultural conditioning remains a ploy to keep many harnessed to the *concrete world of getting* rather than taking charge of their lives and plugging into the *abstract world of giving*. The talent is there. The opportunity is there. Yet many hesitate. They do what they hate and punish themselves every day, justifying the penance for the money. Marsha Sinetar has exposed this deception in *Do What You Love, The Money Will Follow* (1987). Service to others is what satisfies, and this is an idea that is subjective and qualitative. You cannot take satisfaction to the bank, nor can you experience it until you take the risks and find out the truth about yourself by doing what you love, no matter what money or prestige there is to the work. You must go against the grain of the objective world of quantitative measurement ("I do this for the money"), the cynical world of greed where "more" is never enough.

Society is on the threshold of having enough leisure time to create a modern Renaissance which could compare with that of ancient society. This is difficult to contemplate, because modern workers are trained and conditioned for a world that no longer exists, and therefore, they appear totally out of control while pretending to have their act together. In the absence of harnessing their creative energies, modern workers overcompensate in frenetic activities. This is the era of conference calls, fax machines, E-mail, message machines, pagers, cellular phones, beepers, laptops, laser printers, home computers, microwave ovens, and the Internet. In a study entitled *Agenda for the 1990s*, it was learned that people are working more and enjoying it less (Figure 6.3). Professional workers are finding it impossible to meet both their personal and professional demands, so what suffers? Of course, their personal lives are in shambles. This study examined the lifestyles of 1,000 businessmen and businesswomen in 14 industries in the United States. What the study showed was that the time-savers and efficiency-enhancing technology, oddly enough, contribute to the problem. Far from simplifying, codifying, and reducing the informational blitz-krieg, these wonders of technology define it instead.

Edward Tenner in *Why Things Bite Back: Technology and the Revenge of Unintended Consequences* (1996) theorizes that these technological inventions take on a life of their own.[13] Tenner calls this the "revenge effect," which are not side effects. A side effect, he defines, is just plain bad—an antidepressant that gives you diarrhea. A revenge effect is ironically bad—an antidepressant that makes you depressed. In connection with time-savers, Tenner claims the more we focus on the computer-powered "paperless office," the more paper we must generate to make it possible.

Modern workers are working for technology rather than technology working for them. With so much information available (most of it not worth the heat it generates) and so little time to deal with it, what do you suppose happens in most instances? Research shows that professional workers become *proactive* (a modern buzzword)—not in data abatement, which you might have reason to expect, but in producing even more technology to accentuate the data flow. This ever-increasing volume of information has become the modern demon, demanding the soul, mind, heart, and will of

---

Working More and Enjoying It Less

- 85 percent said they work more than 45 hours per week
- 48 percent feel stressed every day
- 65 percent work more than one weekend a month
- 89 percent take work home with them
- 53 percent spend less than two hours a week looking after their children
- 4 percent said child-care facilities were available at their workplace

---

Figure 6.3   Agenda for the 1990s: Survey of professional men (650) and women (350).

the worker. It has created a decision-making dilemma, where machines ultimately decide the fate of their creators.

Panic is in the air. When genuine leisure is possible, "leisure society" remains a myth. In 1989, the sales of the Filofax Company, whose elaborate notebooks help people navigate through the clutter of their lives, hit $4.2 million, double its sales figures in 1987. Meanwhile, more executives, professionals, self-employed people, journalists, consultants, and bureaucrats confess in unison to thriving on a 60- to 70-hour work week schedule.[14] The electronic workplace is more a demanding mistress than ever was the sweatshop. Economists who make a business of studying the beneficial impact of such activity on the national economy fail to find any. People are spinning their wheels, because those around them are spinning theirs—the herd mentality is alive and prospering. Working longer and harder is a way of avoiding the issue altogether, a way to avoid the pain of working smarter. It is also a way of avoiding an ugly confrontation with the boss. Few are willing to take the risk of being labeled a trouble-maker, agitator, or malcontent. In the average professional worker's career, he is destined to spend three years in meaningless meetings, two years writing reports that nobody reads, six months in performance reviews that contribute little to development, and two years in training programs that prepare him for the way it was, but no longer is.

Preoccupation with superficial activities deprives professional workers of the time to be creatively self-reliant. Ralph Waldo Emerson expressed this unique spiritualism in his famous essay *Self-Reliance* (1844). Here he emphasizes the wisdom of self-trust and the power of perspective: "To believe your own thoughts, to believe that what is true for you in your private heart is true for all men…that is genius."[15] Where is our genius today? Why such a merry rush to madness when our transcendental past—the world of Emerson, Thoreau, Melville, Poe, and Hawthorne—promises a more sane society? Emerson had a different vision of the educated man than the professional-technical elite. He envisioned a person with a strong bent for experience, supported by a spiritual insight into being, a person with a sense of balance. Emerson believed, too, that education should promote the ability of the common man as much through experience as from books. For him, the basis of a democratic education was the cultivation of ordinary experience to its spiritual essence. From this qualitative faith in the sovereignty of the individual sprang Emerson's vision of the *unity of self, nature, and society*—everything is connected to everything else. He could see experience melting into the essence of the national character, producing a model of the possibilities of a democratic culture for the world. Repeatedly during Emerson's long career, he expressed the sanctity of individualism along with the responsibility of self-reliance. Late twentieth century man has drifted far afield of such a course.

Consider the arrogance of individualism today and the conspicuous lack of self-reliance. Where is the sense of place and space, the sense of experience and self-determinism? Many workers, by their own admission, find little joy in work, less joy in educational experience, and still less joy in their private lives. They are essentially miserable, preferring to be well-paid wretches than happily unemployed.[16] But of course that is not the point. They are being taken care of, and they resent this codependent bond with their employer. So what do they do? They lash out at phantom nemeses, failing to see themselves as both the enemy and ally of their own situation. As the enemy of the company, their behavior becomes the silent killers of lost momentum, and as the company's ally, their behavior becomes the secret weapon to newfound hope. They live the sorrows poet Eugene O'Neill captures: "We talk about the American Dream, and want to tell the world about the American Dream, but what is that dream, in most cases, but the dream of material things? I sometimes think that the United States, for this reason, is the greatest failure the world has ever seen."[17] But if O'Neill is right, who can change this but the American worker?

Enter the Manic Monarchs of the Merry Madhouse!

Termites destroy a person's home with no one the wiser until irreparable damage is done. Termites are invisible to the naked eye working diligently and effectively beyond anyone's awareness. But what of social termites, otherwise known as the *six silent killers* of the organization's infrastructure? We note and are alarmed with the tens of billions of dollars lost to sick leave misuse due to substance abuse every year. We also note with concern the tens of billions of dollars lost due to stress and emotional-related problems, including accidents, heart attacks, strokes, seizures, and mental illness. Then we note with an astonishing amount of tolerance others who manage to make it to work every day with diminished capacity due to smoking, eating, or drinking too much. Their major achievement is showing up for work and precariously piloting their way through the day. Still, these problems are visible and definable. No surprises. Awareness takes the form of Employee Assistance Programs (EAPs) and generous medical insurance benefit programs. But the infrastructure damage caused by the *six silent killers* is beyond the pale of anyone's imagination. Social termites are unconscionable, mainly on automatic pilot, literally eating away the hand that feeds them. Social termites choose to deny reality, to become inauthentic to themselves, and to become obsessively negative to others. Social termites look for what is wrong, not right; for what they can get, not give; for what they don't have, not possess; and the glass for them is always near empty. Social termites develop political cunning just this side of amazing, displaying an incredible facility to manage, influence, and manipulate colleagues and superiors indiscriminately. They conveniently choose to see themselves as victims of a system that fails to appreciate them or satisfy their needs. Without knowing it, they have been seduced by the *six silent killers*, behaviors that can kill a career before it is underway, undermine all they could become, and literally destroy the enterprise for which they work. Organizations plagued with these social termites find management preoccupied with damage control without dealing with the source of the problem. Managers, as manic monarchs, take ownership of the wreckage, while the social termites treat the workplace as their merry madhouse. It is like the plague all over again, a disease that contaminates everyone and everything, but the source of which no one seems to recognize. It is too obvious.

Silent Killer No. 1: *Passive Aggressive Behavior*

Examples are coming in late, leaving early, doing as little as possible to get by, or not as much as one is capable of doing. This silent killer is invoked somewhere in the world at least ten million times every hour of every work day, at a cost in productivity loss in the trillions of dollars. Small wonder bankruptcy is such a booming business. Passive aggressive behavior has several interesting components.

Perceiving Oneself Being Wronged!

Passive aggression is a strategy, seldom conscious, of punishing someone for a real or imagined slight. Passive aggressive behavior is actually an oxymoron—"passive" and "aggressive." While in a passive mood, the mind is racing with some kind of hostile thought or punishing conduct meant to put a hurt on someone or something. The perception of being wronged totally justifies any amoral conduct. This perception builds to a defiance that is manifested in poor performance.

The Need to Challenge the Rules!

Authority is symbolized as the enemy. The mind nurses the idea of being powerless and lacking self-esteem. It is the fault of authority that one thinks so lowly of oneself, and it is the fault of authority that one has little power. How to get back at authority? Nip at the rules, not enough to break them and get into major trouble, but enough to cause havoc in the workplace—such as smoking in the rest rooms, not wearing safety goggles in designated areas, dumping hazardous wastes into the sewer system when no one is looking, or not maintaining proper hygiene. The point is to violate as many rules or policies as possible to cause extreme irritation, but not enough to be considered flagrant. One engineer of such a mind, who had a comfortable five-figure income, chose to live in his car on the company parking lot. It took security and management nine months to get him to cease and desist. After all sorts of touchy-feely approaches—he had recently been divorced—management gave him an ultimatum either to live elsewhere or to turn in his security badge. He found a place to stay that very day and never caused this kind of trouble again. His anger against his ex-wife was turned against the company's authority until the company lost its patience. In a strange involuted way, the company took responsibility for this engineer's fouled-up personal life and played rag-tag with the problem for nine months.

Fixation!

Occasionally passive aggressive behavior takes a strange turn back on the person. These people become so fixated with being wronged that they take it out on themselves—by eating too much and becoming fat and disgusting (because thin is in); or by drinking too much and causing friends to avoid them (see what a waste I am?); by disregarding normal hygiene (the engineer who lived in his car quit bathing, yet no one in his lab, including his supervisor, could muster the courage to tell him how bad he smelled, because appearance is in and smelling refreshed is expected);

by using uncouth language and telling coarse jokes to display self-contempt (professionalism demands a certain refinement); or by doing, saying, or behaving in any way to mount self-deprecation to the extreme. In the twisted logic against the self, the idea is to punish the system by making it apparent that it (system) made this behavior necessary. Self-humiliation in public epitomizes this fixation.

What triggers this behavior could be anything from a failure at home, work, or school or in a relationship to a death in the family (yes, being mad at God can trigger this behavior), failure to be appreciated or recognized for some act, failure to be included in a select group or event, or failure to earn an expected promotion. Even self-contempt for not being healthier, happier, more attractive, more intelligent, younger, or a better lover or athlete can produce such reactive behavior, along with being upset with a national or international event only remotely related to the person in question. It isn't what triggers the behavior which is important, but how the behavior, once revealed, is dealt with. Being contemptuous of healthy, happy, productive, important, and engaged people can take the form of being antagonistic to persons who display these attributes.

Passive aggressive behavior is often a failure to communicate with oneself, which precipitates this ambivalent and destructive behavior. It rises out of an imagined sense of being powerless and lacking self-esteem. It is a way of getting even without getting hurt too badly or being discovered too quickly. Passive aggression is devastatingly disruptive, and yet most organizations cultivate it by first choosing to ignore it and then, once noticed, to deal with it ambiguously.

Silent Killer No. 2: *Passive Responsive Behavior*

Examples are never doing anything until one is told, then doing only that and standing around waiting for further instructions before doing anything else or bringing one's body to work while leaving one's mind at home. One word describes how a manager or co-worker is likely to feel about this person—frustrated. No matter what you do to or for them, nothing happens:

- You flatter them—nothing.
- You reprimand them—nothing.
- You give their pay a boost—nothing.
- You cut their pay—nothing.
- You praise them before their colleagues—nothing.
- You reprimand them before their colleagues—nothing.
- You give them a letter of commendation for their personnel file—nothing.
- You threaten to put a critical letter in their personnel file—nothing.
- You give them a vacation day with pay "to think it over"—nothing.
- You give them time off without pay—nothing.
- You promise them a promotion—nothing.
- You threaten them with a demotion—nothing.

- You threaten to fire them—nothing.
- Nothing, nothing—nothing!

Not a single thing management does or colleagues attempt to do seems to get through to this person's passive responsive behavior. He appears inexplicably beyond the skills of comprehension and communication. Too frequently this person's manager becomes obsessed with him. The manager is convinced that he is going to *save* the person from himself! The rescuer's mentality is just what the passive responsive person thrives on. Paradoxically, the tough-minded mentality, who would bounce the person off the wall, falls equally into this person's grasp. The passive responsive person is circulated from one department to another, never staying long, always with approval of his worth to his next manager. He endures, leaving in his wake tired, beleaguered, victimized witnesses.

Ultimately, in total frustration, a manager documents his every action. The cost of this documentation in terms of time wasted, energy expended, and money lost is beyond calculation. The rationale, which usually justifies this obsession, is never candidly disclosed. When asked, a manager will say he is trying to save a lost employee. That, of course, is an impossibility. Only an employee can save himself. That happens when the employee chooses to act differently on purpose. Perhaps closer to the truth is that a manager devotes so much time to this person because of the principle of the thing. He deludes himself into believing his job is to motivate workers to become top performers when that, too, is an impossibility. A manager's job is to create a climate for productive effort, then to facilitate that process. The rest is up to the worker. If the worker does not respond, the worker should suffer the consequences, not the organization. That means nipping the passive responsive person in the bud, not when he is a thriving menace.

One manager documented a person who was tardy for work for the 167th time. This documentation, submitted to the Marginal Employee Program, ran to seven typewritten pages, single spaced. When asked what was so magical about the 167th time, the manager scratched his head and said, "I really don't know."

Characteristically, such a manager takes ownership of the passive responsive person's problem. As far back as anyone could check, this person had had a manager who served as a sympathetic surrogate parent. Over time, the passive responsive person's sensitivity erodes to the point that he becomes totally insensitive to everything and everybody. No matter what the stimuli, he is utterly beyond responsiveness. Every time the passive responsive person had an opportunity to fail, somebody broke his fall, rescued him from the incident, or saved him from a learning experience. Such protectionism may rise out of duty, love, guilt, a sick need to dominate, or many other shades of human conduct that prevent growth through self-knowledge and self-understanding. It is a diabolical deception to cut a person off from the struggle of his own experience and then have someone else carry him on their shoulders. Life is struggle, and without this essential component, there is no life, only vegetation, atrophy, and passivity.

How, then, do you turn a passive responsive person around? You don't! You cannot easily overcome the disadvantage of 20 to 30 years of mismanaged development. There are no miracles. You can neutralize the impact of such a person on operations by cutting him off from the mainstream and placing him in an inconsequential job. If there is any flicker of behavioral change, and there may be some, reward him immediately, not in a big way, but in a way which indicates progress is in the desired direction. If he completes an assignment before it is expected, give him slightly more responsible tasks and then monitor his activity. If he shows little or no improvement, it is not the organization's problem. It is his only. The organization's mission is to establish a productive work climate, not save workers from themselves.

Generally speaking, Time and Attendance (T&A) is not a very meaningful performance gauge. Focusing exclusively on punctuality projects the implicit message that conformity and obedience count for more than contribution and that showing up on time fulfills the principal requirement of work. Western society is brimming with workers who have never missed a day or have seldom been late. Many of these same workers are great socializers, coffee break specialists, rumor mill facilitators, and unlikely to make a smidgen of difference to the bottom line. Showing up is their major contribution.

The passive responsive person is an emotional cripple who causes pain to everyone he touches. The irony is that he generates so much concern that people want to help him when only he has that capability. There are basically three types of workers in any organization at any one time (Figure 6.4):

- There are those variously known as *hard-chargers, winners, curve-setters, leaders, or victors*. These workers represent about 15 percent of the workforce. No matter what management does, what state of stability or instability the organization is in, or what the majority of workers are doing, including their peers, they go forward successfully. They are usually well ahead of the learning curve, understand and accept the naked reality in which the organization finds itself, and deal with it accordingly. They use the organization to foster and promote their own personal and professional agenda without any compunction. There are obviously climbers amongst their ranks, but these hard-chargers are not exclusively climbers. They are doers and make up about 75 percent of the positive energy. Were it not for them, the organization would be dead in the water.

- At the opposite end of the curve, there are those known as *feet-draggers, losers, lagers, or victims*. These workers also represent about 15 percent of the workforce. The *six silent killers* nest here but spread well beyond the bounds of this category. Not only are passive responsive persons card-carrying members of this distinction, they are perhaps the biggest losers of all because they not only visit this haven, but live here. Losers fail to understand the organization or their own

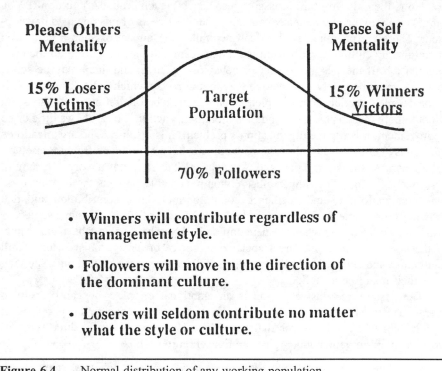

- **Winners will contribute regardless of management style.**

- **Followers will move in the direction of the dominant culture.**

- **Losers will seldom contribute no matter what the style or culture.**

Figure 6.4   Normal distribution of any working population.

motivation. They are the walking wounded, unable to see what the organization can do *for them*, choosing instead only to see what it does *to them*. The feet-draggers have a great deal to do with forward inertia because the organization is unable or refuses to cut them loose from the fold. The remarkable thing about this category is that many in it survive the most drastic cuts in downsizing and restructuring. Upwards of 90 percent of these losers manage to share equally in wage and entitlement benefits that accrue to the true contributors. Evidence? Consider performance appraisal results (discussed later).

The balance of the organization, 70 percent, falls into the broad category of the *followers, soldiers*, or the *obedient many*. No organization can succeed without rallying this group to its cause. Followers move in the direction of the prevailing winds. If the wind is at management's back, it will be blowing followers in management's direction and on course to its goal. If it is not, followers will scatter, and management's ability to forge ahead is nigh impossible. Most of management's energy is devoted to sequestering this group to some semblance of order and purpose. The organization is a dynamic entity, so that means members of the followers category are likely to be moving in both directions of losers and winners. What direction (forward or backward) should display the greatest momentum is a factor of training and development, workplace culture, and the structure of the organization. Given the current dominant structure and workplace culture in most organizations, the chances of moving in the direction of winners are slim. If anything, most organizations neutralize the winner potential by imposing frustrating policies and procedures, ambivalent promotional schemes, and rigid rules for the conduct of business. The timid back away and play it safe, finding security well within the bounds of this category. Others who are just waiting for a chance to trash the organization retreat into the losers category.

The winners, hard-chargers, leaders, or victors are winners usually despite rather than because of the organization. They are in your face, some with great subtlety and others with annoying style. Winners know their worth and use it to their advantage. What is desirable about these hard-chargers is that they get the organization to take risks it might otherwise not take. What is undesirable is that their personal victories are not always in the best interest of the organization. This implies that they, too, must be managed and supplied with limits in a conducive workplace culture and organizational structure. It is not prudent to allow them to play "lone ranger" in support of their personal agenda. Yet they are essential to organizational success. Too frequently management prefers followers to these winners because they are easier to handle. When management plays "cute" and ambivalent with winners and followers and fails to create a climate in which both can be productive, invisible behaviors take center stage, and the *six silent killers* raise their heads and play havoc with operations.

Passive responsive persons think several of the things actually said by passive defensive people. While passive responsive persons give the appearance that they could care less, the fact is they have been hardened to the vicissitudes of life. Robert Smith captures this in his book about children with the catchy title *Where Did You Go? Out. What Did You Do? Nothing* (1974). Passive responsive persons are suspended in adolescence. It is a safe place youngsters learn to go early in life, for it is easy to say, "I don't care," or "You don't understand." Most of us visit this place as a temporary haven when we are hurt and confused and have yet to develop the emotional maturity to deal with pain. We are in trouble, however, when it becomes home.

Silent Killer No. 3: *Passive Defensive Behavior*

Always having an excuse for why something isn't done ("Not my job!" "Nobody told me!" "How was I supposed to know?" "I never got that training!" "I didn't get that memo!" "I can't read your handwriting!" "I wasn't there when you gave the order!" "You must have told somebody else, thought it was me, and forgot!" "I can't read your mind!" "I'm waiting for somebody to tell us what to do. This is where they told us to go." "I'm new around here, okay?" "All I can say is I followed instructions!"), pointing fingers ("I did my job. Is it my fault that Sally didn't do hers?"), playing "show your ass" (SYA) or "cover your ass" (CYA) games by pointing out errors or having a memo to cover yours, and doing other people's assignments as an alibi for not doing your own ("I didn't have time. Sam asked me to give him a hand. What was I supposed to do, turn my back on a colleague?"). The passive defensive person is the passive responsive person with brains. They possess an interesting psychology. They appear to have their act together but have a faculty for getting into one unfortunate situation after another. As the conflict between what is valued in the organization and what is not grows more acute, distorted, and confused, persons of a passive defensive persuasion appear to flourish, taking these forms:

- *CYA games*—Practitioners have an amazing faculty, no matter what they do or fail to do, to make everyone else feel responsible. The passive defensive person puts his adversary off balance and on the defensive by exploiting a known weakness of his accuser, which may or may not be relevant to the situation. The point is that the accuser has lost his advantage and the passive defensive person now rules the game.

- *SYA games*—Practitioners go from self-love to self-hate to self-pity to the attack before the target of such attention can catch his breath. The practitioner sees himself as the hunted and immediately goes into a survivor's mode. He realizes that the only way to throw the hunter off his scent is to use "smoke and mirrors" by adopting the guise of the hunter rather than the hunted. Having painted himself into a corner, through some stupidity, he comes out with a "red pencil," caustic remark, or the phantom exception. His singular strategy is to throw his hunter off scent and off stride and on a wild goose chase. Once his adversary is off in the wrong direction, he plants innuendos, rumors, and "he said/she said" tales along the trail, which puts his hunter in the cage of his deception.

- *Reckless abandon games*—Practitioners of this passive defensive behavior have used SYA games for all that they are worth, have come up short, and find themselves still under paralyzing scrutiny. They have reached the point of a zero-sum game as well as the point of no return. Psychologists call this person a Type "T" personality with a high risk-taking, thrill-seeking, rule-breaking, creative-abandon persona. Being primarily left-brain dominated, his reasoning easily gravitates to the bizarre. Paranoia, which is busily fermenting under a contrived calm surface, comes to dominate his mind. He is looking for trouble, for any justification to act as weirdly as possible, and invariably finds it. He finds that he is surrounded by enemies. He convinces himself that he is under siege and has no recourse but to act, if necessary, cruelly or absurdly, but, by all means, decisively.

The first two forms of passive defensive behavior are common. There are times when we all resort to CYA and SYA games. These brief lapses are part of our normal defense mechanism, a mechanism that many organizations unwittingly encourage by the way they are designed. Because most of us don't reach the limits of our emotional resources, we seldom encounter "reckless abandon" games. It is a stage where the person leaves the herd and the social barriers that restrain him and enters the wilderness of his primordial being where there is seldom any escape. It is a most dangerous place to be, yet an improbable number of talented people, as well as very disturbed types, are rushing into it in increasing numbers today.

We read about a "T" type personality who walks into a McDonald's and guns down an innocent lunch crowd, a disgruntled post office employee who blasts his way into his supervisor's office and kills her, the failed graduate student who kills his dissertation professor, or the unemployed handyman who throws gasoline on shoppers in a supermarket and then torches them. We seldom read about reckless abandon games where the scars are invisible and the victims carry them forever. Nor should we confine CYA/SYA and reckless abandon games exclusively to individual behavior. Many organizations are seduced by the same intoxicants of passive defensiveness. Intoxicants of money, power, status, glamour, immortality, fame, ambition, lust, or any number of variations of the seven deadly sins can play a role in this sinister silent killer.

Reckless Abandon Games—When the Scars Are Not Visible!

What do Martin Siegel, Ivan Boesky, John DeLorean, Gary Hart, Dr. John Darsee, Jim Bakker, President Richard Nixon, John Dean, The Johns Manville Corporation, Continental Bank, E. F. Hutton, and Chrysler Corporation have in common? The answer is passive defensive behavior.

The Siegel/Boesky Connection

While still in his thirties, Martin Siegel had everything—a Harvard education, a prestigious position with Kidder, Peabody & Company, a $3.5 million home, a $4 million annual income—but it wasn't enough. Siegel had the whole world in his hands and dropped it![18] He agreed to share privileged information (inside trading) for a price with Ivan Boesky, the legendary investment king. Why did young Siegel break the law and put his comfortable existence in jeopardy? Why did he turn his back on life's promise for a few silver coins? Why did he deceive himself that it was okay and, in so doing, cheat many? Only he knows. But the fact remains that he was enamored of power and flattered by the attention of heavy-hitter Boesky. "Imagine," he must have thought, "I am a confidant of the fabulous Boesky!" Siegel was heady, being important and successful and being professionally accepted by one of the pacesetters of the market.[19] With the cosmic soaring of his income, he spent with a compulsive fever to match it. He was hooked on the narcotic of money. If you have money, his behavior implied, people will love you, pay attention to you, and cannot hurt you. This passive defensiveness translates into a deep disabling spiritual want that no amount of money can satisfy. It is the domain of insecurity without wisdom.

John DeLorean

If ever there was an ideal type to depict the reckless abandon passive defensive personality, it was John DeLorean. This tall, handsome man with a coiffure helmet of steel gray, chiseled features, dark eyes, and ever-smiling lips resembled a swash-buckling hero from the Sunday comics more than a General Motors executive. Yet he took GM by storm with his creative flair, dress, and style. His more conservative, low-profile associates would cringe when he took over a room and accentuated the atmosphere with his latest story. He was a successful salesman through and through, a winner in a business where anything goes as long as you can sell automobiles.

When DeLorean left GM and formed DeLorean Motors in Northern Ireland, he was moving away from his strength into the no-man's land of his weakness. He was not a detail man, not interested in the labyrinth of minutiae that went into the bottom line. That was for others to handle. Just give him the facts! Soon, not long after this newest adventure was underway, problems started to mount. He found that there was much to the business that was foreign to him. He was impatient and found it necessary to cut corners with reckless abandon. Before, he had played the capitalistic game of business with panache and humor, mainly within the rules, because others were covering his ass with the boring details of the business. He couldn't be bothered. Once outside GM's broad protective umbrella and on his own nickel, DeLorean took on Nietzschean dimensions, personifying himself as the self-made, capitalistic super-man. He believed the myth and then tried desperately to make it real.

DeLorean was always a self-promoting supersalesman, never truly a business-man. He looked down on the species with minor contempt. Nevertheless, he con-vinced Northern Ireland to stake him with $100 million with the promise that he would bring hundreds, then thousands of jobs to the six counties of Northern Ireland, a region that hungered desperately for economic development. He betrayed that trust by going out of business not long after the paint dried on his first production run. Before the failure was finalized, however, he did a merry dance into the underworld of crime, attempting to rescue the misfired venture by being implicated in cocaine-trafficking charges.[20] This behavior demonstrates, as business writer Craig Waters so aptly points out, a profound naivete about the nature of small business and the role of the entrepreneur: "He (DeLorean) had no appreciation of the role GM had played in his success during his 17 years there, no understanding of his limitations, and no comprehension of the finite nature of capital."[21] DeLorean got caught up in the high-risk, high-roller game of self-deception and fell like a stone to the bottom of his dreams.[22]

Gary Hart—The Inside Outsider

No political leader on the American scene was better prepared, harder working, or more focused on national issues than former U.S. senator and presidential candi-date Gary Hart. His devotion to new ideas about American life brought depth and vigor to an otherwise lackluster 1988 presidential campaign.[23] Enter the femme fatale in the person of Donna Rice, and you have the beginning of Hart's demise. Who shot down Gary Hart? Was it Donna Rice? The press? Or was it the reckless abandon of Hart's passive defensiveness?

A half century ago, in the 1940 campaign for the presidency, Republican candidate Wendell Willkie openly campaigned with his mistress.[24] He had a good relationship with the press and refused to hide the complexity of his marriage. Even President Roosevelt had ceased to have an intimate relationship with his equally famous wife, Eleanor, and carried on a rather open relationship with Eleanor's secretary that was well known to the press, but not to the nation.[25] Hart's error was that it was a different time. His reckless abandon passive defensiveness was his refusal to acknowledge the morality of his time. For one thing, the press was much less inclined to practice journalistic voyeurism in 1940 than it was in 1988, and for another, the presidency had taken on the glamour of celebrity that did not exist in the earlier period. Willkie was soundly defeated in that 1940 election, but the war in Europe was already underway, and the United States has never shown an inclination to change leaders in a time of national crisis. So, Willkie's behavior had little to do with his defeat.

No, Ms. Rice did not shoot down Gary Hart.[26] His reckless abandon did the trick. He is an interesting study.[27] His fall from grace perhaps started with him changing his name, then progressed to being coy about his age, and moved on from there to finding it difficult to level with his friends.[28] Hart was an introvert who tried to wax the hearty fellow well meant, when his greater inclination was that of the scholar and idealistic thinker. He was an inside outsider who never joined the club but fought hard to acquire the credentials. He came to prominence when the world needed him, only to find he was playing on another circuit. In sharp contrast to Gary Hart, there is President Bill Clinton, who is the complete extrovert. President Clinton makes Hart's indiscretions look like child's play. Whereas Hart may have had too much soul for his own good, facile writer Garry Wills suggests Clinton "may not have any interior to withdraw to."[29] Martin Walker, author of *The President We Deserve* (1996), argues that Clinton survives brutal onslaught after onslaught because of his peculiar strengths of stamina, resilience, and unstoppable determination.[30] Wills adds that "Clinton looks like a person so external to himself as not to have met himself."[31] Hart, on the other hand, took himself far too seriously and became, in the words of a friend, "a time bomb waiting to explode." And of course, it did. Reckless abandon passive defensiveness is not only the act, but a perspective as well.

Dr. John Darsee—The Far Side of Paradise

Dr. John Darsee had a spectacular career from 1974 through 1979.[32] His research and hospital charts were written with bold, impeccable handwriting. One senior medical colleague described his writing as "meticulous, beautiful, almost like calligraphy." An envious peer went even further to suggest "you could almost photograph his notes and publish them in a text book" they were so complete. The clarity of Darsee's mind and the scope of his vision was legendary, and he was only 30. Dr. Darsee had it all, a quicksilver grasp of complex scientific concepts, high skill and compassion as a physician, the drive of a perfectionist, and the charisma and charm of a born teacher. He was popular among his younger colleagues and much respected by his influential seniors. Dr. Paul Walter, a prominent heart specialist whose name appeared as coauthor on 15 of Darsee's published scientific works, thought of him as "clearly one of the most remarkable young men in American medicine." Dr. Walter was right, but for the wrong reason. It appears that most of Darsee's convincingly presented data were, in fact, cunningly crafted lies. Walter, like dozens of other researchers, was dazzled by Darsee's talent, productivity, generosity (sharing credit), and skillful use of flattery. Consequently, they were remiss in closely scrutinizing the data he churned out.

Lengthy investigations at Harvard Medical School, where he graduated with honors, and at Emory University, where he did his residency, have uncovered a pattern of deception that is remarkable in the expanding annals of research fraud. Seventeen of his full-length scientific papers have had to be retracted from the scientific literature, as have 47 abstracts (short summaries of research results). But it goes beyond this. Many scientists have used Darsee's published works as reference to their own research, so more than 241 scientific reports have been compromised. Yet, the scientific community of medicine is asking, "How could it happen?" That is the wrong question. Why it happened is more appropriate.

This demonstrates the laxity and, indeed, the naivete and preference of the medical profession to be more quantitatively than qualitatively driven. Because medical research, like research in so many other fields, is structured to be captivated by quantitative indices, the system is vulnerable to this type of deceptive manipulation. Making a clever impression with brightness and hard work, coupled with imposing credentials and a matching bibliography, is the passport to academic success. This gets closer to the why of Darsee. The drive to succeed at any price in the shortest span of years promotes cheating. There are no shortcuts. While these good doctors are lamenting how they have been deceived, it might be well for them to explore why they so readily accepted a byline to scientific work they did not conduct themselves. Even more to the point, they might wonder why the system encourages such behavior, and why the workplace culture and structure of the organization is not more diligent.

For every Dr. Darsee discovered there are literally scores preparing to take his place. Darsee represents a reactionary frame of reference that is the realm of reckless abandon passive defensiveness. How sad that Darsee didn't take his keen imagination and sculpt it into something authentic and meaningful, as have Michael Crichton and Somerset Maugham. Crichton, too, was a brilliant medical student at Harvard. He, too, had a flair for the written word. So much so that he wrote pulp fiction while he was a medical student to help defray the cost of his education. Upon graduation and the completion of his internship, Crichton wrote a most successful novel (*The Andromeda Strain*, 1969), as did Somerset Maugham (*Liza of Lambeth*, 1897), when he completed his medical studies. They both used their medical studies to breathe life into their literary careers, where fiction gives you the right to tell stories and to be lionized for the telling. This is the other side of paradise that beckoned Darsee but which he lacked eyes to see.

Jim Bakker's Ladder is Gone!

Irish poet William Butler Yeats writes, "Now that my ladder is gone, I must lie down where all ladders start, the fowl rag-and-bone shop of the heart."[33] Some of us scale to great heights, only to avoid ever running into ourselves. But, there is a time when crashing reality cuts through the fog, and we are face-to-face with our own humble selves as naked, exposed, and truly wretched beings. It is a wonder we don't have more compassion in our hearts for those that fall because everyone falls at some time in their lives, be it off a footstool or a mountain. Jim and Tammy Bakker were designed for falling off a footstool, but somehow found themselves falling off a mountain. How such totally ordinary people could rise so high and fall so far is a telling index of our times. Their "Praise the Lord" (PTL) television club was a resounding success, largely due to its commonplace familiarity and genius for understanding what may broadly be called the spiritual or emotional life of individuals as people.

Jim Bakker possessed something that intellectuals scorn as "common con," when it is actually an exceptional sensitivity to the heart of the lonely and lost, which includes most of us. He possessed antennae to troubled souls, something perfectly ordinary, empirical, and quasi-aesthetic. This gift entails the capacity for integrating a vast amalgam of constantly changing events—too many, too swift, too inter-mingled to be caught and pinned down—as elements in a single pattern where simple prayer is the pragmatic answer. Denomination, dogma, liturgical scripture, and even the Bible were not the common focus. Indeed, Bakker brought followers into his flock beyond Christianity. To be able to do this well seems to be a gift akin to that of the creative artist. He gave the impression that he was directly acquainted with his listeners' pain and texture of their lives, not just the sense of the chaotic flow of experience, but a highly developed discrimination of what matters most to the wounded. Above all this, he had an actual sense of what fits with what, what springs from what, what leads to what, how things seem to vary to different people, what the effect of such experience upon them may be, and what the result is likely to be in a concrete situation of the interplay of human beings and impersonal forces. No, this was not the raving of a "common con." Bakker demonstrated a sense for what is qualitative rather than quantitative, for what is specific rather than general in the lives of his listeners. Bakker epitomized a direct acquaintance with pain, distinct from a capacity for description of pain or calculation of what the pain might mean to a Freudian psychoanalyst or a social engineer. He presented no credentials as an expert. Nor did he attempt to present himself as beyond being flawed. He possessed what is sometimes called "natural wisdom" as opposed to scholarly erudition. What he possessed was an imaginative understanding, insight, perceptiveness, and intuition into the matter of ordinary lives of ordinary people. With this practical wisdom, he demonstrated a capacity for synthesis rather than analysis. His troubles began when he tried to analyze his own success and, with it, his audience's tolerance for his family's flaunted, blatant, and escalating eccentricities.

Somewhere between the Bakker home and the homes of millions of Americans, Tammy's mascara and war paint and Jim's cherubic grin became diabolical.[34] Essentially nice people in common with most, the Bakkers got caught in the war of ratings and the insatiable appetite for more glorious projects, which required more and more television dollars. Long before Jim's sex escapade and scandal surfaced, the PTL club had become "show biz," departing from its practical message and spiritual intent. The PTL club became entertainment with a capital "E." There is no way to substitute the perceptual gift, the capacity for taking in the total pattern of the human condition, or an understanding of the way in which things hang together—a talent which Bakker possessed, then neglected—and expect to stay on course. When Bakker started listening to advisers with uncanny gifts for analysis and stopped using his natural wisdom, he embraced alien if not hostile forces. When that happened, the Bakkers commenced to behave like superstars with other people's money. The mansions, the Mercedes, the elaborate vacations, Tammy's shopping sprees—all became part of a growing scam that led to Jim's dalliance with Jessica Hahn.[35] Reckless abandon passive defensiveness—"you can't touch me!"—had come to dominate their lives and lifestyle. When that happened, the Bakkers became a "born-again disaster."[36] Jim Bakker forgot that his rise had little to do with him personally and everything to do with his acquaintance with the ghosts that haunt us all. Failure came from his resistance to what worked best for him and from ignoring it in favor of systematic verification—polls and ratings—and then becoming enamored of and overwhelmed by his own genius. What happened to Jim Bakker could happen to anyone who climbs off the stool and starts trekking up the mountain.

President Richard M. Nixon

The thirty-seventh president of the United States was born in Yorba Linda, California, of a lower middle-class Quaker family of Irish descent. His father ran a combination small grocery store–filling station on land he was unable to develop. Dirt poor, his father had to sell, only to have the land turn out to be rich in oil. So, instead of the family becoming rich and prosperous, it struggled with dignity. Nothing came too easily to the Nixons, especially Richard. He lacked athleticism and made up for this with brutal courage on the football field. He lacked social grace and made up for this with brilliance in the classroom. He carried the wounds of being "almost rich" and the death of his brother at an early age as the yoke of his life's responsibility—to live and perform always as two.

While a law student at Duke University, where his diligence as a student earned him the nickname "Iron Butt," Nixon's drive betrayed him, as it would several times throughout his remarkably long and successful career. One night, not able to handle the suspense of waiting until grades were posted, he broke into the dean's office to see his grades, only to be caught. He had top grades and was to finish third in his class, yet an anxiety at not knowing became a telling flaw that was to master his destiny.

His political career, much like his prowess on the football field and in the classroom, was marked by courage—fearless outspokenness and brilliant political tactics. Reckless abandon passive defensiveness marked every segment of his career—from his vicious campaign as successful candidate for the House of Representatives in 1946 to his crushing debacle with the Watergate Affair. Perhaps his finest hour was in

1960 when he lost the presidency to John F. Kennedy by the tiniest of margins, so tiny that there was broad suspicion that the election was stolen in the Chicago precincts of Mayor Richard Daley's machine. Nixon refused a recount and conceded gracefully.

Yet, the low state of his birth, the poor luck of his family, the anxiety over how he was being perceived, and his paranoia of Eastern seaboard money and its intellectual crowd haunted him. No matter how successful he was, this knowledge seemed never able to give him peace. Far ahead in the polls in the 1972 presidential campaign, he allowed his advisers to attempt (unsuccessfully) a break-in of the Democratic National Committee's headquarters located in the Watergate Hotel, Washington, D.C. The purpose of the break-in was to place telephone bugs and acquire information damaging to the presidential campaign of George McGovern. Countless Nixon biographers make much of this in terms of his legendary paranoia. By their own assessments, Nixon—known for his achievement in foreign policy (establishment of China–American accords)—is credited with making great strides in terms of civil rights and social welfare programs. Still, he demonstrated a disconcerting capacity for senseless behavior.[37] Nixon lost credibility with the American people by claiming executive privilege for senior White House officials to prevent them from being questioned and by refusing to hand over tapes of relevant conversations. He resigned under the threat of impeachment after several leading members of his government had been found guilty of involvement in the Watergate scandal. Obviously, there are many contradictions in President Nixon's character, from a Quaker upbringing to a tough-minded hawkishness, from an extreme discomfort around people to a public boldness bordering on bravado. It is within this veiled context that his reckless abandon passive aggressiveness resides. Columnist Tom Wicker captures the essence of Nixon and his time in his book *One of Us* (1992), which puts the American people on notice that he is much like the rest of us and that there is no way we can distance ourselves from what he was and came to be.

John Dean and Blind Ambition

John Dean was one of the actors on the Nixon stage. He was counsel to the president—the president's lawyer—and essentially young and untested in life. There is a tendency, like an invisible magnet in our makeup, which draws us to like-minded people, and which is sometimes a fatal flaw. When values and beliefs are poorly defined or essentially malleable to the situation, one is always on the threshold of the no-man's land of reckless abandon. Dean, in his autobiography *Blind Ambition* (1977), candidly admits that "making it" took precedence over everything.[38] Cheating became not only the rule of convenience, but a necessity. Cutting corners became an art form of Machiavellian perfection, with the ends justifying any means. Dean was hooked on hoodwink. He operated quite successfully in this cynical world where cunning, duplicity, and bad faith were part of the arsenal of deception. When he was made to take the fall for the entire Nixon administration, he reneged and sang like a songbird. Several White House officials of the Nixon administration who were indicted, charged, sentenced, and imprisoned have gotten "religion" as their way to expiate their fall and win back some social grace. Dean has chosen a quiet withdrawal from ambition, blind or otherwise.

Corporate Malfeasance—Johns Manville Corporation et al.

It would be inappropriate to end this discussion on passive defensiveness without including its corporate character. The corporate landscape is as vulnerable to its seduction as is the individual to its appeal. The examples cited are not mutually exclusive but rather represent a disturbing trend that seems to grow with time. When a major company is under attack, as are tobacco companies at the moment, reckless abandon and CYA passive defensiveness appear to act like a hypnotic enchantment. The same might also prove true with regard to the recent White Water investigation in the House of Representatives. The cases referred to here, however, are now part of history and are presented for what might be learned from them.[39]

Johns Manville Corporation once enjoyed the status of a corporate giant. It has now disintegrated into a shadow of its original size, brought down by its principal product, asbestos. For many years, it seems the Johns Manville medical department took it upon itself to doctor data regarding the dangers associated with the inhalation of asbestos. This duplicity goes back at least to the end of World War II. Consequently, the sheer magnitude of the time span makes it impossible to estimate how many former employees suffering from debilitating diseases can be traced to their having worked for Johns Manville. The cover-up, in any case, falls into CYA passive defensiveness.

What is particularly disturbing about this case is the motivation behind it and the amorality displayed by those implicated. A lawyer recalls how, 50 years ago, he confronted Johns Manville's corporate council about the company's policy of concealing chest X-ray results from employees. He asked, "Do you mean to tell me you would let your people work until they dropped dead?" The corporate attorney replied without a quiver, "Yes, we save a lot of money that way." Such reckless abandon and CYA passive defensiveness represent, to those who advocate this course, the least troublesome way to solve a punishing dilemma. The focus is on how much the company could lose if exposed, not how it could gain in goodwill if it came clean. Time is the enemy of such a policy, making it increasingly difficult to do the right thing. By all standards of decency, a company is held to higher ethics than the individual. The pure absurdity of thinking that anything is justified as long as it saves the company apparently never occurred to anyone. Nor were human rights ever considered, only corporate survival. Concealing information, whatever its nature, is considered a way of protecting proprietary products and services and, therefore, the company. In the case of Johns Manville Corporation, this strategy became its death knell.

The Continental Illinois Bank

Before the savings and loan scandal, long before banks became ranking predators in their own right, the ninth largest bank in the United States was eclipsed into oblivion by its own chicanery. Similar to the gigantic fiasco of the thrifts and the multibillion-dollar "bail outs" of 1989–91, this bank now belongs to the Federal Deposit Insurance Corporation (FDIC) to the tune of more than 80 percent of its assets.

It was a different matter in 1976, when Continental Illinois had a dream that, through leveraged lending, it could become the seventh largest bank in America. To climb into the "top seven" was a heady goal. Corporate officers became recklessly aggressive in pursuit of borrowers everywhere with only one thing in mind—the realization of their dream. A banker's caution was deserted for the cocky flair of the salesman.

Their fearless diligence paid off.[40] Continental Illinois found a rich captive market in poorly capitalized areas, such as Oklahoma's oil producers. With this discovery, the corporate officers began to bet enormous sums on their dream. Eventually, a cool $1 billion worth of dreams found its way into Continental Illinois' portfolio, and another $1 billion of depositor's money flowed out to pay for the business. The trouble started when the price of oil collapsed. A combination of OPEC members cheating on each other, competition from non-OPEC nations, and conservation efforts of consuming nations, including the United States (introduction of compacts by American manufacturers), drove the price per barrel of oil down by nearly 50 percent. No one anticipated or prepared for this possibility.

Continental Illinois had become spellbound by lending and the growth it produced. It seemed disinclined to look too deeply into how that growth was achieved or how stable it was. When borrowers produced dry holes, which left their drilling equipment idle, the fat interest rates dried up, too. Under the reckless abandon of passive defensiveness of growth—growth that was not subject to harsh scrutiny but which relied largely on luck—the sharp shrinkage of assets caught the attention of internal auditors. The dream died almost immediately. The auditors, without even trying, stumbled on the bottomless pit of deceit upon which the dream was built. One loan officer had purchased $800 million in gas loans from Penn Square Bank in Oklahoma City, where he had also borrowed $565,000 personally. He was issued a minor reprimand for this behavior. It wasn't until federal prosecutors entered the picture that such incidents of charity were called what they were—kickbacks.

As with Johns Manville Corporation, internal control mechanisms flashed danger signals, but they were either ignored or treated as routine. No one wanted to know. The bank was on a roll, and nothing was going to stop it. Once the word got out, however, the bank's instability nearly put it under, saved only by FDIC. The big losers in this, of course, were the bank's thousands of shareholders and more than 2,000 employees who lost their jobs. Continental Illinois is now a small bank made modest by a big appetite for delusions of grandeur and cover-up.

E. F. Hutton & Company

No fall from grace was more shocking to the national television audience than that of E. F. Hutton & Company.[41] The symbolic sense of this company was captured in a television commercial: "When E. F. Hutton speaks, everyone stops to listen." This was a financial institution to be trusted. E. F. Hutton, the nation's second largest independent broker, finally pleaded guilty to more than 2,000 counts of mail and wire fraud. This brokerage firm systematically and with full awareness of its culpability bilked 400 of its own banks by drawing against uncollected funds or, in some cases, against non-existent funds. It would cover these funds after enjoying 24-hour interest-free use of the money. It was a scam treated as a normal conduct of business. Perfect. Who knew of the scam, how many knew, or when they knew nobody will ever know. Yet, it rivals Watergate and Whitewater in the sheer complexity of the cover-up. E. F. Hutton paid a modest fine of $2 million plus government investigative costs of $750,000. Additionally, $8 million has been placed in reserve for restitution to the banks in question. This is nothing but a pittance, a slap on the wrists. True, many officers lost their jobs. Several others are now or have been under indictment— the case is still not closed. Yet, it demonstrates that white-collar crime or crimes against property receive neither the attention nor the judicature that crimes against persons receive.

Meanwhile, investors' confidence level in E. F. Hutton is quite another matter. The corporation still suffers from the sting of this scandal. People don't forget something as spiritual as trust or as emotional as money. The irony is that most television viewers are not investors. They were offended, not because they lost money, but because their trust in an image was violated, and that's even worse. In that respect, then, not only E. F. Hutton was tarnished by this act, but an entire industry.

Chrysler Corporation

Thanks largely to Lee Iacocca, Chrysler Corporation had again become a household name, with automobile sales setting new records.[42] At the height of the recovery, when all the depressing struggle could be put to rest, a story of odometer tampering and damaged vehicles being sold as new automobiles shook this image.[43]

In one case, a 1987 Turismo driven by a Chrysler executive hit a pocket of water on a highway, flipped on its side, slid for several feet, and landed in a ditch, rolling over.[44] The executive luckily escaped serious injury, but the automobile was to have another fate. Instead of reporting the incident as it happened and then auctioning off the automobile as damaged goods, the executive and his co-conspirators decided to repair the car and to ship it off as a completely new vehicle. No mention was made that it was shuttled between executives for their convenience. This was far from the exception. An investigation found that at least 40 Chrysler automobiles were shipped as new after being involved in collisions or accidents severe enough that frames were bent and doors damaged. Moreover, during an 18-month period (July 1985 through December 1986), this investigation uncovered that Chrysler sold more than 60,000 vehicles as new cars that had been driven routinely by company managers and executives with their odometers disconnected. The hidden odometer mileage often exceeded 400 miles, as these employees drove these automobiles to and from work and some even on personal trips. When caught in this deception, the Chrysler chorus sang, "Everybody takes a free ride. What's the big deal?"[45] When there is a tendency to explain away clearly unacceptable behavior or when the attitude is to ignore what is happening that is unacceptable or in violation of corporate conduct, the behavior is in the realm of passive defensiveness. It matters not whether the behavior is intentional or accidental, corporate or individual; passive defensiveness is at work.

Silent Killer No. 4: *Approach Avoidance Behavior*

Examples are volunteering for assignments one doesn't intend to complete or to complete on time; proffering one's support for important initiatives and then withdrawing such support at the last moment; taking on special projects and then not showing up for the required work and necessary meetings; punishing others with one's knowledge to mask one's inability or unwillingness to learn new things; indicating a desire to be challenged but avoiding all the sacrifices and inconveniences required (such as working late, taking courses on one's own time, taking risks); appearing to be dedicated to doing something but, in actuality, refusing to do it; and displaying high RPMs for "whatever" but a low torque. Approach avoidance behavior is much more common than one might suspect. It represents a flirtation with what is expected or required but with no real intention of performing at that level. A person inclined toward approach avoidance behavior counts on obscure directions and forgotten orders. Work is a game to be avoided at any cost, only no one is intended to be able to either decipher the avoidance or make claim against the deadbeat for it. That is where the pleasure comes—in outfoxing the system!

This is the equivalent of the student who consents to do his homework but avoids it by going to his room and gabbing on the phone instead. The behavior involves *approaching* (agreeing to act), then *avoiding* (evading the necessary action) by whatever means come to mind. Telethon campaigners know the behavior well—a person feels obliged to make a generous pledge to say, public television, then ignores the frequent mailed reminders of this commitment. To the approach avoider, it is no big deal! It takes a special constitution to display this behavior. The classic form of approach avoidance behavior in an organization is when a person committed to a project fails to contribute his part. Such failures mean others have to take up the slack, which lets the approach avoidance person off the hook. It might be a report not completed on time, an important reference not checked out, the right people not invited to a crucial meeting, failure of memos to be distributed, or any number of important "little things" that make for the successful completion of projects and thereby spell organizational success.

Most of us are guilty of approach avoidance on occasion, but the seasoned approach avoider consciously strives to find ways to dissemble his motivation. What may trigger this behavior is the conflict between the need to please others and the need to please self. The self-antagonism generated is demonstrated by keeping the organization and the people in it (especially those in authority) off stride and at bay. Irritation is the highest form of reward and is perfected to an art form. Of all the "Manic Monarchs of the Merry Madhouse," this is the most ambiguous and most difficult to comprehend. A morality play is going on in the head of the individual. At once, he is driven by what he should do and should be (*ideal self*), only to be stopped short by what he is and feels inclined to do (*real self*). This conflict between *self demands* and *role demands* causes him to misdefine the situation. He prefers to see things as he would like them to be, not as they are. This finds him accepting assignments (*role demands*), only to be stopped short by *self demands*—"How could they ask me to do that? Don't they know that job is beneath me?" Self demands take precedence over role demands when it is a case of approach avoidance. If this seems confusing, imagine the individual who experiences this ambivalence. If he can misinterpret the demands made on him, he will. When captive to such wrong-headedness, he is seldom apt to do what is expected or when it is expected. He is too busy massaging his delicate ego.

It is the old game of fight or flight—with one side of his mind wanting to fight (*approach*) and the other wanting to take flight (*avoidance*). It is the problem Philip Slater illustrated in the last chapter—engagement versus non-involvement. Approach avoidance creates stress and anxiety. When a person is in the throes of approach avoidance conflict, the practitioner's pulse quickens and his temples throb, while he puts on a front that everything is under control. He feels the psychic need to avoid whatever is demanded of him, but cannot escape the fact that "it is his job"—thus the conflict and confusion (Figure 6.5).

"Anxiety is how the individual relates to stress, accepts it, interprets it," writes Rollo May in *The Meaning of Anxiety* (1977). "Stress is a halfway station on the way to anxiety. Anxiety is how we handle stress."[46] The problem with people subject to approach avoidance behavior is that their emotional circuits become flooded, and they are crippled by distress. This inability to deal with role demands, because of brutalizing self demands, finds them getting less meaningful assignments. Because they cannot be depended upon or trusted to do the job, management unwittingly reinforces the behavior. At the extreme of approach avoidance behavior, the person is labeled and then treated as irresponsible and ultimately becomes non-responsible.

Silent Killer No. 5: *Obsessive Compulsive Behavior*

Examples are always wanting to be and have what someone else is and has, being obsessed with what one does not have and is not at the expense of what one does have and is, always seeing the grass greener on the other side of the fence, and being consumed with jealousy and envy. Obsessive compulsive behavior is characterized by obsessive ideas and compulsive actions. It can be diagnosed as psychosis—a severe mental or personality disorder in which the person loses contact with reality and is unable to participate in ordinary social life. The cause may be either organic or functional. Obsessive compulsive behavior is, however, much more prevalent in the organization as a neurosis—a mild personality disorder or chronic emotional difficulty. A neurosis is much less serious than a psychosis and is considered functional in character rather than organic. There are at least four ways to examine obsessive compulsive behavior as it affects organizational health: cultural,

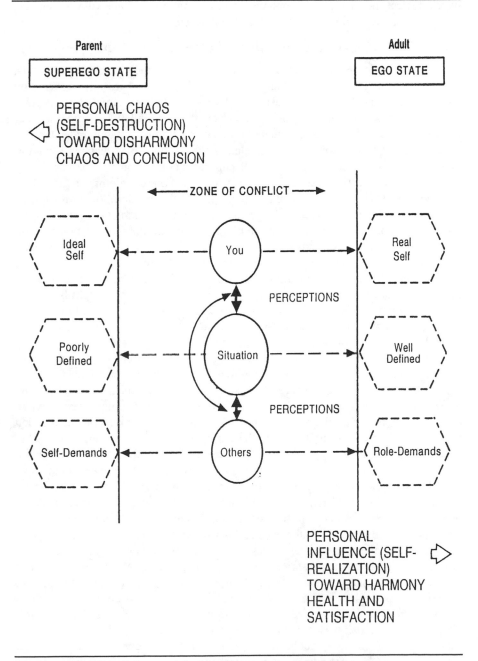

Figure 6.5　The Fisher model of conflict and stress resolution.

psychological, political, and economic. It has become the silent killer of choice, which appears to aggravate all the other silent killers.

Obsessive Compulsive Behavior—Cultural

Culture, as defined here, is the workplace climate and the shared values, beliefs, and expectations of workers. Culture is a recent managerial obsession, triggered by its emphasis by HRD. Over the past several years, HRD has attempted, unsuccessfully, to untangle the sins of organization with cultural manipulation. Senior management can now mouth the words, such as climate and culture, without understanding their meaning. What is not communicated is that cultural bias dictates behavior. Unless the focus is on cultural bias, all cultural modification will be essentially cosmetic and ineffective. Established rites, rituals, and rhetoric dominate the will of the organization, with the informal group controlling the ebb and flow of how these established practices are working. Inherent in this informal structure is the current mind-set, not only toward these cultural biases but toward the organization as well. The combination of this mind-set and these biases dictates behavior—what is tolerated, expected, believed, valued, and experienced. There can be no discernible change without first understanding and then dealing with this reality. It is natural for the organization to resist change no matter how good the change might be—logic does not operate at this level—because it prefers to sustain its known value and belief system. To ignore this fact and to go plunging ahead without first dealing with it is to spell inevitable doom for the change process.

The formal organization is essential to generate an appropriate operating philosophy, consistent policy with a mission focus, and a fair-minded value system for growth and development. It creates the rites of passage, the rituals of operation, and the message of the mission. Once this is done, the informal group reacts to these directives and interprets them in its own best interest. The interpretation and reaction to this set of interventions determine the workplace culture. It is this relationship between senior management and operating personnel that spells success or failure in any organization. Culture is always created from above and interpreted from below. If both are on the same page, everything runs as smooth as silk; if not, operations bound out of control. Management exerts little real influence on informal behavior once the cultural variables are defined and assimilated. Should they be changed, workers must be involved in the process for verification, acceptance, and support.

What we have seen in recent times is that circumstances have forced organizations to change quickly to stay afloat. Expediency became policy. Panic was reflected in a series of faddish activities—from "T" groups to QCC's, from team building to sensitivity training, from Muzak to ergonomic work centers, from worker-wellness programs to company-sponsored beer blasts on Friday night, from MBO to TQM, from 40-hour work weeks to flex time, from company day-care centers to EAPs, from shared management to symbolic management...and on it goes! There is nothing wrong with any of these interventions except for one thing—they were done to the workers and for the workers with little or no input from the workers before the fact.

They were gratuitous interventions—like giving candy to a baby not to cry—which made workers feel even less in charge of their destiny than ever before. Workers didn't show their resentment up front. They went underground and surfaced with the *six silent killers*.

These were tactics, not grand strategies. They demonstrated the panic of buying time. Work has changed. Workers have changed. Real work has gotten a bad name or gotten lost in the shuffle. *Value change*, which is essential to behavioral change, is served poorly by cosmetic changes. Fad merchants know their clients and their impatience. The quickest way for them to lose a sale is to tell senior management that it has to change first before anything else changes. Management, consequently, has gotten what it expected and wanted—quick fixes and non-involvement. Management remains obsessed with the idea of culture while becoming compulsive in its actions toward it. There is no point in assessing blame. No one could have predicted the incredible changes or the demands of these changes in the workplace in so short a time. Management, in its naivete, thought that whatever it did would get it to where it wanted to go. That has proven false (see Figure 2.1). Preoccupation with fads has found the workplace going from the Culture of Comfort to the Culture of Complacency, at the expense of the Culture of Contribution.

Obsessive Compulsive Behavior—Psychological

The psychological is defined in terms of relationships within the organization. Most executives are more adept at managing technology (things) than in managing, motivating, and mobilizing human resources (people). Management deals best with what it knows, which means people are often managed as things. People do not behave, react, or forgive the way things do, which is the basis of conflict. Relationships imply conflict. As sociologist Georg Simmel observed, conflict can be the very glue which binds people to a task. Yet conflict is considered a pejorative. Disagreement is considered disruptive when it is a vital precursor to agreement. *Managed conflict* keeps the organization on course and is essential to its health. Where conflict is taboo, dissatisfied employees are ignored, not heard, and given a short tether, not access to the councils of power. Too frequently, elitism sponsors favoring one group over another (engineers over administrators), while authority hides behind position power—a psychological climate ripe for backlash. The implication here is that loyalty to authority must take precedence over loyalty to self, that they cannot co-exist. Human nature has trouble with this. Perversity of relationships contributes to a psychologically sick organization. The more the organization resists the demands of human nature, forcing standards by which all must abide without recourse, the greater the intensity of internal stress and strain, and the less the organization (and its people) is able to respond to accelerating external demands. Given this predicament, the organization becomes easily polarized, traumatized, and dysfunctional. It becomes obsessed with its survival and compulsive in its actions to endure. Management may say the right words to defuse the situation, but its actions are likely to tell a different story.

Contribution is the key to organizational success. It is based on the authenticity of relationships. This means behavior must first pass through the filter of politeness, followed by the filters of suspicion and fight before arriving at cooperation. This is the route to communication and cooperation. There is no bypass route to this kind of consensus. Attempts to go from politeness to cooperation, avoiding suspicion and fight, achieve compliance instead of cooperation. Compliance is realized always through coercion or involuntary submission. Compliance propagates the *six silent killers*. Cooperation is given freely and voluntarily, and generates contribution (Figure 6.6).

The Personification of the Obsessive Compulsive

Going from politeness to cooperation requires work on the part of the person in question and the facilitator managing the process. It is not a neat, clean, and predictable relationship. Relationships are often messy, volatile, inconclusive, and troubling to those involved. Consider this against the obsessive compulsive individual who expects everything to fit. Imagine what drives this individual—avoidance of conflict, unpleasant or opinionated people, work that is inconclusive, and situations which are uncomfortable and unpredictable. There is a fatiguing preoccupation with the negative—what to avoid rather than what to embrace (Figure 6.7). In contrast, this person may use lifestyle as a distraction from fatigue—spend as much as you make, live for Saturday night, and find an opiate in whatever. This includes being obsessed with losing weight, getting into shape, or becoming more cosmetically attractive. Diet books are

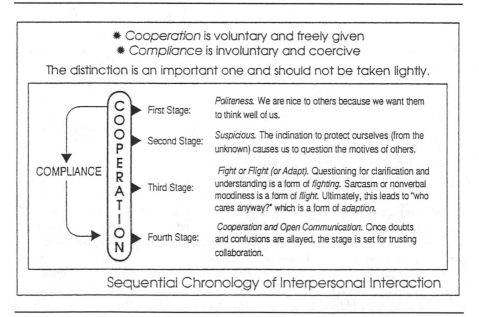

Figure 6.6   Sequential chronology of interpersonal relationships.

bought and not read, exercise equipment is purchased and not used, and medical advice is sought but not followed. Obsessively compulsive people keep psychotherapists, psychologists, dieticians, astrologers, and palm readers in business. Many are in love with their sickness and consumed with seeing it prosper. Others are awaiting a miracle pill, which will allow them to go on living self-abusive lives without consequence. *Redux Regimen*, the first diet pill approved by the FDA in 23 years, seems to be the answer to the fat world's prayer. Or is it? *Time* magazine (September 23, 1996) reports "Redux has side effects. Some are merely annoying: fatigue, diarrhea, vivid dreams, dry mouth. But some are patently dangerous. The drug has caused significant, possibly permanent brain damage in lab animals..."[47] This will hardly deter the obsessively compulsive.

The late Jackie Gleason bragged that his six-pack-a-day cigarette addiction and voracious capacity for booze and food were justified because "You only live once!" Such obsession is not living, but suicidal. Other celebrities equally compulsively addicted were John Wayne, Humphrey Bogart, Yul Brynner, Nat "King" Cole, Steve McQueen, Edward R. Murrow, Richard Burton, Desi Arnaz, Sammy Davis, Jr., Chet Huntley, Betty Davis, and Mickey Mantle. All died before their time.

Work continues to suffer due to obsessive compulsive behavior. Take AIDS. The current obsession with this disease has spawned a new disease, pseudo-AIDS. This disease is described as the anxiety that occurs when people experience recurrent fatigue, diarrhea, night sweats, and prolonged fevers, which are also early symptoms of AIDS. Given the sickness in society, this could one day blossom into hysteria.

Drug and alcohol abuse in the workplace is compulsively out of control. Research indicates that as many as one worker in four, at some time, uses dangerous drugs on the job. Seven young people out of ten join the workforce having used illegal drugs. In the United States in 1988 alone, alcohol and substance abuse cost the U.S. economy more than $100 billion in lost productivity.[48] In 1996 it was estimated to be approaching $150 billion. Even worse, 95 percent of business owners surveyed said they had direct experience with drug abuse among their workers. Not only do these predilections translate into increasing operational costs, but they are serious contributors to "the enemy within" or liver, lung and colon cancer, strokes, heart disease, and heart attacks. Against this reality, does behavior change? Not necessarily. Many go for transplants. According to a 1996 study, transplant possibilities include cornea and sclera (coating around the eyeball), cartilage, lung, liver, pancreas, kidney, blood, artery and vein allografts, knees, pericardium (membrane sac that encloses the heart), heart, heart valves, hip, bone marrow, skin, muscles, and tendons. Medical science is capable of producing the bionic man but, alas, not the balanced man.

Obsessive Compulsive Behavior—Corporate

Corporations reflect similar inclinations. Obsessive compulsive behavior is common if not sometimes comical. Take the controversy over the Procter and Gamble trademark. For more than 140 years, P&G enjoyed the distinction of having

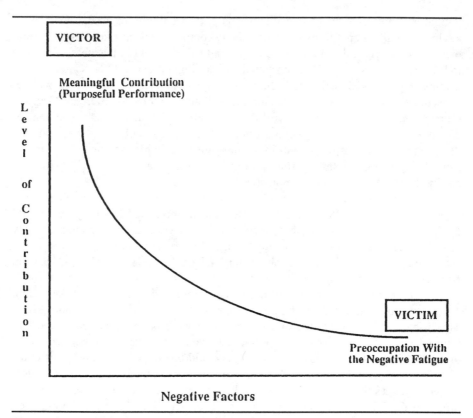

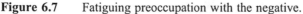

Figure 6.7   Fatiguing preoccupation with the negative.

a trademark that featured a man in the moon with 13 stars representing the 13 original American colonies. Anyone who saw this trademark immediately thought of P&G. It was that distinctive. Then one day this logo was condemned by certain accusers as being a symbol of satanism and devil worship. These condemners urged a Christian boycott of all P&G products nationwide, including such popular brands as Pampers, Duncan Hines cake mixes, and Folger's Coffee. This grew into a P&G litigious fixation of considerable cost and inconvenience.[49]

Accusers went so far as to point out that when a mirror was held up to the logo, the curlicues in the man's beard became "666"—the sign of the anti-Christ (Figure 6.8). To refute these claims, P&G filed a three-inch-thick brief that included a map of the United States showing the sweep of the rumors geographically; tallies of all the rumors, state by state; compilations of all the queries to consumer service departments; computer printouts of the day-to-day complaints and the precise nature of the complaints; and literally tens of thousands of follow-up tally sheets. P&G's obsession was compulsively out of control. Rather than ride out the hysteria of its accusers and let nature take its course, for the problem was far bigger in P&G's eyes than in

Figure 6.8   Procter and Gamble's original trademark.

reality, expensive and compulsive denials and paranoid counterattacks were insti-
gated. Less than one percent of P&G's customer base was aware of this attack and
were it not for P&G's own counterattack probably would never have known. This
seasoned organization allowed itself to become unglued by a psychological threat of
little substance. In defeat, P&G modified its logo, although it is not known to this day
who the accusers were. One lingering epitaph is this: "In the beginning God made the
tree. Where does Satan get Charmin?" This demonstrates that any organization can be
reduced to rubble if its collective psyche becomes obsessively compulsive.

Obsessive Compulsive Behavior—Political

Lee Iacocca, perhaps unintentionally, reveals in his autobiography, *Iacocca*
(1984), how obsessively self-absorbed we can become. The book, in places, reads like
a television soap opera. Iacocca constantly talks about himself in obsessional terms.
In its conclusion, the following could have been lifted from "As the World Turns":

> *I never expected a showdown, but if it came to that, I was ready. I
> knew how valuable I was to the company...I was far more important than
> Henry (Ford). In my naivete, I held out hope that because we were a
> publicly held company, the better man would win. I was also greedy. I
> enjoyed being president. I liked having the president's perks, the special
> parking place, the private bathroom, and the white-coated waiters. I was
> getting soft, seduced by the good life. And I found it almost impossible to
> walk away from an annual income of $970,000...I wanted that million
> dollars a year so much that I wouldn't face reality.*[50]

It was this self-mocking candor that made the book a resounding best-seller. Yet,
behind the candor was an obsessive compulsive man. Iacocca didn't invent the
condition. He happens to be one of its more celebrated practitioners.

A less compulsive word than political is influence. As much as Iacocca made of his perks, his obsession was power, the more obvious form of influence. Dr. Lawrence Peter identified the cruel "pecking order" game in his book *The Peter Principle* (1969). Promotion, Peter found, is one of the more cynical ways of neutralizing an adversary, making it a common practice to promote people to their level of incompetence.[51] There they can do far less damage and are easier to control. Peter was looking at the organization in terms of competence, not influence. To an educator, competence is more meaningful than influence. Professors have little power and less influence, so they typically judge each other in terms of competence. Professional workers see themselves in a similar light—competence is everything! This sponsors a lot of nit-picking among the ranks, with mountains being made out of mole hills. Meanwhile, power, which they would have if only they exercised it, gets short shrift. The *six silent killers* first found life in academia and then spread from there into industry, government, and every other fissure of society. Professors, forced to conform to the whims of unenlightened superiors, rebelled covertly so as to avoid losing tenure or their meager perks. This resulted in an obsessional and, ironically, incompetent educational system. Page Smith illustrates this in *Killing the Spirit* (1990)—professors focus on publishing indistinguishable scholarship at the price of educating students.[52]

Obsession with influence is well documented in John Kenneth Galbraith's *The Anatomy of Power* (1983). Galbraith devotes 90 percent of his narrative to the origins of power, much less to why it is amassed or even how it is used. Users of power, as a rule, don't write books. They are too obsessively involved in the power game. Galbraith, a distinguished economist and academic, is perhaps fascinated, like Peter, with how power players come to play the game. Galbraith, who was himself a U.S. ambassador to India, former dean of American economic liberalism, and adviser to several presidents, has had to use power. Both men agree, however, that corporate heads may be power-hungry if not power-mad.[53]

If power generates madness, it doesn't stop at the top. Nor is the obsession confined to results. The focus is far more entangled, convoluted, and fraternal, as the maddening web of intrigue and gamesmanship plays in the transfer of power. The *Divine Rights of Friendship* display the politics of obsessive compulsive behavior. When Lee Iacocca asked Henry Ford why he was being fired after leading Ford Motor Company to its two greatest years in history, Ford shrugged his shoulders and replied, "Well, sometimes you just don't like somebody." That was it! The rights of friendship are powerful and can exceed the transfer of power of royalty. And as with royalty, there are no guarantees that friendship will produce leadership. Like a toss of the dice, friendship is a risky business, but remains an important player in the power game.

Obsessive Compulsive Behavior—Economic

There is a saying that "the Japanese are obsessed with people and realize profits. Americans are obsessed with profits and realize people problems." This is not necessarily true, but it is commonly thought. It is reputed that the Japanese understand and play the business game far better than its inventer, the United States. History is more kind to these commonly accepted remarks than one might like to admit. Alfred Sloan, the legendary leader of General Motors, once boasted that GM, although forced to lay off tens of thousands of workers during the Great Depression, continued to pay stockholder dividends. A Japanese industrialist, even if circumstances dictated such action, would never think to say, much less boast of, such a deed. Openly valuing profits above people would destroy his relationship with his workers and produce chaos. What is unremarkable about the Japanese executive's confession is that Sloan's boast has the same impact on American workers and with a similar long-range effect. It is not limited to a company or a country because it plays the same way worldwide:

- Focus on workers, and they will focus on the needs of the company.
- Form a partnership with workers, and they will work to sustain that partnership.
- Practice what you preach, and workers will preach what you practice.

There is no great mystery here. Workers can be channeled to do good or imploded to do great damage.

Managing things is easier than managing people. So people are often left to chance. The Japanese have divined that the only way they can keep up with a world favored over them is to tap into *people power* for the good that it can bring. Working with and through people is essential to organizational success. It is not so much that the Japanese do it especially well. It is the fact that they do it at all. The perception persists that management thinks first of stockholders, then itself, next the company's image, and finally the customer. Workers are believed to be taken for granted. Japanese management, in contrast, is perceived to think first of its country, then its company and its people, and lastly, of itself. Edward Wolff in *Top Heavy: The Increasing Inequality of Wealth in America and What Can Be Done About It* (1996) adds credence to this mixed perception. He does so by showing the salaries American management pays itself—CEOs make 225 times the compensation given to average employees under them. But it doesn't stop there! Add to it the trauma caused the average employee by executive perks; the panic with quality; the continuing restructuring, downsizing and streamlining; and the constant rumor of redundancy exercises, mergers, or leveraged buyouts, followed inevitably by forced bankruptcies and plant closings. If this were not enough, wealth is skewed so that the top 1 percent of the population owns 48 percent of the nation's wealth, while the bottom 80 percent is shown to own only 6 percent. Wolff suggests that a passive reactive workforce, like the American majority, fails to see itself as wealth creators and that reversing this psychological block could be a first step toward greater equity.[54]

When the organization is in trouble, as many are now, how often does management seek the advice and support of workers for ways to increase performance? It isn't that management is this great monster, and workers cower before it. The answer is simpler. Management has little confidence in its ability to communicate meaningfully with workers on crucial topics. It is even less confident in its ability to improve performance through people. It has more confidence in cost avoidance issues and cost reduction proposals or the world of things. Being obsessively analytical and quantitatively compartmentalized, management is compulsively driven to redundancy exercises and resetting objectives. This is a way of dealing with workers without being involved with them. HRD, as the agent of such exercises, contributes to this folly by constant "worker satisfaction" assessments (see Chapter 7), which result in cosmetic changes and even greater dysfunction. There is no question that great energy is being put forth to make workers more productive. The only problem is that they need to be put in the equation, not forced to digest the prescribed medicine. With management thinking of workers as "things," its behavior suggests, "If we throw enough money at it, the problem will resolve itself." If this seems unfair, consider that more than $4 billion annually is spent on training and development alone by *Fortune* 500 companies—solutions looking for problems, as successes clearly show. Management's overriding flaw is its Presbyterian sense of being morally right, coupled with its need to be earthly right no matter what the cost. It could be argued that management is more interested in being right than effective.

If workers are to make a difference, making a difference must be important. As argued elsewhere, there appears to be a cultural bias against making a difference, the emphasis instead being on making an impression. This is illustrated each time workers are trained with new tools.[55] With the shift toward TQM, workers are now trained in Juran Methodology (handling chronic problems), Deming's 14 points of Quality Management,[56] Taguchi's Design of Experiments (focusing on the critical difference),[57] Nominal Group Technique (everyone involved), statistical process control, process flow analysis, teaming, listening, and coaching and counseling skills. These training modules represent splendid tools that are extremely useful in establishing quality if the workplace culture and the structure of the organization are supportive of such standards. But consider that:

- TQM represents a holistic approach, while most organizations insist on being operationally departmentalized and focused on MBO.
- TQM is a process of incremental, continuous improvement, while most organizations are programmed to hasty schedule changes.
- TQM is qualitative, force-fitted into quantitatively driven workplace cultures.
- TQM is subjective, while primarily measured in terms of objective standards.
- TQM is an attitude, a mind-set, a philosophy of doing business. It is not doctrinaire, nor dogma. To enforce quality is to miss its point.
- TQM has a cultural bias for quality and a long-term commitment to quality standards. This conflicts with a bias for quantity and a short-term perspective.

When this worker, trained in new quality skills, attempts to implement them in the old culture, he confronts dominant cultural biases. These biases prevent him from using his new tools. This puzzles the trainee as to why he was trained. It leads to an attitude of "Why bother? Nobody cares anyway. It's just a game. Go along with the game, and I'll be okay. Fight it, and I'll be out on the street." This trainee knows in his gut if it is a matter of quality and shipping on time, that schedule is going to win every time. Failure of training to make a difference is due largely to leaving out workplace cultural biases. It is culture that either supports or discourages workers from making a difference. This is the rule, not the exception. Cultural biases must be dealt with accordingly. Otherwise, no matter how sophisticated or how sincere management is in providing training, the results will be training for training's sake.

When Influence Falls Between the Chairs

The complex organization is a twentieth century phenomenon. If society doesn't have it quite right regarding the relationship between workers and managers, it is because the organization is still in a learning mode. Once management was tapped to be surrogate owner as operator, the relationship between workers and managers changed. Managers took on the responsibility for the organization's success. From that sense of duty, it is easy to see how management might take advantage of workers or take them for granted. Management became the stick that stirred the drink. Wrong or right, that is what evolved. Workers went along with it, to a point. Then the unions stepped in to complain that all wasn't quite kosher. The union movement was meant to look out for the interests of workers. It contributed instead to the current dilemma by surrendering to management the control of work in exchange for wage and benefit concessions. Unions are disintegrating at an alarming rate because that function is no longer necessary. Workers are adrift psychologically, however, and remain essentially reactive, hurting spiritually, if not economically. They hunger for the nostalgia of work when they controlled what they did.

To understand this shift, consider William H. Whyte, Jr.'s *The Organization Man* (1956).[58] Whyte profiled a new breed of elite managers dedicated to the goals of their leaders without question. These managers sacrificed family, personal comfort, and ego for the company. The organization man was loyal, obedient, conforming, hard working, dutiful, and dedicated. He put the concerns of the company ahead of his own. Over time, a peculiar thing happened. The *organization man* came to feel "he was the company!"—that the company belonged to him because he had more of a stake in it than anyone else. As organization men moved up the ladder, they perpetuated the myth, behaving as if they owned the company. Leaders, such as Iacocca, are custodians of the myth. With the shift in the knowledge base of the organization in the 1990s and with knowledge being much more critical to success, this arrogance has often found organization men running the company into the ground. The *organization man* mentality persists in *Fortune* 500 companies. It is revealed every time a reporter asks a senior manager how he can justify an eight-figure income. A typical response: "When I came into this company, the company had lost money for five years, the stock price and market share had been cut in half. We just had our second record year in a row, the stock price is at an all-time high and we have regained our position in the market. Considering that, I am underpaid." An *organization man* thinks he does it alone and feels little guilt for doing whatever to put the company back on its feet. Nor does he apologize for taking the compensation derived for his efforts. He sees his obligation to stockholders, not stakeholders—not the workers. Yet the role of the *organization man* has faded. His influence has shifted to institutions that manipulate the symbolic economy. Money, credit, and capital are no longer tightly bound to the real economy of produced goods, services, and trade. We are seeing the collapse of traditional power and the introduction of synthetic power. Who would have thought that multibillion-dollar corporations could end up on the trading block or be driven to criminal activities for survival? Archer-Daniels-Midland was just fined $100 million for price fixing of lysine, a feed additive. Meanwhile, Texaco agreed to a record $176 million settlement for racial biases. It is relevant to this discussion to mention how this came about. Richard Lundall, a senior personnel executive, lost his job in a Texaco cutback in 1994. In 1996, he released tape recordings of a Texaco senior management meeting, which took place in 1994. These recordings depicted him and other company officers belittling black employees and plotting to destroy evidence in a race discrimination suit. It became the basis of the nine-figure settlement. Now, it seems portions of these tape recordings were erased, reminiscent of the famous 18-minute gap in the Watergate tapes. The plot thickens! Indeed, who would have thought the *Age of Capitalism* would descend to such vulgarity? But it may be happening in your own backyard. In the Tampa Bay area, Publix Supermarkets, Inc., which dominates the food supermarket business in the Southeast and enjoys a reputation of being a first-class, first-rate employer, agreed to pay its 150,000 women employees $81.5 million to settle a sex and race discrimination lawsuit brought on by 12 former and current female store employees. What is reminiscent of the Texaco lawsuit is that senior management first took the class action suit as a joke and behaved badly. Senior management overrated its importance or imagined power, while it underrated, in both instances, the impact of modern workers once they get their dander up.

Profits have taken on the appearance of imagined power. Organizations are either more or less profitable, so traditional leaders are either enhancing or losing their imagined power base. The frantic search for profits finds many companies surviving on the basis of how well they play the money market. Galbraith predicted this catastrophe many years ago, envisioning capitalism giving way to a mandarin-like technocracy, where moving money would take precedence over making things.[59] Sony Corporation chairman Akio Morita, addressing the 1990 graduating class of the Wharton School of Business of the University of Pennsylvania, warned that America will never get back on course if its best continue to "chase the buck" instead of producing quality goods.[60] Only 50 out of an MBA graduating class of 840 planned to get into manufacturing, keeping Galbraith's prophecy extant.[61] Peter Drucker, while more philosophical than Galbraith, sees the world economy in a state of flux, with classical economic theories no longer applying. "The new symbolic economy of financial flow," he says, "outweighs by a ratio of more than 35 to 1 the real economy of traded goods and services."[62] What is causing the demise of the real world economy is the uncoupling of the primary products economy from the industrial economy and of the industrial economy from employment. The result is that capital movement rather than trade is driving the economy. Moreover, information technology and services are taking precedence over traditional labor. In light of these shifts, we are seeing a steady shedding of blue-collar jobs, with more than 5 million such jobs disappearing in the United States since 1975. America is experiencing what the world economy will eventually experience, and that is an accelerating substitution of knowledge and capital for manual labor. "Without such a substitution," Drucker argues, "no modern nation can remain competitive."[63] Yet, the obsessive attempt to first preserve blue-collar jobs and then to treat all workers as if they are blue-collar workers has become a prescription for disaster.

The problem, then, is that the professional worker, who has made both the blue-collar worker and the organization man obsolete, continues to be treated as if it is still 1945. While professionals have an edge on the knowledge curve and, therefore, influence, and managers are now the equivalent of co-workers, the cultural biases of organizations insist on treating management as if it still has the power. The result is the donnybrook we see and the reason why the *six silent killers* are thriving. Management valiantly attempts to exercise control and cannot, so influence falls between the chairs.

The Color-Blind Approach to Managing Professional Workers

Modern technology is responsible for creating the professional worker. It is now the organization's job to get inside these workers' heads and to manage them in a way which serves their needs and the requirements of organization. Management sees white-collar workers (professionals) in blue-collar terms. How could it be otherwise?

Blue-collar workers are conditioned to expect to be managed. Professionals expect to manage themselves. Professional workers cannot be managed. The nature of their work is primarily qualitative, not quantitative; subjective, not objective; symbolic more than substantive; informational rather than product-oriented; and more abstract than concrete. The workplace culture and the structure of the organization are more critical to success than ever before. In the current competitive world, if these workers do not respond to challenges promptly and effectively, business can suffer. Therein lies the critical difference between blue-collar workers and professionals.

When the nature of the business is stable, routine, and predictable, blue-collar workers have responded positively to the formalized nature of QCC problem-solving (Figure 6.9). Definite production standards exist, with discrete performance criteria with which to gauge performance. Small groups of workers meet regularly to solve work-related problems. The problems they solve relate to climatic factors—more light in working areas, less noise, or more privacy from other operations—and procedural considerations—more visuals in blueprints, better gauges, or better qual-

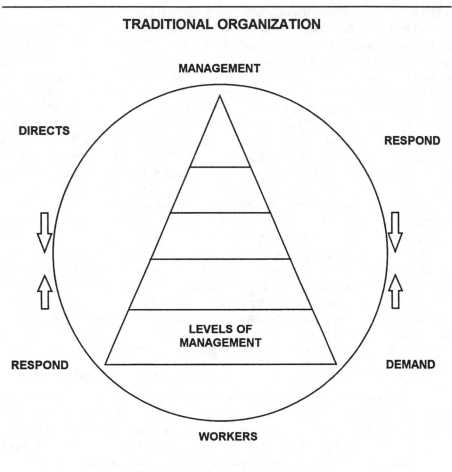

TRADITIONAL ORGANIZATION

MANAGEMENT

DIRECTS

RESPOND

LEVELS OF
MANAGEMENT

RESPOND

DEMAND

WORKERS

CLOSING COMMUNICATIONS LOOP

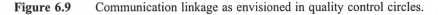

Figure 6.9   Communication linkage as envisioned in quality control circles.

ity raw material. It is the nature of their work to deal with things, and so they think in terms of things.

Work, in the case of professionals, is an integration of thinking and doing, which is often complex. The work they perform is more specialized and personalized and is situationally controlled. Not only are the thinking and doing integrated, but the managing and performing are as well. Managers and professionals are part of the same team, partners with differing skills but a common objective.

Thinking is the critical mass of work today, as doing was in the past. Thinking becomes a problem when position power takes precedence over knowledge power, when the approach to work is not consistent with its demands. You cannot preach quality in one breath and practice expediency in the next, nor can formality take precedence over informality. The mechanistic mind-set, which set the precedence in the past, now gives way to the organic. The organization is not a fine-tuned clock of many discrete parts, but a single organism with multidimensional, interdependent, integrated, and simultaneously supportive functions. Moreover, the archaic problem-solving formula of linear logic, cause and effect analysis, and concrete data that are popular in QCCs is not sufficient for today's problems. QCCs were designed as a voluntary system of worker participation, giving workers the opportunity to contribute to the decision-making process. J. M. Juran has observed such efforts directed at solving the trivial many problems and not the vital few. Juran states that only 15 percent improvement can be effected if blue-collar workers are 100 percent successful. This leaves 85 percent of the problem untouched, which Juran sees as only germane to management and professionals. Juran and W. Edwards Deming introduced the team concept to the Japanese in the late 1950s.

More remarkable is the fact that Joseph Scanlon introduced this same concept to Empire Steel and Tin Plate Company in Mansfield, Ohio, in 1932.[64] *The Scanlon Plan* was responsible for saving the company from bankruptcy by promoting union and management cooperation. This teaming was aimed at reducing costs and improving quality. The wholehearted cooperation which ensued was instrumental in Empire Steel's turning the financial corner. The plan also included profit sharing with all employees. The Scanlon Plan hoped to establish a free-enterprise system in which every worker could become a capitalist. The cultural bias of the organization, however, doomed this innovative idea. Once Empire Steel was back on its financial feet, it went back to managing and operating as if nothing had changed.

This still happens. A General Motors assembly plant in the Van Nuys area of Los Angeles instituted the Japanese approach to the team concept in 1987. Three years later, an incident indicated how badly it was failing. Reporter Barry Stavro of the *Los Angeles Times* (January 28, 1990) tells this story:

> *It was only one of the 3,000 or so parts that go into a new Chevrolet Camaro or Pontiac Firebird. But for Larry Barker, a welder...one part summed up all that is wrong with the way GM builds cars. One night last fall Barker, along with the rest of the shift, was sent home early after GM ran out of a reinforcement panel that is welded next to the wheel wells near the motor compartment...The panels came in pairs—one for the right side, one for the left side—and when the plant ran out of panels for one side, the assembly line stopped. A night shift supervisor came down and actually took one of the panels from the other (wrong) side and literally tried beating it into place with a hammer and then welding it. The Rube Goldberg fix-it took so long, Barker said, that GM decided "it wasn't worth it, so then they sent us home." If the wrong part could have been forced into place faster, they probably would have run the assembly line.*[65]

What is important about this story is that GM immediately put into place procedures to prevent this from happening again. But procedures do not replace a mind-set. The Saturn automobile, produced by GM, demonstrates how a quality product is possible in a workplace culture if the mind-set is totally committed to quality, whatever the circumstances. Workers at Saturn plants have the right to stop the assembly line and fix the problem. This is part of GM's continuous improvement plan to make better cars. It works when it is practiced, and it is practiced when the workplace culture supports the company philosophy.

The team concept didn't prepare the workers at the Van Nuys plant for trying to force a wrong part into an automobile, but the lingering management style did. "There's a difference between having a part a little wrong, and beating one into place with a hammer," Barker confided. "They want quality, and they want you to be proud of what you're building. How can you when you see stuff like that?" Such confusion creates cynicism, and cynicism leads to the *six silent killers*. At the Van Nuys plant on a typical day, 17 percent of the workforce are no shows. The team concept and the drive for quality are a joke to them. Morale is poor. Workers want to believe in what they do. They want to be able to stop the assembly line and fix what is wrong. This gives them pride in what they do. Workers also want to be cross-trained to do different things, which breaks the routine and monotony. Barker confesses sadly, "Management is too busy keeping the line moving."[66]

Professionals are even more cynical of such devices. They see themselves being expected to function in a one-dimensional world when the demands of work are multidimensional and being buried in information with little opportunity to have input into conceptual designs. Information overload is a common problem, but professionals have ideas on how to handle it. These ideas are foreign to management, because it is not privy to the subtleties of their work. The challenge is to find a way to integrate professionals and managers—with diverse talents and complex personalties—into effective teams. Attacking the trivial many with blistering energy at the expense of the vital few problems is a reflection of obsessive compulsive behavior.

Vanishing blue-collar workers are not the problem. They have seen their jobs disappear and their lives ruined, believing in a system that no longer exists, a system which regarded them as interchangeable parts in a complex machine. Education, training, orientation, and continuing support are now essential components to them in the new world of work. Blue-collar workers were never considered shareholders in the sense that Scanlon dreamed. This lesson has not been lost on professionals. These workers, however, lack the maturity to take hold of their new opportunity. They want the power and authority denied them before, but with the comfort and security they have always enjoyed. Power and influence will continue to elude them if they do not accept the responsibility and consequences of their actions.

Silent Killer No. 6: *Malicious Obedience*

Examples are withholding information that is critical to the success of an operation; hiding information required by colleagues to perform their jobs; giving false information; doing precisely what instructed to do even when one knows it is wrong; circulating disinformation about the company, colleagues, or superiors which frustrates the organization from its purpose; playing games of divide and conquer; talking behind people's backs; inciting distrust by spreading rumors; toying with colleagues' natural suspicions; and misusing company property, all while having the appearance of doing nothing wrong. Malicious obedience is aimed at punishing and thwarting the efforts of others. It is the most insidious of the silent killers.

Take malicious obedience as reported by David Brand in *Time* (February 1, 1988).[67] Laurie Bernstein, 30, started work at a small Southern law firm, getting distinctly icy treatment from the only other woman lawyer on the staff. When Bernstein was given one of her female colleagues' cases to handle, resentment turned to spite. She discovered, to her frustration, she was not given the court documents and other important papers needed to handle the case. Late one evening, she accidentally uncovered them hidden in the other woman's mailbox. Ms. Sabotage was severely reprimanded. "I felt terrible," recalls Bernstein. "I expected a camaraderie to emerge between us as the only two female lawyers at the firm. Quite the opposite occurred."

Malicious obedience is not exclusively a feminine complaint. Men have been doing this to each other for centuries in their roles as principal breadwinners. Now women are equally involved in the competitive jungle of making a living. What authors Luise Eichenbaum and Susie Orbach write about in *Between Women: Love, Envy and Competition in Women's Friendship* (1988) applies as readily to men.[68] With promotions stalling, amalgamation of job categories, and management opportunities disappearing, professional workers have become known to turn their considerable skills on placing land mines in the way of each other. This irrational behavior is fueled by fear, hysteria, and rumor, yet professionals have far more opportunity than ever before. Cooperating with co-workers is the key to job satisfaction, morale, and greater job security. Even so, more professionals are falling on their own swords exercising malicious obedience.

The idea of malicious obedience is so repugnant that many choose to be unaware that it is in their arsenal of competitive warfare. It is far more common than most would like to admit, and chances are many of us have practiced it on occasion. The word "malicious" describes the intent, while "obedient" describes how the behavior appears. Malicious obedience is a paralyzing emotional trap in which the perpetrator becomes the victim of his own experience. With such a venomous mind-set, the perpetrator cannot clearly define his situation and moves blindly in a fog of malicious contempt. His frame of reference is clouded by competitive zeal, envy, jealousy, or self-hatred. What protects the person from malicious obedience are emotional maturity and healthy self-reliance. These buffers come into play when we accept ourselves as we are and others as we find them. We don't own other people's problems. We realize there is plenty of space for us in the universe. We don't become defensive because we haven't made the progress we would like. Instead, we maintain a sense of humor about what we're doing with what we have. We don't compare ourselves or our progress with where others are. We realize if we haven't made the progress we want, it is because we haven't needed to. It wasn't as important as we would like to believe. We don't play games with ourselves. We are aware of ourselves as we are, accepting in that awareness, choosing (or not choosing) to act on that awareness to change (or not change) our circumstances. We know, after all, it is up to us to make our own way, that the only freedom and joy in living is to seek opportunity and move away from repressive dependence, which is the domain of malicious obedience.

What goads the maliciously obedient person is the game of success and failure, appreciation and ingratitude, inclusion and exclusion. It is not easy to make the correct inference as to what goads the maliciously obedient, for success to one is failure to another. The truly maliciously obedient person is evil, but such a person represents only a small segment of this silent killer. The real carriers of the venom are people who are neither too malicious nor obedient, but passively indifferent. They operate mainly on automatic pilot. These people have little understanding of the severe consequences of their behavior. They operate from spite. They have been wronged, and they must hurt back. This urge is fueled more by impulse than conscious desire to destroy. "I don't get angry," they coo, "I get even." Vengeance is a corrosive disease, but so is indifference. With indifference, we encounter the personification of disrespect and disengagement. To wit: secretaries in a high-tech company use computer-aided design (CAD) computers as word processors rather than personal computers. The cost of the CAD computers is ten times that of the PCs. If they are doing this in ignorance, it is one thing. If they know the relative cost, it is *malicious obedience*. If an engineer observes the secretaries doing general correspondence on these computers and does nothing, this is also *malicious obedience*. If the section supervisor is aware of what is going on but chooses to do nothing because he doesn't want to cause alarm and draw attention to the budget, it is *malicious obedience*. If the director is complacent because the program is a "cost plus" program with the government footing the bill, it is *malicious obedience*. This situation might appear hypothetical, but it is in fact true. It wasn't until the situation reached the vice president of operations that something was done. *Malicious obedience* was practiced at all levels below him. What happened to the offending parties who had cost the customer tens of thousands of dollars? Nothing. Was the customer informed of the wrongdoing and reimbursed? What do you think?

Malicious obedience grows out of a contempt for the civilized needs of others and a scornful disregard for the interdependent nature of all things. Companies need workers, and workers need companies. Sometimes this simple declarative truth is lost in the emotions of the moment. It doesn't take much for an employee to feel a right to malicious obedience. *Working Women* (September 24, 1996) carried a survey of cancer survivors who worked while undergoing treatment.[69] According to the article, employees with cancer are fired or laid off five times as often as others. Those who keep their jobs, the article continued, are often stripped of important duties by supervisors who believe the treatment will slow the worker down. Such information feeds malicious obedience because the rumor mill carries the implicit dread far beyond the scope of this article.

Many readers are too young to remember Ralph Nader's frontal attack on General Motors for what he believed was a cavalier disregard for automotive safety. This young lawyer wrote a book about the dangers of driving a Corvair automobile, *Unsafe At Any Speed* (1956), which caused GM to go ballistic.[70] GM's first response to the accusation was neither to verify nor refute the claim. GM sought to compromise Mr. Nader by invading his privacy and, hopefully, to discover some scandalous deviltry. When no shameful activity was uncovered, GM became obsessed with Nader and compulsive in its strategy to deal with him. The result was that Nader grew to national prominence while GM looked ridiculous. Nader was an independent contractor who felt a responsibility to set the record straight. This is the opposite of malicious obedience.

When a manager is operating on a tight budget, scrambling for breathing room and feeling compelled to make his numbers creatively, he practices malicious obedience. The Chrysler executives who rolled back the odometers on 60,000 automobiles were maliciously obedient. They were guilty of knowingly doing something that hurt their customers. Anyone who was aware of the activity and failed to report it was also guilty. The Watergate cover-up was a classic example of malicious obedience, with every level of the executive branch—all the way to the presidency—arrogantly disregarding ethics and common sense. Similarly, the Iran/Contra scandal was incomprehensible to most Americans, who could not conceive of their government selling arms to terrorists—to a nation that had held Americans hostage for more than three agonizing years. Holding Americans hostage gave the terrorists a paralyzing grip on the American psyche. As with the Great Depression, this rekindled the psychological fixation of helplessness in the face of adversity and of innocence in the face of doubt. To learn that the American government was a partner with these criminals was more than many could fathom. In order to cope, many American workers have become hardened to duplicity, chicanery, and bad faith. This is evident in how they are reacting to the Whitewater investigation. "Why wouldn't President Clinton and the First Lady be involved in that exposé...?"

Malicious obedience often starts with surprising innocence and builds to spiteful deception, climaxing in consequences clearly out of control. Lt. Col. Oliver North, with his steel-hammer commitment to following orders, saw any means as justifying the end. Patriotic zeal was shielded behind the American flag. North grew to epic proportions on television as the American people, failing to see his behavior for what it was, malicious obedience, became captivated by his ramrod confidence as he appeared before the Senate's Iran/Contra Hearings. Elevated to epic hero, North was forgiven, for the moment, on a wave of patriotic emotion. But in 1994, when he ran for a senate seat in Virginia, the emotion had faded, and he was defeated.

Shakespeare's Contribution—Iago in the Tragedy of *Othello*

Malicious obedience has intrigued man for centuries. William Shakespeare froze this deception in the character of Iago in the tragedy of *Othello, The Moor of Venice* (1622).[71] Othello is a good man who struggles with good and evil in his soul. Iago, the villain, perhaps the most sadistically evil character in all literature, is maliciously obedient. On the surface, he is an obedient and dedicated liege to Othello, but in his heart he is a malicious viper. The tragedy takes place shortly after Ensign Iago is passed over for promotion in favor of Cassio as Othello's chief of staff. What follows is an intricate pattern of skullduggery in which Iago means to settle the score.

Like most men of an evil heart, Iago makes it his business to know Othello's vulnerability. He knows that Othello is hopelessly in love with his wife, Desdemona, and is intensely jealous, keeping a diabolical register of Othello's possessive looks on his wife and his obsessive attention to her. Iago has noted that Cassio, too, loves Desdemona, but that his love is pure and innocent and no threat to Othello. Taking these delectable circumstances to heart, he schemes. Iago tells Cassio that Desdemona loves him and not Othello. He arranges a meeting of Cassio with Desdemona to confirm the truth of this. Desdemona is ignorant of the purpose of the meeting, nor has Cassio any intention of presuming that it is so. Cassio agrees to meet Desdemona when and where Iago has scheduled the rendezvous. While they are talking, Iago brings Othello in full view of the pair but too far to hear the conversation. Iago whispers into his ear vague innuendoes as to what they might be saying.

Afterwards, on a regular basis, Iago makes references to the meeting and asks questions of Othello in a manner meant to cause him to wonder if Desdemona has been intimate with Cassio. Once the seed is planted in Othello's jealous heart, Iago exploits the doubt. Othello questions Desdemona's fidelity by wondering after her most innocent comments or movements. Anxiety mounts while treachery smolders. When Othello complains to Desdemona of a headache, she offers to bind his head with her handkerchief, Othello's first gift to her. Later, she inadvertently drops it, only to have Emilia, Iago's wife, pick it up. The opportunity nearly blinds Iago with joy. He seizes the handkerchief from his wife and deftly hides it in Cassio's room.

When Othello finally asks Iago for proof of Desdemona's unfaithfulness, threatening to kill him if he cannot, Iago states with great calm that he has such evidence. He claims only that day he slept in Cassio's room and overheard Cassio speak sweet words of Desdemona in his sleep. Moreover, in his presence, Cassio wiped his beard with a handkerchief which was not unlike the one Othello had once given to Desdemona. With the evidence at hand, overcome by passion and madness, Othello vows revenge. He orders Iago to kill Cassio, appointing the ensign as his new chief of staff, while he goes on to smother Desdemona to death in her sleep. Learning too late of Iago's treachery, mad with grief over what he has done, Othello plunges a dagger into his own heart.

Profile of the Maliciously Obedient Person

Shakespeare's kind of malicious obedience is a whispered presence in most washrooms, company cafeterias, local eateries, social hangouts, board rooms, and dinner tables across the globe. Psychologically, the maliciously obedient, whatever their age, are not satisfied. They don't know why they are not satisfied, but they know it is not their fault. They don't expect anything to last—not love, work, family, or life. They are in it for right now, and everybody is on their own. It amuses them when serious people ask them their opinion. The fact is they don't think. They scheme—

how to get what they want from whomever with the smallest risk and inconvenience to themselves. They lie, cheat, steal, deny, ignore, covet, or confiscate if they think they can get away with it. There has been so little uplifting grace to their time, they rationalize, that they don't need a conscience or a soul to ponder. Economically, they come from every class and every segment of society. Malicious obedience is democratic. They are more clever than wise, but consistently bright. They are more prominent among professional ranks than blue-collar workers because the majority of the latter still believe. The maliciously obedient have long ago given up belief and are in it for what they can get. Politically, they cover the spectrum, but not in the sense of a party or ideology. Malicious obedience is a scheming strategy. It requires the cunning of a politician and the heart of an executioner. The maliciously obedient are as likely as not to be narrow-minded, intolerant, self-pitying, extroverted, politically sophisticated, and materialistic. Few can escape its pull if the circumstances are right. So, labels offer few clues as to the maliciously obedient. They think more than they feel, act more than they react, operate more on a scheming strategy than automatic pilot—precisely the reverse of other passive silent killers. Malicious obedience can be seen as a crippling disease of an otherwise resourceful population. That is why it is so damaging to the organization.

Identifying the Six Silent Killers Before They Take Hold

What makes this problem so difficult to deal with is that it is endemic to our existence. Two things drive us: one is fear and the other is desire. While we are going to school and developing our personalities, we are programmed daily by peers, parents, teachers, preachers, friends, and relatives as to what is important and what is not. This conscious stimulation we absorb or fend off because we encounter it directly. Less obvious but equally constant is the subliminal bombardment of television, radio, and the Internet, which support or refute our ethnicity and its rites and rituals of passage.

The predominant characteristic of our conditioning is to please others, invariably at the expense of pleasing ourselves. Many find this a "catch-22"—our greatest desire is to please while our greatest fear is to fail to please. In an effort to please everyone, we end up pleasing no one, especially ourselves. Without knowing it and before we can express it in words, we find ourselves a victim of circumstances not of our choosing, existing but not living, and exercising someone else's agenda, not our own. We are bitter without having a reason. Angry without having a cause. We go to school because we have to, we go to church for the same reason, and we take this mind-set to the job. The cumulative effect of always living up to what others expect skews our behavior toward the negative, expecting to be disappointed, exploited, defiled, taken for granted, or worst of all, ignored. Nowhere do we find a place for pleasing ourselves. We are told that pleasing ourselves is selfish and being selfish is a cultural curse. So, we lie. The war between desire and fear rages on silently in the shadows of our mind with our real self being hidden from the eyes of others. Without consciously desiring it, we find ourselves seeking solace in schemes beyond the accepted. Without a carefully worked out plan, we become the instrument of the *six silent killers*. There are several discernible signs of this social debility. The most discernible is that the social character of our personality appears to change as our desires and fears conflict. When our fears become our desires, we are no longer in control. We:

- Dress differently or appear careless about our appearance for the first time.
- Avoid long-time friends, no longer share lunch with co-workers, or always find an excuse to be left alone.
- Begin to curse, to flower our speech with colorful, earthy expletives, or to tell dirty jokes to shock others, when previously we didn't swear or listen to such stories.
- Take up smoking, drinking, or start doing drugs, or if we have stopped, we start again.
- Put down people absent from the group, bad-mouth the company or our manager.
- Attempt to convince others to be deviant with us or to violate established norms.
- Become promiscuous after being considered just this side of a prude.
- Gain or lose weight dramatically.
- Lose interest in what before were consuming interests.
- Become especially careless with money as opposed to being miserly before.
- Are given to spontaneous and inappropriate eruptions of rage without provocation.
- Become especially talkative or quiet—both abnormal behaviors for us.
- Lose long-time friends and don't seem to mind.
- Commence to hang out with those considered losers.
- Stop going to church if a church-goer.
- Start lying a lot, which was not characteristic of us before.
- Bad-mouth our mate, if married; extend the same to family and friends.
- Show an inclination to cruelty uncharacteristic before, especially to animals.
- Let the quality of our work break down with little concern.
- Become argumentative about nothing.
- Start missing work.
- Become accident prone.
- Develop credit problems.
- Become a supervisor's pet project to save us.

If you can see yourself in some of these behaviors, don't be surprised. They are common to most of us at one time or another. The conflict that desire and fear can generate can go beyond frustration to draw us into a web of self-defeat. The way "in" to this behavior is alone, and the way "out" is alone as well. What we will now show is how workplace culture and its cultural infrastructure sponsor comfort and complacency. This cultural conditioning produces dependency that is as repressive as any prison. It also sponsors the immaturity necessary for the *six silent killers* to breed. Without intending to, this places workers in suspended adolescence from cradle to grave. Prevention of the *six silent killers*, as you shall see, is a monumental task.

Endnotes

1. Henrik Ibsen, *Peer Gynt* (Act IV, Scene 13) in *Works of Henrik Ibsen,* Vol. 1 (New York: Scribner's, 1911), pp. 228–229. This play is about the human *will*. Our *will* is broken up into specific wishes, wants, desires, and appetites. For Peer Gynt, the basic drive of that *will* is a will-to-power. In the scene alluded to here, Begriffenfeldt seeks to make Peer "Lord of the Lunatic Asylum." As Peer sinks down into the mire, a wreath of straw is pressed on his brow, as "Monarch of the Madhouse." This chapter on the *six silent killers* shows parallels to the reality of our times which make this unsettling.

2. W. W. Rostow, "To Compete, Americans Must First Cooperate," *Minneapolis Star Tribune*, March 16, 1987, Commentary section, 1. Note also: Michael Elliott writes, "American Competitiveness Is Out of Style," *International Herald Tribune*, February 23, 1987, Opinion section, 1.

3. Willard and Marguerite Beecher, *Beyond Success and Failure* (New York: Pockett Books, 1966), pp. 56–65.

4. Erich Fromm, *Beyond the Chains of Illusion* (New York: Simon & Schuster, 1962), p. 41.

5. Ibid., p. 41.

6. Ellen Goodman, "Once-Rebellious Baby Boomers Dread Their Kids' Q&A," *The Tampa Tribune*, September 15, 1996, Commentary section, 6.

7. Karl Zinsmeister (American Enterprise Institute), *The Tampa Tribune*, April 10, 1980, Nation/World, 18.

8. Daniel T. Rodgers, "Work Ethic Has Long Been Resisted," *The Tampa Tribune*, October 4, 1981, 4-C. This article draws heavily from the work of Robert and Helen Lynd and their classic 1920s study of Muncie, an Indiana factory town, which they made famous in their study *Middletown* (1959).

9. John Strohmeyer, *Crisis in Bethlehem: Big Steel's Struggle to Survive* (New York: Penguin Paperbacks, 1987). He writes, "They had practically every benefit you could think of, including 13-week vacations every five years for the senior half of the workforce. Anybody on the outside could see this would not possibly last, that the bubble was going to burst, that these people had really negotiated themselves into a corner and had, in effect, crippled the goose that was laying the golden egg."

10. Lance Morrow, "What Is the Point of Working?" *Time*, May 11, 1981, 93–94.

11. James O'Toole, "The Meanings of Work," *The Tampa Tribune*, September 6, 1981, 4-C.

12. Studs Terkel, *Working: People Talk About What They Do All Day and How They Feel About What They Do* (New York: Avon Books, 1972), p. xiii.

13. Edward Tenner, *Why Things Bite Back: Technology and Revenge of Unintended Consequences* (New York: Knopf, 1996).

14. Karen Cherry, "FiloFax Feeds a Trend," (study by Priority Management Systems, Inc.), *St. Petersburg Times*, January 20, 1990, Business, 1.

15. *The Complete Essays and Other Writings of Ralph Waldo Emerson* (New York: The Modern Library, 1950), p. 145.

16. Marvin Harris, *Why Things Don't Work: The Anthropology of Daily Life* (New York: Touchstone Books, 1987). The author wonders if America is dying of a broken part. He sees

change as the culprit as disparate aspects of change form an unintended coherent pattern of poor performance.

17. "Give Me Liberty And...," unpublished play by Eugene O'Neill as reported in *Time* (Source: Alan Valentine, *Age of Conformity*, p. 95).

18. Jim Henderson, "Young, Rich—and Deep in Debt," *USA Today*, March 31, 1983, Business, 1.

19. Michael A. Hiltzik, "As Boesky Sings, Evidence Trebles," *International Herald Tribune*, December 16, 1987, Business/Finance, 1.

20. Alexander Cockburn "Of Cocaine, Capitalism and the Martyred De Lorean," *The Wall Street Journal*, October 28, 1982, 31.

21. Craig R. Waters' comments appeared in the De Lorean cover story for *Inc. Magazine*, April 1983.

22. Columnist Joseph Kraft is quoted in the Cockburn piece, stating that "high rollers are on the loose. Greed at the top has been systematized and even sanctified."

23. Kevin Phillips, "Hart's Withdrawal Gives the Republicans a Boost Against 'Seven Dwarfs,'" *Los Angeles Times*, May 15, 1987, Op-Ed, 33. The seven dwarfs alluded to were Governor Michael Dukakis of Massachusetts, the Reverend Jesse Jackson, Representative Richard Gephardt of Missouri, Senator Joseph R. Biden, Jr. of Delaware, Senator Paul Simon of Illinois, Senator Albert Gore, Jr. of Tennessee, and former Governor Bruce Babbitt of Arizona.

24. William van den Heuvel, "When the Other Woman Wasn't a Flaw," *New York Times*, May 11, 1987, 30. Heuvel writes, "A reporter approaches Mr. Willkie after his nomination and told him that he had information that he was living with a woman other than his wife. 'Yes,' Mr. Willkie reportedly replied. 'I am in love with another woman—and I don't intend to apologize for that or to pretend that it isn't so. If you print this story, my campaign for the presidency is probably over. But that is your decision. I have made mine.'" Obviously the story was never published.

25. "European Press Has a Field Day," *USA Today*, May 30–June 1, 1987, Washington/World section, 4. Ben Franklin, JFK, and FDR were mentioned as great philanderers in a piece appearing in Brussels' conservative *Libre Belgique*.

26. A. M. Rosenthal, "Gary Hart Ought to Know Who Shot Down Gary Hart," *International Herald Tribune*, May 12, 1987, Op-Ed, 4.

27. Gregory Katz, "Rice Skirts Questions on Hart, Says He'll 'Survive,'" *USA Today*, June 20, 1987, 1.

28. David Maraniss, "To His Friends, Hart Was Often Reluctant to Tell It 'Straight,'" *International Herald Tribune*, May 9–10, 1987, Op-Ed, 10.

29. Garry Wills, "A Tale of Two Cities," *The New York Review*, October 3, 1996, p. 22.

30. Martin Walker, *The President We Deserve: Bill Clinton, His Rise, Falls, and Comebacks* (New York: Crown Books, 1996), p. 217.

31. Wills, op. cit., p. 22.

32. Richard A. Knox, "Medical Fraud: Rise & Fall of a Medical Legend—Former Co-workers Are Left in the Rubble of Dr. Darsee's Discredited Research," *Boston Globe*, May 23, 1983, pp. 46-48.

33. William Butler Yeats, *Bartlett's Familiar Quotations,* No. 22 (Boston: Little Brown, 1992), p. 599.

34. Richard N. Ostling et al., "TV's Unholy Row: A Sex-and-Money Scandal Tarnishes Electronic Evangelism," *Time*, April 6, 1987, 38–43.

35. Andrew L. Yarrow, "Jessica, Donna, Fawn and Fame," *International Herald Tribune*, September 29, 1987, 13.

36. Timothy McQuay and Jack Kelley, "IRS Says Bakkers Took PTL Funds for Own Use," *USA Today*, June 6–8, 1987, featured story.

37. An insight into President Nixon's reckless abandon passive defensiveness is last section of *The Memoirs of Richard Nixon: The Presidency 1973–1974* (New York: Grosset & Dunlap, 1978) pp. 761–1090, compared with Bob Woodward and Carl Berstein, *The Final Days* (New York: Simon and Schuster, 1976).

38. John Dean, *Blind Ambition* (New York: Simon & Schuster, 1979).

39. Saul W. Gellerman, "Why Good Managers Make Bad Ethical Choices," *Leaders of Humanity* (New York: Center for International Leadership, Bell South Management Institute, 1986).

40. Ibid.

41. Ibid.

42. Lally Weymouth, "Has Chrysler Been Saved?" *Parade Magazine*, cover story, September 12, 1982.

43. Philip Greer and Myron Kandel, "Chrysler's Miracle: Iacocca Doesn't Merit All the Credit," *USA Today*, August 30, 1982, 13.

44. Howie Kurtz and Warren Brown, "Chrysler Named in Indictment on Odometer Fraud," *International Herald Tribune*, June 25, 1987, 11.

45. The Associated Press, "Chrysler Defends Practice: Says All Makers Take Free Ride," *International Herald Tribune*, June 26, 1987, 11.

46. Rollo May, *The Meaning of Anxiety* (New York: W.W. Norton, 1977), p. 113.

47. Michael D. Lemonick, "The New Miracle (Redux Regimen) Drug?" *Time*, September 23, 1996, 60–67. Update: Christine Gorman writes in *Time*, "Redux on the Ropes," June 23, 1997, p. 47: "…bad news, bad luck and too high hopes add up to disappointing sales for last year's hot new diet pill."

48. National Institute on Drug Abuse, Research Triangle Survey, *The Tampa Tribune*, January 15, 1989, Commentary section, 1-C.

49. Sandra Salmans (*New York Times*), "Procter & Gamble Exorcising Devilish Rumors: P&G Gossip—'In the Beginning, God Made the Tree. When Did Satan Get Charmin?'" *The Tampa Tribune-Times*, August 1, 1982, 2-E. Note: We see demonstrated here corporate obsessive compulsiveness which is constantly repeated with unintended consequences. Take the obstreperous attempt of the Southern Baptist Convention (June 1997), the largest Protestant denomination in the United States, to have its 16 million members boycott Disney Enterprises. The corporate complaint here is that Disney lets gay and lesbian groups have the same run of Disney World and Disneyland as other groups, that the company gives partners of homosexual employment the same benefits it gives the spouses of heterosexual ones, and that ABC-TV (which Disney owns) let "Ellen" (Ellen DeGeneres) out of the closet in her weekly situation comedy. Generally speaking, corporate obsessive compulsiveness has the same impact that it has on individuals, which is a negative if not an embarrassing one.

50. Lee Iacocca, *Iacocca* (New York: Bantam Books, 1984), pp. 120–121.

51. Lawrence Peter and Raymond Hall, *The Peter Principle: Why Things Always Go Wrong* (New York: Morrow, 1969).

52. Page Smith, *Killing the Spirit: Higher Education in America* (New York: Penguin Books, 1990), pp. 177–198.

53. John Kenneth Galbraith, *The Anatomy of Power* (Boston: Houghton Mifflin, 1983), pp. 44–46, 48, 59, 62, 63.

54. Edward Wolff, *Top Heavy: The Increasing Inequality of Wealth in America and What Can Be Done About It* (New York: W.W. Norton, 1996), pp. 32–45.

55. J. M. Juran, "Product Quality—A Prescription for the West," *Management Review*. June & July 1981; "International Significance of the QC Circle Movement," *Quality Progress*, November 1980, 18–21.

56. Myron Tribus, "Deming's Way," *Mechanical Engineering*, January 1988, 26–30. Deming's famous 14 points are: (1) create consistency and continuity of purpose; (2) refuse to allow commonly accepted levels of delay for mistakes, defective material, and defective workmanship; (3) eliminate the need for and dependence upon mass inspection; (4) reduce the number of suppliers—buy on statistical evidence, not price; (5) search continually for problems in the system and seek ways to improve it; (6) institute modern methods of training using statistics; (7) focus supervision on helping people do a better job—provide the tools and techniques for people to have pride in workmanship; (8) eliminate fear—encourage two-way communication; (9) break down barriers between departments—encourage problem-solving through teamwork; (10) eliminate the use of numerical goals, slogans, and posters for the workforce; (11) use statistical methods for continuing improvements of quality and productivity and eliminate all standards prescribing numerical quotas; (12) remove barriers to pride of workmanship; (13) institute a vigorous program of education and training to keep people abreast of new developments in materials, methods, and technologies; and (14) clearly define management's permanent commitment to quality and productivity.

57. Genichi Taguchi, *Introduction to Quality Engineering: Designing Quality into Products and Processes* (White Plains, NY: Unipub/Quality Resources, 1986).

58. William H. Whyte, Jr., *The Organization Man* (New York: Simon & Schuster, 1956), p. 53.

59. John Kenneth Galbraith, *Money: Where It Came, Where It Went* (Boston: Houghton Mifflin, 1975), pp. 268–283.

60. "Sony Chairman Commencement Address," *Wharton School of Management Review*, June, 1990, 16.

61. John Kenneth Galbraith, *The Culture of Contentment* (Boston: Houghton Mifflin, 1992), pp. 154–165. Galbraith writes of what might be called "incipient catastrophe" in Chapter 13, "The Reckoning."

62. Peter Drucker, "World in Flux: Drucker Dissects Global Change," *Time*, April 7, 1986, 48.

63. Drucker, op. cit. By reference to the "symbolic economy" is meant that money, credit, and capital no longer are tightly bound to the real economy of produced goods, services, and trade.

64. Frederick G. Lesieur, *The Scanlon Plan: A Frontier in Labor Management Cooperation* (Boston: MIT Press, 1964).

65. Barry Stavro, *Los Angeles Times,* as reported in the *St. Petersburg Times*, January 28, 1990, Business/Finance, 1.

66. Ibid.

67. David Brand, "Love, Envy, and Competition in Women's Friendships," *Time*, February 1, 1988, 56.

68. Luise Eichenbaum and Susie Orbach, *Between Women* (New York: Viking, 1988), p. 133.

69. Judie Glave (The Associated Press), "You Can't Do That," *The Tampa Tribune*, September 25, 1996, featured story. From *Working Women*, September 24, 1996, featured story, 1.

70. Ralph Nader, *Unsafe at Any Speed* (New York: Grossman, 1965).

71. William Shakespeare, *The Tragedy of Othello: The Moor of Venice* (New Haven, CT: Yale University Press, 1961).

The Culture of Comfort

The brain uses the principle of "the match" by which incoming information matches, more or less exactly, the patterns stored in the brain, or else it is not recognized...Biasing involves all that is stored in the brain, relevant to a program decision, from experience, from plans, aims, fears, and from the current situational input. To effect change of behavior, or "open a new door" to learning, we must try to change biases, not behavior directly...Present learning depends heavily on previous learning and biases stored in the brain of each individual. Giving individuals uniform instruction without regard to what they bring to the learning effort virtually guarantees a high incidence of failure.[1]

Leslie A. Hart

The lust for comfort, that stealthy thing that enters the house a guest, and then becomes a host, and then a master.[2]

Kahlil Gibran

Sisyphus Alone!

Imagine a small high-tech operation in which 400 employees conscientiously come to work. This operation, once a leader in its field, finds itself in a survival mode with executives working seven days a week (some 10–12 hours a day), struggling to keep the operation afloat. In this situation, work means executives cordoning themselves off from other employees, running from meeting to meeting, from marketing to sales, from engineering to production, from crisis to crisis. The operation is under siege; no one has time to think, much less kid, as morbid activity fills a humorless void.

Meetings provide the worry beads for this anxious group, with preparation for meetings leaving little time for calm reflection. Work, undeniably laborious, finds no one with either the inclination or courage to call "time out" for a sanity check. Yet, at this most critical moment, the focus is shifted suddenly from the problem and refocused on the corporate fathers' demand for a management review. All energy is

143

redirected to an elaborate presentation of the "state of the business," combining CYA and SYA "show and tell" documentation. A veritable magnum opus of 1,300 pages is generated with copies for all. The text is then featured in a four-hour, 400-viewgraph presentation in living color. Someone from another planet observing this whole affair might conclude, "There is no intelligent life on planet Earth."

The corporate fathers, numbed to the bone by the presentation, suffering jet lag and overload, reciprocate by directing the staff to return to the drawing board—"simplify, codify, and verify your findings." After weeks of Herculean effort, reduced to raw nerves and little else, the shock of this demand might be expected to break the staff's composure. Instead, faces of weary resignation greet the news, except for the secretarial pool. Their marriages on hold for weeks, they cry jointly, "Enough already!" One secretary says, "It's as if all my energy was poured down a black hole without any hint of light."

This was the effort of 80 men and women against an organization of 400. Eighty self-appointed company saviors operated without the support, input, or involvement of the other 320 employees. Yes, 80 people were observed daily pushing the great stone of Sisyphus up the slope, while four times that number stood about and watched

Figure 7.1　Sisyphus in Hades—condemned to roll a stone up a hill, only to have it roll back down again as it nears the top...for all eternity.

with derisive smiles. "It's not our problem," the multitude sang, "management got us in this mess. Let it get us out!" These workers, so glib and righteous, so comfortable in their ignorance, are non-responsible. No scornful observer stopped to think that it was his job that was on the line. From these workers' viewpoint, management takes care of its own. "They'll all get golden parachutes if worse comes to worse," one worker reflected, "while we'll get two weeks severance pay and a couple hours of outplacement counseling. You see, it ain't our show, so why bother?"

When Getting Fired Looks Pretty Good to Some...

Obviously, there is some truth to what this worker says. The golden parachute, at least in theory, is meant to keep management honest with its focus primarily on the interest of business rather than on its own security.[3] That has not always materialized in practice. With the growing trend toward golden parachutes, getting fired looks pretty good. Take Sidney Jay Sheinberg, the CEO of MCA, Inc. Should he lose his job within a year of the company going through a "change in control," he takes home $16.8 million in cash or roughly 23 times his normal annual salary. The severance package for MCA's top five executives could cost a minimum of $33.45 million. Add to this another 364 MCA employees guaranteed lump sum parachutes of three times their normal annual salaries, plus benefit packages and stock options. These additional parachutes approximate another $82 million.

Not to single out MCA, John W. Amerman, CEO of Mattel, faced with a similar firing, would get $5.5 million. Irvine-based Fluor Corporation guarantees its top executives two to three times their annual pay plus cash payments to compensate for lost benefits. Los Angeles–based National Medical Enterprises would give its top three people a total of more than $11 million plus stock and incentive items. Apple Computer would give its CFO Joseph A. Graziano $2.4 million if he were fired and senior vice president Delbert W. Yocam $1.6 million. Carlsbad-based Decom Systems, Inc. guarantees its top officer four times his base salary if he is fired, twice his salary if he is unable to return to work because of a disability, and a year's salary if he just decides to quit. The late Armand Hammer of Occidental Petroleum, who lived well into his nineties, was given a severance package which exceeded $16 million. The IRS tried to make this pay seem excessive and got into the act. Occidental Petroleum turned around and agreed to pay all of Hammer's tax bills.

Meanwhile, those employed continue to see their executive compensation rise. Anthony O'Reilly, CEO of H.J. Heinz, received $75,085,000 in 1991 or about $300,000 every working day and $37,500 every working hour. Had O'Reilly been doing the same job in Japan, he would have been paid about $400,000 and received about as much again in fringe benefits.[4] The next ten best compensated American executives received at least $11 million, while 1,200 directors of Wall Street firms earned (on average) $1.1 million in 1991.[5] To put this issue in perspective, in 1989 the richest 1 percent of families owned 36.2 percent of America's private wealth, 5 percent more than they did six years before. The next 9 percent owned about the same, while the remaining 90 percent together owned $1 trillion less than the richest

1 percent.[6] Albert Dunlap of Scott Paper[7] and Robert Allen of At&T[8] have the dubious distinction of being superstars in *management by downsizing*. Their corporate scouring has sent stock prices soaring. With it, their corporate salaries climb, even though downsizing has proven a failed strategy.[9] Author Ralph Estes blames it on the "tyranny of the bottom line."[10]

...And Is an Economic Holocaust to Others

When a plant closes, it is an inconvenience to the management team and a veritable disaster to the rank and file workers. Yet these workers do very little extra in response to crises because they see themselves as outside the decision-making process. There are many horror stories that might illustrate the devastating impact of a plant closing, but none more graphically than that of the grocery chain Safeway Stores, Inc.[11] The leveraged buyout (LBO) of Safeway Stores epitomizes a new level of employee cold-heartedness. Working in a food chain used to give the worker a sense of security. Everyone has to eat. Safeway's longtime motto was emphatic: "Safeway offers security!" After the LBO, management changed Safeway's motto to "Targeted returns on current investment." Employees went from being people to being things.

More than 63,000 managers and workers were cut loose from Safeway Stores through store closings, sales, or layoffs. Many workers, when they finally found work again in the grocery industry, went from an average of $12 to $4 per hour. Many lost their homes, went through divorce, serious illness, or bankruptcy. A few attempted suicide, some successfully. The majority, however, took the misfortune on the chin without complaint as they watched the three investment banks that worked the LBO cash in. These banks received a total of $65 million, with law and accounting firms sharing another $25 million. Peter Mogowan, CEO of Safeway, along with other Safeway directors and top executives, received $28 million for their shares in the company. Mogowan alone received $5.7 million. He and 60 other Safeway executives also got options to buy a total of 10 percent of the new Safeway stock at $2 (1986) per share. Today those options, ten years later, are worth more than $200 million or $25 per share.

Meanwhile the corporate raiders of Herbert and Robert Haft have managed to make $100 million by selling their Safeway shares they accumulated to Kohlberg Kravis Roberts & Co. (KKR), the LBO specialists who managed the reorganization. Incidentally, KKR charged Safeway $60 million in fees just to put the deal together. Everybody made money and continues to make money as the buyout group aggressively sells assets and consolidates profits, all at the expense of the long-term, loyal, and dedicated employees who remain out in the cold. Safeway was an economic pogrom for these 63,000 managers and workers, no less psychologically damaging than the Holocaust of World War II was to the survivors.

Workers' perception of their role is to dutifully put in eight hours and the company be damned! For more than a half century the company has taken care of them, and that is what they know and what they want to continue to experience, all evidence to the contrary. "Let management worry about the health of the company. It's not my problem," the average worker cries. But it is his problem, and it is his to worry about, for the worker's cry should be, "I AM THE COMPANY!" Without workers, there is no company, only buildings and things. Management's role, especially with the advent of the professional worker, is to lead and to serve workers as its first customer. Workers, in turn, must serve each other in user-friendly terms as first customers, too. The combination of leadership and service is the key to success: Lead and the organization will realize its opportunities and adjust to its challenges; serve and the organization will serve everyone. This cannot happen, of course, when a cultural bias promotes style over substance, conformity over contribution, and loyalty over leadership. Such a bias thwarts workers from doing their best and fosters instead the nightmare described above.

An Exception Which Could One Day Prove the Rule

It is only fair to mention that this dark cloud sometimes has a silver lining. Michael Ryan in *Parade Magazine* (September 8, 1996) features Aaron Feurestein, the CEO of Malden Mills, a plant located in Lawrence, Massachusetts.[12] On December 11, 1995, this 90-year-old family business burned to the ground, which seemed certain to put its 3,000 employees out of work permanently. But Aaron Feurestein did something that astonished his workers, so impressive that President Clinton invited him to sit with Hillary and Chelsea Clinton during the President's State of the Union Address in 1996: he announced that he would keep all of his 3,000 employees on the payroll for a month while he started rebuilding the mill. The following month, he announced he was extending their pay for another month. This generosity was repeated for yet a third month. By the end of the third month, most workers were able to return to the mill full-time. Why did he do it? He could have taken the insurance money and run with it, but he didn't. "The fundamental difference," he said, "is that I consider our workers an asset, not an expense. I have a responsibility to the workers, both blue-collar and white-collar." He added, "I have an equal responsibility to the community. It would have been unconscionable to put 3,000 people on the streets and deliver a death blow to the cities of Lawrence and Methuen. Maybe on paper our company is worth less to Wall Street, but I can tell you it's worth more. We're doing fine." That is what the CEO did for his people; what is equally dramatic is what his people are now doing for the firm.

Before the fire, the plant produced 130,000 yards of material a week. A few weeks after the fire, it was up to 230,000 yards. "Our people became very creative," Feuerstein points out. "They were willing to work 25 hours a day." When employer and employee form a bond of trust and mutual respect, nothing can stop them from achieving their goal.

What Aaron Feuerstein possesses is a value system that serves him well. He is a deeply religious man whose command of biblical Hebrew is impeccable. But beyond that, he is a man versed in the liberal tradition of Western society—that is, a man unabashedly educated in the liberal arts. "If you think the only function of a

CEO is to increase the wealth of shareholders, then any time he spends on Scripture or Shakespeare or the arts is wasteful. But if you think the CEO must balance responsibilities, then he should be involved with ideas that connect him with the past, the present and the future." Feuerstein understands and practices Robert Greenleaf's servant leadership, and providence rewards him more than tenfold.

The Law of Entropy

It would be nice to leave the matter on this high note, but that would be dodging reality. Something is terribly wrong in many organizations. The organization has become "The Prison of Panic called NOW!" This drains and depletes many organizations of their most critical resource, people. Attempts to manage enterprise out of this insane economic hell, as illustrated earlier, may drive it only deeper into the divine inferno of Sisyphus. Rather than joining forces to attack the problem, workers and managers in such a situation too frequently choose to declare war on each other. No one seems to understand what is happening or why.

What may be wrong is that *entropy* has set in. Entropy is the Second Law of Thermodynamics and what Einstein referred to as "the premier law of science." The law of entropy states that energy can be changed in only one direction, or from available energy to unavailable energy, from usable energy to unusable energy, from order to chaos. Entropy, in other words, is the law of limits (everything created ultimately changes and eventually dies). Paradoxically, out of chaos comes order, creativity, growth, development, and a new level of consciousness.[13] It is like the phoenix rising out of its own ashes. Ernest Becker reminds us in *The Birth and Death of Meaning* (1971) that when what we think and how we think no longer serves our purposes, meaning must die to give birth to new meaning which supports a more relevant, valid culture.[14] Becker points out that the road to this realization is replete with booby traps and false starts.

This finds organizations creating "The Prison of Panic Called NOW!" This is because the pathology of normalcy stubbornly maintains the status quo, when it is the status quo that is destroying organization. This is demonstrated each time management imposes its fiction on a problem by overcontrolling it. Such behavior plunges the organization into a new kind of chaos. Being aware and understanding demand a kind maturity often missing, a consciousness that embraces the pain and risk of new experience. This moved me to write an editorial for the *St. Petersburg Evening Independent* (January 1, 1976) as America was about to celebrate its 200th anniversary:

> *America is dead! Long live America!...On the eve of our 200th birthday, we have been shocked awake from our illusory dream. We have discovered belatedly that success is in the mind and not the body politic; that being "Numero Uno" is reaching after a child's fantasy; that progress carries the seeds of its own destruction...America remains like a child. And like a child, the focus of America's existence has always been on becoming, rather than being; on the competitive drive, rather*

than on cooperation; on the illusion of progress, rather than reality...But alas! Thanks to a decade of corrupt and incompetent leadership, the wasting of our natural resources, the impatience of youth and discriminated minorities, the dream has died...And in doing so...we have embraced despair...despair is the only cure for illusion. Without despair...we will not grow up. Thus, on the eve of our 200th birthday, we are in a mourning period for our cherished illusions and protected fantasies...In the end, time runs out on a nation's adolescence. The youth must die to give birth to the man. That is why I proclaim, America is dead! Long live America!" [15]

In one sense, the American century is over, but in another, it is about to be born. What is still open to speculation is whether America has the mind, heart, and soul to leave its adolescence and to assert itself in its maturity.

Cultures, be they societal or organizational, begin with the confidence of shared values, beliefs, and certain expectations, and with the appropriate cultural infrastructure to support them. Once established, cultures move irrevocably in the direction of random chaos and crippling waste. Waste, in this case, can be defined as dissipated energy. Cultures are born spontaneously out of the collective energy of their people, flourish with a distinctive identity and idiosyncrasy, and then die with a reverberating groan, leaving their footprints in the sand. Out of their ashes comes new life as surely as the seed must die to give birth to the flower's bloom. Cultures across the planet are in the throes of this confining reality, as they have been since the beginning of time. In America:

- Where the American dream is economic security and where most Americans appear economically well off, 25 million go to bed hungry every night, another 25 million are about to go below the poverty line, and the standard of living for another 100 million teeters perilously toward decline.
- Where science and technology are prided and lead the world in most categories of excellence, where there are some of the greatest universities of the world, where public education is free and the investment in that education rivals other nations of the world, 75 million adults, or one in three Americans, cannot read adequately to function in society. That number could rise to two in every three by the turn of the century. Many professional athletes, who command multimillion-dollar contracts, cannot read at the sixth grade level.
- There is little sense of this problem because economic survival and literacy remain a phantom that is not felt. Therefore, the dying status quo, the culture which sponsors this deception, is resolutely maintained.

Put tersely, using the United States as an example of a dying culture, an inevitable process that embraces all cultures, America's prosperity is a false god, and the bills are coming due. The illusion of normalcy resides in the nuclear organizations of society—the family, the church, the school, the body politic, and commerce—which are dying from the inside out.

Economist Robert Heilbroner finds the United States not only losing ground to Europe and Japan economically, but losing ground with respect to America's capacity as a society.[16] What Heilbroner sees as impoverishing America is "the inadequacy of our infrastructure, the public underpinnings without which society cannot be healthy or an economy prosperous." Following World War II, spending on the infrastructure absorbed 6.9 percent of the non-military federal budget. This share has declined ever since, plummeting to about one percent today.[17] The neglect will now cost (1985 dollars):

- $50 billion to repair the nation's 240,000 bridges.
- $315 billion to repair the nation's highways.
- $25 billion to modernize air traffic control.
- $20 billion for public housing.
- And inestimable billions for water supply and waste treatment.

And these totals relate only to hard investments.

The soft portion of the nation's infrastructure, especially public education, is also badly neglected. Spending on elementary and secondary education reached 4.4 percent of GDP in the 1970s and fell by more than 10 percent from this level in the past two decades. This is important because the quality of our labor force is deteriorating rapidly both at the bottom and at the top. Tamara Henry in *USA Today* (September 10, 1996) writes that "underachievement at school is as big a problem for middle- and upper-income youth as it is for the poor" according to a new Carnegie Report. Two out of three U.S. dropouts are not poor at the time they leave school. Most children who drop out have never been poor. "What America must come to terms with is that many middle- and upper-income children are failing to thrive intellectually," the *Years of Promise Carnegie Report* says. The report goes on to say that by the fourth grade, the performance of most children is below grade level. To counteract this trend, the Carnegie study proposes adding two years of high-quality preschool education to the basic kindergarten to 12th grade school pattern for all children. It is also recommending programs to show parents how to be effective as their youngsters' first and most influential teachers.[18]

Heilbroner looks at the whole infrastructure problem strictly in economic terms. He insists it has happened because America has been unwilling to impose taxes on income, consumption, or even sin to pay for public improvements.[19] Consider this against the fact that Sweden's 1985 tax structure was 51 percent of its GDP, Germany's and Great Britain's were both 38 percent, while ours was only 29 percent. As of 1994, the United States had the lowest tax rate of any government in the G-7 (Western Confederation), roughly 15 percent below the median government (Germany); only Japan's rate of taxation remains below at 28 percent.

Additionally, fear of deficits and the Russians has immobilized the United States, while military spending more than doubled between 1980 and 1989 ($143 to

$300 billion) as the deficit continued to climb. Heilbroner argues that the public, without new taxes, could pay for improvements to the infrastructure by doing what corporate America does for plants and equipment—*borrow*. Corporations finance by writing a check against earnings. Precisely the same avenue of finance is open to the government. Investing in the infrastructure contributes directly to economic growth. Still, the fear that deficits will bankrupt the country is a built-in state-of-the-mind bias which is hard to escape. And now that peace is breaking out all over the world, much of the military budget can be redirected for infrastructure repairs. Applied in this manner, the results could be reflected in an improvement in the quality of life, a reduction in the number of school dropouts, cleaner air to breathe, a more productive economy, and a more dynamic and growing society. The reason for emphasizing this here is to point out how it could be if the public and private sector were dedicated to the same ethical agenda. But little of this is likely to occur if the dominant cultural biases of society are stubbornly sustained, and if the pathology of normalcy is held to be valid.

Many organizations are obsessed with *tradition-structure-order-control* as if written in stone. They fail to see that these obsessions could keep them from responding to changing demands. It is easy to understand the appeal of the known. It is comfortable, whereas change is ambiguous, ambivalent, and chaotic. The merry madness which traditionalists embrace is that of "a place for everything and everything in its place." They prefer to ignore the *Law of Entropy* rather than resist it. The law implies that the best way to restore order is to first accept the lack of order, even to embrace disorder and the natural inclination to resist it.[20] Most readers have experienced the paradox of control—the more controls are tightened, the sooner chaos dominates. What follows the tightened controls are islands of dissension, disorder, confusion, and mounting discord. It is a repeat of the fate of the legendary King of Corinth, Sisyphus, who rolls his heavy stone up the hill of Hades, only to have it roll back down once he is near the top, over and over again for eternity.

This is illustrated by an organization of 4,000 employees in which everything is changing and nothing is changing at all: The TQM theme is promoted, but because the cultural bias is being ignored, the organization is very much in the embrace of the *six silent killers*. Where it intended to go was toward continuous quality improvement. Management, in its frustration, however, made decrees as if it were 1945, so the workforce has a 1945 cultural psychology: "Do everything right the first time…or else!" Today, this turns professionals off and tunes them out. TQM fits the requirements of professionals when it is implemented appropriately:

- TQM requires a process orientation, which means shifting the emphasis from results to a focus on dealing with the problems of process as they occur.
- *Results orientation* reflects the old-style commitment to quantitative standards, linear objectives, obsession with costs, and a mania for chronological time. This orientation is also saddled with MBO and

top-down authority and control. Planning of this orientation is around antiquated Goals and Objectives (G&Os) with precise printouts and explicit action items, assignments, and neat schematic flow charts and benchmark reviews. What is implied in this orientation is that this is management's game from the get-go.

- *Process orientation* is subjective in concept and collegial in its execution. The process and workers are one. There is consensus on what constitutes the qualitative standards. The integrity of the operation is set by psychological time, not chronological time. Because the focus is on mutual respect, trust, competence, and shared values and attitudes about work, chronological time takes care of itself. There is no problem meeting schedule because in this teaming environment the work teams respond quickly to process change requirements without fear of stepping on toes or violating protocol.

- *Results orientation* demands constant checking and waiting for approval.

- *Process orientation* requires trust and risk-taking.

- Structure is sacred to a *results orientation*.

- "Ad hocracy" is the driving force for a *process orientation*.

- Order, control, conformity, formality, and discipline are orchestrated as the vanguards of *results orientation*.

- Creative problem-solving, managed conflict, natural enthusiasm, and shared credit are the sanctuary of a *process orientation*.

With this contrast in orientation, TQM has found an uneasy existence in most organizations. What is amusing, if it were not so enervating, is how management often reacts to TQM failures—re-emphasizing the performance appraisal process. In one instance, 350 managers and supervisors spent literally tens of thousands of hours on this effort. The purpose was to make quality the critical index to promotion and salary adjustment. This intervention, of course, took workers and managers away from productive work.

Recall from Chapter 6 the normal distribution curve of workers (Figure 6.4). A typical workforce finds 15 percent hard-chargers, 70 percent middle-of-the-roaders, and another 15 percent totally out of the picture. Of the 4,000 workers in this sample, these 350 managers should have found roughly 600 (15 percent) workers needing some type of improvement. In actuality, after much time and great expense, they found a total of six employees who were declining in rating and another four who needed improvement. This total exercise was a sham, a charade of absolutely no value whatsoever. It could even be implied that it increased the level of cynicism a few more notches. Obviously, getting workers and managers to talk to each other is invaluable, but when the discourse is one-dimensional, counterfeit, and cosmetic, then it is a mocking expression of organizational life.

With most workers currently of the professional class, the autocratic parent–child management relationship is no longer appropriate. The interdependent adult–

adult relationship is obviously more suitable. Workers are now a critical asset to an organization, no longer interchangeable parts in a giant machine. Yet the critical shortage of highly skilled knowledge workers is reaching 20 million in the United States alone. These workers have the power but have not been trained to recognize or deal with it. They are in control, but they only understand how to take orders. What complicates the matter further is that with all their confusion and frustration, *do they have the will to work?*

Author Jeremy Rifkin sees this as a matter of entropy. He claims in *Entropy: A New World View* (1981) that entropy must be felt as well as understood.[21] It is easy to intellectualize the matter of entropy, he insists, but unless it penetrates the worker's conscience, nothing changes. More to the point, the greater the effort expended to improve order, the more likely chaos is created. If chaos is felt, it can be dealt with creatively, giving it room to dissipate and order to be re-established. Often, calm heads and patience offer the remedy. Conversely, attempts to maintain formal structures "because of the principle of the thing" can cause chaos to gravitate to disorder and explode into disaster. Informal processes make up to 90 percent of all activities. To use them by first being aware and accepting of them, and then respecting their impact on collective behavior, can lead to the miracle of synergy. The most dangerous course, Rifkin points out, is the safest course, the one that permits no risks, but sponsors instead a set of contrived civilities. Nature cannot be so easily fooled.

Entropy is a natural phenomenon that should not be ignored. It is natural for an organization to decline and to slip into chaos. Denial does not change this. The best way to reverse the chaos and re-establish the desired order is to deal with people problems with maturity, patience, and insight. An organization is not a thing. It is a human group. People got the organization where it is, and people are responsible for its decline. Therefore, it follows that people can get the organization back on track. The fiction holds today that technology is the answer, that technology can get the organization back on track. It cannot. It will not. And it has not in the past. Robotics, computers, creative finance, telecommunication in all its wonder, capital manipulation, mergers, leveraged buyouts, and acquisitions, among other means, are temporary measures. In the beginning as in the end, people make the difference. As long as the organization is guided with this truth, it will survive. People will find the answer if given an opportunity to see themselves as part of the problem. Technology is solution-driven, often at the expense of people. In truth, technology can unwittingly foster social disruption, discontinuity, and finally incipient catastrophe— which is maximum entropy or organizational death.

The Changing Cultural Landscape of Work

Author Charles D. Hayes in his excellent *Self-University Newsletter* (Fall 1996) writes,

> *Traditional education in America has caused millions of people to conclude that education is something you can "finish"...The external push for degrees in order to qualify for high-paying jobs often blinds us*

to the fact that education is as necessary for our general well-being as it is for economic opportunity...even though full employment is increasingly problematic, many of us are better at "earning a living" than we are at "living a living."[22]

Imagine the frustration of J. M. Juran (who came to America from Romania as a small boy), Peter Drucker (from Austria), and native-born W. Edwards Deming when they had to go abroad to test their ideas. There was no market for them in America. These three historic personages have changed the landscape of work but have had to work the unimaginative American mind for more than 60 years, and still their contributions are more appreciated abroad than at home. As Charles D. Hayes points out, Americans are knowers, not learners, and are dedicated to the status quo at almost any cost.

Think of it. Juran and Deming worked at Western Electric's Hawthorne Works in Chicago with industrial psychologist Elton Mayo in 1927 in the famous *Hawthorne Study*. They began with a conventional industrial-engineering approach, treating workers as part of the machinery to be manipulated by efficiency experts.[23] Their initial experiments varied the lighting in the factory to observe its effects on production. But no matter whether they turned the lights up or down, production seemed to increase. Mayo's associates hit on the idea that the workers were responding to being studied. Instead of treating them like cogs in a machine, someone was interested in them personally, and the workers appreciated the attention.

To test this so-called "Hawthorne Effect," the Mayo team set up further experiments in the factory in which they paid attention to the personal reactions of workers. Results verified their original findings. Unfortunately, these researchers "threw the baby out with the bath water." They concluded that studies of organization were no longer appropriate for technologically oriented engineers and management scientists. They reasoned these studies should now be placed in the hands of human relations experts. Moreover, the emphasis should be placed squarely on the dynamics of informal groups with none of the brutal clarity of Frederick Winslow Taylor's *Scientific Management* (1911).[24] The "human relations movement," however, was simply as one-dimensional in the direction of the irrational as Taylor's scheme was one-dimensional in the direction of the rational—an equal nightmare in terms of the *deus ex machina*. Nothing is either/or but always either and or.

America has a penchant, once it decides to change, to treat "what was" with disdain and "what is to be" as if divine. This is a powerful error and a cultural flaw. Juran-Deming-Drucker are right about quality, but they show a disregard for culture. "Don't change corporate culture," Drucker writes in *The Wall Street Journal* (March 28, 1991). "What we need is to change organization behavior."[25] This displays a total ignorance of the way human beings perform in a group. It is as impossible to change behavior without changing the workplace culture as it would be to defy the laws of gravity and attempt to jump off a mountain and expect to survive. The reason the Asian societies profited so much from the work of Juran-Deming-Drucker is because these societies had cultural climates conducive to their ideas. These societies sustain cultural institutions to perform basic cultural tasks, ensuring that their children are well educated, keeping the sanctity of the family paramount, systematically diverting money from consumption to savings, and attracting highly talented citizens to government service. These behaviors are possible because their cultures create a climate for such behaviors and an infrastructure which supports them. The American culture does not, cannot, and will not as long as ignorance and arrogance are esteemed over humble exploration.

This absurdity is captured by Hayes and confirmed by a 1995 National Survey of College Freshmen put out each year by UCLA's Higher Education Institute.[26] Incoming college students "are increasingly disengaged from the academic experience," according to the study.[27] Only 35 percent of the students said they spent six or more hours a week studying or doing homework compared to 43.7 percent in 1987. And the 1995 survey reports 33.9 percent of the students claim to be bored with their studies. "During the last decade, college students have changed for the worse," chemistry professor Henry Bauer of Virginia Tech said in a paper presented at an academic meeting in Orlando, Florida. "An increasing proportion carry a chip on their shoulder and expect good grades without attending class or studying," he adds. "The real problem is students who won't study," writes a Penn State professor. Another professor from Southern Connecticut State adds, "I found my students progressively more ignorant, inattentive, and inarticulate." Still another professor from Virginia Tech admits, "Unprecedented numbers of students rarely come to class. They have not read the material and have scant interest in learning it." Another professor states that many students come to class when they have nothing better to do. At one of his classes, no students at all showed up. Peter Sacks, the pseudonym for a California journalist, depicts the prevalent attitudes in his new book *Generation X Goes to College* (1996). Sacks produces a devastating portrait of bored and unmotivated students unwilling to read or study but feeling entitled to high grades because they see themselves as consumers "buying" an education from teachers, whose job they see as delivering the product of a degree to them. Disengaged rudeness is typical of these students. Sacks found students often chat loudly, sleep, talk on cell phones, and even watch television during class, paying attention only when something amusing or entertaining occurs. *Getting an education is the job of students, every bit as much a job as being a wage-earner. The decline of the work ethic was culturally institutionalized with grade inflation, along with the human relations of hand-holding (the assumption that teachers would solve students' personal problems as surrogate parents), social promotions (allowing students to be promoted to the next grade who demonstrated none of the skills required of that level of education), and the watering down of educational standards to accommodate a generation of students who are increasingly disengaged from anything resembling an intellectual life.*

Equally disturbing is that students show the same inclination that workers display when reacting to opinion surveys: the number one quality students want in a teacher is to be entertaining and for education to be fun. Education, as is the workplace, is in the midst of a profound cultural upheaval that completely changes everything.

What is amusing about this scene is displayed in the reaction of many baby-boomer parents. Tom Jackson of *The Tampa Tribune* (September 8, 1996) reports the same baby-boomer militants who made school grunge possible now blame the way kids dress for everything from declining SAT scores and hallway violence to rampant truancy and lousy cafeteria manners.[28] Alas, it is an interesting time!

In *The End of the American Century* (1990), Steven Schlossstein confirms this in his comparison of East Asian societies with the United States.[29] He finds a disproportionate number of children in America fail to learn the basic skills of modern life, claiming this as America's greatest weakness. On the other hand, he sees academic standards in the best American colleges and the schools that feed them as far above those of these same Asian nations. Schlossstein makes it clear, however, that putting pressure on elite schools to reverse the trend is not the answer. It is the pervasive culture that dominates which makes the difference. This is graphically illustrated in one aspect of Asian education. According to scholars of Asian educa-

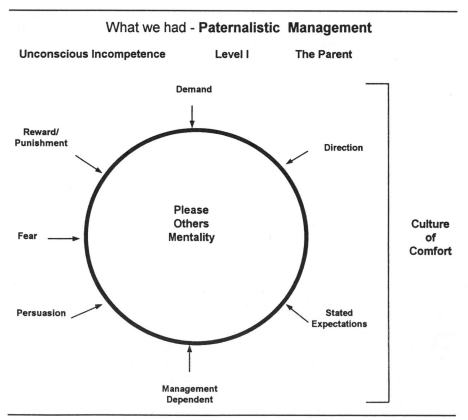

Figure 7.2   The Culture of Comfort—Management acts as a parent in creating a management-dependent workforce.

tion, what makes education function so positively, while supplying Asian societies with the type of workers to remain competitive, is that their worst graduates are so well educated. No matter where we start, we always end in the same place—the culture of comfort has a lock on America!

The Culture of Comfort

"The lust for comfort," Kahlil Gibran notes, "enters the house a guest, and then becomes a host, and then a master." So true. The Culture of Comfort (Figure 7.2) snuck up on America in the dead of a winter's night in 1950 when all was quiet and America was the envy of the world. America was slumbering in the twilight, the city on the hill, looking down on an adoring world, tranquilized by the narcotic "what America touches, America makes holy." It was an American illusion transposed to a 1950s conclusion.

For those who have forgotten the 1950s or weren't yet born when America passed through them, that was the decade which saw Rosa Parks, a tired black working lady, refuse to move to the back of the bus in Montgomery, Alabama. America was unconscious of its fatigue, incompetent to deal with changing social demands. This ushered in the Civil Rights movement, which was to forever change the American landscape. America was paralyzed by comfort, ruled by management but not led anywhere. Corporate America lacked vision, will, understanding, and purpose as it failed to perceive the shifting forces within the working middle class. More Americans than ever before entered the workforce with professional credentials after lengthy educations. In the 1950s, armed with the G.I. Bill from World War II, veterans stormed the American campuses with a passion to learn, mature beyond their years. Meanwhile, Dwight David Eisenhower, the custodial president, ruled with the magnetic smile as the baby-boomer generation, which was to carry America into the next century, was being born. The combination of too much, too many, too soon invaded the American culture and took possession of it.

Against this backdrop, a new phenomenon was taking hold—everyone wanted to be a manager! Having a title after one's name became as important as the money the title commanded. *Management creep* started out metaphorically like the flu and by transmutation became a cancer that metastasized throughout every fissure until the organization was essentially immobilized. Typically, an organization in the 1950s that employed 4,000 people had a general manager, who was not a vice president; a manager of operations, who was not a director; a manager of administration and finance, who handled personnel as well; and department foremen, who were not managers but supervised all activities. The total management staff of an operation with 4,000 employees was unlikely to be more than 50 people. Before the downsizing, redundancy exercises, streamlining, re-engineering, and policies of attrition of the 1990s, that same 4,000-base company was likely to have a minimum of 250 to a maximum of 400 managers. Even with the radical surgery of the 1990s, however, most companies of 4,000 employees have at least 200 managers. Little has changed beyond the rhetoric.

The irony of this malignancy is that it has paralleled the rise of the professional working class. Better educated than managers of the 1950s, these workers remain programmed as if this were the 1950s. Little note has been taken that these workers need much less supervision. There is a scandalous excess of people at the top and at the bottom in management roles. Middle management takes the rap for excess, with some justification, but top management brings in an army of MBAs to replace it, while the ranks of first-line supervisors have hardly thinned at all. If anything, these supervisors discourage work or get in the way of it.

Nonetheless, you would think that it was management that made the difference and not the workers. *Business Month* (November 1988) wailed the plight of management with the headline: "The Management Purges—Although the recent wave of corporate streamlining has greatly improved profit margins, it has so decimated executive ranks that America may never recover."[30] Not to worry. Management continues to take care of management, if not business. In one multinational corporation of 100,000 employees worldwide, downsizing was launched in 1986 with a vengeance. HRD was in charge of managing this process. By 1988, the workforce was reduced to 74,000 employees—a reduction of 26 percent. Meanwhile, the management staff across multinational operations was reduced by less than 3 percent. As for HRD, it profited by the exercise—going from four to nine vice presidents.

Human nature expects survival to be the prime motivator in a downsizing process. Obviously, management could not be the culprit, right? The culprit is the workplace culture. But is it? More to the point, how can you separate culture from management? After all, the workplace culture evolved over time to support management's agenda and self-interests, possibly at the expense of the organization. Then too, operational behavior is consistent with management's edicts and declarations. Ironically, crisis management receives great kudos when successful (such as downsizing and subsequent re-profitability). Few note that management solves primarily those crises it creates through ineptitude. Yet, those sought for positions of CEOs in American firms must be great problem-solvers. Problem-solving ability is equated with top executive performance.

Robert McNamara, who epitomizes this profile, was recruited from Detroit by President Kennedy to be Secretary of Defense. McNamara and his band of business-school whiz kids processed numbers well in the Vietnam War that defied processing. Stubbornly determined to demonstrate success quantitatively, body count was used as an index of the war's progress rather than political reality. Failing to understand the culture of the enemy, the war leaders became bogged down in the steamy muck of an unstoppable and incomprehensible guerrilla war, one that claimed 58,000 American lives.[31] Vietnam was reminiscent of the American Revolution in which the British, in full bright regalia, marched like splendid paraders in open plains against the Minutemen snipers, who hid in bushes, trees, behind rocks, and in river beds and shot the enemy like sitting ducks. America had evolved a culture foreign to the British, a culture which fought war in its own style, not in the enemy's. The more things change, the more they remain the same.

Some readers will remember the crisp, rigid, self-assured McNamara as he appeared daily on American television, the man we felt ideal to guide an undefeated military machine. But now we know that he knew early on that it would never work. He just never disclosed the truth. He confesses in his 1995 biography *In Retrospect* that he was soldiering in a job in which he no longer believed.[32] The mockery of this admission is that it displays an executive arrogance which has tainted leadership most of this century. Leadership can no longer play the parent and carry the burden of society as if no one else is capable. Nor can leadership expect to avoid crises by overcontrolling or playing to human weakness and ignorance for comfort. What is most scary about McNamara's book is that he openly admits to being unsophisticated, culturally speaking, and this misled him into thinking that North Vietnam and China were a common monolith, not actually the century-old enemies that they were. Taking this out of the context of politics and into the frame of commerce and industry—and noting that it is now internationally driven—you get a sense of how sophisticated and culturally urbane leadership must be today for survival.

Worker disenchantment is built into worker comfort. Professional workers, in particular, seek education as the vehicle for attaining freedom and satisfaction in work and for gaining control of their lives. Workers are given, instead, money for what is increasingly non-work, counterfeit work, or simply "make do work." This adds to their disappointment and resentment while it gives them a sense of being trapped—imprisoned by their dependence on money. Comfort pervades the spirit of the educated, who are often not educated at all. They claim their right to that distinction for staying in school for a number of years, but the skills they bring to their function are frequently of a marginal nature. The result is that inflation has invaded the job market. Work previously performed by technicians now requires a graduate engineer, and so on.

Given this scenario, what do professionals do? Do they empower themselves by seeking more challenging work? Do they demand more responsibility? No. They know work is driven by money, and so they seek more money to bring attention to their angst. Privately, they will admit they are being paid more than they are worth, doing what they are doing, but money is a means of self-protection. It isolates them from the ugliness around them and justifies (to themselves) the reason they come to work every day. It is a cynical attitude displayed in a self-mocking comeback: "Making money demands gets management's attention. Besides, money is the only game in town."

Money is a hedge against personal commitment or communal involvement. If money doesn't materialize, the *six silent killers* are produced instantaneously. Professional workers are in a frantic search for status, role, place, and comfort (Figure 7.2). The higher their anxiety, the deeper their depression, which invariably spills over into their private lives. They are often angry, unhappy workers without a cause, unaware of the basis of their anger or the reason they feel helpless to extricate themselves from their circumstances. They accept the label of *victim* cheerlessly and without humor, then go on to play the role.

Management Dependence and the Culture of Comfort

The seeds of comfort grew out of the Great Depression of the 1930s. Many felt too helpless to control their own destiny and were relieved when government took over. The Public Works Administration (PWA) and the Works Projects Administration (WPA) put a lot of people to work, and the Social Security Act of 1935 gave citizens a safety net of sorts. This was a modest effort, however, compared to the momentum gained by the 1950s, when corporate America took up the burden. Benign paternalism now reigned supreme, playing the surrogate role of strict parent to the worker's obedient child. Motivation now is promoted by fear-based rewards and punishments. Hell's fire is put under workers, not into them.

The whole cultural conditioning process of the Culture of Comfort is designed to please the authority of management. The controllers of behavior are fear of failure (failure to please), fear of discovery (guilt or shame for deviancy), and fear of success (failure to sustain pleasing). Most readers know something of these fears. We sign up for fear's rewards and punishments at an early age. Cultural conditioning is designed to maintain proper behavior, to sustain a social fit with others, and to accept, even relish, the confinement of organization. Individualism, an American characteristic, obviously becomes somewhat confused in these contradictions. The result is social instability, uncertainty of purpose, insecurity, and a dependence on authority where consistency resides—i.e., *management dependence.*

With the perpetuation of the "should not's" and the "don't do's," the 1950s institutionalized the negative as a manifestation of parental wisdom and caring. This unwittingly sponsored a disconnect between what a person could be and what he was, between what he wanted and what he needed, between what he thought and what he felt. No longer did a person naturally turn to himself to inquire as to the status of these dimensions of his being. He no longer felt confident that he had the answers or even a right to ask the questions. This self-estrangement, which was culturally inculcated by the workplace culture and the cultural infrastructure, was branded into the worker's psyche by his work. He no longer was involved in planning, organizing, controlling or managing his work but was given a piece of a complex whole with which he felt no ownership and little identity with the final product. Fifty years later, contrary to what empowerment advocates would profess, *paternalism* has not relinquished its hold, resulting in the most persistent behavior in organization, that of the obedient 12-year-old child in a 50-year-old body.

The Culture of Comfort looks for the exception, not the rule, for what is wrong. Comfort is motivated by failure, not success, more inclined to look for what is not working than what is. Comfort is addicted to problem-solving and, therefore, is solution-driven. Comfort will never run out of problems because "problems are its most important product."

This spills over into relationships. There is a dread of giving compliments and, therefore, a fear of dispensing reprimands. There is a false modesty associated with success because there is always a fear of failure. "Think the worst," the comfortable say, "and you will never be disappointed." Pleasure is also suspect. If what one is doing feels good, it must be wrong, unhealthy, or illegal. Comfort demands that we see ourselves as victims, not responsible for our own actions, as ploys in someone else's game. Comfort finds it easier to complain than to create, to take criticism personally rather than try to understand how behavior offends. The comfortable take others' opinions of themselves more seriously than their own. They wear physical pain as a badge ("See my scar!") while avoiding the hazards of psychological pain (confronting an adversary). The comfortable see everyone better off than they see themselves—having more money, better looks, or more advantages. On the other hand, the comfortable have a fear of letting the group down (family, church, school, club, gender, race, country, religion, company, and friends) but little fear of letting themselves down, which compels them to do just that. The comfortable feel obliged to have an answer to everything because they have a fear of not being smart.

Against this cultural umbrella of comfort, a privileged few (paternalistic hierarchy) orchestrate the demands of the organization to the passive many (management-dependent workers). In another time, this system worked reasonably well. Paternalism champions the belief that knowers (management) understand what doers (workers) need and want. The educated minority (managers) saw themselves as responsible for the contributions of the ignorant majority (workers). Now, education is equally distributed throughout the organization and requires a new game plan. In some cases, the roles have actually been reversed, with management as the ignorant minority and workers as the knowledgeable majority. The 1950s cultural bias and belief system, in any case, is no longer apropos.

An Army of the Night

When the twentieth century was young, when times were simpler and everything moved more slowly, management was reasonably effective as surrogate parent to workers. Management made demands, gave directions, stated expectations, controlled rewards and punishment, and played on workers' fears and their need to please. The workers, whatever their age, behaved with the emotional maturity of children. They went quite naturally from parental dependency (home) to teacher dependency (school) to management dependency (work). Like children, workers exercise little responsible behavior without direction. Peter Drucker, who comes from a paternalistic vintage, states that, "The only things that evolve by themselves in an organization are disorder, friction, and malperformance."[33] Obviously, with this paternalistic perspective, workers need managers to guide, direct, control, counsel, and coach them to effectiveness. This is the bias of the Culture of Comfort. What management sows so shall it also reap.

By the mid-1950s, an army of the night was quietly positioning itself to dominate. Tens of thousands of spirited management trainees, engineers, and other technicians, with fresh diplomas in hand, marched into organizations to seek positions, not jobs; security, not opportunity; comfort, not challenge. Incredibly, they found it all waiting for them as expected. America was booming, and by the accident of their birth, they were coming of age when nothing was impossible.

This army of the night was politically naive and spiritually dull; seekers, not explorers. While most failed to find true purpose or happiness, they had no trouble finding comfort. This first iteration of professionals in the twentieth century was not the obedient 12-year-olds described earlier. They weren't mature either. More likely they were wrestling with some doubt and unconscious rebellion. World War II had changed the world, and they were stepping into no-man's-land. This ambivalence and confusion was captured in a popular film of the time, *Rebel Without a Cause* (1955), with the quintessential confused kid of the era, James Dean, along with Natalie Wood and Sal Mineo.[34] These actors portrayed teenagers dissatisfied with a world they didn't create. They didn't know what they wanted, only that they didn't want to be boot-lickers like their parents, groveling to authority.

This army of the night was turned on by the "Beat Generation," reading William Burroughs's salacious novel *The Naked Lunch* (1954) with picaresque guilt,[35] the nihilistic (1950s) poetry of Allen Ginsberg,[36] and Jack Kerouac's insouciant novel *On The Road* (1958).[37] Life was pointless with "the bomb" (hydrogen) hanging over everyone's head. The primal urge was "in" and expressed in scatological terms. No one succeeded better at this than J. P. Donleavy in *The Ginger Man* (1959).[38] Donleavy's chaotic humor caught its fancy, as did J. D. Salinger's contempt for the status quo in *The Catcher in the Rye* (1951).[39]

Comfort was endemic to this army of the night as it displayed a timid soul and a preference for being spectator to the real. Reckless experience was as foreign to it as combat would be to the Pope. This army was into comfort, not pain, and vicarious adventure, not risk. It carried in its soul the spirit of enterprise but found no safe place to put it. So, its rebellion was mainly whimsical, safely expressed through books, films, and "irreverent thoughts." This army marked the end of America's extended innocence—the protected isolation from the world beyond its oceans—and the end of its safety net. Yet, true to its colors, it had no intention of letting reality get in its way. This army would continue to seek comfort, which only increased its discomfort. Erich Fromm saw this shifting in terms of dependency—a mass social movement from home (family) dependency to organizational (employer) dependency. The seekers sought psychological and physiological sanctuary without encountering the world of uncertainty. In other words, seekers wanted a sure thing. Fromm cautions in *To Have or To Be?* (1976) that freedom demands embracing uncertainty, not comfort, for freedom can be realized in no other way:

> *Not to move forward, to stay where we are, to regress...to rely on what we have, is very tempting, for what we have, we know; we can hold onto it, feel secure in it. We fear, and consequently avoid, taking a step into the unknown, the uncertain; for, indeed, while the step may not appear risky to us after we have taken it, before we take that step, the new aspects beyond it appear very risky; and hence frightening. Only the old,*

the tried, is safe; or so it seems. Every new step contains the danger of failure, and that is one of the reasons people are so afraid of freedom.[40]

Management understood the army of the night and was ready to employ it. Explosive growth was in the air, and management had an appetite for empire-building. "More is better" became the accepted practice. Promotions and compensation were based on the size of one's staff, not necessarily what the function accomplished, for only token reference was made to performance. Growth blinded nearly everyone. As organizations swelled with people, so did job titles. An enterprising supervisor could work the system to build an organization and see his job status and title change progressively—section head, department head, manager, director, vice president, even president of operations. This writer has seen this happen on more than one occasion. Such a supervisor creates an army of like-minded individuals, who subscribe to the same belief and value system, and who have an equal ambition. So, each of these lieutenants goes about building an organization, creating a network of pyramids, all reporting to the initial supervisor. Network marketing never had a better showcase.

What first disturbed this "Camelot" world was not economic constraints, but working women.[41] With men away in World War II, tens of thousands of women did the work of men in defense plants, proficient at spot-welding, drafting, electrical circuiting, and so on. With the war's conclusion, women failed to leave the workforce in the numbers expected and by the early 1960s were returning to industry in droves. Automation, which was labor unions' greatest fear, was changing work requirements, placing more emphasis on skill than brawn. Labor unions argued that automation would destroy the workforce and create an economic catastrophe. It didn't. It merely started the process of changing the collar of workers from blue to white. Yet, after 30 years of virtual dominance in the world market (1945–75) with American products, the surge was over; product demand had peaked and declined precipitously. Suddenly, Japan and Europe started to replace traditional American products at home as well.

By 1975 the economic decline in the United States was certain, but not apparent. It was not apparent because optimism continued to command the American psyche. In retrospect, it seems incredible that as:

- Wages soared, productivity declined.
- Grades in school escalated, student performance bottomed out at embarrassingly low levels. Socially promoted high school graduates couldn't read, write, or handle simple computations.
- The standard of living ceased to be a function of productivity, it became, instead, a function of borrowed optimism on the future. America moved from a creditor to a debtor nation.

In a more specific sense, management fed this optimism. Nor was there any shortage of writers to encourage management in its fainthearted practices. No one wrote that management was being cowardly, ignorant, or arrogant in its approach to business. The books produced in this era were safe, not risky, and as Fromm might put it, were "an escape from freedom." A plethora of motivation and productivity books illuminated the way, including Saul Gellerman's *Management by Motivation* (1968),[42] Frederick Herzberg's *Work and the Nature of Man* (1966),[43] David McClelland's *The Achieving Society* (1961),[44] Douglas McGregor's *Human Side of Enterprise* (1960),[45] Rensis Likert's *The Human Organization* (1967),[46] Kurt Lewin's *Field Theory in Social Science* (1951),[47] and Abraham Maslow's *Motivation and Personality* (1970).[48] These books were variously descriptive, analytical, quantitative, judgmental, value-laden, logical, searching, informational, and critical. They were also complete with categories, classifications, dichotomies, definitions, and generalizations. In other words, they were locked into problem-solving discovery, not into designing a departure from conventional thinking—not a single one of them. Yet, pick up any business journal today, and precisely the same malaise that tormented the cultural landscape of work 50 years ago persists to torment it today. Industry is still desperately seeking a dose of productivity. The sad performance in the late 1990s has already lifted the cost of doing business because wages and benefits of workers continue to grow faster than productivity.[49] This finds Drucker lamenting, "We know nothing about motivation. All we can do is write books about it."[50]

Even so, management watchers, with few exceptions, persist in considering money as the greatest motivator. The belief endures, despite the fiasco of Bethlehem Steel and Alcoa, despite the experiences in the automotive industry, despite the callous behavior of well-paid entertainers and professional athletes. As many of the latter's private lives break into print (e.g., failure to pay child support despite multimillion-dollar incomes), it becomes obvious that money has not produced Nirvana.

True, money succeeds in getting workers' attention, but what impact does it have on their psychology, on their behavior? The psychology of pay is derived from what satisfaction work brings to the person and how it enhances the person's sense of individual worth. Perhaps one reason the world is so angry, hostile, violent, and self-pitying is because money is not the imagined panacea. The horror stories of many lottery winners find money is their "Alcatraz," a barren prison surrounded by a sea of avaricious sharks. In the end, if work is not satisfying and spiritually renewing, money only aggravates the dissatisfaction. From steel workers to baseball players, there is an echo: "I want the organization to respect me as a person and to recognize me for my contributions." Money is never enough. Money does little to assuage dissatisfaction. And money cannot be a substitute for being treated with respect and dignity. Having said that, the beat goes on, as it is:

- Easier to increase wages of workers than to yield to the workers' demands for control of their work and the freedom to operate in a trusting environment.
- Easier to replace workers than to provide workers that now exist with the training, opportunity, and challenge of meaningful work.
- Easier to serve the needs of senior management than to support the requirements of workers to do the job. What often prevents workers

from being productive is the lack of the appropriate tools and training to use such tools properly.

- Easier to remain parochial and proprietary than to adapt to a changing world.
- Easier to focus on profits than to treat workers as assets and deal with them accordingly.

The consequence of this fixation with things at the expense of people has led to unconscious incompetence and the Culture of Comfort—unconscious because all motivation is derived from external stimuli—putting a fire under workers, not into them. This is the way four-legged animals are motivated. Without a fire in the belly of the worker, there is no sense of individual responsibility. Incompetent because most work is counterfeit work or "make work," work that has always been done "this way" even though such work has only a marginal function or little real purpose. Included in such descriptions are most of the functions of supervisors, paperwork, reports, meetings, conferences, and even training sessions. Incompetency prevails because the need to please others remains central to "the way to get along is to go along." Pleasing others never put a fire in the belly in the history of man, and it is unlikely to do so now. Pleasing others may put a fire under a worker, but this takes an enormous amount of energy, constant surveillance, and still doesn't last very long. Incompetency also prevails because the prescription of most jobs is to learn the job, which then becomes behaviorally fixed rather than part of a continual learning experience. The worker produces, grows for 2 years, and coasts for 38. This was acceptable in industrial society, but not in this post-industrial age.

In the Culture of Comfort, the pain of new experience is avoided because the price is too high.[51] The risk of failure is considered greater than the reward for trying. Safety, security, and comfort dominate motivation so that a victim complex is not unusual. Comfort has resulted in cultural drift and institutional collapse, but without paternalistic authority loosening its hold on society. Comfort continues to foster non-responsibility and learned helplessness as benign paternalism suspends workers in terminal adolescence. In organizations, this is shown as being more important to fit than to soar, to impress than produce, to be passive than assertive, to avoid conflict than manage it, to follow than lead, to seek comfort than challenge, to sacrifice than gain, to meet the needs of others than one's own, and to go with the flow. This cultural inculcation has been eminently successful, however inappropriate. Mediocrity is celebrated while brilliance is suspect.[52]

Nearly 40 years ago, deep in this dilemma and fighting the phantom challenge of comfort, the organization turned to human resources, the people's advocate, to extricate itself from this crippling abomination. Management was comfortable with issues involving things, but not issues involving people. It abdicated its role and delegated without precedence its function to a group that had never known such power. HRD rose out of the human relations movement, a movement that created a stir, as pointed out earlier, but which never delivered. A worse nightmare is about to unfold as HRD sought to achieve the Culture of Contribution, only to embrace the Culture of Complacency.

Endnotes

1. Leslie Hart, *How the Brain Works: A New Understanding of Human Learning, Emotions & Thinking* (New York: Basic Books, 1975), p. 100.
2. Kahlil Gibran, *The Prophet* (New York: Knopf, 1972), p. 32.
3. Kathy M. Kristof (*The Los Angeles Times*), "The Golden Parachute," *The Tampa Tribune-Times*, May 27, 1990, Business section, 1.
4. James R. Fisher, Jr., *The Taboo Against Being Your Own Best Friend* (Tampa: The Delta Group Florida, 1996), pp. 85–87.
5. "Greed Clearly Back in Style for CEO Pay" *(Wall Street Journal Report)*, *The Tampa Tribune,* April 13, 1995, Business/Finance, 1, 8. Carl E. Reichardt, Wells Fargo ($16.4 million); Reuben Mark, Colgate-Palmolive ($15.8 million); James E. Cayne, Bear Stearns ($14.6 million); Hugh L. McColl, Jr., NationsBank ($13.7 million); Eckhard Pfeiffer, Compaq Computer ($13.2 million); Lawrence A. Bossidy, AlliedSignal ($12.4 million); Maurice R. Greenberg, American International ($12.1 million); and Roberto C. Goizueta, Coca-Cola ($12.1 million). What is a bit humorous about this is that in an attempt to get CEO compensation under control, several companies have linked the boss's check to the firm's stock price. Here is a sampling of 1996 CEO compensation on that basis: Nolan Archibald, Black & Decker ($6.5 million, 83% salary increase, return to shareholders –13%); Gilbert Amelio, Apple Computer ($23 million, return to shareholders –40%); Lawrence Coss, Green Tree Financial ($137 million, 109% salary increase, return to shareholders +47%); and Michael Eisner, Walt Disney ($204 million, 1,283% salary increase, return to shareholders +10.9%). Source: *Time*, April 28, 1997, 59.
6. Donald L. Barlett and James B. Steele, *America: What Went Wrong?* (Kansas City: McMeel, 1992), pp. 1–30. The authors present a disturbing picture of the dismantling of the middle class.
7. "After Layoffs, Should CEO Get Pay Raise?" *(A Wall Street Journal Report)*, *The Tampa Tribune*, April 16, 1995. Albert J. Dunlap, CEO and chairman of Scott Paper, Inc., cut the company staff of the second largest consumer products company in the United States by a third, or nearly 12,000 jobs. This resulted in the company stock doubling in value or appreciating $6.5 billion. Dunlap took over the helm in April 1994 and was able to accomplish this turnaround in 19 months. For it, he received a salary of $1 million and a bonus of $2.5 million. His predecessor in 1993 received a salary of $617,918 and no bonus. Was Dunlap happy? On the contrary, he was quite incensed. He felt he was grossly underpaid, and says so in his book *Mean Business: How I Save Bad Companies and Make Good Companies Great* (New York: Random House, 1996). Compared to colleagues, he may have a point (see endnote #5).
8. Associated Press report, *The Tampa Tribune*, April 18, 1996, Business section, 1. AT&T CEO and chairman Robert Allen eliminated 40,000 jobs and accepted a $16 million compensation package, confessing, "I feel no pain."
9. David M. Gordon writes about Mr. Allen in *Fat and Mean: The Corporate Squeeze of Working Americans and the Myth of Managerial "Downsizing"* (New York: Free Press, 1996).

10. Ralph Estes, *The Tyranny of the Bottom Line: Why Corporations Make Good People Do Bad Things* (San Francisco: Berrett-Koehler, 1996).

11. Susan C. Faludi (*The Wall Street Journal*), "The Leverage Buyout of Safeway Stores," *St. Petersburg Times*, May 27, 1990, Business section, 1.

12. Michael Ryan, "They Call Their Boss a Hero," *Parade Magazine*, September 8, 1996, 4–5.

13. Jeremy Rifkin (with Ted Howard), *Entropy: A New World View* (London: Paladin Books, 1985), pp. 16, 76, 90, 141.

14. Ernest Becker, *The Birth and Death of Meaning* (New York: The Free Press, 1971), p. 29: "By the time we grow up we become masters at dissimulation, at cultivating a self that the world cannot probe...We have become victims of our own art. We touch people on the outside of their bodies, and they us, but we cannot get at their insides and cannot reveal our insides to them. This is one of the great tragedies..." And later, "A large part of the evil that man unleashes on himself and his world stems not from a wickedness in his heart, but from the way he was conditioned to see the world and to seek satisfaction in it" (p. 185).

15. James R. Fisher, Jr., "America Is Dead! Long Live America!" *St. Petersburg Evening Independent*, January 1, 1976, Op-Ed, 13.

16. Robert Heilbroner, "Seize the Day," *The New York Review*, February 15, 1990, 30–31.

17. U.S. Statistical Abstract Table No. 1397, 1985.

18. Many parents, disgusted with the failure of public education, have resorted to a throwback to the nineteenth century, "home school."

19. Heilbroner, op. cit., p. 31.

20. Rifkin, op. cit., p. 274.

21. Ibid., p. 50.

22. Charles D. Hayes, "Real Education Begins in September," *Self-University Newsletter*, Fall 1996. Charles Hayes is an American phenomenon. He has written two books, *Proving You're Qualified: Strategies for Competent People without College Degrees* (1995) and *Self-University: The Price of Tuition Is the Desire to Learn. Your Degree Is a Better Life* (1993).

23. Randall Collins and Michael Makowsky, *The Discovery of Society* (New York: Random House, 1972), pp. 165–166. See also George C. Homans, *The Human Group* (New York: Harcourt, Brace & World, 1959), Chapters 3–6.

24. Frederick Winslow Taylor, *The Principles of Scientific Management* (New York: W.W. Norton, 1967), pp. 72–78.

25. Peter Drucker, "Don't Change Corporate Culture," *The Wall Street Journal*, March 28, 1991, Op-Ed, 32.

26. Charles D. Hayes, *Proving You're Qualified* (Wasilla, AK: Autodidactic Press, 1995), pp. 7–13.

27. John Leo, "Many Students Just Want to Be Entertained, Professors Complain," *The Tampa Tribune*, September 14, 1996, Commentary page. This finds English majors at Georgetown no longer study Shakespeare or Chaucer; Emerson College has abolished its Western Civilization requirement, while Yale offers 50 courses in homosexual studies (Jeff Jacoby, *The Tampa Tribune*, May 31, 1997, Nation/World, 16).

28. Tom Jackson, "Clothes Make the Student—or Do They?" *The Tampa Tribune*, September 8, 1996, Commentary section, 1.

29. Steven Schlossstein, *The End of the American Century* (New York: Congdon & Weed, 1989), pp. 219–243.

30. Paul Hirsch, "The Management Purge," *Business Month,* November 1988, 39.

31. Paul Hendrickson, *The Living and the Dead: Robert McNamara and Five Lives of a Lost War* (New York: Knopf, 1996).
32. Robert S. McNamara, *In Retrospect: The Tragedy and Lessons of Vietnam* (New York: Random House, 1995).
33. John J. Tarrant, *Drucker: The Man Who Invented the Corporate Society* (New York: Warner Books, 1976), p. 311.
34. *Rebel Without a Cause*, 1955 film. Prototype 1950s-generation movie with James Dean, Natalie Wood, and Sal Mineo. Cast also included Jim Backus, Corey Allen, Edward Platt, Dennis Hopper, and Nick Adams; directed by Nicholas Ray.
35. William S. Burroughs, *The Naked Lunch* (reprint of 1954 edition) (New York: Grove Press, 1969).
36. Allen Ginsberg, *Reality Sandwiches. Poems: 1953–1960* (San Francisco: City Lights, 1963).
37. Jack Kerouac, *On the Road* (reprint of 1958 edition) (New York: Penguin Books, 1979).
38. James Patrick Donleavy, *The Ginger Man* (reprint of 1959 edition) (New York: Dell Publishing, 1970).
39. J. P. Salinger, *The Catcher in the Rye* (reprint of 1951 edition) (New York: Bantam Books, 1977).
40. Erich Fromm, *To Have or To Be?* (New York: Harper & Row, 1976), p. 95.
41. Some of the activities which followed the war now seem comical. Returning veterans were promised their old jobs back, creating a glut of unemployed women, many of whom were reluctant to step aside. A propaganda campaign followed. For instance, the government came out with recipe books with instructions on how to prepare a three- to four-hour dinner, which replaced 30-minute recipes promoted during the war. Home-centered activity booklets of all sorts were produced. These were promoted over the radio, in newspapers, through the mail, and in movie newsreel clips, to encourage women to be homebodies and homemakers. The hidden agenda was to discourage women from remaining in the workplace and competing with returning veterans for a limited number of jobs in industry and commerce.
42. Saul Gellerman, *Management by Motivation* (New York: AMACOM, 1968).
43. Frederick Herzberg, *Work and the Nature of Man* (New York: World Publishing, 1966).
44. David McClelland, *The Achieving Society* (Princeton, NJ: D. Van Nostrand, 1961).
45. Douglas McGregor, *The Human Side of Enterprise* (New York: McGraw Hill, 1960).
46. Rensis Likert, *The Human Organization* (New York: McGraw Hill, 1967).
47. Kurt Lewin, *Field Theory in Social Science* (New York: Harper & Row, 1973).
48. Abraham Maslow, *Motivation and Personality* (New York: Harper & Row, 1970).
49. James C. Cooper and Kathlene Madigan, *Business Week*, February 19, 1990, 27–28.
50. Tarrant, op. cit., p. 312.
51. Paul Kennedy, "Fin-de-Siecle America," *New York Review*, June 28, 1990, 31–40. Kennedy covers the debate between those who see America in decline and those who foresee a new millennium for America.
52. Paul Kennedy, *The Rise and Fall of the Great Powers: Economic Change and Military Conflict from 1500 to 2000* (New York: Random House, 1987). Kennedy sees the United States committing the same mistakes as other great powers of the past.

The Culture of Complacency

In place of the traditional ethic of self-denial and sacrifice, we now find an ethic that denies people nothing.[1]

Daniel Yankelovich

Once upon a time, when you were asked things you didn't care to talk about, "mind your own business" was a perfectly acceptable reply. Then came Phil and Oprah and Maury and Geraldo and Ricki and Montel and the gang, and nothing, it seems, is too private, too hush-hush, anymore. The walls—not to mention your bathroom and bedroom doors—have come tumbling down.[2]

Gary Reinmuth

The United States woke, after a 30-year nap, to discover that it wasn't a nightmare, but a catastrophe. On the dawn of Independence Day, 1976, America's 200th anniversary, the country awoke with an economic and spiritual hangover. For 30 years, America had been intoxicated with the spirit of invincibility. It had ignored the ominous signs of economic discontinuity and personal despair, reassuring itself with characteristic optimism. Double-digit inflation and unemployment found tens of thousands without jobs, while millions more were possessed with psychological terror. Two decades later (April 19, 1995), that terror became palpable with the bombing of the Federal Office Building in Oklahoma City (168 people lost their lives). That tragic act of terrorism by Timothy McVeigh was followed by the mysterious mid-air explosion of TWA Flight 800 (July 17, 1996), in which all aboard were killed. This tragedy continues to confound the experts. Paranoia and conspiracy theories seep through the complacent mask society wears as the Dow Jones Industrials hover around 8,000. Nothing is as it seems. The National Institute of Mental Health reports (1996 figures) that 16 percent of the U.S. population is suffering from a major mental illness or substance abuse in any given month. Severe mental illnesses are more common than cancer, diabetes, or heart disease. One out of four families is affected by severe mental illness in their lifetime, and more than 21 percent of all hospital beds are filled by patients with mental illness.[3] Meanwhile, according to the World Bank (1996), chronic health problems plague workers because of lifestyle propensities, including respiratory infections, heart disease, major depression, strokes, brain aneurysms, and chronic lung disease.

A climate of fear pervades our schools, with criminals in the classroom as the hard lesson of the 1990s. According to the Florida Education Coalition, the number of criminal offenses—from homicides to assaults and thefts—at Florida schools soared more than 34 percent in just one year, from 46,088 incidents in the 1990–91 school year to 61,842 in 1991–92. Those numbers don't include hundreds of thousands of incidents classified as disorderly conduct or other minor occurrences. Looking at schools at another level, in 1983 the National Commission on Excellence in Education released "A Nation at Risk."[4] This report warned of the rising tide of mediocrity that threatens the "very future as a Nation and a people." It went on to say, "If an unfriendly foreign power had attempted to impose on America the mediocre educational performance that exists today, we might well have viewed it as an act of war. As it stands, we have allowed this to happen to ourselves."

The slide into economic and psychological decline seemed gradual because the buffers were so great. It wasn't until the humiliation of Vietnam reached the nation's consciousness that reality started to break through. Staggering out of Vietnam, platitudes could no longer cover embarrassment. Nor was it an accident that the economic collapse coincided with a sudden withdrawal into personal searching. Introspective psychology, an enigmatic invention of the East, became a mainstream parlor game—from EST to Gestalt therapy, from psychoanalysis to reality therapy, from Rolfing to biofeedback, from bioenergetics to genetic research. Scientists were looking for the soul to quantify, while the average citizen was looking to escape reality. A conspiracy of madness-as-normalcy, more appropriate to a Jean Genet novel, became a $3 billion industry with 29,000 psychiatrists (M.D.'s), 26,000 clinical psychologists (Ph.D.'s), and more than 31,000 mental-health professionals ready to probe the nation's narcissistic psychic fixation. America had lost its confidence as well as its way.[5]

Social chronicler Daniel Yankelovich in *New Rules: Searching for Self-Fulfillment in a World Turned Upside Down* (1981) notes a perceptive shift in American values. He finds that from the mid-1960s to the mid-1970s, positive responses to "hard work always pays off" dropped from 72 percent to 40 percent for college students and to only 58 to 43 percent for the general public, suggesting that college-educated workers had grown more cynical.[6] Cynics today are in the Jeffries and Boeskys, the Siegels and Bakkers, the Harts and the Norths, the Darsees and the DeLoreans. Cynicism is common, but it is veiled with optimism, which leads to complacency. A growing number of people are indifferent to what they do, what they make, or what they become. Cynics or not, many have retreated into the protected clime of the Culture of Complacency (Figure 8.1).

What is happening and why? Downsizing has become labeled "dumbsizing."[7] Peace and tranquility, once taken for granted, has been supplanted by the image of

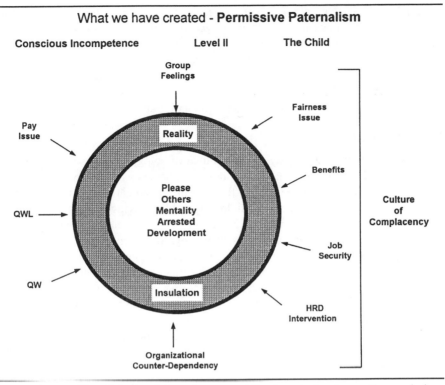

Figure 8.1   The Culture of Complacency: All attempts to change the workplace culture lie outside the individual.

"terror in the streets." Trust and love has been downgraded to cynicism while despair and mediocrity has graduated and gone to college. Reminders that there is trouble in Camelot are so frequent that a complacent public accepts them as part of the noise of modern life.

The Danger of Complacency

When the organization could no longer ignore the economic and psychological collapse of enterprise, it turned to social engineering to relieve it of its anxiety. HRD (originally the personnel function was handled by the finance department) was a post-1960s phenomenon. Even today, HRD remains unclear as to its role, being an eclectic function of recruiting, selecting, orientating, training, and placing personnel, along with tracking talent demographically, organizational development (OD), and wage and benefits administration. HRD is essentially a staff function. It lacks the acumen to be operational, yet that is what it was asked to do. Caught in humanistic psychology, HRD became solution-driven, proposing one intervention after another, which was to hold employees in arrested (adolescent) development. The Culture of Complacency was a conscious process. So the permissive paternalism that grew out of it can be viewed as conscious incompetence, compared to the Culture of Comfort and its unconscious incompetence. The "parent" (*paternalistic management*), which dominates the Culture of Comfort, producing management dependence, now is superseded by the dominance of "the child," generating counterdependency on the organization. Judith Bardwick identifies in *Danger in the Comfort Zone* (1991), without taking HRD to task for fumbling the ball, the high toll which the entitlement mentality has taken on the nation's productivity and morale.[8] Let us now examine how this happened.

The Pay Issue

Research shows it is not pay per se but the symbology of pay that is important. Make no mistake, workers want to be paid fairly. They expect to derive an adequate income from what they do to satisfy their financial obligations and can become obsessed with pay out of personal pathology (gambling, living beyond their means, failure to save, or credit card mania). The second part of the mania is management's obsessive belief that workers think only of money. Such a mind-set believes it can do anything with, to, or at the expense of workers and be tolerated as long as workers are well paid. Not so. The two most time-consuming and least productive activities of management are its pay programs and its performance appraisal reviews. Management spends far too much time on both. As executed, these activities reflect a joint cynicism, creating more problems than they solve. To management's obsession that pay is the prime issue, workers obligingly respond by demanding more money for doing less. What workers would like is appreciation for their work. They wish to be treated in the same manner as management—to share in the company's success and participate in the bonus process. *Workers know that money is the language of management.* To get management's attention, they attempt to hit the organization in its pocketbook. Therein lies the fallacy. Workers are treated as if the company belongs to management and resent management playing with the company's money as if its own. Workers take offense at management acting like Santa Claus at performance reviews. What motivates mature workers, with money the currency of value, is productive work. Mature workers are interested in gain-sharing in the same manner as the CEO. "Forget performance appraisals! Forget salary increases! Get real!" is their message. They see pay programs as patronizing and condescending. They no longer make widgets with a grammar school education. Mature workers know the company's health as well as any executive. This is the information age. There are no more secrets!

Put the pay issue on a reality basis—company performance—and take the trump card of performance review out of the hands of management, and workers will start acting more mature. The same holds true of education. Originally, grades were meant to measure teachers' performance. If students didn't acquire the skills expected, the teacher was obliged to get the flunking grade. If performance appraisals are to be given, managers should be accessed as to worker effectiveness accordingly.

The argument that workers are not ready to handle a reduction in pay due to poor company performance is not without merit. It is about time they face up to that reality. In Drucker's words, "We may now be nearing the end of our hundred-year belief in the free lunch."[9] What mature workers are saying with their money demands is "I want to be part of the action. Money tells me the company is taking my contribution seriously. Pay me more, and you have to pay more attention to me and my ideas." Workers are learning to express themselves in the language of money because it translates into a sense of worth and usefulness. Management plays into this as it gives coin more easily than compliment. Compliments are subjective and qualitative, not objective and quantitative. Compliments are also value-laden and reflect personal bias. Management has an image of itself as being fair-minded, impartial, and objective—a myth. Management would rather distribute pay arbitrarily than deal with this ambiguity. The angst this behavior produces is a major contributor to the *six silent killers*.

Frederick Herzberg was right. Money is an ineffective ploy, not a motivator but *a hygiene factor. Workers are dissatisfied if money is taken away, but not necessarily satisfied if more is received.*[10] Management is reluctant to deal with the broader issues of concern to workers—ownership and control of what they do. By circumventing this imbroglio, it acquires complacent rather than contributing workers.

Group Feelings

Groups have feelings. We call this morale. Individuals have feelings. We call this attitude. Morale is the predisposition of a group to act in a given way, as attitude has the same impact on individual behavior. What is interesting to consider now, in retrospect, is how the "touchy-feely" intervention was expected to work with groups when it had failed miserably with individuals. From the workers' point of view, there was a reluctance to open up, a skepticism of the process, along with a belief that what they said might be used against them, so they were coy, but attempted to please by saying what they thought management wanted to hear. Most managers are poor listeners, poor decoders. Meaning goes beyond what is said to what is felt. What managers are good at employing is felt phrases, which get workers' attention—cost-of-living increase, merit rate increase, upgrade of benefits, expansion of staff, new product line, vacation policy, a wellness program. Workers translate felt phrases into something for nothing. Management thinks it has "broken through" when it has not even broken in. Here is a verbatim exchange of one sensing session:

> **Management**: *"I get the feeling you are concerned about a possible layoff. Yes, well, we have had to cut back 120 people since last quarter. But that is it. We should hold steady the remainder of the year with a modest employee increase in the 4th quarter."*
>
> **Employees**: ...*(no comment)*
>
> **Management** *(after a several second pause)*: *"As to a freeze on promotions. Well, Henry (CEO, always designated on first name basis) just issued a management bulletin (bulletin that concerns everyone but goes only to management) indicating that it (the freeze) is off. The salary*

forecast calls for 80 percent of all employees to be considered for a merit increase." (management smiles appropriately)

An employee: *"On what basis?"*

Management: *"Pardon?" (smile fades)*

Same employee: *"What is so magical about 80 percent? Why couldn't it be 90 percent or 60 percent?"*

Management *(not understanding or perhaps not able to decode the employee's question): "I don't think you appreciate what Henry is trying to do here. We have just come through a difficult financial period. To be able to release funds for distribution among 80 percent of our population is almost a miracle when you think about it." (Broad smile, sweeping gesture with hands to encompass entire group, soliciting approvable nods as eye contact is made with individual employees. Employees drop their eyes.)*

Same employee *(not impressed): "I don't think you've answered my question."*

Management *(tension showing on management's face): "I'm sorry you feel that way (turning away from questioner to the other side of the room). Are there any more questions?" (management's eyes boring into the group, no response.)*

All employees: *(turn to look at agitator accusingly, who disturbs their comfort)*

Management: *"If not, thank you very much. Check with your HR representative for our next (sensing) session. Now let's all get back to work." (grimace smile)*

Literally thousands of such sessions have been conducted with similar results. The employee in question may or may not have intended to annoy. We will never know. Management's agenda was on display, not that of the workers. The session was an end in itself, not a means to a mutually satisfying end. It was a monologue, not a dialogue. The four-step process to communication and cooperation is always in this order: politeness, suspicion, fight, and communication (see Figure 6.6). A question symbolizes the fight stage and provides a means to break through suspicion to cooperation. Confrontation is conflict. Conflict is not to be avoided. *Conflict management is the clue that holds an organization to its purpose.* What purports to be harmony is more often contrived resentment, which gives birth to the *six silent killers*. Communication is the key to everything. Understanding, on the other hand, is not agreement. Too often management reasons that when it asks for questions and there are none, what has been stated is understood and, if understood, is agreed to. Not so. Management and workers are now two sides of the same coin. If not, the coin is a slug.

Unfortunately, even as the twentieth century comes to a close, management appears near panic at the thought of not being in control. The chance for spontaneous and frank exchange in sensing sessions is only remotely possible. HRD's error was that it allowed management to believe its agenda was being bought by employees instead of showing management the fallacy of its thinking. Carl Rogers in *On Becoming a Person* (1961) provides management with a blueprint for engaging the employee. He calls it "enabling."[11] Enabling is a *person-centered* approach aimed at uncovering a person's agenda and assisting that person in dealing with it. What a wonderful tool for management! If change is to occur, change must be initiated by the person—a worker or a manager. Enabling does not necessitate brilliant diagnostic skills on the part of management. Enabling involves a workplace culture that is conducive to *worker-centered* work. Enabling involves treating workers as authentic human beings, on terms that are meaningful to them, enabling them to get in touch with themselves and their own experiences and then assisting them in making choices on that basis. One aspect of this enabling process has been perfected by Thomas Gordon, author of *Leadership Effectiveness Training* (1977)—active listening.[12] Gordon, who studied under Rogers, has made an impact on management becoming more sensitive to the needs of its employees because of the development of this listening skill.

A number of theorists on managerial performance have not survived as well as Gordon. Robert Blake and Jane Mouton became famous with *The Managerial Grid* (1964), which emphasized the relational aspects of Rogers' model.[13] These authors— improving on the work of Douglas McGregor,[14] who came up with *Theory X* (task-oriented manager) and *Theory Y* (people-oriented manager)—developed a grid to demonstrate four dominant management styles (Figure 8.2). For the next 20 years, management attempted to avoid the "country club" management style—the manager who attempted to meet the needs of the people at the expense of the organization's mission—and also the "hardheaded taskmaster"—the manager who attempted to meet the mission of the organization at the expense of the people. Everyone wanted to be seen as the "9-9" manager, the manager who had wonderful relations with the people and an equal focus on the mission.

Out of this fixation with *management style* grew the language of "participative management," "teaming," "employee involvement," and "empowerment." Many organizations put management on notice that it would change its style "or else." What this obsession with management style produced was mass confusion. Many managers simply managed by abdication, interpreting these demands as "You can no longer kick ass or take names to get things done, but you must kiss ass and treat workers with kid gloves to hold your job." Paradoxically, senior management, which promoted this style change, continued to play the "hardheaded taskmaster." Obviously, senior management had no intentions of abandoning its heavy-handed, autocratic style. *Yet, cultural change will not occur unless it becomes of symbolic value to senior management, its architectural designer, building contractor, and principal advocate. Senior management cannot live in the old castle and expect workers-managers to behave as*

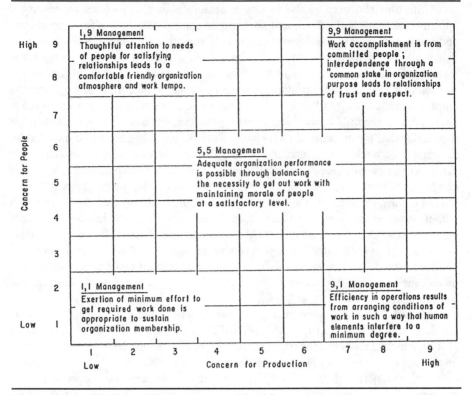

Figure 8.2   Blake and Mouton managerial grid.

if operating in a modern arena. They will behave as if they have never left the castle. No amount of reward or punishment will change the mind-set.

The down side of group feelings is that many workers become immersed in socializing. You would think their principal reason for being at work was to make friends. HRD plays into this mania by advertising the workplace as a "fun" place to work with lots of interesting people and comfort-satisfying facilities (promotional brochures with campus-like pictures of handball and tennis complexes and recreational centers, with expansive lawns and trees as an idyllic setting for meetings outdoors)—a veritable country-club atmosphere. Whatever the intention, this display does not energize work cells. If socializing is in fact a driving behavior sponsored by the workplace culture, complacency will be its principal outcome, not contribution. The culture speaks loudly: "It is important to be liked, more important to be a winning personality than a contributor, to be friendly more than functional."

Selection in a complacent organization follows a very select criteria without being consciously aware of it. The most important to the least important criteria are likely to be revealed in the following descending order:

- Do I (interviewer) feel comfortable with this individual?
- Will this individual fit comfortably in my (our) organization?
- Is this person qualified (to do the job)?

If the answer to the first two questions is positive, chances are the interviewer will find a way to make the third answer positive as well. It is amazing how the resumé implies non-existing credentials once this is the determination. Conversely, if the candidate is highly qualified and causes the interviewer to feel uncomfortable, perhaps even intimidated, there is absolutely no chance the candidate will be selected in a Culture of Complacency. To illustrate, I participated in the selection of a communications director with the stated requirements of a Ph.D. in communications, ten years of progressively more important work assignments, a number of publications in the discipline, and relevant work in the high-tech industry. Age was not mentioned, but we were looking for a candidate in their late thirties or early forties with the maturity and presence to do the job. One candidate had all of the above, and then some. If he had a fault, it was that he was interviewing us more intensely than we were interviewing him. All other interviewers, save myself, considered this a negative. Their consensus was "he is not a safe hire," meaning he will be difficult to control and might one day be our boss—perhaps sooner than later. The person hired was fresh out of the U.S. Air Force, a sergeant who was the attaché to a general, with slightly less than two years of college, no publications, and no contact with our industry. He was 28 and obsequious to a fault. He shared a hobby of deep-sea diving with two interviewers and held a license to teach the skill. He got rave reviews and the job. When it was apparent, after six months, that he wasn't up to the job, these interviewers were astonished as to why. When I was asked, I put it simply: "He is an enlisted man in officers' country," which was true. Besides not having the apparent credentials required, he had been trained to react to orders, not give them. Carl Rogers created a little confusion when he pointed the workplace culture in the direction of being worker-centered as opposed to management-centered. The same problem has developed in education, with the classroom becoming student-centered at the expense of being teacher-centered, and in the field of medicine, being patient-centered as opposed to doctor-centered. Lest we forget, it is not either–or in any case or in any circumstances, but either and or.

Fringe Benefits and Entitlement Programs

Fringe benefits are still not part of taxable income as this is being written, and so they are largely taken for granted. They are treated as inalienable rights and not as the privileges that they are. They include medical and dental insurance, life insurance, sick leave and paid vacations, retirement programs, paid holidays, incentive savings and stock option programs, day care allowances or facilities, maternity leave allowances (for husband as well as wife), credit union banking, and school tuition reimbursement. A study of the *Fortune* 500 (1988) indicates fringe benefit and entitlement programs will cost these companies, at the present rate of growth (1988 baseline), $3 trillion by the year 2000. These costs threaten the very survival of many of these companies. To illustrate this more graphically, a division of one *Fortune* 100 company, which employed 4,000 people, saw its medical costs alone escalate from $780,000 in 1978 to more than $8 million by 1982, with no significant increase in personnel. To pay for these increases, without dipping into profits, would require an increase in business of $70 million in new business for a $200 million operation or a growth rate of over 35 percent. Not realistic!

Fringe benefits have proven successful in recruiting top people. Operationally, however, they have proven a motivational nightmare. Benefits and entitlements are not seen as hard currency and are not included as taxable income. Therefore, the average worker does not consider them as real money. Yet, for most companies, especially those in the *Fortune* 500, these costs represent 50 percent or more of the worker's actual taxable income. Frederick Herzberg has explained this problem with his "two-factor motivation theory." Fringe benefits and entitlements, according to Herzberg, are hygiene factors—having these benefits doesn't necessarily mean the worker will be satisfied, but to take them away is guaranteed to make the worker dissatisfied (Figure 8.3).[15] These non-productive costs are causing many companies to fiscally bleed to death, necessitating some radical policies, such as outsourcing and redundancy exercises, which have become endemic to the times.

HYGIENE FACTORS	MOTIVATORS
Environment	**The Job Itself**
Policies and administration Supervision Working conditions Interpersonal relations Money, status, security	Achievement Recognition for accomplishment Challenging work Increased responsibility Growth and development

Figure 8.3   Herzberg's two-factor motivation theory.

Cost control is one of the quick fix strategies now much in evidence. In fact it has become a recycled new discipline—cost control management. This is an emergency strategy because the leadership of most organizations failed to envision a restrictive market, global competition, or the radical change in technology, all of which have necessitated a more sophisticated workforce. There is no point in finding fault with the leadership. This miscalculation is already causing many established old firms to regroup or dissolve. Reducing costs is a short-term strategy. It may help an organization get a second wind, but it will not sustain growth, ensure market share, or protect the business. It is easier to reduce costs than to generate new business. *It is also easier to cut benefits and staff than it is to increase productivity or to establish new markets. In order to survive, a more difficult strategy must be embraced, and that strategy must include creating a new workplace culture and a new infrastructure that resonates with the workforce. This involves creative risk and perhaps the greatest challenge of all—to understand human chemistry and how to tap this resource for growth and profit.*

Workers who have never been self-employed have little sense of the cost of time (vacations, holidays) or things (medical/dental insurance). They resent take-aways, even if the company reduces its medical benefit from 90 to 80 percent. Take-aways are often camouflaged as "flexible benefit programs" or "extended choice programs." HRD would be better off to level with employees, absorb their anger, and educate them to realize the "free lunch" is over. Management might cut the fog between itself and workers if it stopped the deception and started to treat workers as partners and adults. To put this problem in graphic terms, imagine that a worker is being paid a salary of $40,000 a year, with the worker's benefit package costing an additional 40 percent or $16,000. Imagine this $56,000 is taxed as straight income. To make the picture more real, imagine that this is the income of the husband and that the wife earns a matching salary. Instead of paying income taxes on $80,000, the couple is paying income taxes on $112,000. Say the couple has no children. Chances are the cost of their benefits will nearly equal their additional income taxes. If that isn't a wake-up call, consider this: it is only a matter of time before benefits will be taxed as real income.

The Fairness Issue

Fairness is interesting, largely because it is not an issue. Whether we are winners or losers, successful or failures, victors or victims is a function of how we see ourselves and our circumstances. There is no magic to the proposition. The issue of fairness is pivotal on how we see ourselves, not on how others see us. What is winning to one is losing to another. Many are obsessed with the idea of fairness and constantly find the lack of it. What they fail to see is that an individual allows unfairness to happen by way of his approach to the circumstances of his life. Everyone experiences "bad breaks," which often are blessings in disguise. It is all in how experience is interpreted. Labeling experience as unfair only makes matters worse. Experience is neither good nor bad. It simply "is." When destiny is tied to someone else's rainbow, life is forever a disappointment. Peter Drucker is emphatic: "To predict the future, one must create it." William Jennings Bryan, the great populist stump-orator, echoes the same: "Destiny is not a matter of chance, it is a matter of choice; it is not a thing to be waited for, it is a thing to be achieved." In the same vein, the great English maverick poet Percy Shelley adds: "As to us—we are uncertain people, who are chased by the spirits of our destiny from purpose to purpose, like clouds by the wind." Robert Louis Stevenson submits: "Wherever we are, it is but a stage on the way to somewhere else, and whatever we do, however we do it, it is only a preparation to do something else that shall be different."[16]

Read about the lives of doers, and you'll discover that adversity is a constant companion and that they embrace their hardships and soar beyond them. Life and work are never fair, but for doers the focus is always on making the most of their situation; of taking charge of their destiny; of looking for opportunity, not justification for complaint; of making things happen, not waiting for them to occur. Steel in the spine is not experienced by filling it with Teflon.[17]

Incidentally, the fairness issue is generally viewed in terms of deprivation rather than excess. If anything, we have too much affluence. John Kenneth Galbraith wrote prophetically in *The Affluent Society* (1959) of the damage affluence has done to our collective soul.[18] Once only a small segment of society, usually children of celebrities, failed to cope with the excesses of privilege, from Dianne Barrymore's *Too Much, Too Soon* (1961)[19] to Lindsay Crosby's suicide *(Parade,* February 25, 1990), and now beyond.[20] Premature death comes more frequently to those with too much than those with too little. The affluent are more likely to be caught up in alcohol, drugs, depression, debauchery, and deviancy than the deprived. They are bored, with too much time on their hands. Once the money tree of family support is removed, they may see themselves as worthless because they cannot face the future without money, and so they either slowly commit suicide by drugs and drink or more quickly with the gun. What once was a celebrity disease has now become a common problem to society-at-large.

HRD has been successful in making the fairness issue a concern to workers. Fairness confirms the thesis that workers are counterdependent on the organization. The organization's sickness is a function of this dependence. Consider this:

* Rather than taking control of their destiny, many workers suffer from a sense of being controlled and, therefore, subjected to the will and whim of management.
* Rather than sensing their own power, these workers find solace in comforting each other by complaining about how unfairly they are being treated.

They play the victim of the system, which insulates them from reality and isolates them from responsibility. Lost in this immersion with fairness is the recognition that workers have the power, that workers are the organization, and that workers are the system they delight in attacking. It would be comical if it weren't so tragic. It is an endless game of control, with those exercising it (management) not having it, while those having it (workers) not exercising it. In praise of fairness, it is reduced to a praise of folly.

Job Security

In *Wisdom of Insecurity* (1951), Alan W. Watts explains that insecurity is a given.[21] Everyone possesses it, no matter how gifted or accomplished. Peter Drucker puts it slightly differently. He claims people of great aptitude also possess great weakness. Once we acknowledge insecurity as part of our makeup, Watts discovered, we miraculously overcome it. We are then able to act—to be and to do. Insecurity, Watts concludes, is simply a mania for control. Consider this against the fixation with "nailing things down," for having people, events, and situations behave predictably. Astrologers, palm readers, and mediums do a landslide business with presidents, their wives, heads of state, executives, academics, and others whom you might think would know better. We don't like surprises. We desire divine intervention to take the suspense out of life, some forecasting tool that will cut through the ambiguity to make sense of things, but something which will cause no pain, discomfort, inconvenience, effort, or involvement on our part. Something sublime! This finds many who live from paycheck to paycheck religiously participating in the state lottery at the rate of $20 or more per week. This is not an investment. This is looking for something for nothing. Even if a person should win, it isn't earned and, therefore, does not contribute to a person's improved sense of worth or even a person's control over life. The lottery feeds an endemic disease—something for nothing—rather than alleviating a mania for control and security.

The irony of this predilection finds us, both in our personal and professional lives, compulsive planners and impulsive implementers. We seem obsessed with order and so create the chaos that intimidates us. We take pride in manicured lawns and dent-free automobiles but throw debris from cars and behave as savages in public. We appear terrified of confusion and public display of emotion, yet if data fail to fit our preconceived notions, we have little problem with refuting them. On balance, the mania for security may find us victims of insecurity. From our earliest days as workers, the rationale for staying where we didn't want to be and doing what we didn't want to do was the company retirement plan. The company's retirement policy is part of its recruitment package. It doesn't end there. Periodically, bright, colorful brochures are produced with clever charts and tables indicating the fruits of retirement some 20 or 30 years hence. The symbology of these products is to reinforce the thinking of how good you have it now and to provoke your sense of insecurity. Obviously, this is an attention-getter. Mention job security and accrued benefits of working "here," and the ears perk up.

It may surprise you but children of the baby-boomer generation are more obsessed with security issues than any generation before. They have a terrifying sense of impermanence, of nothing lasting for very long—jobs, relationships, and their health. They have a quest for money that they associate with security and nothing else. Moreover, they are frightfully conservative, and they will quickly justify staying in a job they hate because they believe they can't afford to take a chance to do what they enjoy for less money. Garry Wills writes in *The New York Review* (October 3, 1996) that the liberal tradition in American politics is "electorally nonexistent":

> *We must choose between a party that neglects the poor and one that savages them, between a party that defects to the rich and one that deifies them, between a party that abjectly apologizes for government and one that demonizes it. One party signs a Faustian contract with the devil. The other party offers the contract...Better Faustus than Mephistopheles.*[22]

Baby boomers and their progeny believe if they have money, they will be secure; if they have money, nobody can hurt them; if they have money, they will be loved; if they have money, they will never be lonely; if they have money, they need never grow old. Samuel Warner anticipated this mind-set with his book *Self-Realization and Self-Defeat* (1966). Warner could see the growing struggle of the young with the reality of limits.[23]

With no precedence to guide them, workers in their twenties and thirties today are competing with other Western societies and emerging Eastern industrial giants for a shrinking economic pie. American workers now net almost 20 percent less in real wages than they did in 1973. "We are the only Western nation to have so retrogressed," writes educator Martin L. Gross in *The Political Racket* (1996). "After taxes, two paychecks in a family barely equal the purchasing power one had twenty-five years ago."[24]

Due to the belief that security can be purchased, if not won in the lottery, many conduct careers parallel to their principal occupation. This dilutes their productivity in both. With the great American dream bombarding their senses, few give much thought to living within their means or challenging the status quo of their primary occupation by being more productive. It is almost a helpless belief that they are stuck, incapable of living or acting otherwise. This produces a "double bind" between work and themselves, diffusing their attention, while making losers of employers and employees. Job security is predicated on the survival of the organization, and then on workers remaining skilled and relevant to the demands of the marketplace. Workers cannot succeed if the company fails, and the company cannot succeed if workers fail. The word is "interdependence"—not codependence, not learned helplessness, and certainly not non-responsibility. Employers and employees are in it to succeed by supporting each other, or if not supporting each other, failing together.

Is this the "Age of Uncertainty"? Perhaps. The stability of many jobs is uncertain; even many professions are in transition. Uncertainty can create an obsession with the future. Meanwhile, workers in this climate may feel contempt for the company because of its imprisoning hold. They may resent the fact that they don't enjoy the comfort and job security their parents once enjoyed. How this may translate in behavior serves neither the interests of either. Much like a young adult living at home who resents the imposition of implied control—critical glances at his comings and goings—the employee may come to blame "the company" for his insecurity and anxiety. This is organizational counterdependence personified and can lead to the *six silent killers*.

Insecurity can translate into inaction or passive behavior. Such workers exaggerate the prevailing norms, becoming obsessed with not messing up, not stepping out of line or on toes, not being the messenger who gets killed, or not seeing or hearing anything. Passivity is justified for survival. Workers bring their bodies to work and leave their minds at home. Yet few get into trouble taking the initiative. Security anxiety is a way to practice "conscious incompetence." The paradox is that the more an organization promotes security, the less workers are able to deal with insecurity. You don't give soldiers guarantees they won't be lost protecting the *common good*.

It is a risk they accept when they put on the uniform. Workers put on a uniform, too. The problem is they don't know it. And so "Russian roulette" is played with their insecurities instead of designing ways to embrace them.[25]

Quality of Work Life

Working conditions once varied from grimy to abysmal. There were blatant, criminal abuses of worker health and welfare. Now with exotic chemicals and gases, breeder reactors, in which the hazards of materials go beyond the ambience of the workplace to the community, even encompassing the globe, quality of work life is paramount. The ecology of environment—in both the community and workplace— has made necessary if not sufficient progress. "Progress" is not an idle word. It is the ecology of mind where the situation has psycho-social as well as physical implications. What negatively impacts most workers is not so much the physical as the psychological climate of work. Problems of workplace health and safety are being addressed. Scant attention is being paid to workers as persons. Quality of Work Life (QWL) is replete with psychological abuse:

- Being asked to do much more with fewer resources because of cutbacks. Little attention is paid to redundant processes or antiquated practices that should be expunged from operations.
- Being asked to work overtime and on weekends because there are fewer people.
- Seeing the ranks of individual contributors shrinking much faster than the ranks of management.
- Contending with redundancy exercises, wage freezes, reductions in benefits—or constant rumors—while seeing top management acquiring million-dollar bonuses. General Motors' board of directors voted to double the pension for retired former chairman Roger Smith from $550,000 to $1.1 million at a time when the company lost 11 percentage points (46 to 35) in market share during his leadership. GM employees know that with each percentage point drop, thousands of jobs are lost.
- Dealing with the rumor and uncertainty of takeover and the frustration of near constant reorganization, restructuring, and reallocation of resources.
- Discovering that loyalty, trust, duty, and seniority count for little.
- Feeling you are always the last to know about things affecting you, while being inundated with information that is only remotely related to your interests.
- Being promoted, then demoted, then reassigned, and then made redundant—not for performance deficiency, but due to organizational restructuring.
- Being asked to maintain copious records that nobody reads and to report to superiors who understand nothing of what you do.

The problem is not resolved by periodically repainting the workplace walls, changing the lighting of the cubicles, or holding a company carnival. These psychological abuses contribute to more than low morale. They pollute the worker's spirit with the poison of deviant behavior. This abuse suffocates pride and crushes the worker's sense of dignity. This loss should not be underestimated. Cyril Northcote Parkinson writes in *The Economist* (September 1957) in connection with Parkinson's Law that "My experience tells me (after nearly eighty years of living) the only thing people really enjoy over a long period of time is some kind of work."[26] Parkinson, you may recall, anticipated "corpocracy" with *work expands so as to fill the time available for its completion.*

With more emphasis placed on QWL in terms of the physical, many workplaces resemble shopping malls more than places of employment. Check out the post-modern high-tech facilities with their computers, robotics, lasers, modern art, and paperless factories—where the ambience of the sweatshop is but a distant mirage. Shopping mall workplace complexes feature piped-in music, soft-colored walls, indirect lighting, soundproof cubicles, sparkling-clean rest rooms, game rooms, full-line cafeterias, coffee breakout rooms, and indoor/outdoor rest centers. QWL would appear as tranquil as a college campus framed in tree-lined symmetry, with picnic areas embroidering man-made lakes with artificial geysers, giving one the impression that the workplace is an idyllic refuge one remembers from reading a nursery rhyme. This festive atmosphere highlights health and wellness days (free physical examinations), carnivals for charity and Special Olympics for the disadvantaged, "shutdown" parties upon the completion of big contracts, TGIF beer blasts, retirement parties, and more. The modern worker is told in so many ways that he has never left home but simply has acquired more considerate parents. Despite the grandeur, ask most workers if they are happy, feel challenged, feel appreciated, have the resources to do the job, and have a free hand in control of work and you are likely to find QWL is still an issue. With regard to managers, downsizing has created an increasingly unstable and insecure workplace for them. A growing number are turning to being entrepreneurs, having experienced two or three job cuts. "Although there are many uncertainties and risks associated with becoming an entrepreneur," states James E. Challenger, president of *Challenger, Gray & Christmas Quarterly Job Search Survey* (1996), "many believe there are even greater risks in entering into another employee–employer contract."[27] Others escape the route of mental depression. Depression cost the United States alone $43.7 billion annually: $23.6 billion in absenteeism and lost productivity, $12.4 billion in direct costs for treatment and rehabilitation, and $7.5 billion in loss of earnings due to depression-induced suicides.[28]

Quality of Work

Quality of work is linked to quality of work life as Yin is to Yang. Yet the problems associated with work seldom involve workers in the creation of the remedies. Work is an enigma to workers and managers alike. Perhaps they are too close.

Work continues to change with improbable speed, which creates the comedic vision of workers and managers on opposite sides of the same treadmill, going to beat the band, but going nowhere. Ideally, management would like to isolate work from the dynamic flow, freeze-frame it, and treat it as a stationary thing. Workers escape the maddening pace of going nowhere by treating work as amusement. Neither disposition improves the Quality of Work. Job descriptions are the most archaic documents around. They have little meaning and contribute less to productivity. Job descriptions had some validity when workers were trained orangutans. With thinking and doing the twin components of modern work, role identity and role relationships are dynamic and essential and already standard practice in professional sport. Once a basketball player received kudos for scoring, and that was it. Today, a Dennis Rodman hardly scores but commands a $4 million annual salary for rebounding. Some players command similar compensation for giving assists, others for blocking shots or having few unforced errors, and still others for being team leaders. The same role identities and role relationships are evident in professional football, baseball, hockey, soccer, and so on. To establish this in work requires a clear understanding of:

- The function (purpose) of work from the simplest to the most complex in terms of how it relates to the final outcome.
- Worker–manager relationships and how this chemistry supports the function and contributes to outcomes. This includes, but is not limited to, how information is shared, how ideas are generated and processed, and who carries the ball when a problem occurs.
- The way credit is shared so that all the critical aspects of work are properly highlighted and duly rewarded.

This is not reinventing the wheel, but taking a page out of professional sport. In many ways, this is a throwback to the pre-industrial guilds. Differentiation of work was on the basis of what needed to be done and who was most skilled to do it. Managers and professionals are now part of the same coin. Managers are doers too. A future challenge is to motivate managers to be reborn to the blessings of work.

Generally speaking, a functional group description, stating the objective of the function and its broad performance criteria, would be more appropriate than job descriptions for individuals. This allows the group to discover their own unique chemistry the same way individual basketball stars become a team. If players don't leave their egos in the locker room, no matter how talented, they will perform miserably as a team. The same is true of the workplace. Not meaning to make a group divisive, that is precisely what happens when the group is not allowed to determine its own center, stability, and balance. When the team, through the chemistry of its individual members, creates, manages, and controls the process, the quality of work improves.

Conversely, the performance appraisal system is the antithesis of quality work. It attempts to impose individual quantitative standards on work which is collegially qualitative, objectivity on subjective components (attitude, morale), and concrete measurement on abstract behavior (team spirit), while being obsessed with *doing*, when timely *thinking* is perhaps the most critical standard of work. Moreover, who is to get credit—an individual or the team? Because work is essentially a subjective qualitative process, performance appraisal has caused more problems than it has solved.[29] For the professional worker, productivity is more a matter of mind-set than activity. A professional in the right frame of mind, along with his colleagues of a similar orientation, can save tens of thousands of dollars by gaining insight into a process *before* it has gone awry. Conventional thinking inspects the final product, then discards the damaged goods. If the product is out-of-specs, conventional practice has a routine of looking for the problem after the fact. No operation can tolerate that practice today.

Performance appraisal was designed as a developmental tool—to support the manager and worker in a coaching-counseling dialogue to improve the worker's skills on the job and to enhance the worker's future career development. In that sense it was a diagnostic tool because the focus was on behavior, not the person, and what mechanics might be modified to move the worker closer to his potential in the job and beyond. For the worker, it evolved to be little more than a session to see how much increase he was likely to get in the next pay review. For the manager, it became a means of establishing his power and control over the worker and to register his satisfaction or dissatisfaction with performance—something that should have been expressed before.

A variation of this process is equally suspect. This has the worker making a self-assessment of his performance, which is then compared to the manager's assessment. The idea here is to create a dialogue between the manager and worker and jointly solve the problem on the worker's career development. What makes this suspect is that invariably the worker becomes the issue and not the manager's role in the process. Performance appraisal is inconsequential in employee development and of little influence on behavioral change. It may seem like a radical idea, but I believe that a discontinuance of performance appraisal will save money and increase productivity:

- As workers and managers focus on work.
- As the artificial worker–manager codependency bond is broken (the process actually encourages this codependency).
- As the role of manager gravitates to one of participation in the work.

Managers typically have 10–15 people reporting to them. Some progressive organizations have upped this to 25. There is no reason that managers in the future cannot be responsible, in a facilitating role, to 200–300 people. There are enough fail-safe processes to monitor performance and predict outcomes without a mass of non-functional managers getting in the way. Again, Drucker seems to have the last word: "So much of what we call management consists in making it difficult for people to work."[30] On balance, job descriptions and performance appraisals create a climate of paternalistic management dependence and a codependent bond between employer and employee, which is mutually dysfunctional.

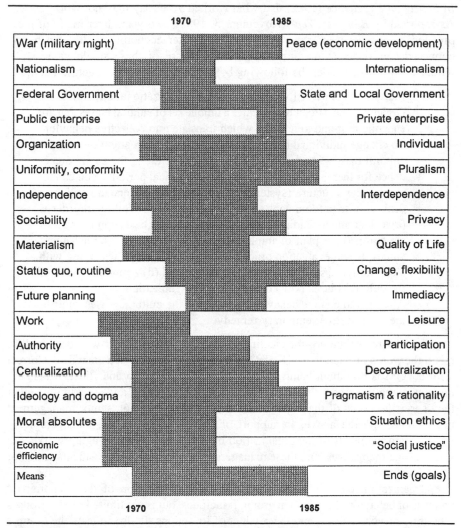

	1970	1985	
War (military might)			Peace (economic development)
Nationalism			Internationalism
Federal Government			State and Local Government
Public enterprise			Private enterprise
Organization			Individual
Uniformity, conformity			Pluralism
Independence			Interdependence
Sociability			Privacy
Materialism			Quality of Life
Status quo, routine			Change, flexibility
Future planning			Immediacy
Work			Leisure
Authority			Participation
Centralization			Decentralization
Ideology and dogma			Pragmatism & rationality
Moral absolutes			Situation ethics
Economic efficiency			"Social justice"
Means			Ends (goals)

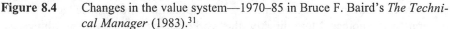

Figure 8.4   Changes in the value system—1970–85 in Bruce F. Baird's *The Technical Manager* (1983).[31]

Quality of Management

We have seen a seismic shift in values within the organization and without an appropriate managerial response (Figure 8.4). There is not a single organization within my memory that has truly realigned and restructured itself in terms of these value changes.[32] I must assume that there is insufficient knowledge to accept this challenge. Obviously, we know from the profiles in Tom Peters and Robert Waterman's

In Search of Excellence (1982) that what worked yesterday may not work today.[33] As reported by *Business Week* (November 5, 1984), two years later many of these profiled companies were experiencing roller-coaster economic cycles that hardly connoted confidence.[34] An organization fully aware of these subtle value shifts would do well to consider the following before attempting to restructure itself:

- Individual behavior follows that of the organizational structure.
- Organizational structure generates a unique set of cultural biases that are endemic to it and to it alone, which translate into collective behavior.
- To change individual behavior requires first giving attention to these cultural biases—understanding the history of them, the social precedence for them, and their function during critical periods. You cannot change the structure (system) before you first understand and then deal with its predominant values. What then must follow in order is (a) a clear understanding of the values that might best support the new structure; (b) a plan of implementation designed to establish these values; (c) an evaluation process to monitor these values, along with a qualitative assessment of value change; and (d) a random check of the cultural biases now common to the organization.
- Attempts to change behavior by ignoring the cultural biases contribute, at best, to a temporary remedy.

In order to restructure for Quality of Management (QM), it would be well to recall the words of Pope John XXIII: "See everything. Overlook a great deal. Correct a little." QM is not about being judgmental, critical, or even analytical. It is about understanding the predominant values expressed by workers and assessing whether they serve the needs of the organization or not. If they do not, senior management must orchestrate the above. In support of such an intervention, managers serve workers and the needs of the organization by listening and encouraging workers to self-manage themselves, and these managers then report their assessments to senior management.

Organization culture is the integration and assimilation of the predominant patterns of behavior of the human group. It includes, but is not limited to, the group's thoughts, speech, actions, and the product of its actions. It also reflects the group's capacity for learning and transmitting new information and knowledge from one generation to another. More directly, the workplace culture is the way things get done. Much like an individual, an organizational culture can deny or resist change. In fact, cultural biases are there to do precisely that—maintain the status quo. They can even ignore the indicators that suggest their survival is in jeopardy. A word of caution: It is difficult to read the culture of an organization from the outside. Consultants are notorious for misreading the workplace culture. Workers in an organization, who personify the culture, are largely unaware there is such a phenomenon. They believe they behave the way they do because they are in control, when clearly they are not. Almost imperceptibly, as a new person experiences a workplace culture, behavior before changes to behavior consistent with everyone else. A new worker once asked me, "Why do all the lights go off automatically at five (P.M.)?" I smiled, "Because the company doesn't want to pay overtime, and this is a union shop." He soon adjusted to working seven-plus hours versus his previous ten-hour days. If he hadn't and couldn't do the work demanded of him in that period, the culture was telling him, "You don't belong! Go elsewhere," without saying it. Working with police, I have seen new police officers join a department with liberal, citizen-centered views. Six months later, overwhelmed by the dregs of society and the hypocrisy of the community, these same individuals sounded and acted like weary, cynical veterans. The mean streets of the community had changed them, and these streets were their workplace culture. That is why novelist and former Los Angeles Police Department Sergeant Joseph Wambaugh, author of *The Onion Field* (1974), claims, "A community gets the kind of police it deserves."[35] The police don't create the culture. Police reflect the culture in their behavior.

One persistent problem of organization is that the demands for cultural change are often drastic, but the organization is painfully slow in recognizing and dealing with these demands. It will do almost anything to maintain the traditional culture that brought the organization to prominence. The conflict, contradiction, and inconsistency that result from this delay cause no shortage of anxiety, stress, and frustration. This can be a costly error in judgment, especially if external demands accelerate— the market changes overnight with a competitor's new product eclipsing market share. The organization is not equipped to react to this situation and can go into a tailspin. Strong workplace cultures can become weak, fragmented, or obsolete.

Take the culture of Company A (Figure 8.5). This company, in business more than 100 years, is structured to promote stability, predictability, consistency, politeness, obedience, loyalty, hard work, provincialism, and a parochial perspective. Company A has grown from a modest product base to a sophisticated high-tech systems line of products. It has established a reputation for service and reliability, with more than 80 percent of its management team coming from engineering. Business has grown moderately but consistently over the years. It has become a multinational with operations around the globe, but its principal operations are located in a major metropolitan area where some 20,000 people work. Return on investment has been conservative to disappointing. Wall Street has been critical of management for its failure to grow the business and the slowness with which it comes out with new products. Wall Street further points out that upstart companies have cut into its market share, which has dropped six points since 1990 or nearly a point a year. The working population is represented by a bimodal curve with the under 25 and over 45 dominating, with the curve skewed toward the over-45 work group. Average service to the company is more than 20 years. Most workers have spent their entire careers at a single facility. The company has downsized from 100,000 to 74,000 employees.

Company B has been in business less than 25 years and has grown at the rate of 30 percent a year since it was in business. It now has 20,000 employees worldwide

Company A	Company B
Quality of Work	
Control	
Quality control is clearly the responsibility of the manager.	Quality control is the responsibility of the person closest to the work.
Teamwork	
Workers work best alone where they are unencumbered by co-workers in tomfoolery.	All work is organized in team work cells, where workers in these teams enjoy autonomy within the limits of time, resources and requirements.
Measurement	
Management designs, monitors, evaluates and tracks performance.	Individuals measure themselves on the basis of customer satisfaction.
Professionalism	
Only managers and select specialists are deemed of this status; all others are considered nonprofessional.	Everyone has a customer, either internal or external, and is therefore considered a professional.
Communication	
What top management decides is what everyone abides.	The central discourse of work is about customers and their requirements, which makes everyone's voice important.
The Bottom Line	
This is the exclusive domain of management, especially top management.	Everyone tracks their own impact on the bottom line, which means everyone should know the state of the economy of the company.
Workplace Cultural Climate	
Have little understanding of what constitutes "culture"; see the workplace in sterile, essentially pragmatic terms. Work is a necessary evil.	The climate allows each worker to paint his own individual workscape on the canvas of communal contribution.

Figure 8.5   Quality of work: Value differences—Company A and Company B.

and sets the pace in its industry. A glamour stock of the NYSE with ever-improving financial indices, Company B has limited fixed resources and few operating plants, preferring to subcontract much of its manufacturing and fabricating work. It is heavily involved in R&D but is equally heavily into high-profile marketing. Its state-of-the-art technology is central to its operation and marketing thrust. The longest life cycle for a product to date is 18 months which, incidentally, matches the average service time

Company A	Company B
Quality of Worklife	
Individual Respect	
Only senior people are accorded this treatment: senior people are "indispensable."	Everyone is esteemed because everyone is valued for their unique skills.
Personal Challenge	
Reserved to high-level people for personal challenge is deemed imperative to keeping senior people operationally sharp.	Everyone is challenged to the level of their capacity or desire; cumulative sharpness is critical to company success.
Personal Growth	
Too abstract a concept to be taken seriously. A job is a job.	Personal learning is seen as a constant requirement of growth.
Enthusiasm	
A "nice" word, but not a requirement of work. It is too touchy-feely for most senior people.	The common belief here is that if people are not turned on to their work they are not productive.
Ethics	
Considered important. A company should be as fair and honest as it can be and still be effective.	Ethics is fundamental to company success. No compromise is worthy of the name to mollify this.
Work/Life Balance	
The job comes before personal life considerations. The job is life until the job is done...whenever that is.	People work to live, they don't live to work. There is a time to create and a time to recreate. Leisure is one of the hardest lessons of the work/life.
Rewards	
Money and career advancement are the most powerful factors in people's expectations during their worklife.	Respect, recognition, one's opinion valued, to be trusted with important information, and given meaningful work are food for the worker's soul.

Figure 8.6   Quality of work life: Value differences—Company A and Company B.

for employees. Several employees have left to head spin-off start-up businesses in direct competition. Far from discouraging this approach, some of these companies have become subcontractors to their original employer. Few employees have more than ten years continuous service. Intensely marketing-driven, with almost all of its top management with marketing backgrounds, the workplace culture is dynamic, unstable, and chaotic. This is verified with a 30 percent attrition rate and a 40 percent

Company A	Company B
Quality of Management	
Business and Organizational Understanding	
Only top management needs a sense of the "big picture."	Everyone understands they are a part of the "big picture." No work is done in a vacuum.
Relating Job to Society	
Consider this essentially a Senior Management concern.	Believe the work of all employees contributes to a final product or service, for which they all should share in the credit.
Trust	
Earned by devoted service by each person over a long period of time.	Every person is assumed credible and trustworthy unless proven otherwise.
Recognition	
Self-consciousness is displayed by special recognition limited to retirement and separation.	Recognition is joyous and spontaneous, frequent and timely.
Relating Past, Present and Future	
History is a club to protect the status quo and to revere tenure and seniority.	History is the window of tradition, connecting the past with the future, while supporting change in the present.
Leadership	
Management sees itself as providing marching orders for the direction in which the workers, as troops, need to move to engage the objective.	Believes leadership involves the personification of the vision which inspires confidence and commitment from workers to that end.
Spirit	
Even the word makes management uncomfortable. It suggests something magical to its pragmatic conscience, which generates cynicism.	Spirit pervades all aspects of work. Nothing is impossible when the passion of spirit is unleashed. Work is love made visible.

Figure 8.7   Quality of management: Value differences—Company A and Company B.

rate of churn (changing jobs within the organization) per year. Besides a marketing perspective, the company is intensely performance-driven and accepts, even encourages, aggressiveness to produce creatively. It stands on no norm, nor will it ride on reputation. Its rallying cry is, "There is an enemy and potential customer behind every tree." Workers are not permitted to rest on their laurels or become complacent. Acceleration is the motto. Domination is the game. Job security and role security are foreign to them, replaced by opportunity and responsibility, not age or seniority. The average worker is in his twenties; the CEO is in his forties.

No two companies are ever the same, nor are two companies ever in the same place or circumstances. *You cannot generalize about culture. You cannot develop a paradigm or model that fits all. In fact, it is likely to fit only one well. It is wrong to project a company's culture on someone else's cultural foundation. No two companies have the same history, values, beliefs, interests, problems, personnel, expectations, and approaches to their respective mission, nor should they.* A 100-year-old company is not where a 25-year-old company is. Nor is any product history the same. Similar industries experience similar problems, but that does not make them the same. Company A and Company B happen to be in the same market; one is fighting for its life, while the other is thriving. One has a clear sense of its past, a tentative sense of its present, and no real sense of its future. The other has little interest in its past and looks at the present in future perfect terms. What is also interesting about these two companies is that the much more veteran company treats business as if it is a respectful parlor game, whereas the upstart company treats business as all-out warfare. The latter takes no prisoners, while the former is prisoner to a philosophy that confines it to a self-imposed cage.

Business today is modern warfare at its bloodiest. It is not a polite game. Weighty assets in plants and equipment slow the modern company down. The "Fall of Rome" discussed in Chapter 4 is not unlike what is happening to many companies. They cannot adjust to the times because their focus and energy are placed on the wrong emphasis, or they stubbornly hold to the status quo come "hell or high water."

The late Seymour R. Cray, a computer industry pioneer and the father of the supercomputer, experienced the cold-blooded nature of modern warfare when he formed Cray Computer Corporation in 1989, which three years later was $300 million in debt and ended in bankruptcy in 1995—a casualty of the rising power of cheap microprocessor chips. On balance, the nature of this warfare demands that companies structure their organizations and workplace cultures to the needs of the marketplace.

Company A concentrates on selling, on being seen as a work hard, play hard culture, depending heavily on its history of past successes and loyal customers to sustain its growth. Company B studies the marketplace as if under a microscope and then delivers product after product to fill that need, irrespective of what the analysts are going to think of its exploitative orientation. Company B spends twice as much of its budget, percentage wise, on R&D than Company A. Embracing risk management, Company B releases products to the market before it is convinced the products will be successful. Company B has a philosophy of "bet your company" culture, but with its risk management tied closely to R&D and marketing research. Which company do you think has quality management and will be around in the twenty-first century?

The Culture of Complacency, under the auspices of parochial management and HRD interventions, has stolen the minds of workers and substituted the catechism of tradition. Complacency has isolated these workers from the pain of experience.

Complacency has filled this void with a doctrine of learned helplessness and non-responsibility. Complacent workers behave, are polite, obedient, punctual, and predictable—or safe hires! Complacent workers are not energetic, confrontational, creative, and unpredictable—or spirited hires! Complacency finds these workers conditioned to be 99 percent robotic, programmed to breathe, sleep, digest, and excrete, with an instinct for reproducing what is expected and to behave as if in suspended adolescence.[36] Beyond that, complacent workers' minds are largely mechanical, for they are living on automatic pilot. T. S. Eliot writes, "Where is the life we have lost in living? Where is the wisdom we have lost in knowledge? Where is the knowledge we have lost in information?"[37] The robot has stolen it. But nowhere is it written that we cannot steal it back and create our destiny.

Endnotes

1. Daniel Yankelovich, *New Rules: Searching for Self-Fulfillment in a World Turned Upside Down* (New York: Random House, 1981), pp. 38–39.
2. Gary Reinmuth (*The Chicago Tribune*), "What Is Normal? Looking to Find Out, An Author Learns People Don't Hesitate to Air Their Dirty Laundry," *The Tampa Tribune*, November 7, 1995, Baylife section, 1, 5.
3. Knight-Ridder, "New Ways Challenge Psychiatry: Medications and Cost Containment Are Retooling the Treatment of Mental Illness," *The Tampa Tribune*, May 6, 1996, Nation/World, 6.
4. Michael Berg, "Still at Risk," *The Tampa Tribune*, April 25, 1996, Commentary section, 1.
5. Judy Jones and William Wilson, *An Incomplete Education* (New York: Ballantine Books, 1987), pp. 425–431.
6. Yankelovich, op. cit., p. 39.
7. "Dumbsizing" firms regret cost-cutting (a *Wall Street Journal Report*), *The Tampa Tribune*, May 19, 1996, Business, 1. Consultant Rick Maurer: "Cost-cutting has become the Holy Grail of corporate management, but what helps the financial statement up front can end up hurting it down the road."
8. Judith Bardwick, *Danger in the Comfort Zone* (New York: AMACOM, 1991).
9. John T. Tarrant, *Drucker* (New York: Warner Books, 1976), p. 318.
10. Frederick Herzberg, *Work and the Nature of Man* (New York: World Publishing, 1966).
11. Carl Rogers, *On Becoming a Person* (Boston: Houghton Mifflin, 1961).
12. Thomas Gordon, *Leadership Effectiveness Training* (Solana Beach, CA: Wyden Books, 1977).
13. Robert R. Blake and Jane S. Mouton, *The Managerial Grid* (Houston: Gulf Publishing, 1964).
14. Douglas McGregor, *The Human Side of Enterprise* (New York: McGraw Hill, 1960).
15. Herzberg, op. cit.
16. Notice the *twin senses* of vulnerability and responsibility of these reflections. It is no accident that great men are sensitive to their own inertia, and bent on overcoming it.
17. James R. Fisher, Jr., *Work Without Managers: A View from the Trenches* (Tampa: The Delta Group Florida, 1991), p. 198. The fairness issue is often more of compulsive excess than concrete deprivation.

18. John Kenneth Galbraith, *The Affluent Society* (reprint of 1958 edition) (New York: Houghton Mifflin, 1984). Galbraith, a quarter century later, still saw the "Affluent Society" as heartless (*St. Petersburg Times)*, September 9, 1984, 1-D.

19. Diane Barrymore and Frank Barrymore, *Too Much, Too Soon* (Cutchogue, NY: Buccaneer Books, 1981).

20. *Parade Magazine*, February 25, 1990, 4. Story of the tragic decline and suicide of Bing Crosby's son, Lindsay. It chronicles how this young man, surrounded by affluence, son of a strict, often harsh, conservative father, found no room for himself. In the absence of interior calm, he used shock as a weapon of deviancy.

21. Alan W. Watts, *Wisdom of Insecurity* (New York: Random House, 1951).

22. Garry Wills, "A Tale of Two Cities," *The New York Review*, October 3, 1996, 22.

23. Samuel Warner, *Self-Realization and Self-Defeat* (New York: Grove Press, 1966).

24. Martin L. Gross, *The Political Racket: Deceit, Self-Interest and Corruption in American Politics* (New York: Ballantine Books, 1996), p. 4.

25. Marsha Sinetar, *Do What You Love, The Money Will Follow* (New York: Dell Trade Paperbacks, 1987). One of the most imaginative titles ever. Sinetar says there is no need to play "Russian roulette" with your life when you listen to your heart.

26. Cyril Northcote Parkinson, "Parkinson's Law Lives," *The Economist*, September 1957, 30.

27. James E. Challenger, "Careers & Workplace," *The Tampa Tribune*, October 22, 1996, Baylife, 2.

28. Despite these sobering statistics from the National Institute of Mental Health (1990 data base, *Time* cover story, "The Evolution of Despair," August 28, 1995, pp. 50–57), the new science of evolutionary psychology finds the roots of modern maladies in our genes. In this age (Culture of Complacency), one is seldom considered responsible for his stress, anxiety, and depression. Blame it on nature! Blame it on our genes!

29. Take this brouhaha that ignorance sponsored. An engineer was downgraded in his section by his supervisor. The charge? The supervisor said all he ever saw him doing was humming and tapping his pencil at his desk, never saw him on the floor. It turned out the engineer was a systems analyst and the key player on a $50 million program. His peers threatened to walk off the job if the downgrade was not rescinded. It was. The supervisor was new on the program and was ignorant of the work of systems analysts.

30. Tarrant, op. cit., p. 312.

31. Bruce F. Baird, *The Technical Manager: How to Manage People and Make Decisions* (Belmont, CA: Lifetime Learning, 1983), p. 75.

32. Jolie Solomon (*The Boston Globe*), "*In Search of Excellence* Author Downbeat About Change: Despite the Popularity of His Ideas, Few Companies Have Instituted Them," *The Tampa Tribune-Times*, March 17, 1991, Business section, 1.

33. Thomas J. Peters and Robert Waterman, *In Search of Excellence* (New York: Harper & Row, 1982).

34. *Business Week*, November 5, 1984, devotes most of its issue to the failure of companies profiled in *In Search of Excellence* to sustain their performance.

35. Joseph Wambaugh, *The Onion Field* (New York: Dell Paperbacks, 1987). It is a sociological study of police and the policed and supports Wambaugh's thesis that a community gets the police it deserves.

36. Donald C. Drake, "Our Destiny, Obedient Automatons?" *St. Petersburg Times*, December 27, 1973, Business section, 1. See also Stanley Milgrin's *Obedience to Authority* (New York: Harper & Row, 1973).

37. T. S. Eliot, *Bartlett's Familiar Quotations* (Boston: Little Brown, 1938), p. 899, "The Rock."

The Culture of Contribution

"The Work Ethic Lives!: Americans labor harder and at more jobs than ever." This was an attention-grabbing *Time* magazine (September 7, 1987) lead-in to an article which, curiously, insisted that hard work is ennobling and that people forced to work two and three jobs to live in style is proof positive that the American work ethic is alive.[2] I don't think so. It suggests quite the opposite, for hard work is scarcely relevant, much less exalted today. Working hard is like treading water in place, knowing if you ever stop treading you will drown. There is a community of workers in conventional jobs who feel precisely like they are treading water. There is a limit to endurance, then what? Working two and three jobs is avoiding the issue. It is not evidence of a work ethic, but of unconscious incompetence or the search for the easy way out. There is no easy way out. Workers who have seen their jobs vanish must either be retrained in more productive work or retire. They cannot keep treading water. If they are unable or unwilling to learn new skills, they may well become a casualty. Conscious competence demands that workers make reality checks periodically, and that they assess their competence against this reality. Moralizing is not the answer. The economics of warfare has no heart. The question every worker must ask himself is this: What can I do now that I am not doing to get out of deep water and onto firm soil? Workers are under siege, and this is no time for half measures.

Unfortunately, there is a jaundiced appetite in worker consciousness for a strenuous schedule. Even if a worker is not making progress, he gets social sympathy for working hard: "Isn't it just wonderful how hard Sam (Sally) works. Why, I believe he (she) is working two jobs." Workers take pride in boasting about how hard they work. It is much less acceptable to boast of how smart one is working: "I only work 20 hours a week and make a good living. Isn't that great?" Most people would not think so. First, they would be suspect of your boast, next they would put you down for bragging, and then they would hate you for making them feel a fool. Few are likely to tell their friends it now takes them half the time it took before to earn a living. People take exception to those who show themselves as clever, while the same people welcome someone who complains of working hard. They can identify with the latter, but not the former. Why?

Workers hate to make hard choices. The fact that hard choices make it easy for them eventually has little impact on their decisions, nor that easy choices make for miserable lives. Research shows that most careers of workers are accidental, not planned. Most workers fall into their jobs and don't consciously seek out their careers. They stumble into their destinies. So, workers recite to colleagues how tough their schedules are, how many hours they work, how many jobs they juggle, failing to see the imbecility of this. Many workers prefer self-deception to committing to something they passionately believe in. Instead, their energy is engaged in menial diversions.

There is graphic evidence of this. The graduate schools of many American universities are the best in the world, especially in the pure sciences and technologies. The students that dominate these graduate school populations are foreign students, primarily Oriental. The mathematics, physics, chemistry, and graduate engineering programs, especially in electronic and computer engineering, have anywhere from 50 to 75 percent of their graduate students from foreign countries. Obviously, one of the reasons for this brain drain is that these curricula require extensive preparation, from grammar school, high school, and through undergraduate school. Europe and Asia excel at preparing students from preschool on for rewarding careers in science and technology. Meanwhile, Americans exalt students with athletic prowess who can throw a ball through a hoop, kick it through a goal post, or hit it out of the park. If not athletic, Americans exalt students who chase the buck in business or law schools. We produce more MBAs than the rest of the graduate schools of the world combined, and in Washington, D.C. alone there are 65,000 lawyers. American universities have some of the finest liberal arts and fine arts colleges in the world, which again draw widely from foreign lands. Schools are here, opportunity is here, but where are the students?[3]

Is Work a Product or a Process?

American society is becoming soft working hard as work has progressed from the assembly line through automation, laser technology, computers, and telecommunications, moving from work being primarily manual to essentially mental. However, the workplace culture and the cultural infrastructure still glorify hard work. American society has taken the cowboy out of the frontier, but not the frontier out of the cowboy. "Rawhide!" The word suggests rough-cut, open, individualistic, tough, uncompromising, brave, unpretentious, blatant, and proud. Americans still insist on behaving as the golden child of the globe, eternally young, unspoiled by time, unsophisticated by civilization, and unsullied by limits—a partial explanation of why Americans take so much pride in working hard and so little in working smart. A society that attempts to solve most of its problems by working harder manages only to exist. This is a form of dementia, a mania for being busy, not being able to relax and do nothing. It reminds me of the film *Magic* (1978) in which a ventriloquist, Anthony Hopkins, becomes obsessed with his dummy.[4] His agent, Burgess Meredith, at one point bets Hopkins that he cannot separate himself from interplay with the dummy for 60 seconds, which, as it turns out, he can't. Americans often display the same mania for keeping busy. My mother was a great reader, and as she got older she turned more and more to books. One day I got a letter from my brother: "We must do something. Mother reads a book a day and does little else. How bored she must be! Can you imagine wasting your life like that?" To me, my mother was the picture of envy; to my brother, a man of action, my mother's behavior was just this side of bizarre.

Living is a process, and work is an important part of it. To have work that is loved is the essence of happiness. It is an expression of joy and sense of usefulness. Even so, many, from the first day of work until they retire, can think of little else than the day they have nothing to do, when there are no demands, no clocks to watch, no criticism to endure, and no conflicts to avoid. They can't wait for the day when they are free! But are they? Struggle is an integral part of freedom, and stress is an integral part of that freedom. Hans Selye's *Stress Without Distress* (1974) is a blueprint for using stress as a positive force to achieve a rewarding life. Selye believes we should embrace and use stress, not be overwhelmed by distress.[5]

Living requires concentration on process. Success is a journey, not an end. From the time we are kids, we are charmed by "Aladdin and his Magic Lamp," thinking if only a genie could give me three magic wishes. Most everyone is given many more than three, yet they are ignored. Why? Because most people are afraid to live, committed only to existing. Existence is driven by results—what do I get for what I give?—the product, not the process. People preoccupied with existing want to get to the top, but without experiencing the joy of the climb. Special perks are the bane of fulfillment, while struggle is its blessing. Existing is to retire in a no-growth job at 21 and coast in comfort to a slow death 50 years later.

Some refer to living as existential, a philosophy of life in which the person finds time for beauty, daydreaming, contemplation, and smelling the roses. It is a philosophy of now, not later. An existential person might enjoy art, literature, architecture, farming, mountain climbing, rafting, or anything else which puts him in touch with himself and his world. Work is a vocation to one, an avocation to another. When a person is able to combine his vocation and avocation, as popular novelist Elmer Leonard has, it brings nothing but joy. Notice that such people are at peace with themselves and have little need to impress or rattle their sabers. Gratitude permeates their presence as they can't believe they are making a living doing what they love.

Are you living or existing? Are you doing what you are supposed to, playing out someone else's agenda, or are you doing what you want to? Existence focuses on performance and results, which is always a disappointment because results are anticlimactic. You are stuck with them. With process, you have flexibility. A student who works for an "A" and pays little attention to the materials may get his "A," but his chemistry doesn't change. People we read about in books struggled to create the world in which we live. Their triumphs and tragedies become our studies. We build our world on their foundation. In learning about them, we better understand ourselves. By reliving their struggles, we discover our own. In the process, we become more human. There is no place for intolerance in an educated mind.

In the "Prison of Panic called NOW!" where workers spend eight hours a day fighting through scrap and rework to produce a product, there is little deviation until someone says, "Enough, already!" And then the results may not turn out as anticipated. One young product assurance engineer, who had just attended a short course at MIT on quality, returned to put into practice what he had learned. He studied the process and checked the amount of scrap created by redesign, rework, and reschedule. He then extrapolated these data year to date and came up with a staggering figure of $5 million in unaccountable waste. For the effort, he was demoted, taken off the program, and shipped to another plant. What the young engineer didn't realize is that the workplace culture was driven by results, not process, and by producing a product, not worrying about costs. It was a cost-plus program with the United States Department of Defense.

Work as a product is essentially lifeless, floating on a sea of uncertainty and red ink. Work as a process is dynamic and conducive to meaningful problem-solving:

- Manage the process, and the product will take care of itself.
- Manage the product, and the process will give you nightmares.

Working harder is a negative coefficient. Fortunately, there have been great strides to correct this, especially in the automotive industry, which has gone from losing its leadership 30 years ago to again being the No. 1 automobile producer in the world.

Work and workers have changed dramatically, while management and the measurement of work have lagged behind. This cannot be blamed on management exclusively, for many workers would rather work hard than take risks and work smarter. Being culturally conditioned to results, they want personal guarantees, to know what they are going to get for what they give. Nor are they likely to be inclined to take a three-, four-, or five-year apprenticeship in electronics, computers, or some other technician program, which pays them less than they would make on the assembly line of some automotive company. Within a company, they are unlikely to bid on a demanding job, which includes high risk and possible failure.

With medicine becoming a high-risk profession due to the rising tide of lawsuits, women are replacing men in medical school. In 1970, only 14 percent of medical school graduates were women. Today, nearly half are women. Women are apparently more willing to take risks and work the process than men, as more than 60 percent of all graduate students are women, with more than 55 percent of all master's degrees issued to women. In 1970, only 5 percent of women earned law degrees; now that number is approaching 50 percent. There is even a greater gender imbalance growing in higher education for minority students. Among black students who earned bachelor's degrees in 1990, fully 60 percent were female; among Hispanic students, 55 percent were female; and among white students, 53 percent were female.[6]

This may have broader implications. Women have always preferred to work smart over brute force. Women don't have the physical strength. Their powers are more subtle. Moreover, women are less prone to be shamed into capitulation than men. A female executive was demoted and given a non-functioning job. She maintained an office, but no longer had a secretary or a private parking space. Otherwise, she continued to draw the same salary and benefits. I would often pass her office, see her doing her nails, smiling broadly, or talking animatedly on the telephone. She continued to dress to the teeth and displayed all the aplomb as if she was still an active power broker. A male colleague of mine, once a revered engineer, was demoted because of a drinking problem. He suffered a similar fate with a totally different reaction. He took on the role of rabble-rouser, attempting to organize the engineers into a union. When that failed, he became a political activist, campaigning throughout the facility. That, too, failed. Then, he became despondent, lost his sense of humor, seldom spoke to anyone, wore a permanent frown, and moped about. One day he had a heart attack at age 50 and died. The female executive spent seven happy years in limbo, giving no indication that she felt any psychological damage, then retired at 65. Today, she is still going strong and still looks beautiful.

It is no mere coincidence that women are adjusting to the new cultural demands more rapidly than men. Women are used to being in charge, not on mahogany row, but as mothers who put their sons there. Women, without portfolios, have had to be problem-solvers with limited resources and have learned to make the most of what they have had. Limits are a new experience for men. From the age of four or five on, men learn the game of bullying and choose their leaders on that basis. Physical prowess, until age 18, commands the attention, respect, and following, especially athletic ability. Gradually, from that point forward, leadership takes on more of a cerebral and psychological character, but hardly intellectual. Men as doers, talkers, and shakers get noticed. With women:

- The cerebral has always been more enchanting.
- It has been their role to listen, to plant the seed of an idea into their sons' or husbands' heads, and watch them go forward with the idea without acknowledgment.

- It has been necessary to be real and to deal realistically with what they have had, not with what their husbands, fathers, or brothers dreamed of having.

Men like to soar like birds. Women prefer to feel the solid earth under their feet. Women have kept the culture extant by practicing the tenets of the culture religiously and consistently. Men fall back on the culture when in dire straits; otherwise they ignore it. Women are unabashedly spiritual because they carry a soul with them wherever they go. Men argue the metaphysics of soullessness. Where men and women are more alike than different is that their cultural conditioning finds them more driven to please others than to please themselves. With women, their drive is to please men. With men, their drive is please power, which usually resides with men.

There is no danger of a unisex gender. It seems clear that the scales are turning toward many of the attributes that are commonly associated with women. These attributes are becoming essential to organization—listening skills, acceptance of limits, dealing pragmatically with reality, using the whole brain, being as comfortable in the abstract as the concrete, not needing to promote "action for action's sake," and not being afraid to respect and play hunches. There is something else going on in organization that is less intimidating to women than men. It is the assertion of individualism in pursuit of collective identity. Collective identity is a mockery unless the individual first relates honestly and completely with himself. He must expand his consciousness without apology before he can relate meaningfully to others. Most workers don't know what they want as they have spent their lives pleasing others:

- It is more acceptable to be a grind or mediocre than to step out of the crowd and be great.
- Only "geeks" love what they do regardless of pay.
- Audacity is discouraged, as is conflict. A person who is willing to admit that he values his own opinion more than what others think about him is considered arrogant. The mask of humility is encouraged.
- Those full of pleasing self above pleasing others are put on notice that this is not acceptable.

Yet the mind-set of pleasing others at the expense of pleasing self comes out of the cultural landscape of comfort and complacency, not contribution. The Culture of Contribution is a very different place. It is the land of giants, giant achievers, giant pains-in-the-asses, and giant contradictions. It is the land where giant inconsistencies rest next to giant consistencies, where there is no such thing as a status quo, and where giant breakthroughs are so common they don't have a name.

Topographical Landscape of the Culture of Contribution

Because the Culture of Contribution is the land of pain, risk, uncertainty, and limits, it represents an entirely new landscape for doing business, a new visage and frame of reference. It is the land of growth and contribution. It is far easier to speak of contribution than to test the measure of its potential. The topography of contribution is enchanting from afar, mysterious and intriguing, but up close it is threatening because it challenges everything we believe is sacred. It has no status quo as it is in a constant state of motion. It is like Brownian movement—fluid, dynamic, and in constant flux. This topography is the next frontier. It is not as mysterious nor as far-reaching as a space probe to Mars, but under our feet, ours to claim if we have the sense and will to claim it.

Old terms are meaningless in this new configuration—CEO, president, vice president, director, manager, supervisor—as the Culture of Contribution is the constant bombardment of "colloidal particles in a fluid state." Even such archaic words as power, empowerment, interdependence, collegial, and teaming fail to capture its essence. Everything moves to the needs of organization. Differences, disputes, arguments, discussions, conflicts, and confrontations are all part of its chemistry. These encounters are not to be avoided, but used and exploited to the organization's purpose. Given that many organizations cut individuals off from expressing their concerns, which results in them worrying more about their identity than doing the job, it becomes easier to complain than contribute. That is why the old configuration is no longer apropos.

Corporate culture has neither sponsored growth nor encouraged purposefulness. It has instead made workers dependent and driven them to pettiness—more concerned with getting than giving, better actors than performers—rather than toward significant contribution. There is no substitute for feeling a sense of usefulness and no greater pleasure than making a contribution to the well-being of others. This cannot be measured quantitatively. It is a qualitative indicator, which corporate culture continues to ignore. Despite attempts to ease operational problems with remedial programs and processes, the delivery and evaluation of these have been mainly quantitative, not qualitative; objective, not subjective; cognitive, not affective; concrete, not abstract. Human beings are qualitative, subjective, affective, and essentially abstract entities. Following leaders is mainly symbolic. People will go to hell and back if you touch their spiritual cords. Conversely, if you ignore their spirit and insist on bombarding their senses with quantitative, objective, cognitive, concrete indices, you enter the realm populated by the Robert McNamaras, not the Abraham Lincolns. McNamara looked at Vietnam and thought like a machine. Lincoln looked at the Civil War and thought like a prophet. Lincoln brought Americans out of themselves and into a common spirit. McNamara brought Americans out of a common spirit and into themselves. The same error is made every day in corporate culture when workers are directed away from their spirit and toward comfort and complacency.[7]

By sustaining the need to please others as a condition of employment, a servile and lethargic culture springs forth from these roots. This culture is not honest, avoids pain and risk, and contrives to be what it is not. As Sigmund Freud asserts, "It is only through pain that our level of consciousness increases" (Figure 9.1). If anything, comfort and complacency reduce our awareness of reality. This finds us seeing what we want to see, hearing what we want to hear, feeling what we want to feel, and thinking what we want to think. Yet it is only through increased consciousness that

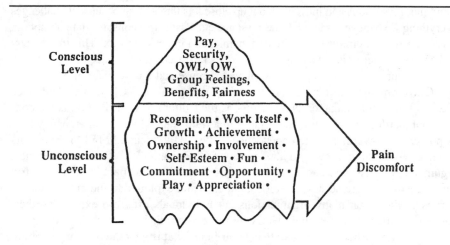

To experience breakthrough or to surface some of these true motivators the worker must experience pain (discomfort). Also, management must decode what people say to what they mean. For example, "pay" is at issue when the person's self-esteem, sense of worth is on the line.

Figure 9.1   The path to increased consciousness.

we can manage change. What increases our level of consciousness other than pain? It is the language that touches our spirit and awakens us out of ourselves into a sense of a common humanity. It overcomes what Leon Festinger refers to as *cognitive dissonance*—when we encounter inconsistent knowledge to what we already perceive to be true, we reduce the dissonance by modifying the information to fit our preconceived notions. This automatic cognitive correcting can put us out of touch with reality.[8]

Comfort and complacency reduce awareness and lull the mind to a false sense of security. Pain and conflict are necessary precursors to contribution. That does not mean we engage pain for pain's sake or become masochistic. There is no glory in an ability to endure pain. We are discussing psychological pain, the pain of discomfort, embarrassment, failure, loss, inadequacy, rejection, or social exclusion. Psychological pain is real. Once we are in the thralls of psychological pain, we find ourselves in the land of "second chances," of personal renewal, and of reinvention. President Bill Clinton has had a life of loss and gain repeatedly, and each time he has encountered a loss, he has found his way to be reborn. He was the youngest governor in the history of the United States to ever be defeated. Had he not lost that election, Clinton-watchers claim, he would have lacked the fortitude or purpose to become president.

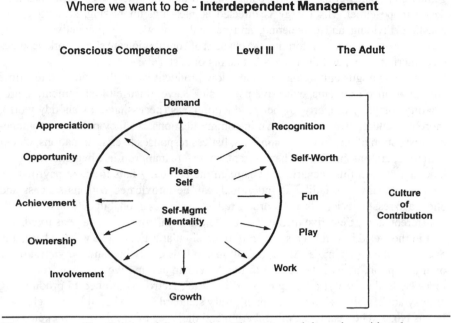

Figure 9.2   The Culture of Contribution: The mature adult worker with a clear sense of interdependence.

Think of your life. What has made you the person you are? If you are pleased with where you are and who you are, and none of us are completely, chances are you have embraced psychological pain and used it to advantage. We learn much more about ourselves from defeats than victories, from failures than successes. Why? When we are successful, we become almost robotic. We fail to reflect much on success unless we are an exception, like Jack Nicklaus. At the height of his career, No. 1 professional golfer in the world, he practiced, practiced, practiced as if he were an amateur. When something goes wrong, and we fail, we are painfully aware of the failure. We become analytical, which, incidentally, is the worst thing we could do. Analysis fragments our sense of the problem and disperses our energy from its source. Better we practice what works for us, and success is bound to return.

If you sense that contribution is an individual commitment, which brings out our collective idiosyncratic talents united to a common objective, we are on the same page. Admittedly, corporate culture, as it now exists, too frequently pressures the individual to conform to arbitrary standards and to wax sincere. This drives the individual to desert his own thinking and feelings in order to behave as others would expect him to behave. Conformity takes a surprising amount of energy. It also increases the level of stress and distress, along with free-floating anxiety. The individual is sitting on pins and needles, afraid that if his true personality evolves, he is in trouble. An artist once said that all geniuses are pains-in-the-asses. A person with a high need to please others has little desire to be either. His energy is directed at pleasing, impressing, stealing credit, cheating, dividing and conquering, and certainly not working productively. When rewards are so great for conformity, the chances of contribution are slim. Work becomes a counterfeit game, and the players but actors on a stage.

It is this bogus culture that produces low productivity, high accident rates, time and attendance problems, excessive use of sick leave, misuse of equipment, appropriating company property, higher production costs (necessitated by shoddy work), more procedural errors, breakdown in communications, we/they polarity, spontaneous disruption of operations by conflicts, listless responses to crisis situations, clock-watching, grab-assing, sexual harassment, cover-up, inappropriate hygiene, and salty language. Given this scenario, downstream the company fails to make payroll.

A company, not unlike an individual, can be intoxicated with its success and choose to rest on its laurels. Back orders tell it business is good, but new business tells a different story. Selective memory can hide the truth from a company as to what is real in the world beyond. This can lead to the circular argument of what, where, and even why the company is. An organization can thus easily become the victim of its own deception, as was the case with the American automotive industry from 1954 to 1979. In the face of a changing world market, Detroit continued to produce big clumsy automobiles with quality an arbitrary standard. Why should Detroit change? It was No. 1. Then came the oil embargo, and the price of gasoline skyrocketed due to the instability of Middle East oil producers and the defiance of OPEC. Suddenly, foreign compacts became popular as economic replacements for Detroit's gas guzzlers. It took a quarter century for Detroit's automotive manufacturers to regain the lead in this industry, but they did it! This indicates that corporations, too, have second chances. Many of the ideas and concepts in this book these manufacturers are now doing mainly because they embraced psychological pain. They didn't run from it. They found the courage to make the hard choices, choices that they had before ignored. What Chrysler, Ford, and General Motors are doing is changing the corporate culture, the performance structure, the cultural biases, and the work standards that better approximate a Culture of Contribution. They are making progress, but they have not reached fruition. Nor can their successes be generalized. The topography of contribution may be similar but not the same.

Proving You Have the Culture of Contribution

Often what seems to be isn't. This is especially true of something as subtle and multidimensional as culture. When I was a boy, there was a radio series called "The Shadow." The entre into each program ran something like this: "Lamont Cranston, while studying in the Orient, learned to cloud men's minds so that they could not see him." A short pause followed, then, "Who knows what evil lurks in the hearts of men?" Another pause. "The Shadow knows," then bone-chilling laughter. At age seven, the Shadow was a fanciful extension to my life, full of mystery and wonder.

I would run home from school, glue my ear to the radio, and listen to the latest exploits of this unseen crime-fighter. That spirit of wondering and mystery, which is so natural in one's innocence, can easily be killed. Somehow, it survived in me. I learned at an early age that men do, indeed, seek to conceal their intentions or deeds for what they are. Albeit trained as a scientist with a reverence for reason, my success in life has been in dealing with human spuriousness, thanks to those enthralling early days of my youth. Human beings, in one sense, remain an enigma; in another, they are painfully obvious. People continue to defy scientists who study them. There is far too much spuriousness to make accurate assessments.[9] Much of the data in *The Bell Curve* (1994), for example, leads to silly assumptions as authors Richard Hernstein and Charles Murray try to make a case that one race is smarter than another.[10] Even the rigorous statistics of polling is loaded with loopholes. Yet politicians follow polls as if the key to the Holy Grail. In many ways, people are as predictable as Newtonian physics. We know from basic physics, for instance, that heat rises and cold contracts, that an object in motion tends to stay in motion, and that energy can be neither created nor destroyed, only transformed. Likewise, we know that people move from discomfort to comfort, and that without struggle, there is little growth. We also know that the more you do for people, the less they do for themselves. The more you supply people with identity, the less they know who they are. This is not rocket science. This is common sense. Everyone who has ever wondered and separated what people say from what they do develops the ability to discern. Discernment is reading behavior. Most people have never gone to the Orient, but they have learned how "to cloud men's minds so that they cannot see them." Their behavior fools us because we don't pay attention. We don't look past the obvious to discern. Yet, the shroud that covers most behavior is transparent, if we would but look. The workplace culture, then, is somewhat accessible if we are looking with our God-given gifts, instead of allowing ourselves to be baffled by the "smoke and mirrors."

Proof that the workplace culture supports contribution is not straightforward but is enveloped in myriad behavioral indicators, among which there are:

- Workers have a sense of purpose with a short-term minor goal and a long-term major goal. They are natural planners without portfolio. Once they have a clear objective, they don't return to confirm and report every little iota of progress made. They have a plan, a schedule, benchmarks to monitor their progress, and a target date to complete. As long as they are working within time constraints and "on plan," they stick to their work. No one develops this schedule for them. It is of their own design and construction and serves their peculiar style of operation.

- They move with confidence, but not cockiness. They don't hesitate to seek help and assistance when they have questions or problems. They are available to help others who have the need of their expertise. The work they turn out is user-friendly and shows evidence of understanding the needs of colleagues in that connection.

- They are learners, not knowers. When someone asks them a question, they don't punish the person with their knowledge, nor are they afraid to say, "I don't know." If they know an alternative source, they add, "but you might check with so and so."
- They have opinions and are not afraid to express them. If they disagree with someone, they tell them. They express their disagreement directly and politely and focus on the subject, not on the person.
- There are no secrets. Trust is the foundation of all relationships in this culture. There is no claptrap of "on a need to know basis." Information is up front and available.
- The focus is on designing, constructing, and building concepts that lace together the important ideas necessary to get the job done. Out of this grow practices that are flexible, relevant, and changeable. Nothing is written in concrete.
- The frame of reference is broad, deep, and diverse. Conventional problem-solving is passé, where the emphasis previously was on cause and effect analysis, linear logic and linear curves, and quantitative analysis. Creative thinking is in vogue, not critical thinking. Critical thinking leaves out constructive possibilities and creates adversarial relationships—winners and losers. Parallel thinking is in, which explores the problem at several levels and creates a solution. It does not discover the solution.
- Change is a natural, not an artificial condition. The atmosphere is collegial and respectful without being pretentious. Cooperation is not the attention-getter, but the product of joint exploration. Change entails creative, constructive, design energy.
- Workers are self-organized and are no longer externally controlled. The fire is within, not under them. They understand that their perceptions are constantly in a state of flux, self-organizing, and changing, as they work and experience new things.
- Workers are free to personalize their work, founded on the trust that they will do a good job. They are in control. Should they fall short of the mark, however, they seek help and correct their errors accordingly.

In the Culture of Contribution, you sense that it is fun to be at work. Problems occur, but there is no panic. What is conspicuously absent is the too controlling, too defining, and too overwhelming manager, who in his effort to motivate instead kills the worker's spirit. Here the focus is on creating a performance climate by reinforcement of the values of contribution: (a) providing the training and tools necessary, (b) presenting workers with an objective and the time constraints to do the job, and (c) then backing off and allowing workers to achieve the objective on their own. What is remarkable about this formula is that (a) and (b) are commonly provided, only to be thwarted by (c).

What is also absent in the Culture of Contribution is finger-pointing. The focus is on what is wrong, not who is wrong. Humility is more common than arrogance—"We accomplished" rather than "I accomplished." Wisdom is much more appreciated than cleverness, so workers don't waste their time being crafty. To an outsider immersed in the flow of this casual chaos, it might seem people are goofing off, but this could not be further from the truth. Work is fluid and dynamic, with action evident by the rate of completion of tasks, with no one standing around waiting to be told what to do next. They know their complementary roles and move to fill them. There is a lot of give-and-take humor but little evidence of complaining. Workers pride themselves in anticipating and dealing with problems. Crisis management is an embarrassment. Managers and workers hold each other in equal esteem and support each other to the point that their roles seem indistinguishable.

The most subtle characteristic of the Culture of Contribution is presence. It is that unspoken quality that you feel more than you see. You have the sense that people wouldn't be here doing this work if they didn't want to and that they have a high personal regard for themselves and feel no need to assert their dignity. They are selfish in the sense that they have a high need to please themselves, but not at the expense of co-workers. If they didn't enjoy the work or like their co-workers, they would clear out and not become a nuisance. They are far less self-centered than those of the please-other mentality. Those with an obsessive need to please derive their satisfaction by complaining and drawing attention to themselves. Those of a please-self mentality are more inclined to enlightened self-interests. This is displayed in their enthusiasm for work, which is catching, and is directed toward the service of others, not because it is the thing to do but because it is how they feel.

Workers in the Culture of Contribution see managers and workers as there to serve each other as first customers. They feel traditional management fails to see workers and managers in complementary roles. Some have attempted to educate management into understanding this new relationship. No organization, within my experience, has been completely successful in this regard. Most success thus far of the Culture of Contribution is *ad hoc* or in the realm of informal group activity. Yet cultural change of this nature is not likely to be accidental. Without the direct involvement of senior management, the full benefits of this culture will continue to linger. Meanwhile, conventional wisdom still holds most organizations to conventional practices, which are described here as Level I and Level II, or the Culture of Comfort and the Culture of Complacency. Level III, the Culture of Contribution, requires conscious competence to establish its behaviors. This compels the organization to make a supreme effort and, yes, a radical departure from the conventional approach to doing business. What we have, at Level III, is mature adult workers, not snivelling workers in suspended adolescence, nor do we have codependent bonds between employers and employees. Obviously, the Culture of Contribution threatens the status quo. With this, culture control shifts from a select few to a network of managers and workers throughout the workplace. The technology is already here begging for this cultural development, but the social dynamics lag, as one might expect, because workers and managers are not ready, nor are they mature enough to fathom its implications.

Conscious Competence

Conscious competence can best be experienced by embracing one's natural resistance to pain, discomfort, difficulty, dissatisfaction, or perturbation, then soaring to new heights because of this embrace. "The dove, as she speeds her way through the air, may marvel at the resistance to her flight by the atmosphere," writes Western philosopher Immanuel Kant, "but we know that but for that resistance she could not fly at all." Nor could a kite fly, a sailboat sail, or an organization move forward. Consider all the posturing that goes on in the typical organization as it vacillates between independence and dependence, autonomy and central control, separation and integration. Meanwhile, open cooperation, collaboration, and communication are rhetorically upheld but operationally neglected. "That didn't happen in my department"..."That didn't happen on my watch"..."We completed our part successfully"...until one day the thinking changes to "We have a problem"..."What resources can we commit to it?"..."What can I do extra to help?"... as resistance is embraced, and there is breakthrough. At that moment, the synergy of interdependence crashes through the barrier of consciousness. Suddenly, the consciousness of the group is that it is not alone—that it is not a splintered reality—that nothing is impossible. We embrace our resistance to the fact that without others, we cannot succeed. As Drucker observes, "People of great strengths have great weaknesses."

Recognition of personal limits and the need for others fosters interdependence. Yet in our culture there is a syndrome known as "John Wayne" or "Lone Ranger" that intimates that we don't need anybody and that being a "stand-alone person" is a positive.[11] Generally speaking, to resist something is a negative. Darlene Goth-Neuman says "Resistance is a positive and powerful force. When you understand that resistance has a purpose in assisting us to create, the habit of resisting resistance will be changed. Resistance enhances our ability to learn and adapt to varying situations. We must not change the object of our judgment, instead we must change the judgment of our object."[12] With our senses being constantly assaulted with the need to change, there is a natural tendency to say to ourselves, "Enough!" and to retreat from change consistent with that pressure. We escape into "iron man/woman triathalons," working two and three jobs, eating and drinking to excess, drugs, promiscuity, violence, crime, depression, becoming television junkies or Internet nerds. We desire to escape, not embrace, freedom, for as Erich Fromm says, "Every new step contains the danger of failure." Alan Watts characterizes modern retreat as "having the accelerator and brake to the floor." This is absurd, but is it accepted as such? Of course not. Machismo covers the silliness, with reality defined as "when rubber hits the road." We might add to Watts's metaphor, "burning up rubber and going nowhere." Is it not societal madness when the culture people embrace burns them out?

The tyranny of technology has turned most things inside out and upside down, finding that which is presumed rational quite ironic. Living in an obsessively materialistic world chips away at our soulfulness and leaves us perversely preoccupied with our clothes, waistline, crow's feet (around the eyes), and abdominal muscles. Content is out. Context is in. Edward Tenner suggests in *Why Things Bite Back* (1996) that technology is out to hurt us. Time and again, he argues, just as we are celebrating having rolled back the mess of the natural world another few inches, whichever gleaming new machine we have just built will take on a life of its own and teach us a lesson in humility. He calls this the *revenge effect*—an antidepressant that makes us depressed; the Chernobyl reactor exploding because the plant was testing a new safety system; high-tech football helmets, designed to protect players' heads, instead provoke an epidemic of spinal injuries; the more roads built around a metropolitan city, the worse traffic becomes; or the overprescription of antibiotics forces bacteria to evolve into drug-resistant superbugs.[13] These are *revenge effects*. In the event of these apocalyptic revenge effects coming to pass, it would force the end of the world to take a back seat to a dreadful irony. Herbert Marcuse calls the growing union between productivity and destruction "the brinkmanship of annihilation."[14]

That is why Mikhail S. Gorbachev's *glasnost* and *perestroika* policy in Russia provided a glimmer of hope to an otherwise cynical and ironic world. Despite this glimmer of light, the horizon remains darkened by technology serving to institute new, more effective forms of social control and political cohesion (scientific management of opinion), telling people what to think and why to think it. Perhaps little of this is done with malicious intent, but none is done without malicious consequences. The swirl of technology is changing everything, while changing nothing.

Modern medicine has had little to do with prolonging life. Diet and healthcare deserve the credit. Modern medicine has had more to do with introducing *revenge effects*. In an evolutionary sense, we certainly aren't getting better as human beings. Organizations society has created to serve it continue to waffle in confusion. Technology has taken over our collective consciousness with such spellbinding speed that society seems at a loss as to how to cope. There is an undeclared war between the individual and society and between the worker and the company. Companies perpetuate the false need for toil at the expense of joy. Communities sponsor aggressiveness at the expense of civility. Most live and work in sick cultures, which, in turn, arrest development. Many feel trapped in their own design, lost in the swirl of what is topical, going backward or sideways but seldom forward. It is for this reason that the Culture of Contribution is important. We need individuals who think for themselves, march to their own drummer. Most organizations see this mentality as a threat. Organizations, whatever the industry, remain essentially naive despite their trappings, with a mania for control and an obsession with predictability. This drives them in the direction of comfort and complacency, dependency and counterdependency, where workers never progress much beyond the emotional maturity of adolescence. So monolithic is this fixation with control that most organizations zoom blindly toward entropy (the disintegration of structures).

The "Please-Self Mentality" Explained

There is no single tendency that causes more frustration and loss of purposeful-ness than the drive to please others. This is actually an indication of a disturbed mentality, which society prefers to see as a state of normalcy. More damage has been done by people consumed with this drive than any other single factor. People who spend an inordinate amount of time worrying about what other people think of them demonstrate an unhealthy preoccupation with self. This is a conditional consequence of upbringing and the curse of our time. Individual growth is from the outside in. Our nascent psyches, as little tykes, constantly react to, internalize, and assimilate what others tell us. We become them long before we become ourselves. This is a process of self-imprisonment or victimization. Many people go through a lifetime never thinking their own thoughts, pleasing themselves, or doing what comes naturally. Their entire orientation is to please someone—a parent, relative, friend, peer, teacher, preacher, or boss. Never in the span of a lifetime does such a person come close to having any idea what he is about. It never occurs to him to wonder. He acquires too much reinforcement, too many accolades, too much approval to do otherwise. He floats through life on a cloud of comfort and never rises off the ground. There is no way a person can be as productive as his potential might allow when his standard is not his own. Such a person has placed himself in a cage, the cage of compromise, conciliation, and concession. He is a chameleon.

So many roadblocks exist within society to self-appreciation, self-discovery, and self-design that what is accepted as an authentic human being is more often an oddball striving for attention—another form of pleasing others at one's own expense. The majority never have the pleasure of knowing themselves. They are many, never one. The reason for this is that our culture has an aversion for rebellion, and yet rebellion is essential to individual potential and identity. There is no substitute. It is only when people take the risk of shedding their conditioning and start sorting out what makes them go that they encounter their essence. This puts them in touch with their *true self*. Their *acquired self* is the facade they assume every day as a mask of safety, called "personality." We live in a time when personality is immensely popular and is treated as celebrity. This epitomizes our sickness—it is more important to impress than perform, to fit than to be qualified, to support than to confront, to accede than to challenge. The irony is that once an individual is allowed to rebel and to find his own way back to society, like the prodigal son, he is overwhelmed by how much his father has learned in his absence. Rebelling is essential to healthy growth and development and the first expression of freedom. Disobedience, which is frowned upon in our culture, is integral to rebellion. A society which produces good little boys and girls is a society of arrested development, because it is unlikely that society will provide the means, motive, and opportunity for them to become mature adult men and women.[15]

The failure of people to grow to their potential or to work out who they are and why they are is epidemic. Take these reflections: "I've spent too many years doing exactly what was expected of me—being a good son, a good husband, and a good father. In my company, I'm known as a 'good soldier.' When I ask myself what I am about, I'd have to say, 'I don't know anymore.' I've tried for so long to fit in; I've held back for so long, and I don't know what or who I am."[16] People purchase millions of self-help books in a desperate attempt to deal with their arrested development. No subject has been treated with greater seriousness. Yet people are afraid to be their own best friend. It is more acceptable in our society to be self-hating than self-loving and more acceptable to give others the benefit of the doubt before we give the same to ourselves. In *The Taboo Against Being Your Own Best Friend* (1996), I write: "We are all authors of our own footprints in the sand, heroes of the novels inscribed in our hearts. Everyone's life, without exception, is sacred, unique, scripted high drama, played out before an audience of one, with but one actor on stage. The sooner we realize this the more quickly we overcome the bondage of loneliness and find true friendship with ourselves."[17]

Think about it. In our culture we constantly try to change others to conform to our personal standards. This diminishes others "as we find them," and in the process diminishes us "as we are." It is a no-gain game. This finds us taking on other people's problems as our own, projecting our problems on them as theirs, and then in a game of compulsive projection, try to make them right with what is wrong with us, when we, not they, are the problem. It is a rare individual, indeed, who can look at another person's situation and see and feel what that individual sees and feels. That is why acceptance is such a powerful tool in listening actively to another person. If there is no emotional involvement in the other person's problem, you can reflect back what you hear and help the other person get a handle on his problem, a problem only he can solve. It all starts with self-acceptance, with liking oneself for what and who one is.

A three-step approach to conscious competence within the framework of the pleasing-self mentality is not new: (1) *awareness* of ourselves as we are, which includes being aware that each of us possesses a separate reality, and which means we view the world differently than any other person; (2) *acceptance* of our awareness in all its naked offensiveness, finding no need to become defensive about it or to make excuses for it, choosing instead to consider the options available to change the behavior (or to live with it); and (3) the *action* we decide to take, given our awareness, and acceptance of that condition.

Choosing to reject the behavior in question is different from denial. A person may admit he has a drinking problem (awareness), but considers it part of his lifestyle. Perhaps he is a traveling salesmen who is required to take customers to dinner, which involves some drinking. When his health starts to go and he has liver complaints, he takes notice. Not until his doctor tells him to either quit drinking or die does he look realistically at his situation (acceptance). At this point, he realizes how denial has been harbored. His mortality threatened, he chooses to reject his lifestyle and commits himself to a chemical detoxification program (action). Notice that once acceptance is fully appreciated, the person rises above the confinement of his separate reality. The thought of dying did this. He rose above being defensive or being angry at himself or others for being in this predicament. His higher conscious-ness has greater tolerance for human frailty than his denial would allow.

Yet as powerful as acceptance is in dealing with self, it is even more powerful in dealing with others. By accepting others as they are, we never own their problems. This is an invitation to be empathetic, not sympathetic. One can never walk in someone else's shoes. Nor should we carry someone else's monkey on our backs. Friends may resent you for not solving their problems, but they will never forgive you when you do. We don't like to owe anyone anything. Nobody makes another person stronger by carrying their baggage.

When a person with a strong please-self orientation is employed in a please-other culture, there are problems. This is not because the please-self person is not moti-vated to perform. It is because this person focuses too heavily on performance and not enough on personality. A please-self person must submit to the predominant culture or leave. A workplace culture is determined to have its members subscribe to its values, and it always succeeds. That is why the workplace culture is such a critical factor in change. The please-self individual will have difficulty in either a Culture of Comfort or a Culture of Complacency. Co-workers will see him as the enemy, as there to make them look bad, the odd man out. Retreat is the only prudent strategy.

A high need to please self is a weighty responsibility in a breakdown culture, where opposing camps are pointing fingers. This person only wants to contribute. His best hope is to find an organization that has a reasonable tolerance for the renegade. Some of the most conservative organizations have skunk works and other renegade work groups. Nearly every organization has some unique contributors or idiosyn-cratic spirits who are allowed to soar. Let the business move away from their expertise, however, and they are gone. These high achievers are a curiosity treated temporarily as luminaries, but never accepted as role models or allowed to become a threat to the status quo. Legions of brilliant men and women have been finessed into believing contribution counts when conformity is the perverse stratagem. Even managers given to display unique but unexpected brilliance are likely to be the first sacked. Most organizations have no sense of humor for managers who display a please-self individualism.

Pleasing Self versus Selfishness

Is the please-self mentality the ultimate in selfishness? Not necessarily. Unself-ishness is a root cultural condition. A case could be made that the ultimate in selfishness is found in the unselfish. The unselfish allows himself to be exploited by being taken for granted, taken advantage of, given faint praise, and treated as a gopher. When a person permits others to bankrupt him emotionally, physically, and spiritually, he does himself no favor, or anybody else. The unselfish redistributes his pain, agony, and self-pity where it is least deserved, on family members and loved ones. This causes deep unhappiness everywhere. In a zero-sum game, those who are the takers are the most unhappy of all. Takers never get enough, always demanding more—more attention, more sympathy, more time, more everything. Worse yet, takers have little respect for givers. There is only one way to be truly unselfish, and that is by being totally selfish. Look at the evidence. If we first meet our own personal needs before we meet the needs of others, we do so with a generous spirit and a sense of freedom. Yet it is considered virtuous to meet the needs of others at the expense of our own. That is how we have been conditioned. It fails to work in the chemistry of being, because it is dishonest and self-abusing. More virtuous is to assert ourselves by meeting our own needs, then meeting the needs of others with a light heart. To submit to social conformity at the expense of one's own free choice does not engender a kind heart.

Sainthood defies the human condition, placing itself above the vanities while reinforcing cultural vagaries. Sainthood is perhaps the most narcissistic of postures. Albert Schweitzer (1875–1965) may not be considered a saint, but many consider him the noblest figure of the twentieth century for his altruism. He lost patience with what he called a "jackass society"—the bourgeoisie of Europe, which included his own intellectual community—leaving a brilliant career as a theologian, musicologist, and organist to study medicine. Upon completion of his studies, he abandoned Europe for Africa, where he undertook the task to build hospitals and clinics. There is no question that Schweitzer was a gentle and deeply religious man. Only 31, he set up his paternalistic service to Africans in a deserted mission at Lambarene in French Equatorial Africa, in a spirit "not of benevolence but atonement" to fight leprosy and sleeping sickness. Even his newly discovered ethical principle, "reverence for life," was fully worked out in relation to the defects of European civilization. Schweitzer's selflessness has always been troubling to me. He turned his back on a "jackass society," but brought European arrogance to Africa. Africans managed to live for centuries without European progress. Moreover, his reverence for life was confusing to the natives, for he couldn't kill the smallest of insects. His hospitals, as a consequence, would never receive the *Good Housekeeping* Seal of Approval. Conceivably, he went to Africa to find himself and to expiate his guilt for being European. Characteristic of the Christian-Judaic culture is for the individual to identify with society, not with nature. The animism of Africans is to yield to nature, not control it. Schweitzer was a totally Western man. Perhaps a sense of life's futility drove him there to pay a humanistic debt to atone for these misgivings. By sacrificing his life to the natives, perhaps he felt he could realize his salvation. Western man is consumed with the idea of debt and repayment, in contrast to the Eastern man who prefers moving from ignorance to illumination. Whatever the motivation, European society, far from being incensed at his rebuke, celebrated him as an altruist. Was Africa improved? Is it better now? It is impossible to say. What is more remarkable about this man is not what he did, but that he had the courage to do it. He had the courage to please self by serving others. In that sense, he escaped European society and its shackling culture.[18]

The most significant characteristic of the please-self mentality is the need to be purposeful. The world outside may be in disarray, but that has little impact on the deliberate individual. The resonance of the individual operates on a separate dynamic—chaos and change. Chaos synergizes effort, as it did Schweitzer, and launches the person into the dynamic of change. One wonders what Schweitzer could have done if he had stayed in Europe and turned his zeal on his own society, a more monumental task.

In the corporate world everywhere, managers and workers are trying to please customers, bosses, stockholders, suppliers, subordinates, peers, community leaders, even confessors, and ending up pleasing no one. They are at their wit's end and still manage to smile through clenched teeth. So, what do they do? Do they say, "Damn it! Time out! Enough already!" No, they open another pack of cigarettes, have a couple of double martinis at lunch, or go on a health kick, giving up one narcotic for another, punishing themselves into a condition they never had when they were half the age. They acquire younger significant others, while carrying a pack of Rolaids in their briefcase, alongside a deluxe container of Extra Strength Excedrin. They drink gallons of coffee, looking forlorn and perplexed. And then they have a cerebral hemorrhage, myocardial infarction, peptic ulcer, colon cancer, kidney attack, liver complaint, prostatitis, or simply retire on the job. Were these same people inclined to please self, the outcome would be quite different, but they are not, and that's the problem. Albert Schweitzer deserted Europe for Africa and lived to be 90. Think about it.

The Price of Pleasing Self

Not everyone has their Lambarene to escape to. Like Desiderius Erasmus (Catholic Counter Reformation), most people with a please-self inclination must seek their destiny inside the system, rather than outside as did Martin Luther (Protestant Reformation). The clash of culture between feudalism, which was first economic and then religious (Roman Catholicism versus Protestantism), and capitalism, which was first religious (Protestantism) and then economic, is once again upon us. We are in the post-modern, post-capitalistic period, and what is evolving is the please-self mentality, which is neither particularly economic nor religious. It is *peoplehood*. The please-self mentality in today's organization stands out like a sore thumb. People of the please-self orientation might agree with naturalist Stephen Jay Gould's message in *An Urchin in the Storm* (1987), that all organic life is programmed to survive only when it is threatened with extinction.[19] Otherwise, there is no instinctual mechanism that preserves a species. Only the sense of danger precedes activation of the survival behavior. Likewise, with people, if there is no sense of danger, or if it is felt the danger is exaggerated, it will be ignored. The human species has a herd mentality that necessitates being frightened to death to act. Biologist Richard Dawkins relates in his book *The Selfish Gene* (1976) that *selfishness is indigenous to survival.*[20] Dawkins studies single-cell organisms and sees an interesting correlation between biology and social theory. He suggests that selfishness is neither good nor bad, but is simply inherently robotic. Evolution, he claims, has always been selfish, and all organic life is a survival machine, on both a molecular (genetic) and mechanistic (human) scale. So, why are we so afraid to be selfish when it is so critical to our well-being?

Advent of the Professional

Social commentator Eric Hoffer reflects, "if you want to understand a society, study the games they play and how they play them." Professional athletes are pioneering a new direction. They understand their power and are leveraging the organization in a new way—they demand parity. They are taking the power away from owners, coaches, and management and reclaiming it as their own. What is dangerous about this is that there are no clear indications that they understand the demands of power and engendered responsibilities. The possibility exists that they could eventually kill their sport, as baseball almost did with the players' strike of 1994, which cut the season short and canceled the World Series. What is true in sport is also often true in life.

We live in a restless age dominated by youth, with half the world's population under 25. It is a time of radical change in which a new professional class of workers is starting to make waves similar to professional athletes. It is increasingly conscious of its power but not yet competent to exercise it. The spoiled-brat generation, children of the baby boomers, is positioning itself to take over. This generation is different than any before it, growing up in the post-modern period and post-industrial age, craving for the simplicity of pre-industrial society, but with a difference. This generation, which has had so much and experienced so little, demands more control of everything, without flirting with risk-taking, while showing less civility to convention and authority. Baltimore Orioles' baseball star Roberto Alomar spitting in the face of an umpire over a disputed play during a 1996 playoff game illustrates the unhappy combination of exquisite professionalism and juvenility. The lack of respect for authority on display here seems endemic to this generation. They think they have a better way, and they may have. They want to define their situation in terms that make sense to them. They, as workers, are tired of hearing growth advocated while incessantly experiencing budget cuts, being encouraged to take the initiative while seeing conformity rewarded. They represent a learned society, because they are better educated than any before them, but they are not yet a learning society. Our schools still produce learned but not learning people. In a learning society, people have neither the time nor the inclination to exploit, oppress, or be uncivil.

Like athletes, professional workers are students of what they do and seek to excel within the limits of their ability, but not without guilt. Guilt has been the main contributor to confusion as pleasing self is made synonymous with self-indulgence. Professional athletes, who are media trained, are careful not to exude too much pleasure at their accomplishments. Humility, even contrived, is in. Likewise, workers have been programmed to experience anxiety over their successes and confusion over their pleasures. Pleasure, according to the Danish philosopher Soren Kierkegaard, is our greatest fear. Pleasure and sin, Saint Paul tells us, are one and the same. Paul makes pleasure the venom of the human spirit and the scourge of the immortal soul. The spoiled-brat generation, otherwise known as "generation X," attempts to escape this by flaunting its pleasure. Guilt is the social sin of pleasing self over pleasing others. Yet, when we truly please ourselves by excelling, striving for excellence, we invariably please many others. Athletes, composers, musicians, singers, painters, writers—the list is endless—please others because they do what pleases them. When a person listens to the wisdom of his own heart, and plays the music of his own talent in concert with kindred spirits, he makes the world a better place.

Yet, it is not easy to have a "please-self" orientation, even if it is more productive and creative than a "please-other" disposition. Others will attempt to pull you down to their level. They will try to cut your legs out from under you. "Please-self" people soar. People who soar are intimidating to those who plod. The "please-self" person is not likely to envy, to harbor jealousy, to covet what others possess, because he loves what he is, and what he is he owns. The "please-self" person is not afraid to disobey. Disobedience was the first act of freedom, the beginning of human history. Erich Fromm in *Beyond the Chains of Illusion* (1962) states, "All that the human race has achieved, spiritually and materially, it owes to the destroyers of illusions and to the seekers of reality."[21] From a distance, most can cope with the "please-self" personality. They can love or hate a Baseball Hall of Famer like Reggie Jackson or radio personalities such as Howard Stern and Don Imus. It is safe. They can secretly fantasize about these celebrities without pain or misgiving. They can relish celebrity gossip and remain untouched by celebrity scandals. Up close and personal is another matter. Confident people are threatening and, therefore, feared. The "please-other" person wonders, "Why are they not afraid like me? Why are they so different?" The answer is because they are alive. They don't own other people's problems. They are not driven to accomplish other people's agendas. They don't worry about disappointing because they are not driven by others' expectations. Their energy is focused on their own pursuits. Fromm says, "Intelligence...is largely a function of independence, courage, and aliveness; stupidity is equally a result of submission, fear, and inner deadness."[22] "Please-self" people dare to be different! This requires, as Fromm sees, "not only a certain degree of inner security, but also a vitality and joy which can be found only in those for whom living is more than releasing tensions and avoiding pain. In order to reduce the general level of stupidity, we need not more 'intellect' but a different kind of character: men who are independent, adventurous, and who are in love with life."[23]

A "please-other" person is looking for safety and ease. People of this mind-set are desperate for a winner with whom to associate—a winning company, profession, university, or mate. Eric Hoffer calls them "'true believers." Belonging to a cause provides authentication. Their orientation is always outside themselves. They are unlikely to venture inside to uncover what makes them go. They beat to whatever rhythm provides a richer, more sheltered inner life. They live with denial and deception. The "please-other" person can dream and hope, but cannot change. Energy is focused on criticizing, analyzing, condemning, seeking, judging, evaluating, and discriminating. It is not directed at generating, exploring, creating, designing, and constructing new possibilities. New ideas are essential to the change process.

We move from possibilities to the direct design of action. As Edward de Bono states, "To deal with the future we have to deal with 'possibilities.' Analysis will only tell us 'what is.'"[24] Therefore, the "please-other" person is imprisoned in *truth* or "what is," not what can be. His complacent arrogance prevents him from seeing the extent of his own failures. The "please-other" person places the emphasis on judging ideas, not on generating them. He may be clever, but never wise. Wisdom is a way of thinking, not simply an accumulation of experience. Contradictions annoy the "please-other" person, while the "please-self" person basks in them. The "please-other" person is interested in a single truth and desires to throw out one side of the contradiction, whereas the "please-self" person is interested in creating truth and seeks to extract the maximum value from both sides of the contradiction.

Professionals, by definition, are "please-self" persons. So, if they are to feel guilt, let it be guilt for not making a significant contribution. If guilt there must be, let it be for holding one's tongue when it is important to speak. If guilt there must be, let it be for being a spectator to life rather than a bold participant. And if guilt there must be, let it be to eradicate the *six silent killers* from the soul of the organization. Not only does this make more sense in terms of conscious competence, but paradoxically, it is more likely to dissolve the turf wars between managers and professionals as they recognize that survival is not somebody else's job.

Endnotes

1. Whitall N. Perry, *A Treasury of Traditional Wisdom* (New York: Simon & Schuster, 1971). Quotes: Rumi, p. 336; Brahmananda, p. 359.
2. George J. Church, "The Work Ethic Lives," *Time*, September 7, 1987, 40–42.
3. The National Science Foundation (*Quarterly Journal*, Spring 1988) reported that 55 percent of 3,375 engineering doctorates went to non-Americans, as did 23 percent of 15,391 science doctorates. Sherry Buchanan, *International Herald Tribune* (July 9, 1987, 8), indicates another interesting trend. Only 65 MBA students at Harvard Business School enrolled in an ethics course, while 400 enrolled in a course titled "Power and Influence." She concludes, "Money, not intellectual challenge, seems the magnet."
4. *Magic*, a film, 1978. Cast included Anthony Hopkins, Ann-Margaret, Burgess Meredith, and Ed Lauter; directed by Richard Attenborough.
5. Hans Selye, *Stress Without Distress* (New York: Signet Classic, 1974).
6. James R. Fisher, Jr., *The Taboo Against Being Your Own Best Friend* (Tampa: The Delta Group Florida, 1996), pp. 14–15.
7. Paul Hendrickson, *The Living and the Dead: Robert McNamara and Five Lives of a Lost War* (New York: Knopf, 1996). Hendrickson shows "The Prince Hubris" (McNamara) got bogged down with measuring the war's progress in terms of "body count" and the steamy muck of quantification, losing sight of the moral purpose of that war.
8. Marvin E. Shaw and Philip R. Costanzo, *Theories of Social Psychology* (New York: McGraw Hill, 1970). The authors give a good summary of Leon Festinger's *theory of cognitive dissonance* (pp. 202–217).
9. Barbara Vobejda (*The Washington Post*), "Book Stirs Debate About IQ Scores, Heredity and Race," *The Tampa Tribune-Times*, October 23, 1994.

10. Richard Hernstein and Charles Murray, *The Bell Curve: Intelligence and Class Structure in American Life* (New York: Free Press, 1994).
11. Garry Wills, "American Adam," *New York Review*, March 6, 1997, 30. "He (John Wayne) embodies the American myth. The archetypal American is a displaced person— arrived from a rejected past, breaking into a glorious future, on the move, fearless himself, feared by others, a killer for cleansing the world of things that 'need killing,' loving but not bound down by love, rootless but carrying the center in himself, a gyroscopic direction-setter, a traveling norm."
12. Darlene Goth-Neuman, *Writings* (Anaheim Hills, CA: Goth-Neuman, Inc., 1980).
13. Edward Tenner, *Why Things Bite Back: Technology and the Revenge of Unintended Consequences* (New York: Knopf, 1996), pp. 73–83.
14. Herbert Marcuse, *Negations* (London: Penguin Press, 1968), p. 268.
15. Stanley Milgraim, *Obedience to Authority* (New York: Harper & Row, 1973).
16. Marsha Sinetar, *Do What You Love, The Money Will Follow* (New York: Dell Paperbacks, 1987), p. 19.
17. Fisher, op. cit., p. 7.
18. Albert Schweitzer, *Pilgrimage to Humanity* (New York: Philosophical Paperbacks, 1983); *Reverence for Life* (New York: Irvington, 1969).
19. Stephen Jay Gould, *An Urchin in the Storm* (New York: W.W. Norton, 1987); *The Mismeasure of Man* (Norton, 1985).
20. Richard Dawkins, *The Selfish Gene* (New York: Oxford University Press, 1976).
21. Erich Fromm, *Beyond the Chains of Illusion* (New York: Touchstone Books, 1962), p. 160.
22. Ibid., p. 154.
23. Ibid., p. 155.
24. Edward de Bono, *Parallel Thinking* (London: Penguin Books, 1995), p. 184.

10 The Difficult Agenda Ahead, or When the Simple Is Complex

> Transformation must take place with directed effort...Failure of management to plan for the future and to foresee problems has brought waste of manpower, of materials, and of machine-time, all of which raises the manufacturer's cost and that the purchaser must pay....The inevitable result is loss of market, loss of market begets unemployment. Performance of management should be measured by potential to stay in business...not by quarterly dividends.[1]
>
> W. Edwards Deming
>
> It is not at all simple to understand the simple.[2]
>
> Eric Hoffer

Mere reform, as W. Edwards Deming reminds us in *Out of the Crisis* (1986), is not enough. The complex organization must be rebuilt from scratch with different thinking and values, a more appropriate workplace culture and infrastructure, a new appreciation of what leadership entails, and a new sense of what constitutes performance. To wit:

(1) The organization needs to process information in a way in which data does not take precedence over ideas. Ideas are tools to deal with reality; information is not.

(2) The organization is aware of a significant change in values. Awareness is not enough. Nobody ever did anything because they knew. Knowledge must be operationalized. To operationalize knowledge, it must be felt. Values are felt knowledge. They shape the cultural biases of organization. Cultural biases are the mechanisms that govern behavior.

(3) The structure of organizations is out of date with the relationship of managers to workers and employer to employees, and work itself is structured for another time.

(4) Leadership of organizations is wrong for the requirements of work, the organization's mission, and the needs of its people.

(5) The nature of what constitutes real work and how it is to be conducted has changed. Work is much less manual, much more mental; much less tied to individual contribution, much more the synergy of collective contribution; and much less conforming to arbitrary practices, much more an "ad hocracy" of activities.

In the absence of agreement on these implications, workers and managers reared on the formula of worker–manager relationship do not appreciate the shift in power. This promotes an adversarial relationship between workers and managers. Even worse, not only is there *unmanaged conflict* between workers and managers, but this conflict has been internalized to a conflict with self. The evidence of this wasted energy is in the *six silent killers*. Workers and managers are confused. They feel damned if they do and damned if they don't. Even the teaming concept, which is designed to promote cooperation, confuses them. The current workplace culture calls for behavior akin to baseball, not basketball. "The American pastime" is a wonderful sport, but its management style is dated and inconsistent with the professionalism of workers today. It is no accident that this sport has had major contract problems between players and owners. Owners still operate in the world of 1945, and players are resistant to this. All other major sports recognize and accept change, if reluctantly, and deal with it accordingly. Not baseball. Baseball is not actually a team sport, in the modern sense, while basketball is.

> *Baseball Team: Nine individual contributors who happen to be on the same team. Baseball is an obsessively statistical-driven sport of numbers—individual and team records—from batting averages to a sundry of minutiae. Quantitative factors have a qualitative significance in this sport—the higher or lower the numbers determines quality. Major League baseball's original owners were the robber barons, otherwise known as the "captains of industry" at the turn of the last century. They had a paternalistic understanding of the correct relationship between players and owners. That orientation continues to the present. Players are paid to play, not to think; to behave like obedient children, not spoiled brats. Baseball is a blue-collar sport, where the simple is made complex with its drive for data.*

Baseball players today often come from the university pool of players. Originally, they were factory workers. It is a tactical sport in which manager is pitted against manager in tactical maneuvers.[3] The manager is very visible. He moves the players about on every pitch on defense, while on offense declares what the batter is to do. Players have little independent behavior, and their survival is dependent on individual statistics. When players are on defense they operate as a team working together; while on offense, they are each individual contributors who have impact on the team's performance. This dichotomy reflects the typical organization today. If a player makes an error on defense, the team suffers, but the individual receives the punishment or stigma. Rewards and recognition are primarily individual and not team-oriented. Baseball demonstrates another societal irony. In an age that claims "time is money," baseball remains popular even though a game, which can last as long as 4 hours, is only about 30 minutes of action. Significant is that the team leader is called a manager.

> *Basketball Team: Five interdependent players irrevocably involved in the fluid dynamics of a process in which success depends entirely on the five players working together as one. Basketball is intuitively and situationally driven by the players with the coach essentially a hapless bystander, whereas baseball is cognitive and tactically driven by the manager. Basketball is a fast-paced sport within strict time constraints. Whereas the origin of baseball is somewhat cloudy, this is not true of basketball. Historians give Abner Doubleday credit for the invention of baseball in 1839, although it was being played in England before that period. This is not true of basketball. We know precisely when basketball was invented. In the winter of 1891–92, Dr. James Naismith, an instructor at the Y.M.C.A. in Springfield, MA, deliberately invented the game of basketball in order to provide indoor exercise and competition for students between the closing of the football season and the opening of the baseball season. Americans introduced the sport to Europe in World War I, and it has become an international sport since. The coach is the designated leader in basketball and has a very different role than the manager in baseball. His role is to facilitate the action and to promote the chemistry between players. The lower the profile he takes, the better that chemistry develops. What produces a winning team is the team without ego—a team in which each player recognizes the interdependent nature of his own personal success. The individual player brings his strength to the team while realizing his weakness. Michael Jordan is a great scorer and play-maker for the Chicago Bulls, but not a great rebounder; Dennis Rodman is a great rebounder, but not a great scorer.*

Generally speaking, then, what sports tell us is that the relationship of players to management and owners is changing.[4] We have a more appropriate model for teaming in basketball than baseball, although the revolution in organization is being played out in all professional sport. Professional athletes make much more money than their respective coaches and managers, and for a reason. These professional athletes recognize their power, which is their contribution to the success of their respective franchises. Workers have never recognized either their power or their contribution. They have instead remained essentially fixed in terminal adolescence and attempted to get even by displaying the *six silent killers*. But there is hope. What happens in sports, as Eric Hoffer reminds us, is bound to eventually follow in society.

No. 1: Thinking Differently on Purpose

Purposeful performance is not something to seek. It is the recognition that you are "it." You don't consciously seek to be purposeful. If you attempt to do this, you will fail. Your whole being—without analyzing, defining, assessing, and quantifying—is purposeful. It involves the spontaneous action to serve others without estimating cost–benefit considerations. The rationally trained mind has trouble with this. "Give me the facts," it declares, "and leave out the B.S." Western thinking is deeply impaled on deterministic logic or the "Blitzkrieg School of Problem-Solving," which is seldom purposeful. With nitty-gritty deductive reasoning, we expect if we find the cause to, say, AIDS, we will eliminate the disease. Medical science will spend an inordinate amount of its resources trying to isolate the AIDS virus, then develop a miraculous vaccine to prevent AIDS. What if AIDS is not a virus? What then? What if AIDS could be avoided with a lifestyle change? This is not true of most cancers, muscular dystrophy, Lou Gehrig's disease, schizophrenia, diabetes, or Alzheimer's disease. According to the U.S. Public Health Service, the government spent $2 billion in 1995 on AIDS research and $2.7 million on prevention. That compares with $800 million allocated for heart disease. AIDS caused the death of less than 2 percent of Americans while heart disease was responsible for more than 33 percent. Moreover, in the past 15 years (1980–95), AIDS has killed 270,000 Americans, while heart disease kills that many every 19 weeks.[5]

People don't want to think differently because they don't want to behave differently. Medical researchers and chemical and pharmaceutical companies recognize this. They go where the dollars are. That is why celebrity-driven AIDS research is a top priority. People will pay a fortune to avoid a lifestyle change. Medical science hasn't found the cure for AIDS, but it now announces a new drug, Redux, that allows fat, lazy people to avoid eating right or exercising and, providing they have the money, to control their weight with prescription drugs. Just three months after the introduction of Redux, doctors were writing 85,000 prescriptions a week, with the drug expected to hit $1 billion in sales in five years.[6] While the focus is on these lifestyle maladies, terrible diseases are given short shrift. The cause of AIDS and being fat does not lie exclusively in the subatomic world of microbiology, but more in the social psychology of behavior. These maladies lie as much in the mind as the body. When we treat the body and ignore the mind, we promote the estrangement of the mind to the body. Mind–body–spirit are part of the same whole. Nature has its own way of getting revenge by creating side effects to these drugs or by the mutation of genes. Consequently, once the AIDS virus is identified, if it is a virus, the virus is likely to mutate to a new, more impervious strain, and so the vicious cycle of problem-solving continues. Only the medicine of behavioral change will complete the miracle.

Analytical thinking is the religion of the modern mind. It is the wholehearted push of Artificial Intelligence (AI). According to enthusiasts of AI, all human thinking, whether conscious or unconscious, is merely the enacting of some complicated computation. There is no room in AI for the mystical, metaphysical, or spiritual. After all, how could a machine possess this orientation? The theology of AI is logical positivism, the dominant philosophy of twentieth century thinking. Logical positivism is a philosophy which holds that truth of any statement lies in its verification through sensory experience—observation or experimentation. Any statement that cannot be verified through sensory experience is meaningless. This philosophy is every bit as dogmatic as any religion. Also known as scientific empiricism, it postulates that everything is a problem, and every problem can be solved. This fuels the erroneous attitude, "Don't worry about pollution, science will come up with the answer!"

Medical science creates more and more sophisticated tools to reinforce the belief of infallibility, including CAT scanners that direct X-ray beams through the skull from multiple directions, computerized blood analyzers with impressive printouts, cardiac pacemakers, renal dialysis machines, and magnetic resonance imaging (MRI). It seems clear that "nuclear man" has gambled almost everything on a mechanistic, quantitative, mathematically pure approach to his greatest dreads. The belief is that the heart of God, if there is a God, resides in science. This allows man to think the way he thinks—separating nature from the human spirit—and to behave the way he does—polluting and destroying what is irreplaceable. Characteristic of this thinking is to identify the individual with society, but not society with nature. Man goes about ravaging his environment in wanton glee or goes about abandoning his body, mind, and spirit to senseless pleasure. Science as Superman is meant to rescue man's mortal body from this reckless behavior. Fritjof Capra in *The Turning Point: Science, Society & The Rising Culture* (1982) presents this as a paradoxical dilemma. He claims the cleaner the scientific methodology, the more complex the ramifications. Take nuclear power plants. Just how dangerous is the waste created by this cheap energy source? Capra claims we don't have the foggiest notion. He writes, "Barges of nuclear waste roam the American continent in the night like 'vessels without a country,' looking for a haven in which to dump their dubious product."[7] Scientific reassurances notwithstanding, each reactor annually produces tons of radioactive waste that remain toxic for thousands of years. Does scientific problem-solving abandon this approach in favor of another energy source? Of course not. Capra observes, "It concentrates instead on solving a solvable problem, doing what we all do in our rational approach to problem solving—ignoring the real problem (safe disposal of radioactive waste), and concentrating on a solution to a problem it believes can be solved (more efficient production of nuclear energy)."[8] What we need is an energy source that is renewable, economical, efficient, and safe. We have it, Capra writes, in solar energy, which meets all these criteria. He claims the main obstacle is not technical, but political. The shift from non-renewable to renewable resources involves dealing with a stubborn cultural bias—compelling oil companies to give up their dominant role in the world economy and to change their function. It is not a rational but an irrational dilemma resulting from the anachronistic biases of that power.

Obviously, logical positivism holds little store with this assessment. It is quick to produce the litany of scientific achievements over the last century, failing to mention that science creates many of the problems it solves. Scientific empiricism arrogantly denies the spiritual component of man. It holds the view that generalizations can be held valid only when tested by objective techniques and verified by sensory experience. This represents the logical progression from the works of three men, Rene Descartes (1596–1650), Isaac Newton (1642–1727), and Ludwig Wittgenstein (1889–1951). Rene Descartes' Cartesian philosophy formed the basis for the division between the mind and the body, the spiritual and material worlds of man. Isaac Newton described man as essentially an intricate machine personified by a fine-tuned clock. Ludwig Wittgenstein, with his dedication to empirical observation, believed man could maintain a value-free and scientific perspective. Each man contributed to building a more persuasive argument for the division of man: Descartes between behaving (material world) and believing (spiritual world), Newton between thinking and feeling, and Wittgenstein between subjective and objective points of view.

Fundamental to purposeful performance in the workplace is the recognition that we are both subject and object and never value-free, that thinking and feeling are part of the same process, and that we live in a concrete world with abstract implications. The drive to separate the part from the whole is losing favor, as is the idea that empiricism is the last word. Lifestyle is connected to many physical and psychological complaints, as is workstyle connected to many organizational disorders. We are learning that you cannot separate lifestyle from workstyle. Difficult as it might be to grasp, purposeful performance grows out of chaos and confusion, not separate from it. To seek order often begets disorder. Purposeful performance is a dynamic process that may reflect chaos in one sense, but order in another. We are an integration of diverse parts:

- Mind–body–spirit
- Subject–observer–object
- Thinking–feeling–behaving

So, to focus on (or deny) one part at the exclusion of other parts is to develop conflict within and to court confusion. Eric Hoffer expresses this poetically: "No one is truly literate who cannot read his own heart."[9] Identity is the beginning of understanding, which involves accepting ourselves as we are. It makes us ready to accept and understand others as we find them. This looking at a person as a whole (system) and not as a collection of finite parts is what J. Krishnamurti means when he writes in *You Are The World* (1972): "In oneself lies the whole world, and if you know how to look and learn, then the door is there and the key is in your hand. Nobody on earth can give you either that key or the door to open, except you."[10] The current jargon of "the systems approach" is consistent with this identity. Systems researcher Russell Ackoff adds,

> *If you take a system apart to identify its components, and then operate*
> *those components in such a way that every component behaves as well*

as it possibly can, there is one thing of which you can be sure. The system as a whole will not behave as well as it can. Now that is counter-intuitive to Machine Age Thinking, but it is absolutely essential to "systems thinking." The corollary to this is that if you have a system that is behaving as well as it can, none of its parts will be.[11]

This new way of thinking has tremendous implications. When a department is trying to outperform all others, it means it is not supporting other departments as well as it might. Or, it is doing well at the expense of other departments. Likewise, when an individual is not accepted on the basis of his unique characteristics, attributes, and talents and is force-fit into a unfriendly culture and irrelevant job, the results will surely be discouraging for all. A systems perspective requires an acceptance of differences—skills, skill levels, attitudes, dispositions, and personalities. Once these differences are accepted, people of difference are more inclined to change, blending into the dominant culture. Force them to fit, and they will resist. *Everything and everybody is related to and connected to everything else.* Many organizations continue to frustrate themselves trying to force-fit people into operations, compounding the problem by shackling the new worker with preordained expectations. Failure is imminent. Obstinacy takes over with everyone working harder to make the new person fit. With logic as its guide, like a horse with blinders, the company plows ahead not realizing it can only lose. The most important thing for the new person to feel is that he is accepted *as he is*, which of course cannot be a fully known thing.

Putting the Macho Complex to Rest

As the world becomes truly a global community, we are put in the imperative position to rethink much of what we have been taught, to blend the possibilities of the Western mind with Eastern maturity. This entails assimilating Western thinking, which is largely left brain, with Eastern thinking, which is mainly right-brain-oriented. Whether you are religious or not, all aspects of society are influenced by the dominant religion of its culture. Religious orientation is a useful model for illustrating the principal patterns of thinking that come to influence all aspects of society in terms of behavior.

Buddhism is a dominate faith of the East, while the Judaic-Christian culture dominates the West. Buddhism has no sense of false idols. There is no need in Buddhism to destroy icons of other religions as it assimilates them naturally. All idols are considered simply manifestations of Buddha consciousness. The Bible, on the other hand, is full of stories of God's anger at worshiping false gods. In Buddhism, it is possible to move in the field of time, but to remain unmoved by time. Past, present, and future are considered one. Contrast this with Western consciousness, which is totally immersed in the direction of space and time. Even the German philosopher Immanuel Kant's *Critique of Pure Reason* (1781) makes a case that everything comes to us in the field of time and space and that the Law of Space is in our own minds.[12]

The Judaic-Christian culture emphasizes sin and atonement, death and resurrection, debt and repayment, loss and recovery. Buddhism features the joyful participation in the sorrows of the world or asceticism. Retribution is also prominent in Christianity, not in Buddhism. A person with Buddha consciousness is not moved by desire or fear, which are major motivators of Western man. In Buddha consciousness, desire and fear are one, confined to an immovable spot. There is nothing in Buddhism commensurate with Christian sin or good and evil. With Buddha consciousness, evil is akin to ignorance, and "The Way" is the road to enlightenment. The Way is designed to get beyond pain and pleasure, gain and loss, fear and desire, you and me. Buddhism transcends duality to cosmic unity. Buddhism doesn't separate love from hate or goodness from evil. Instead, oneness is realized when a person moves from ignorance to enlightenment, what a Christian might call "spiritual purity," or a State of Grace.

The seasons of the year differ for the East and West. The West has essentially four seasons, which explains the emphasis on time. The East is largely in tropical zones, especially India, where the emphasis is on stillness. So, Buddhism is the tale of ignorance moving to enlightenment, while Christianity is the story of being driven from Paradise and seeking salvation through the unique Godhood of Christ. This presents yet another distinction. Christians can only participate in this Godhood by imitation. *Imitation of Christ* (ca. 1429) by Thomas à Kempis remains a viable guide to this day in most Christian denominations.[13] With Buddhism, we are all Buddha beings, but don't know it. Buddhism is also comfortable in its mythology, whereas Christianity insists on its historicity.

The West prides itself on its authoritarian order and rational control. This is a prominent theme in the Bible. Buddhism lacks a similar theme. With Buddhism, chaos and order are different faces of the same thing. Buddha consciousness makes a case for getting to know you are "it." Joseph Campbell, a scholar of Eastern mythology, claims that Western society "keeps telling you, you are not it." He adds, "How are you going to find your own track, if you are always preoccupied with what society is telling you is your social duty?"[14] To the Buddhist, all things are within the self, and social duty emanates from that source as the person resolves the self; finds the capacity for delight, austerity, and discipline; and then becomes food for others. Buddha consciousness allows a person to participate in life and in the play of life. Nor is any distinction made between the spiritual and material world in Buddhism as it is in the Christian West. These two dominant cultures differ significantly, but at the same time seek similar accord.[15] In a shrinking world, it takes wisdom to make room for diverse thinking and belief systems. How people think and believe is how they will behave.

As we turn our attention to the brain, we find the left brain resists the intuitive hunch that emanates from the right brain because it is not founded on facts. The right brain resists the left brain because there is little display of sensitivity. It is a war within each of us and between us, which has been waged since the dawn of man. The clash of these two brains can also produce insight, inspiration, and creative genius.

The left brain is the home of science and technology. The right brain is the home of art, music, mysticism, and religion. Both brains are involved in most activities, even though one or the other tends to dominate. It is this war between the two brains that has produced languages, cultures, societies, nationalities, and civilizations. Buddhism may be a more tranquil faith, but it has been the Judaic-Christian West that has grabbed the thunder of this clash of brains to produce the modern world. Now we have the religion of technology driving a wedge between the left and right brain again, between the worker and manager, employer and employee, Western and Eastern thinking. Traditional religions failed to produce a better world. It is equally unlikely that science and technology will. We keep slipping through the great divide between these two brains.

Workers and managers are struggling with each other, as are employers with employees. Meanwhile, productivity in terms of the GDP hovers around 2.3–2.4, when it should be a full point higher. Were this so, there would be no reason for this book. Find the answer to the individual and his relationship to himself, and you are on your way to finding the answer to the problem of performance. How to establish a sense of this is another matter. Once a person recognizes the interdependent nature of his brain, this could lead to an integration into purposeful performance.

The left brain is associated with the male. The right brain is identified with the female. In human biology, masculine and feminine characteristics exist in everyone. Sex roles are learned behavior, not genetic consequences. Nobody has a predisposition to be male or female. Yet all men are supposed to display masculine characteristics, all women feminine ones (Figure 10.1). This has meant, for the past several centuries, men having leading societal roles and most privileges. There are several stereotypes that go with such identification. Men are expected to be rational. The rational mind is linear, focused, and analytical. It belongs in the realm of the intellect, which functions to discriminate, measure, categorize, and label. Rational knowledge tends to be fragmented. Women are expected to be intuitive. The intuitive mind is

EXPECTATIONS OF MEN	EXPECTATIONS OF WOMEN
Active and Productive	Passive and Receptive
Rational and Cognitive	Irrational and Intuitive
Aggressive, Competitive, even Ruthless	Responsive, Cooperative, and Consolidating
Conscious of Themselves	Conscious of Environment
'Thinkers'	'Feelers'
Inclined toward Science	Inclined toward Mysticism

Figure 10.1 Traditional societal expectations of men and women.

based on direct, non-intellectual experience of reality arising out of the state of expanding awareness. Intuitive knowledge tends to be synthesizing, holistic, and non-linear. Holistic refers to an understanding of reality in terms of integrated wholes whose properties cannot be reduced to those of smaller units. Western culture favors the masculine brain (left brain) over the feminine brain (right brain), rational knowledge over intuitive wisdom, science over religion, competition over cooperation, exploitation over conservation (Figure 10.2).[16] This emphasis has justified a paternalistic management system and has led to the organization's resistance to authentic cultural change. Many things have challenged this traditional orientation, but with little impact. The world has shrunk. Global competition has become real. Limits are a valid concern. Pollution is an encroaching nightmare. World hunger is a possibility, not because of economic limitations but because of social and political obstructionism. Massive worker rebellion is on the horizon, not of poorly educated blue-collar workers but of well-educated professionals. Minorities and women are now the majority. Women bring unique skills and a much-needed extra dimension to the workplace. The lethargic and predictable industrial age is gone. The factory mentality is obsolete. The information age is here.

To the Eastern mind, there are two kinds of activities: harmony with nature and activities against nature. The Eastern mind chooses the former. The Western mind is inclined to the latter and takes pride in the conquest of nature. It exploits nature and makes nature conform to man's requirements. Manhandling nature is often a mirror image of life in the organization. A recurring misconception is that the Eastern viewpoint is passive, the Western active. The Eastern view seeks a balance between man's needs and the requirements of nature. This is parallel to the concept of the workplace culture being a balance between the needs of workers and the requirements of the organization.

The Western view is aggressively scientific. Much pride is taken in this being the "Scientific Age." Science is the instrument used to make Nature submit to its will.

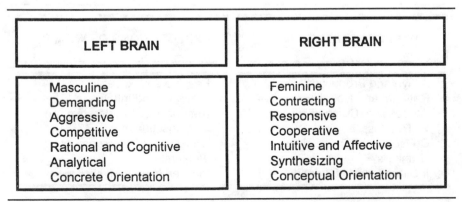

LEFT BRAIN	RIGHT BRAIN
Masculine	Feminine
Demanding	Contracting
Aggressive	Responsive
Competitive	Cooperative
Rational and Cognitive	Intuitive and Affective
Analytical	Synthesizing
Concrete Orientation	Conceptual Orientation

Figure 10.2   Common identities and properties of left brain and right brain.

Nature, in this scenario, is the enemy, and the guns of science are trained on her. The natural has all but disappeared in food, with chemical additives and preservatives robbing Nature of its natural flavors. There is no telling how much damage science, aided by technology, has done to ecosystems and the ecological balance. Literally hundreds of species of plants and animals are becoming extinct every year. America leads this charge, while Europe attempts to slow down America's thrust. In Europe, farmers in many countries still use natural fertilizers, and these same countries refrain from adding chemical preservatives to milk and bread. The shelf life of these products is limited and requires daily shopping for staples. The taste is well worth the bother.

America is captivated by rational thinking and scientific inquiry. Scientific knowledge is considered the only acceptable knowledge, which makes intuitive knowledge just this side of suspect. Hunches are often the beginning of creative thinking, and to trust feelings is often discouraged or not taken seriously. The motor to thinking is feeling, as passion is its fuel. Eric Hoffer writes in *The Passionate State of Mind* (1954), "It is impossible to think clearly in understatements. Thought is a process of exaggeration. The refusal to exaggerate is not infrequently an alibi for the disinclination to think or praise."[17] Many are afraid to think, to wonder, to suggest anything that cannot be easily corroborated. We are mesmerized by the near magical powers of science, unwilling to consider the cost of this adulation. Nor are we able to see it as dogmatic as religious faith. Science is the religion of education, which is failing; of the workplace, which is in a state of disarray; of our social contracts, which are falling apart; of the political process, which is perverted; and of our ethical system, which has lost its way. Science is the only game in town—not power, not money, not sex. These are diversions of our central preoccupation. Like any religion, what science wants is our soul. Perhaps the greatest mind of our century, Albert Einstein, confessed, "I have no special talents. I am only passionately curious."[18] Ironically, his theory of relativity may restore balance between man and Nature.

Since the celebrated declaration of Descartes, "I think, therefore, I am," we have, as Capra reminds us, "retreated into our minds, forgotten how to think with our bodies, how to use them as agents of knowing."[19] What left-brain macho dominance has meant is that virtually everything gets passed through a quantitative filter, which throws everything out of proportion. The idea that more is better, or if something works well in the laboratory, let's mass produce it, is a common occurrence. In a more direct way, we have come to expect scientific knowledge to go hand in hand with wisdom, ethics, and spiritual well-being, when this has not always been the case. Sociologist J. A. Barnes writes in *A Pack of Lies* (1994), "Up to half the scientific papers in the United States may be contaminated by data manipulation."[20] Obviously, scientists have tremendous pressure to produce in this frenetic climate of our times.

From another perspective, science has unwittingly sponsored the decline in cultural creativity by the myriad inventions of sexual contraceptives. It is unfortunate that so much emphasis is placed on sexuality and sexual preference. Consider how little time is actually involved in sexual activity and how much more time is preoccupied with it. Nearly a half century ago, sociologist Pitrim Sorokin envisioned how obsessive compulsive sexuality would create a major fantasy industry. Sorokin observes in *The American Sex Revolution* (1956), "Overindulgence of the sex urge tends to undermine the physical and mental health and vitality of the individual, destroys his sense of morality, brings misery and shame upon himself and his family and friends, diminishes his creative energy, and ruins his prospects for happiness."[21] Sorokin urges society not to condone, but to rally its forces to bring sense, balance, and creative growth into the life of its citizens. If not, he warns, "there will be moral and social decay." Unhappily, he has become a prophet.

Given this situation, people inclined to right-brain thinking would have an insight into this matter, although be equally vulnerable to the problem. They have a different perception and perspective than the "macho man." Contact has been made with their feminine nature, which we all possess. A right-brain-thinking person tends to be more aware of his surroundings, whereas the left-brain thinker is more aware of himself in these surroundings. Right-brain thinkers tend to have a gentle persuasion and an affinity for the aesthetic—from poetry to painting, from drama to didactics, from architecture to music. We need more poets in the board rooms of commerce and industry, as well as in education and government. Scientists, technologists, engineers, economists, and political scientists have done magnificent things and have changed our world, but they are not too good at damage control. Economists, for one, readily admit they operate in a fog. A former chairman of the Federal Reserve writes, "The rules of economics are not working quite the way they used to." Nobel Laureate Milton Friedman adds, "I believe that we economists in recent years have done vast harm by claiming more than we can deliver." Former Secretary of the Treasury Michael Blumenthal agrees. "I really think the economic profession is close to bankruptcy in understanding the situation, before or after the fact."[22] One-dimensional thinking has reached the alarm stage. Their candor is encouraging, but not too consoling. Meanwhile:

- We can control a soft landing of a space craft on distant planets and take pictures of Mars, but cannot control the toxic fumes emanating from our automobiles and factories.
- We propose utopian communities in splendid space colonies, but we cannot manage crime in our cities.
- The business community salutes the growth of the pet food and cosmetic industries as signs of economic progress, but we cannot feed the homeless or provide healthcare for the needy.
- We are considered among the best educated of Western nations in terms of per capita high school and college graduates, with arguably the best university system in the world, but few Americans read books; are multilingual; have hobbies; are students of culture, history, or geography; or are the least bit curious.

Our inability or refusal to think differently on purpose has polarized society, and most of us with it. The "law of polarization," according to Sorokin states that, *when a society experiences some frustration or calamity or emergency, the bulk of its members who in normal conditions are neither too saintly nor too sinful, tend to split and polarize, some becoming more religious, more moral and saintly, while others become more irreligious, more cynical, sensual, and criminal. In this way the ethically mediocre majority of the normal times moves toward the opposite poles of religious and moral ennoblement and degradation. This ethical-religious polarization has almost invariably occurred in all societies of the past when some important frustration, catastrophy, or emergency has fallen upon them.*"[23]

Put otherwise, Sorokin envisions us becoming a society of zombies and fanatics.

No. 2: Recognizing and Dealing with the Ambivalence of Values

Some 300 years ago, America broke away from the confinement of European society to establish a new identity. Some 200 years ago, America produced an incredible body of men who were multidimensional and dedicated to giving substance and direction to the American spirit of individualism. They were not afraid to be different, not afraid to be outsiders, not afraid to cultivate the inner world of expression as they sensed it. American poet Walt Whitman captures this spirit when he proclaims with innocence, "I am larger and better than I thought. I did not know that I held so much greatness."[24] Yet we bristle when someone makes such a proclamation. We think greatness is rare, whereas Whitman knew that the seeds of greatness are in everyone. Where are the Walt Whitmans today? Where are the voices of outsiders who march to their own drummer as did Henry David Thoreau? Many of the giants of our republic lived in the late eighteenth and early nineteenth centuries, including John Adams, John Quincy Adams, William Cullen Bryant, Aaron Burr, John Calhoun, James Fenimore Cooper, Ralph Waldo Emerson, Benjamin Franklin, Horace Greeley, Nathaniel Hawthorne, Oliver Wendell Holmes, Andrew Jackson, John Jay, Thomas Jefferson, Abraham Lincoln, James Madison, Herman Melville, James Monroe, Henry David Thoreau, George Washington, and Daniel Webster. These men were essentially aristocrats in temperament and democrats in spirit. They had a quiet reverence for things mystical, a consuming passion for living practical lives. America was young and had not yet succumbed to mediocrity, nor to self-conscious self-approval.

From Ralph Waldo Emerson's *Self-Reliance* (1844)[25] to Henry David Thoreau's *Walden* (1854),[26] there was a transcendental connection between the spirit and Nature. Transcendentalism was a popular religion of the time. It flourished in New England during the first half of the nineteenth century. Never a systematic philosophy, it held the romantic view that individual intuition was the highest form of knowledge and that God was within Nature. Much influenced by Eastern religious teachings, many of these early American thinkers held a mystical belief in individualism in harmony with all things in Nature. The word that best describes them is "balanced." They would never exploit Nature for their purposes, but would rather maintain themselves in consonance with it.

It was during this same period that the Frenchman Alexis de Tocqueville came to America to study its prison system. From his diary of that visit in 1831, he returned to France to publish a penetrating political study, *Democracy in America* (1835). He outlined in this classic study the advantages and shortcomings of a democratic political and social system. Tocqueville saw values and perils of the democratic way of life that remain pertinent insights to this day.[27] This found contemporary journalist Richard Reeves reliving Tocqueville's journey in candid appraisal of the America he saw and the America today in *American Journey: Traveling with Tocqueville in Search of America* (1982).[28] Reeves reaffirms Tocqueville's perceptions and notes that the seeds of comfort and indifference were already in the soil when America was a young nation. A case could be made that America has been trading off its early greatness for the past 160 years.

Look today, and you are likely to find the same dismal landscape Tocqueville warned could develop if America was not attentive to its democracy. He stressed the importance of education in maintaining this vigilance. Historian Page Smith echoes his sentiments in *Killing the Spirit* (1990).[29] He finds America's most prestigious universities failing to educate because teachers are not personally involved with students. Students get instruction, he claims, not education. This is in the form of information transferals, communication techniques, or some other impersonal and antiseptic phrases to cover *non-teaching teaching* to facilitate *non-learning learning*. Interaction between professors and students is minimal or non-existent, Smith says, because professors are preoccupied with scholarly research and publication. Career-minded faculty, Smith notes, cannot afford to spend time with students. They must publish or perish by having their scholarly tomes appear in the right journals. This helps them win promotion and tenure, which means they stay employed.

Boston Globe journalist Jeff Jacoby paints an even gloomier picture in "The Low State of Higher Education" (*The Tampa Tribune*, October 16, 1996). He writes,

> *At Bristol Community College in Fall River, MA, students can enroll in five levels of basic math, starting with—this is not a misprint—addition. At Boston's vast Northeastern University, more than 30 percent of entering students take remedial English. They study spelling, punctuation and, as the English Department chairman puts it, how 'to get from the subject to the predicate without harming themselves.' The situation is hardly better at the top of the higher-ed ladder. Of the 50 leading American universities, only one offered a remedial writing course in 1939. By 1993, 70 percent of them were teaching the equivalent of 'Sub-Freshman English.' Meanwhile, the history courses that were mandatory at 60 percent of the institutions in 1964 were required by 2 percent in 1993. Literature requirements, which existed at 50 percent of the schools in 1964, had vanished entirely by 1993...Rigor has all but disappeared from the American campus.*[30]

As disturbing as this is, cultural bias of another kind is prominent in the curriculum. Jacoby continues:

> *So what do college students take? The Virginia-based Young America's Foundation examined the 1996 course offerings at dozens of prestigious universities to find out. What it discovered was a bizarre array of political correctness, victim chic, and down-with-America "multiculturalism." At Georgetown University, where Shakespeare is out, "Prison Literature" is in. Students read books by criminals…Haverford scholars can take "Sex and Gender on Film: Screwballs, Devil Dames, and Closet Cases"…Brown University offers "Christianity, Violence, and Victimization,'" which teaches that "Christianity has helped to create and perpetuate a culture of violence, especially against women." Religion-bashing is also big at the University of Pennsylvania, which gives credit for '"The Historical Origins of Racism: Views of Blacks in Early Judaism, Christianity, and Islam."*[31]

Education, it would seem, has become a venting place of frustration, anger, and disillusionment. It seems to be moving away from its original focus of providing tools for life.

Smith calls this a "cult of dullness," in which clear writing and inspired lecturing are deviant and suspicious behaviors. Nothing is done to challenge the student, but apparently everything is done to entertain and remove his angst. Smith believes academic research would be defensible if there was some sense to the product of the research. "The vast majority," he writes, "is mediocre, expensive and unnecessary." This fits nicely into the post-industrial model of *non-thinking thinking* to do *non-doing doing* of *non-thing things*, which was covered earlier, because what these professors have to say, according to Smith, amounts to practically nothing at all. This has even been the curse of one of America's most acclaimed writers, John Updike. The late Granville Hick's of the *Saturday Review of Literature* laments upon reading Updike that "he writes like an angel, if only he had something to say." Style eclipses substance, impression takes precedence over making a difference. Smith calls this "scientism," a devotion to the scientific approach in all fields of study, including the humanities. This has driven the spirit out of enterprise, leaving life an empty shell to be filled with noise as entertainment. We don't seem to be moving from ignorance to enlightenment, in the Buddhist sense, but instead seem to be building our dream house on ignorance's foundation.

Who pays for this? At first blush, you might think it is borne by parents who make sacrifices for their children's education, which now can run as high as $120,000 for a four-year degree. It is future generations of Americans who will pay in the form of the society this education generates. What Tocqueville observed and reported more than 150 years ago has largely come to pass. What will America be 150 years hence? Cut across American society, from the academic community to the government, from industry to commerce, from religious institutions to charitable organizations, and without exception, there is no easy sanctuary for greatness. An individual of greatness must spend much of his energy fitting in, coping, and not offending the mediocre. Organizations are obsessed with internal politics, which are often vicious, leaving little energy for individual or collective excellence.

The real hope for America is the growing professional class of workers, who are aristocratic in temperament and democratic in spirit. This workforce must take hold of its power in consort with management, acclaiming differences and diversity, and channel its power to a common purpose. The traditional formula for continuity and succession planning will not accomplish this. It has succeeded instead in holding the organization back, giving relevance to Thomas Babington Macaulay's refrain in *Lays of Ancient Rome* (1842),

> *Was none who would be foremost*
> *To lead such dire attack;*
> *But those behind cried "Forward!"*
> *And those before cried "Back!"*[32]

We need leadership as much today as we did when we were a young nation. We need greatness as it once existed. We need real change, not cosmetic change. We need thinking that uses all our faculties and all our people. What we don't need is an organization of like thinkers and doers, who have rarely experienced an original thought or dared to wander far from the crowd. Nor do we need people who know how to get promoted far better than they know how to work. Many young men and women enter the working world with their idealism in tact and their values on display. If these values are in conflict with the prevailing values of the organization, they either give in, give out, get out, or tune out. A workplace culture has a low tolerance for dealing with conflict in values. Throughout American history, greatness has come in strange packages. Walt Whitman, an acknowledged homosexual, would tail President Lincoln all about Washington as if obsessed with capturing a glimpse of this great man. Whitman was a strange and wonderful man, and today many critics consider him America's greatest poet. He proclaimed the dignity and freedom of the common man as he sang the praises of democracy. His style, which Hawthorne thought clumsy, has had incalculable effect on later poets, inspiring them to experiment in prosody and subject matter, as he did. Could Whitman function in today's corporate society? Would his genius be allowed? Would anyone acclaim his work?

A One-Dimensional Society

To discover the source of this aversion to greatness, you need look no further than our educational system. In its quest for egalitarianism, education has substituted skill-building for knowledge-building and diversionary entertainment for challenging study. Instrumental education has taken precedence over classical education. Workers and managers have received vocational training at the expense of a humanities foundation. Page Smith accuses our most prestigious universities of reducing education from thinking to technique and from teaching to instructing. Because you can only deal with what you know, the organization and its people are vocationally led and trained.[33] This presents a problem. If management and workers think primarily in terms of utility or from a vocational perspective—with management thinking what it can get out of the individual, and the worker thinking what he can get out of the organization—they share a common cynicism about work. At another level, vocational education puts the emphasis on doing only what makes people successful, not necessarily what is best for the organization. "That is what the company values," workers and managers tell themselves, "and that is what I am going to do." This attitude existed before the downsizing and redundancy panic, which only reinforced it. "Hey, I could be out of here next month," the survivor thinks, "If you're not out for yourself, who are you out for, right?" And thus workers and managers gravitate toward a one-dimensional society.[34]

The MBA degree is essentially a vocational degree in the same sense as a trade school education. MBAs scoff at the idea that their work has cultural implications. They find the concept of workplace culture suspect—too abstract. Being trained in a set of skills—finance, information systems, macro economics, statistics, computers, and management practices—they find little time and less inclination for background reading on culturally related subjects. "What's the point?" one young man said to me in exasperation, "Why should I read a lot of dead authors?" Because the masters of the ages dealt with many similar perturbations in their times. Here is a short list:

- Homer's *The Iliad* & *The Odyssey*
- *The Bible*
- *The Trojan Women* by Euripides
- *The Torah*
- *The Birds* by Aristophanes
- *The Bhagavad Gita*
- *Oedipus Rex* by Sophocles
- *The Holy Crusades (History of)* by Joseph F. Michaud
- The works of William Shakespeare
- *The Republic* by Plato
- *Alexander the Great* by John K. Anderson
- *The Gallic Wars* (Commentaries) by Julius Caesar
- The Epistles of St. Paul
- *Paul: Mind of the Apostle* by A. N. Wilson
- *Meditations* by Marcus Aurelius
- *The History of the Decline and Fall of the Roman Empire* by Edward Gibbon

Reading these works reminds you of the French saying, "The more things change, the more they remain the same." This cultural tip of the iceberg would probably surprise the novice reader, reflecting as did Solomon, "There is nothing new under the sun." We are the product of thousands of years of acculturation, and yet, our evolution is seemingly incomplete. Knowing something about our heritage is much more useful than being obsessed with our family genealogy. The family of man is technically and culturally a true family. We are all related. The better we understand this, the greater the possibility we have to live and work together in harmony.

The Hunt for the American Character

Given our one-dimensional mentality, it comes as little surprise that the answers sought to poor performance of the workforce are likewise one-dimensional. Trust is placed in the rational solution to purposeful performance. Half the brain is put to the problem, resulting in half-baked solutions. Circular logic dominates as we attempt to solve the problems with the same type of thinking that caused them—like a dog endlessly chasing its own tail. Over the years, the deficiency in this approach has produced *Reader's Digest* minds and McCult-type systems for closing the gap between the left and right brain:

- There is the *Aspen Institute* approach in which executives gather in picturesque surroundings to get in touch with Nature over cocktails and the drone of glassy-eyed consultants in accustomed psychobabble.
- *The Great Books Clubs* in which a common herd mentality of like-minded culturally deficient minds ponder the syllabus of their misspent education.
- The satellite cultural-fix operations, such as *The Center for Creative Leadership* (Greensboro, NC) and *The Tom Peters Group* (Silicon Valley, CA), which attempt to make a difference, but only make an impression.

As Edward de Bono puts it, "They are in the business of attempting to discover a solution when the only way out is to create one."[35] These retrofitted strategies sell well, but nothing changes. We are in the throes of a cultural dilemma. We need change, but we would prefer to adjust the limits and call it "change." Integrative thinking, cultural awareness, service-oriented leadership, and value change will take many years. The only thing that might accelerate the rate of change would be a cultural catastrophe, the size of which the workplace has never experienced. You cannot overcome a century of progressive cultural neglect by the miracle of some McCult-type solution. Only time and attention, and much patience, will overcome the cultural biases that no longer serve the American character. It will be decades before the American psyche will:

- Re-establish the sanctity and stability of the family or some appropriate alternative.
- Advocate creativity over discovery.
- Accept the necessity of rebellion over conformity.
- Prefer cooperation over competition.
- Celebrate greatness over mediocrity.
- Encourage students with original ideas over "A" students.
- Award high school diplomas only to students who are proficiently bilingual.

- Promote, mobilize, and utilize diversity in support of effectiveness.
- Sponsor, recognize, and reward team performance over individualism.
- Promote a global perspective over a parochial point of view.
- Support fine arts in high school as much as athletics.
- Support high school debate, essay, and speech events as much as athletics.
- Start language education in French, German, and Spanish in pre-school.
- Make the teaching profession the highest paid profession of all.

If this sounds ambitious, compare it to what our world competitors are doing today.[36]

No. 3: Changing the Organizational Infrastructure from Physical to a Psychological Climate

If the organization knows what it wants to accomplish and is structured to accomplish that goal, behavior will be purposeful, and the goal will be achieved. If the organization knows what it wants to accomplish but is not structured to accomplish that goal, behavior will become the focus, and the goal will not be achieved.

Goal or Objective + Proper Workplace Culture = Purposeful Performance

The infrastructure of the organization should be designed to support and facilitate its strategy. That seems simple enough, but it happens to be difficult, because it is more symbolic than substantive, more psychological than physical. Piped-in Muzak, warmly painted walls, excellent lighting, ergonomically designed work stations, sound-proof cubicles are wonderful, but goals will not be realized if the workplace culture is not equally engineered. The workplace culture should facilitate three-way communications. It is imperative that everyone who needs to know does, preferably before, not after, changes are made. Communication is more a qualitative than a quantitative matter. Throwing unfiltered information at workers indiscriminately tends to overwhelm. It defeats its purpose and contributes to worker frustration, confusion, and anxiety.

The actual information requirements of employees follow common sense:

- Employees want enough information to do a good job.
- Employees want to make the right decisions in their work, which means they need to have a clear understanding of what is expected, when it is expected, and where it is to be performed.
- Employees want information that affects them personally and professionally.
- Employees want information that helps them improve their performance: information must be true, accurate, and necessary. To simply rally them to work harder will have a negative impact.

- Employees want information that will contribute to their growth and development.
- Employees want to know the status of the company in terms that affect their situation, not senior management's. No snow jobs!

The four common sense principles of communication:

- How does the information affect me personally?
- How does the information affect me professionally?
- How does the information impact what I am now doing?
- How does it feel (sound)? Is it believable? Does it make sense?

When the workplace culture facilitates decision-making at its lowest level, it is possible to expedite real-time response to changing work demands. Paternalism and fear—employers and managers acting as surrogate parents—are not conducive to workers taking charge and becoming responsible. Once employees are secure in their jobs, know the parameters of their responsibilities, and understand the relationship of their function to other critical functions, they need only to be given room in the form of trust to do their jobs. The dividends can be astounding. Critical decisions will be made expeditiously at the right level, with the right people, and at the right time. How do you know what is right? Right is a function of knowing what is expected to occur at a given level. As managers operate more like coaches, this type of insight will be common. When the workplace culture and the infrastructure are congruently designed to support the goals of operations, the roles of the workers will become fluid in response to these demands. Once role demands are understood and appreciated, authority and responsibility flow naturally to the requirements of the situation.

Perhaps a basketball analogy might help. One player's role may be to penetrate the defense as a point guard to create offensive opportunities for other players. Another player may have the role to set a screen for the weak side forward for a three-point shot. Pat Riley, successful NBA coach, tells a story on himself as a player, which illustrates the importance of knowing your role, responsibility, and relationship to the other players. It was in his playing days with the Los Angeles Lakers. The Lakers were playing for the NBA championship, and it was the championship game of a best of seven final. Only seconds remained on the clock, and if the Lakers scored, the championship was theirs! The ball came to Riley at the top of the key. He was wide open and took the shot. He missed. The Lakers lost. In the dressing room after the game, trying to console himself on the missed shot, he said to nobody in particular, "I was wide open." Wilt Chamberlain, the great seven-foot center, put his hand on Riley's shoulder. "You were wide open, Patrick, because nobody was guarding you." It was sharpshooter Jerry West's role to take the final shot. Riley's role as point guard was to get the ball to West. But he didn't because, momentarily, in the heat of the contest, he forgot his role and tried to assume a role for which he was not qualified. Self-demands won out over role demands. This happens every day in the organization and with similar consequences. Yet it can be avoided by constantly defining and facilitating these roles, relationships, and responsibilities.

Role identity is based on the special skills and knowledge required to do a particular job. The relationship of roles is based upon the changing demands of the workplace situation. A basketball team has five role identities—two guards, two forwards, and a center—and an infinite combination of those roles, given changing situations. Many of these have been experienced many times, and so there is some comfort in what is to be expected. The work situation, similar to the basketball team, never has the same mix of capabilities or the same chemistry between workers. The manager as coach compensates for individual weaknesses and utilizes apparent strengths of the group to the fullest. Each worker contributes on the basis of complementary roles, not on position power. A particular role may find an individual taking charge in one situation and being supportive in another. This is a much more demanding job than traditional management because the manager, as coach, needs to be teacher, preacher, cheerleader, counselor, facilitator, and arbitrator to strong-willed and ego-driven workers of extraordinary capacities—the professional worker of the post-modern, post-industrial age.

Provide workers with the psychological climate conducive to role identity, and workers will organize themselves consistent with the demands of work. They will self-manage. The psychological climate:

- Advances an easily understood philosophy and creates a sense of mission that workers can understand and commit themselves to, along with a set of guiding principles that support the organization's philosophy.
- Cultivates a common work language that reflects the shared values which all workers can understand and support.
- Presents a consistent message no matter what the level of stress and strain or how accelerating the demands which are placed on the organization.
- Walks its talk in virtually everything it does, recognizing the tremendous indicative power of symbolic interaction in creating desired perceptions.
- Harnesses the workers' power and their "will to do" by paying close attention to them as people.

It is never the perfect organization that succeeds, but the happy and healthy one. Such an organization has a sense of humor about itself, along with the wisdom to balance risk and opportunity with prudence, which brings everyone on board. This is not to suggest that streamlining and general organization trimming are not necessary. Most organizations have gotten too rich for their blood. This is meant only to point out the value of the psychological climate. Nor should this be confused with touchy-feely interventions. The psychological climate produces concrete results, not cosmetic effects. Implementing the psychological climate, however, requires a new set of skills—counseling, coaching, listening, communication, conflict management, employee assessment (potential), team-building, cheerleading, and facilitating— which most senior, middle-line, and staff managers lack.

The Cultural Infrastructure as a Psychological Entity

An automotive company has made a major turnaround in a ten-year period. So remarkable was this resurrection of the phoenix from its own ashes that I called on this company to learn more about its success.[37] The morning of the visit, when I tried to start my rental car, it wouldn't start. When matters were finally in hand, I was 30 minutes late for my appointment and expressed this frustration to the security guard upon my arrival at the company's international headquarters in Detroit. Looking me in the eye, the guard asked, "What kind of car are you driving, sir?" He breathed a sigh of relief when I told him. "I would have been very much surprised," he said, "if it had been one of ours." With a serious look on his face, he said, "You see, it's our intention to make the best automobile in the world." I smiled and thought to myself, "They do a good job of public relations here."

The security guard gave me my visitor's badge and directions to the office of my contact. At the elevator, I engaged in conversation with two engineers, bringing up my recent experience, not knowing what else to say. They looked at each other, then one spoke. Her response was quite similar to that expressed before. Her companion nodded his head in agreement as she spoke. Intrigued by this, wondering at the coincidence, when I reached my contact's office, I shared the same story with his secretary. Again, her response was similar to the others. Without fanfare, each person, I learned later, was reflecting the philosophy and mission of the Ford Motor Company. This was not an accident or some rehearsed agenda. It was something felt, believed in, and lived by. Nor was it coincidental to learn that everyone spoke a similar language in terms of meaning. Considerable effort had gone into creating a consistent message and language in support of that message.[38] The psychological climate is established here and producing results. Every worker I encountered was an ambassador for the company. As one United Auto Worker union official put it, "We've always had these banners around 'Treat People With Respect.' Now, it is clear that we mean it."[39]

The Problem with Mixed Messages

This caused me to look more closely at some mixed messages that have been advanced in other organizations with which I have been associated—companies that were finding it difficult, literally, to decide what business they were in, to the confusion of all. In conversation with these employees, this is a sample of typical responses:

- *"We're told one day we want to grow the business, and the next we've gotta make pay cuts. Hello! Anybody home?"*
- *"Hey, my boss tells me, ' be innovative,' right? Even thinks it's cool.*

So I get creative. Boss comes back, "No, no, no, not like that!'
Practically does my job. It figures, right?"

- *"We have this big meeting. Everybody's there. Whole plant. What,*
4,000, something like that. Guy gets up from corporate. Tells us how
important we are. Wants us to bust our balls, which is all right by me.
Lot of deadheads around here. All fired up. Get back to the plant. Boss
tells me I need a haircut. That's right, a damned haircut! If that's not
enough, tells me I'm on the block next cutback. Well, friend, guess
where my motivation went?"

- *"We play games around here—say one thing, do another."*

- *"I wish I had a dime for every time the boss mentions trust. Doesn't*
trust me, you, anybody any further than he can throw 'em. How do I
know? Gives me an assignment, then the same one to my buddy, can
you believe that? Thinks he's being cute."

- *"This idea of teamwork. Big around here. Did you ever see a team*
player get anywhere? Come on!"

- *"Took this course on planning. You know, plan your work, work your*
plan. That stuff. Well, in 30 years I've only seen one kind of planning,
by your ass handles. Know what I mean?"

There is a perverted consistency in these remarks from diverse workers, ranging from senior managers to engineers, from administrators to custodial workers. The psychological climate is pervasive, driven by prevalent cultural biases. It can be positive or negative, managed, or out of control. People are not bricks, mortar, and cement. They are not buildings. They require cultivation, a suitable workplace climate, and attention, but the payback is many times greater than the costs.

Psychological Forces within the Infrastructure

Each employee is a complex organization within himself, the nucleus from which the organization builds itself. The cumulative effect of these workers as a unit is either purposeful or dysfunctional:

- You cannot treat some employees with respect and not others.
- You cannot favor some employees and expect other employees to applaud your efforts.
- You cannot share company secrets with some employees and put other employees in the dark with the rationale, "They don't need to know." (There are exceptions, but not nearly as many as some would like to believe.)
- You cannot make demands on some and treat others with kid gloves.

All employees must feel that they are special, important, and making a meaningful contribution. Some basic psychological forces within the infrastructure determine if people are in control of their lives:

MISSION

To win the Proposal and dedicate all our energies to that purpose. We are a single team in which the focus is always on what is best for the team to win.

VALUES

How we accomplish the mission is as important as the mission itself. Fundamental to our successes are

- People - Team members are the source of our strength, their skills the core to our winning.
- Results - The quality of our results will be the result of our joint efforts, the differentiator.
- Winning - Winning as a team is the ultimate achievement. It secures everyone's future.
- Fun - A spirit of fun surrounds this opportunity, giving everyone room to express their talents.

GUIDING PRINCIPLES

- Quality of the proposal comes first - To win, the quality of our joint efforts must be top priority.
- Members of the team are our first customers - Our work must put our team members first in order to do a quality job.
- Continuous improvement is essential to our success - We must create a climate for innovation and doing things differently to make this a unique and winning proposal.
- Total involvement is a key to our success - We are a team with everyone participating. We must treat each other with trust and respect.
- Integrity is never compromised - We must conduct ourselves in a responsible and ethical manner.

Figure 10.3   Team mission, values, and guiding principles of an aerospace proposal team going after a big defense contract. All team members carried a card like this in their wallets or purses.

- The forces within the individual's self—the "ideal self," or the way the individual has been programmed to think he should behave, and the "real self," or the way the individual actually behaves.
- The forces within the work situation and how the situation will be defined. If the individual's "ideal self" is dominant, the tendency is to define the situation the way it "should be," but isn't. If the individual's

"real self" is on display, chances are he will define the situation as it actually is (see Figure 6.5).

If the organization fails to communicate a clear *mission*, to develop a common workplace cultural *language*, and to resonate a consistent *message* in that language, there is a likelihood employees will be confused. They will be in a constant struggle within themselves—whether to go with the flow and let problems take care of themselves or to speak out when something goes wrong. Cover-up starts with one person, not a gang. If workers constantly attempt to make an impression, which their mind tells them is the only way to survive, less attention will be paid to the job. Workers react to the workplace culture in complex ways, many of which are not clearly apparent to them, but which have real impact on the way they behave. These are essentially unconscious responses to dominant stimuli. It all starts with how they see themselves, how they think they are expected to be seen, and how comfortable they are with being themselves in this particular workplace culture. Operating deceptively starts with self-deception. Because such workers choose to define their situation poorly, not as it is, the *six silent killers* become their ammunition for survival. If workers are self-accepting of themselves as they are, there is no need for deception. They can admit when they drop the ball or when they don't know. There is no need for pretense. The *six silent killers* vanish when this is their orientation.

Consultant Paul Hersey uses maturity and readiness to describe purposeful behavior in *The Situational Leader* (1985).[40] Maturity is a useful term. When the organization treats employees as adults, their readiness to behave as adults increases—they behave responsibly. The key here is how the organization views employees in terms of maturity and the type of workplace culture it creates. Mature workers are more inclined to be flexible rather than rigid and better able to deal with challenges. They don't panic. Providing the forces within the situation are clearly defined, and the forces within the individual are in a healthy state, then workers are likely to have little trouble balancing self demands and role demands. Self demands rise out of ego demands, which can get in the way of the job. Role demands relate to the job itself, or what workers are hired to do. If the situation is poorly defined, because the individual thinks, "This is not my job," or "Do they know who I am?" or "This is not what an engineer is paid to do," self demands are muddying up the works. Erratic behavior follows. There is a natural conflict between these demands, which depend largely on the maturity of workers as to how they are handled. The more mature (ready) workers are, the more appropriate the behavior is likely to fit the situation (see Figure 6.5). Self demands and role demands may be summarized:

- *Self demands*: The person needs to protect his fragile ego, needs to let people know how important he is, needs to identify with people who personify his ego ideal by name-dropping or forming or associating in cliques, and needs to project personal biases.
- *Role demands*: The person perceives the situation in terms of what needs to be done, works to focus colleagues on the same objectives,

---

Survey of 900 United States Executives

- 93 percent said managers were not rewarded for developing subordinates for leadership. On the contrary, managers are often rewarded for killing off talented managers who are threatening their own jobs.

- 87 percent said it was impossible to make lateral moves in their companies, an essential for developing leaders who will know how the whole company operates, not just a portion of it.

- 80 percent said they had inadequate programs to identify what people needed in order to develop leadership skills.

Figure 10.4   A call for leadership, adapted from John P. Kotter, *The Leadership Factor* (1988), a survey of 900 U.S. executives.[41]

demonstrates competence and earns the group's trust, sees himself in the service of others, shows an easy grace under pressure, and assists others to discover and use their own skills.

Self demands reflect an adolescent disposition. Role demands reflect an adult inclination. Role demands find the individual is very much a self-manager. Workers make a contribution when their personal system (values) is working in consort with the workplace culture. When the forces within the workplace are in balance, everyone knows what is expected of them and why. Work is organized to meet common goals, not structured to create conflict, confusion, and dissension. The infrastructure supports teamwork and fosters cooperation, collaboration, and communication. Work is stimulating, but it is still work, not play. Everybody enjoys what they do, or they would be somewhere else.

The problem with structure, then, is less physical than psychological. The pyramid is already flattening and will continue to flatten. It is the cultural climate that needs attention. Role identities, role relationships, and role responsibilities are part of the team concept, which we know from the athletic model has much to do with intangibles in building toward success. Ford Motor Company is representative of what has been happening in the automotive industry.[42] A revolution is underway, and the results to date, throughout this industry, are astonishing. The automotive industry is again No. 1 in the world because of many things. One thing for certain is its psychological climate.[43]

Figure 10.5   The Cry of the Future. Cartoon by Bill Day, *Detroit Free Press*, reprinted with permission (*International Herald Tribune*, February 24, 1988).[44]

No. 4: Coping with Leaderless Leadership

The paradoxical dilemma is that we cannot lead and we do not want to follow. Do you want to lead? Probably not. Do you want to follow? Again, probably not. Most want to neither lead nor follow anyone anywhere. Why is it most people don't like to lead? They want to believe they are in charge. Then why don't more people lead? They don't know how to lead. Most organizations have a management system and call it leadership.[45] The central issue of leadership is what is meant by it. Does it mean compliance? Coordination of a multiplex of tasks? Does it mean management?

Compliance suggests arbitrary standards to influence desired behavior and involves the generous use of coercion and manipulation, neither of which suggest leadership. Generally speaking, people follow a leader, not because they have to, but because they want to. Where there is coercion, leadership is of a most limited duration. Ultimately, people come to resist the yoke of repression and rebel. Before they rebel overtly, they rebel covertly. Like social termites, they commence to sabotage operations from within via the *six silent killers*. Obviously, coordination is involved in any leadership activity. When coordination is the central thrust of leadership, however, it becomes simply management. Prior to the information age, we were a managed society. Since it worked reasonably well, we felt no compunction to call it leadership.[46]

The Subtle Difference - Leadership versus Management

Leaders are not concerned about leadership qualities, but with purposeful performance.

Think in terms of their followers. Followers are the best guide to how leaders lead.

Understand the work climate. Know the organizational culture and are prepared for an open and trusting climate.

Use the human resources they have. Invest in their development. Know 99 percent of their people are capable, but as much as 90 percent are either not challenged, or lack opportunity.

Know the more outstanding the employee, the greater the problem. Understand employees must be guided by their own lights.

Better that leaders lose good people than have them go sour. The job of leadership is always development. Therefore, leaders should not punish themselves for doing a good job.

The subtle difference between leadership and management is the psychology, not the functionality. Management does mechanical things well — planning, budgeting, organizing, controling — through formal authority. Leadership, while doing these same things, educates its people, inspires confidence and motivates them to take ownership of what they do.

Figure 10.6   Leadership is committed to growth and development.

Management is a mechanistic function and involves the maintenance of an organization in terms of the status quo. When the German philosopher Nietzsche declared that "God is dead," he was proclaiming the shift of Western society from the domination of the church to the secular realm. Capitalism was the new religion, founded on materialistic scientism with management at the controls. The hierarchies of the church now became the bureaucracies of commerce. German sociologist Max Weber in *The Protestant Ethic and the Spirit of Capitalism* (1920) identified the intimate connection between secularism and ethics, which Calvinism fostered, and the rise of capitalistic institutions.[47] The twentieth century verified the relevance of Weber's model.

Bureaucracy is often used in the pejorative sense, but it has been very important in the conduct of society in all its dimensions. Many of its fundamental features are now fragmented or struggling to hold on to tradition. Weber feels there is little danger that long-term bureaucracies, such as the Roman Catholic Church, will vanish any time soon. He believes that the larger the bureaucracy and the longer it exists, the longer it will exist. The church is now 2,000 years old. He claims institutional survival is the combination of size and age. This protects most established bureaucracies from early demise. A traditional bureaucracy may be characterized as a large-scale formal organization with highly differentiated bureaus, within which formalized rules are vigorously enforced. Each bureaucratic department is headed by highly trained experts, whose primary role is to coordinate activities in the hierarchical chain of command. Here central authority is supreme, and the emphasis is on total efficiency, with the approach to the business being rational, technical, and highly impersonal. If this resembles the church, government, or military, it is no accident. Bureaucracy has prevented impulsive change and given stability to the discharge of its functions. True, bureaucracy is wasteful, cumbersome, and lethargic, but these characteristics have enabled this structure to maintain continuity in society. Much of the criticism today was actually the reason for rejoicing in the past. Now, the military, government, and church are out of sync with commerce and industry in the information age. We are in new territory, a place society has never been before. The result is, at the same time, the disappearance of and the call for leadership. How could it be otherwise? What is unsettling, too, is if you think one day bureaucracy will disappear, think again. By early in the twenty-first century, nearly one out of every two American citizens will be working for some bureaucratic institution.

A Difference of Perspective

There is a certain amount of moral courage to followership, which somehow gets displaced as we move up the ladder. Take the case of the woman who was working at her station when the CEO of a major corporation, along with his executive entourage, stopped to chat with her during a ceremonial plant visit. "And how are you today, young lady?" the CEO beamed with a great smile. She turned, looked at him eye-to-eye, hands planted firmly on her hips, and said, "Horseshit!" Then she turned back to her work station to continue her work. The stunned CEO, neck turning red, clearly flustered, removed his safety glasses, wiped them studiously, and finally regaining his composure, said in almost a whisper, "I'm sorry, miss," and moved on.

One of the executives broke ranks and talked to the woman. She was a single parent with two preschool children. Her setup man didn't show up, and her foreman just told her she would have to work at least two hours overtime to meet the shipping schedule. She had no idea who could pick up her children at day care. It was winter. "That damned woman (at day care) will put my kids out in the cold if I'm not there. Done it before." She started to cry. She was at her wit's end. The executive first checked with the shift foreman to gain his approval and then organized somebody to pick up her children. This blue-collar worker was not impressed with the brass. She had had it and wasn't fearful for her job in expressing her dismay. "He asked," she said simply, "I told him (how I felt)." She was full of her problem and unloaded. To the executive who stayed behind, she claimed no sense of courage or regret. "My kids come first." It was an honest admission not tempered with pretense. Nor was frustration charged with malicious intent. Stunned as the CEO was, he found the empathy to be gracious.

Change the scenario. Substitute a distraught professional or manager. Then imagine the reaction of the CEO to a similar candor. The psychodrama might unfold differently. Self demands could easily take precedence over role demands for the CEO, with him getting equally ugly or causing him to say to an aide, "Get that bastard's name and see who he works for!" Why are executives and professionals not allowed to show feelings or to lose it? Can you imagine how fast a person's career would go in the dumpster if he had been so inclined? Milliseconds. The CEO has symbolic power over the masses, but real power over the elite. Imagine how much more powerful the CEO would be if he exercised his symbolic power over everyone. There is an axiom: the less you exercise influence, the more power you have. If CEOs could learn this simple but vital lesson, staff people would go to hell and back for them. The problem with this happening is that the CEO probably imagines two things: that he owns the elite, but the rank and file own him; he can't afford to lose it with them, but he had better show his dander with his people or else. He knows his behavior with the young woman will be common knowledge to every member (2,000 workers) of this plant within 24 hours. Each shift will pass it on to the next. By the following day, the CEO will be either a hero or a heel. CEOs and other senior management can either launch or eradicate the *six silent killers*. Symbolic behavior is that powerful. The reason is that senior management sets the climate and establishes the culture, which is then replicated.

Unfortunately, CEOs have been programmed to believe empathy with staff is a sign of weakness. The natural paranoia of top management is further exercised because self demands can easily take precedence over role demands: "My staff will use this against me. They'll take advantage of me. I'll lose control." True, the possibility exists. Remember, the CEO first did a slow burn, then recovered his composure and acted prudently. Discretion surfaced as a result of giving himself pause and letting intuition guide him. We are discussing the right brain once again. There will be times when the CEO will feel he is being taken for a ride. That is when he must put his foot down and blister the air. As long as the focus is on behavior rather than the person, and on what is wrong rather than who is wrong, this will serve him well.

The working elite have much to offer and cannot be managed as workers of the past. If they are, it will kill their spirit and turn them into cynics and problems. Once a person is given permission to be a thinking and feeling worker, he will behave as a responsible, accountable contributor, not a self-indulgent worker. "Leadership," suggests James MacGregor Burns in *Leadership* (1979), "represents the complete follower."[48] To lead, one must first learn how to follow. Burns remembers prominent leaders who spent much time as ardent, passionate followers. Following gives leaders an understanding of people. Leaders sense where people want to go, then rally them in that direction. Peter the Great single-handedly brought eighteenth century Russia into the modern Western world. He did this by wandering amongst his people in disguise to learn what they were thinking. He checked the pulse of his nation first-hand rather than through loyal sycophants. His driving passion was not to see his people left behind an advancing world. He was successful because that was the fear of his people, too.[49]

The Triangle of Growth

With man, everything begins in the singular and progresses to the collective. With growth, there is no stasis. When growth stops, atrophy sets in. This is the law of Nature. Struggle is indigenous to life. It starts when we learn to walk and continues as we strive to talk, attempt to master a three-wheeler, try to roller skate, etc. Struggle is never-ending. Ever know anyone to look graceful when first skating? Roller skating is embarrassingly difficult. The reason is that the center of gravity changes

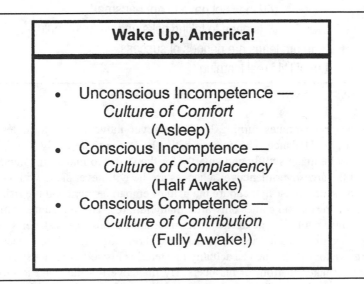

Wake Up, America!

- Unconscious Incompetence —
  Culture of Comfort
  (Asleep)
- Conscious Incomptence —
  Culture of Complacency
  (Half Awake)
- Conscious Competence —
  Culture of Contribution
  (Fully Awake!)

Figure 10.7   The three cultures in terms of "being awake!"

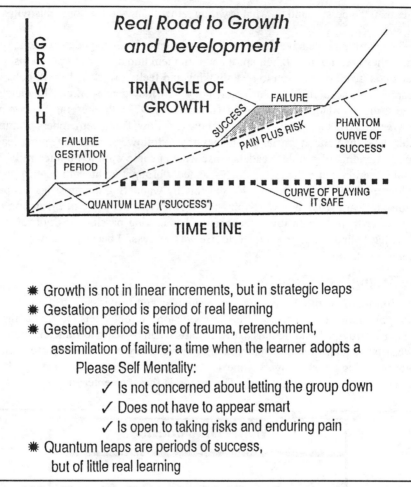

Figure 10.8   The real road to growth and development.

as the skater negotiates turning by a crossover move of his legs, leaving him precariously off balance. The more tentative he is, the more likely he will fall. The move must be made swiftly and smartly for the skater to maintain balance. Should he avoid the crossover maneuver, chances are he will never skate with confidence. A graceful skater must first endure the pain of embarrassment and the risk of falling on his tush. Perfection comes only after many failures. This encounter with embracing resistance could be one of the most important lessons of the skater's young life. It requires letting go and trusting intrinsic psychomotor skills. When successful, this is a huge victory. What he has actually mastered is his self-consciousness or acceptance of mistakes in front of his peers. By maneuvering the mind to embrace his resistance to self-consciousness, he has given himself a psychological edge when the next challenge comes along. Skills that cause embarrassment are best learned when young. When we are young, we are less intimidated by failure. Failure is not actually relevant; pain is. Yet our aversion to physical pain seems to level off at an early age. Psychological pain is another matter. It never crests. Psychological pain becomes increasingly haunting as we get older—the pain of relationships, failures, successes, losses, or gains. Past hurts become barriers to new experiences. If we gave a speech in the sixth grade and everyone laughed, we may never give a speech again.

Organizations behave similarly. Apple, Inc., in its early days, demonstrated an incredible penchant for doing bold things. Today Apple is as cautious as IBM. A young organization is usually idealistic. Once it gets a little long in the tooth, it commonly gravitates to guarded cynicism and encroaching conservatism. If it releases a product that bombs, it tends to lose confidence and behave less decisively.[50] This neutralizes its greatest advantage. Success is the outcome of careful attention to process. The focus of a young company is invariably on process because it has little experience with outcomes. Once success comes, the focus shifts to results. Downturns and plateaus are considered a curse. Yet they are essential components of growth. Every individual and organization experiences plateaus as part of growth. If they play it safe, they can remain on the plateau indefinitely, the plateau of arrested development. The period of stasis, or when nothing seems to be happening, could be called the "plateau of failure." Plateauing is a period when the individual or the organization finally confronts itself and its reality. Processing information and knowledge gained during this period is critical to growth. Judith Bardwick writes correctly in *The Plateauing Trap* (1986) that plateauing can be the beginning, not the end of things. She writes, "We mature only when we face our issues and conflicts, and those, too, never end. Change is the only constant if only because we age. Change is the only healthy response to the unalterable bottom line that nothing is ever forever. And change takes courage" (see Figure 10.8).[51]

Plateauing is a remarkably meaningful stage in development. All growth has an appropriate gestation period. The "plateau of failure" is ours. It is the place where we are on edge. Things aren't going right. We are alone with ourselves in a way we have avoided before. We have suffered a setback—been made redundant, demoted, gone through a divorce, suffered bankruptcy, had a heart attack, lost a major account, or lost a loved one, and the list is endless. It is during this period when some failure causes us to wonder, to break through the wall of reflex behavior to our consciousness. What is nice about the "plateau of failure" is that we don't have to worry about letting the group down. The group is long gone! People are uncomfortable with failure, as though it is a communicable disease. We are alone. Remember how we didn't have to be smart when we were a child? Well, it is like that once again. No one expects us to have answers. All see us as consumed with problems. This puts us in a learning mode. We can now explore, think differently, create, design, and build anew to our heart's content. We can take risks we never dreamed of taking, say things we only thought but were afraid to say, confront people we could never look in the eye before, venture outside our profession or area of expertise, consider lifestyle changes, go back to school, or even leave the country. When things could not look more cloudy, the sun breaks through. We feel a kind of freedom we never dreamed possible. Something wonderful has arisen out of what we thought was the terrible end of everything. We have been reborn. This is truly the first day of the rest of our lives.

When someone plateaus, we think of them going nowhere. This is not true. Or if it is, it is because that person has misinterpreted their own experiences. The plateau is a period of incubation and gestation. We are pregnant with the past, both successes and failures, and inclined toward introspection, taking inventory of ourselves. We may not be able to explain it, but during this period, when by all rights we think we should be miserable, a kind of calm comes over us. Much as we try to be anxious in a way we have been programmed to be, calm sets in. It is similar to the calm we feel after we have an automobile accident. There is nothing we can do about it right now but wait, and our body and mind respond by calming down and giving us relief, a kind that we may not have had in months. Circumstances have forced us to take a time out—much as they do in athletic contests—to regroup and assess the situation. On the "failure plateau," attention is focused on being, not becoming. "Being" means that the person discovers how to please himself and what makes him tick (Figure 10.9). This is a healthy form of self-involvement as opposed to self-indulgence. The

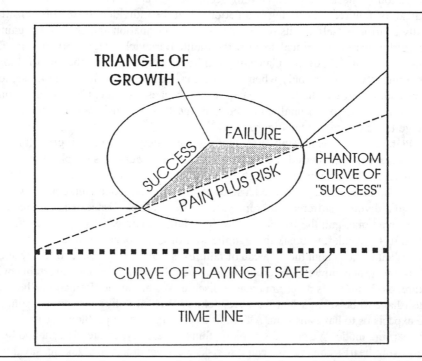

Figure 10.9   The triangle of growth (note the place designated "failure" is the locus of the plateau).

person encounters and deals with real psychological pain and does not attempt to escape this pain in some distraction. "Becoming" involves the person with others—the frantic effort to please others by meeting their needs and to live up to their expectations. This is an unhealthy form of self-involvement and can become obsessive.

Corporations go through similar periods of plateauing. They can experience healthy or unhealthy self-involvement. Instead of using a period of stasis in the business to look hard at the organization, the market, the focus of their concerns, corporations can (and often do) go through periods of denial, projecting their difficulties, only to be buried by them and forced to regroup. J. Eugene Haas and Thomas E. Drabek capture this dilemma in *Complex Organizations* (1973).[52] They explain the "organizational normative, interpersonal and resource structures are never totally consistent. Strains of varying intensity are always present. By organizational strain we mean inconsistencies among and within (these) structures." An analogy to this stress–strain breakdown might be the conflict between managers and professionals about participation in decision-making. The corporation acknowledges the problem between these workers–managers, but chooses to put it on hold. Meanwhile, professionals engage in the *six silent killers*. The corporation continues to conduct its business and cope with customary market demands. Suddenly, out of the blue, the demand level accelerates. A discrepancy develops between these demands and the corporation's capacity to meet them. A competitor launches a new product which captures 10 percent of its market share in one quarter. Its stock price plummets. The level of stress increases as the degree of discrepancy between these demands and its capacity disintegrates. Operating at maximum capacity, corporate structure cannot cope with these increased demands—normative patterns break down, personnel problems mount, and product mix is wrong for the market. The corporation is forced to retreat and regroup. During this period, it learns that the initial disintegration coincided with the stress and strain conflict between managers and professionals. Professionals knew of this new technology but withheld it from management (malicious obedience). Until the collapse, the corporation was powered by forward inertia.

Breaking the Loop

Many individuals and organizations are stranded on a plateau at this moment, experiencing the nightmare of either comfort or complacency. What got them there will not get them off. This is not a time to complain, justify, or rationalize. Nor is it a time to panic. It is a time to learn. The internal dialogue of delay and denial is a vicious circle that must be broken. This dialogue becomes a closed loop that finds us going around and around, producing little movement and no progress. Breaking this loop involves embracing our resistance to right-brain thinking. The right brain accepts our status without defensiveness. It is our left brain that defends the cyclic thinking. We become comparable to an outsider looking in on our dilemma. It gives us perspective and some distance from our emotions. In the corporate sense, the outsider, usually a consultant, convinces the organization to focus on its processes because he has no vested interest. This can be described in terms of freedom.

The outsider has no interest in the "concern to be free" but is passionately committed to the ideal of "becoming free." Rejection of the status quo is the first step toward freedom. This is negative freedom—to be free of too much fixed costs (corporation) or to be free of too much debt (individual). Most criticism is directed in terms of negative freedom. Rebellion is expressed in terms of negative freedom— "to be free of parents." With the outsider, it is not enough to repudiate. That only signifies that there is a problem. Anything not acceptable to us is our problem. We own it. American culture has been pushing negative freedom for 50 years and has accomplished forward inertia. "To become free" (positive freedom) recognizes the need to do something differently—dispense with analyzing the problem to death and create something new. What is created may not be the final solution, but it is a start. For the individual "to become free," the first step involves getting off his duff and doing something—writing a letter, helping a friend, cleaning the house, cutting the grass, doing a crossword puzzle, reading a book, volunteering to serve, getting a haircut, jogging, or any number of things. Things take the person out of himself. What he wouldn't want to do as a first step is become more self-absorbed. Say he was made redundant. Not to panic, which means he wouldn't go to the library and frantically research new careers or obsessively study the *Wall Street Journal* for job opportunities as a first step. Nor should a corporation in trouble go ballistic. For the corporation as a first step "to become free," it might celebrate a corporate anniversary, hold a career fair, call a conference of workers and managers to promote their interdependence, sponsor an essay contest of what is right with the corporation, ask for nominations of best team players, acclaim the first little victory after the storm, and decorate the workplace with ribbons and bunting. Positive, not negative. What we have and what we are, not what we lack and what we aren't.

It is not the end of the world when a new struggle presents itself. Change is needed, but change cannot be expected to occur without regrouping and, yes, retreating to regain composure and energy to go forward. A change in direction requires the positive faculty of imagination to be brought into play. Colin Wilson in *Access to Inner Worlds* (1983) says that imagination is actually "the ability to recreate experience, in all its complexity and richness. And the right brain is able to do precisely that."[53] The company, like the individual, is often comfortable, even complacent, until survival is in question. Then, panic sets in, and all sorts of disruptive behavior follow. "To become free," to recreate experience, involves recognition of the natural interdependence of everyone in enterprise. It involves doing something positive (what is possible) rather than being preoccupied with the negative (what isn't possible). Workers and managers start by seeing themselves as part of the problem so that they can become part of the solution. To deal with this struggle as a single force, which may not produce a final solution, is "to become free."

Gregory Bateson describes this battle between negative and positive freedom as a double bind derived from contradictory messages.[54] One organization of professionals (50,000 workers) was asked to take a voluntary 10 percent pay cut across the board, only to read in the quarterly report that the CEO and all vice presidents were given 20 percent pay increases. The rationale was that "these adjustments are overdue. Our senior management is not compensated competitive to the industry." Such information, Bateson suggests, causes people "to feel lost in the labyrinth of roadblocks, detours, and new construction across the main thoroughfares of their minds." As justifiable as these corporate raises were, and they were, the timing couldn't have been less favorable. No one accepted the explanation. Morale became a problem. The corporation rapidly downsized, got out of secondary businesses and regrouped. It is a much smaller company today. What happened? Some decided to pack it in and leave the company, but the majority decided to come to work and to leave their brains at home. It wasn't the raise that did it, I'm sure, but an accumulation of mixed-message fatigue.

No. 5: Finding Our Way Back to Purposeful Performance

Chris Argyris wrote in *The Failure of Success* (1972) that "We have designed organizations which ignored individual potential for competence, responsibility, constructive intent and productivity."[55] Valiant attempts have been made to change this assessment, but, unhappily, it still holds true. Everything was done to make the worker more productive, save involving the worker in the design. The psychological infrastructure of organization has changed little. True, physical plants have been redesigned, functional practices re-engineered, and a series of employee interventions and creative concepts have been employed to change behavior. These initiatives have not involved workers in either the creation, planning, or implementation phases. Argyris's contention still holds true. The psychological infrastructure has not been touched. It differs little with the 1945 model. At a time when workers need to think and behave differently, they have not been invited to the party. They are the subject, not the predicate. No one knows the difficulty with performing more purposefully than workers. They know that the structure of work is wrong for the requirements of work. They know that the function of work is often at cross purposes with the form work takes. Consultants study them, as if they are a laboratory specimen, and they resent it. This is not the 1930s, and they don't behave like the Hawthorne plant workers of Chicago. What is wrong with the current quest to make workers more responsible is that they remain essentially peripheral to the process. Workers should be a decisive part of the focus group, along with management. The problem will never be solved alone, either by consultants, academics, or executives, but only with all of them in the crucial focus group.

The function of work follows the structure of work. Design an organization in which there are discrete departments—engineering, marketing, production, sales, administration, and personnel—and work will follow with implicit territorial imperatives, out of which develop unquestionable pecking orders, levels of elitism, and status. An organization can boast that work has been designed with the latest scientific ergonomics to enhance productivity and worker satisfaction, proclaim the structure of the organization is streamlined to pose minimal barriers to productive work, and refine the selection process to attract the most able, yet it is all for naught, if the psychological perception of workers is not consistent with this. There are no half measures.

Discrete departmentalization is the product of the mechanistic mind-set, a practice outdated by 50 years. Holistic concepts and pivotal ergonomics do not work when superimposed on departmentalization, any more than senior management can put itself in an ivory tower, remote from the core of business, and expect to be perceived as in the center of things. Nor can management proclaim the importance of safety and environmental protection, then establish the function in an isolated area, staffed with over-the-hill personnel. A similar frustration is experienced when attempts are made to promote user-friendly practices to treat co-workers as first customers, while engineering is encouraged to compete with production, and so on. Pronouncements provoke cynicism when the structure is a contradiction to function. HRD is not a department. It is a philosophy. When structured as a function and operated as a department, we have horror stories. When HRD operates as a philosophy, we have the autonomic nervous system of enterprise.

Team work cells represent an organic as opposed to a mechanistic configuration. The structure of work includes the integration of engineering, marketing, production, sales, administration, and personnel. When an organization has this configuration, psychological perceptions bring about optimum worker satisfaction. Worker satisfaction translates into maximum productivity. How? It goes something like this:

- Engineering designs things that can be easily made by production.
- Engineering designs what is needed as indicated by marketing.

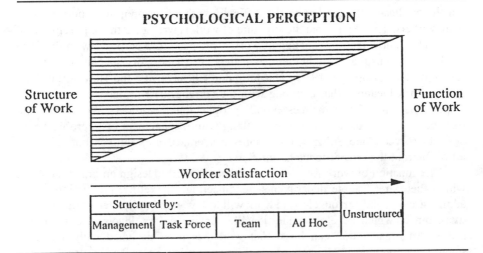

Figure 10.10   Control and satisfaction as a function of structure.

- Sales follows the design, marketing, and production input and confirms or challenges this information on the basis of what will sell.
- Production expresses its capacity and limitations to engineering, sales,
  and marketing, after evaluating the design requirements of engineering.
- Administration tracks all this input and creates the matrix design to
  see that everyone has the information they need and when they need it.
- HRD follows these interactions, facilitates the teaming, learns training needs and resource requirements of respective disciplines and sees
  that they are provided, updates the teams on manpower issues and
  requests for personnel, and makes status reports of recruiting, selecting, training, and orientation.

Ideally, to make such a team truly effective, each team member spends a
specified period of time in each discipline during orientation. The purpose of this
exposure is to facilitate learning, understanding, and appreciation of the interdependent nature of work.

Obviously, there are organizations aware of this dichotomy and which attempt
to make the structure and function congruent. H. Ross Perot, founder of Electronic
Data Systems Corporation (EDS), established a credo that brought considerable
success to his firm. After he became a significant stockholder of General Motors
Corporation and saw how it was being operated, he published a manifesto in *Fortune*
magazine (February 15, 1988)—"How I Would Turn Around GM":

- First feed the troops, then the officers. The bonus system is ludicrous
  and self-serving.
- The running of the corporation belongs to the workers. It does not
  belong to custodial power or management.
- If there is to be a bonus rule, the same rule should apply to the workers
  and managers alike. (EDS has gain-sharing.)
- Management believes it holds the keys to the kingdom, gives itself
  Nobel Prize–like awards, while it gives the troops baubles and beads.
  This is not only senseless, but poor business.
- Management, as a word, should be eliminated. Inventories can be
  managed, people led.[56]

Ever combatant and irascible, Perot took on General Motors as a project worthy
of rehabilitation. At the time (1988), Perot saw GM operating "in a blanket of fog."
For his conspicuous attack, GM dumped him off its board of directors with a payoff
of $700 million for his stock and resignation.[57] The irony is that GM today practices
much of what Perot preached a decade ago and again is the leader in the world of
automotive sales.[58]

This Business of Empowerment

The difficult agenda ahead relates to the ability of the individual to grasp his own
power and to channel his energy to useful purpose. We are put on Earth to prove

useful in the service of others. This does not involve worrying about being used, but being useful. Happiness and fulfillment are tied to this single factor. The more we serve ourselves at the expense of others, the more we are diminished. Why would anyone resort to the *six silent killers*? No one knows the answer. Each individual is different and displays a different justification for punishing himself by destroying others.

There is little point in blaming the family, the school, the church, the government, the company, or God. Each person is born with a set of individual aptitudes uniquely his own. His attitude and personality are acquired as he is exposed to life. Hopefully, these enhance his awareness, acceptance, and inclination to use his talents to a useful purpose. Most of us fall somewhere in the middle between what we are and what we desire to be. Those able to breathe life into their aptitudes have a grasp of their power.

It would be nice to say that society blesses he who exercises his power, but that would be a lie. Society is driven by its own fears. It programs the individual into a state of dependency so it can control him. The individual survives by pleasing others, often at the expense of diminishing what he truly has to offer. He gives up his power for security. He surrenders his will to fit in. Because of this, he is a stranger in his own body, who has dreams of a person he has never met and wanders through life carrying baggage that he never purchased. What leaks through these fissures is the poison of the *six silent killers*. Society has difficulty with genius, greatness, and self-love.

We elect people to public office whom we believe are like us, crippled but not too crippled, part of our herd, but slightly separated from it, who stand out, but not too much. Adlai Stevenson was nominated several times for the presidency, but never stood a chance. He seemed too European, too sophisticated, too intellectual, and too urbane for our tastes, yet he was from the Midwestern farm belt. The same kind of people ascend the ladder of an organization. Those who rise in our culture are people afraid of positive freedom. Early on, they tested the waters for positive freedom and discovered that negative freedom and fear won out.

The problem of empowerment can be frightening. In the United Kingdom while I was working in Europe in 1987, the press related how some 60 fifth-form youths (16-year-olds) who had been at a roller-skating party were robbed of their money, clothes, rings, and other possessions by five young toughs as they left the roller-skating rink. They were commanded to line up, and those who hesitated were kicked into line. The 60 youths obediently followed. A few dominated the many. Were the young toughs leaders? No. What about the 60 youths? Great Britain, it appears, is still very much a repressive society, with children conditioned to be obedient, to be literally kicked into line by the time they are 16. Rebellion is out, as is confrontation. So, to get even, they probably resort to the *six silent killers*, first at home, then on the job, then in marriages, and beyond. It all starts with not being able to show a little fight when young, not being able to discover their own power. These young people were used to being kicked into line—at school, church, and in the community. Like many elsewhere, including the United States, chances are they will never grow up, lock stepping to terminal adolescence because that is where it is presumed safety resides.

Empowerment is not a program or a process. It is a state of being. The rare chance that empowerment is apparent is in an individual known in society as the "outsider." It was no accident that an unknown writer, Colin Wilson, became an international sensation 40 years ago with *The Outsider* (1956). He touched a cord of society. Outsiders today are everywhere pretending to be insiders. They are change agents committed to truth and patiently moving in that direction, while holding valiantly on to their slipping power. Imagine the climate when Wilson wrote these words:

> *The problem for the "civilization" is the adoption of a religious attitude that can be assimilated as objectively as the headlines of last Sunday's newspaper. But the problem for the individual always will be the opposite of this, the conscious striving not to limit the amount of experience seen and touched; the intolerable struggle to expose the sensitive areas of being to what may possibly hurt them; the attempt to see as a whole, although the instinct of self-preservation fights against the pain of the internal widening, and all the impulses of spiritual laziness build into waves of sleep with every new effort. The individual begins that long effort as an Outsider; he may finish it as a saint.*[59]

Endnotes

1. W. Edwards Deming, *Out of the Crisis* (Cambridge, MA: MIT Center for Advanced Study, 1986), first lines of preface.
2. Eric Hoffer, *The Passionate State of Mind* (New York: Perennial Library, 1954), p. 125.
3. George F. Will, *Men at Work: The Craft of Baseball* (New York: Macmillan, 1990). Baseball is a game, Will shows, which acts out our dreams, frustrations, and temperament. It is an individualist ritual in a team setting, rich in quantitative statements but simple to follow, with strategies as convoluted as warfare.
4. Steve Buchholz and Thomas Roth, *Creating the High Performance Team*, ed. Karen Hess (New York: John Wiley & Sons, 1987).
5. U.S. Public Health Service, *General Report*, 1995.
6. Michael D. Lemonick, "The New Miracle Drug," *Time*, September 23, 1996, 60–67. See also Christine Gorman, "Redux on the Ropes," *Time*, June 23, 1997, 47.
7. Fritjof Capra, *The Turning Point: Science, Society & the Rising Culture* (New York: Simon & Schuster, 1982), pp. 261–263; 37–48.
8. Ibid., pp. 41–62.
9. Hoffer, op. cit., p. 91.
10. J. Krishnamurti, *You Are the World* (New York: Harper & Row, 1972), p. 158.
11. Russell L. Ackoff and Fred E. Emery, *On Purposeful Systems* (Seaside, CA: Intersystems Publications, 1972), pp. 4–5.
12. Isaiah Berlin, *The Crooked Timber of Humanity* (New York: Alfred Knopf, 1991), p. 161.

13. Thomas à Kempis, *The Imitation of Christ* (Garden City, NY: Image Books, 1955). Perhaps the most telling phrase of this devotional is, "I had rather feel compunction of heart for my sins than only know the definition of compunction."

14. Joseph Campbell, "Transformations of Myth Through Time," The Learning Channel, hosted by Peter Donat, February 15, 1996. Series is repeated several times a year and represents an invaluable resource for the Western mind to glean an insight into Eastern thinking.

15. Fritjof Capra, *The Tao of Physics: An Exploration of the Parallels Between Modern Physics and Eastern Mysticism* (London: Fontana Paperbacks, 1983). Capra writes, "In modern physics, the universe is thus experienced as a dynamic, inseparable whole which always includes the observer in an essential way. In this experience, the traditional concepts of space and time, of isolated objects, and of cause and effect, lose their meaning. Such an experience, however, is very similar to that of the Eastern mystics. The similarity becomes apparent in quantum and relativity theory, and becomes even stronger in the 'quantum-relativistic' models of subatomic physics where both these theories combine to produce the most striking parallels to Eastern mysticism" (p. 93).

16. Sally P. Springer and George Deutsch, *Left Brain, Right Brain* (San Francisco: W.H. Freeman, 1981).

17. Hoffer, op. cit., p. 105.

18. *The Quotable Einstein*, collected by Alice Calaprice (Princeton, NJ: Princeton University Press, 1996).

19. Capra, op. cit., p. 45.

20. J. A. Barnes, *A Pack of Lies: Towards a Sociology of Lying* (New York: Cambridge Books, 1994).

21. Pitrim Sorokin, *The American Sex Revolution* (Boston: Porter Sargent, 1956), p. 56.

22. "Interviews with Economists," *The Washington Post*, November 5, 1979, Business section, 1.

23. Sorokin, op. cit, p. 183.

24. Walt Whitman, *Leaves of Grass* (New York: Signet Classic, 1958), p. 49.

25. Ralph Waldo Emerson, *Writings* (New York: Modern Library, 1950), pp. 145–169.

26. Henry David Thoreau, *Walden & Civil Disobedience*, ed. Thomas Owen (New York: W.W. Norton, 1966).

27. Alexis de Tocqueville, *Democracy in America* (Vol. I) (New York: Knopf, 1945). In the spring of 1997, C-Span sponsored a revisiting of Tocqueville's 1831–32 visit to the United States, commencing in Newport, RI, where it all began.

28. Richard Reeves, *American Journey: Traveling with Tocqueville in Search of America* (New York: Simon & Schuster, 1982).

29. Page Smith, *Killing the Spirit: Higher Education in America* (New York: Penguin Book, 1990), pp. 199–222.

30. Jeff Jacoby (*The Boston Globe*), "The Low State of Higher Education," *The Tampa Tribune*, October 16, 1996, Nation/World, 16

31. Ibid.

32. *The Oxford Dictionary of Quotations* (London: Oxford University Press, 1950), #22, p. 323: Macaulay's "Lays of Ancient Rome."

33. Christopher Lehmann-Haupt (*New York Times*), *The Tampa Tribune*, May 13, 1982, Commentary, 6. He sees the absurdity of this vocational mind-set in his review of *The One Minute Manager* (New York: Morrow, 1982) by K. Blanchard and J. Johnson. He writes, "Despite

this book's claim that people are not pigeons, it implies that people are like pigeons, only more complicated to the *degree they don't like to perceive they are being manipulated.*"

34. Herbert Marcuse, *One-Dimensional Man*, reprint of 1964 edition (London: Ark Paperbacks, 1986). Marcuse writes, "We are again confronted with one of the most vexing aspects of advanced industrial civilization: the rational character of its irrationality" (p. 9).

35. Edward de Bono, *Parallel Thinking* (London: Penguin Books, 1995), p. 127.

36. Regarding school attendance alone, Japanese public school children go two months longer than American students, while German and South Korean students go at least a month longer. Only great Britain and France have equivalent school terms. U.S. educators, however, are pushing for longer school years.

37. Beverly Geber, "The Resurrection of Ford," *Training: The Magazine of Human Resources Development*, April 1989, pp. 23–32.

38. Paul A. Banas, "Employee Involvement: A Sustained Labor/Management Initiative at the Ford Motor Company," *Productivity in Organizations*, ed. John P. Campbell, Richard J. Campbell and Associates (San Francisco: Jossey-Bass Publishers, 1988), pp. 388–415.

39. James R. Fisher, Jr., "Trip Report of Ford International Visit," July 18, 1989 (unpublished).

40. Paul Hersey, *The Situational Leader* (New York: Warner Books, 1985).

41. John P. Kotter, *The Leadership Factor*, Free Press, New York, 1988.

42. Geber, op. cit., pp. 23, 32.

43. Fisher, op. cit.

44. Bill Day, "The Cry of the Future—Leaders!" *International Herald Tribune*, February 24, 1988 (editorial cartoon).

45. Sherry Buchanan, "A Call for Leadership: Managers Need Not Apply," *International Herald Tribune*, February 11, 1988.

46. Garry Wills, *Certain Trumpets: The Call of Leaders* (New York: Simon & Schuster, 1994). Wills has a splendid but simple definition of leadership: The leader is one who mobilizes others toward a goal shared by the leader and followers.

47. Max Weber, *Protestant Ethic and the Spirit of Capitalism* (reprint of 1920 edition) (New York: Scribner & Sons, 1977).

48. James MacGregor Burns, *Leadership* (New York: Harper & Row, 1978).

49. Henri Troyat, *Peter the Great* (New York: Dutton, 1987).

50. Andrew Pollack (*New York Times* Service), "Can Steven Jobs Pull It Off This Time?: Apple's Founder Seeks Comeback with 'Next'-Generation Computer," *International Herald Tribune*, November 14–15, 1987, Business/Finance, 1. Jobs did pull it off, while Apple computer has been stumbling ever since. In 1997, Apple rehired Jobs as a consultant. Why? To rediscover Apple's old magic. Thus, the irony continues. The beleaguered chief executive officer of Apple Computer, Gil Amelio, was ousted in July 1997, while Jobs and the chief financial officer, Fred Anderson, were elevated to new roles. There is an important lesson here. Macintosh operating systems, from the beginning, were not made compatible with competitors' products. This failure to perceive the atmosphere of compatibility in the competitive marketplace today may eventually lead to Apple's demise.

51. Judith Bardwick, *The Plateauing Trap* (New York: AMACOM, 1986), p. 110.

52. J. Eugene Haas and Thomas E. Drabek, *Complex Organization: A Sociological Perspective* (New York: Macmillan, 1973), pp. 95–121.

53. Colin Wilson, *Access to Inner Worlds* (London: Rider & Company, Ltd., 1983), p. 125

54. Gregory Bateson, *Steps to an Ecology of Mind* (New York: Ballantine Books, 1972), pp. 206–212.

55. Chris Argyris, "A Few Words in Advance," *Failure of Success*, ed. A. J. Marrow (New York: AMACOM, 1972).
56. H. Ross Perot, "How I Would Turn Around GM," *Fortune Magazine*, February 15, 1988, pp. 22–26.
57. "Insiders: General Motors—Perot's Impatient," *USA Today*, January 30, 1988, Business, 1.
58. Thomas Moore, "Make-or-Break Time for General Motors, *Fortune*, February 15, 1988, pp. 14–20. In 1988, GM decided to be a different company. For that decision, and the concomitant commitment to excellence, GM in 1997 is again the leader in its industry.
59. Colin Wilson, *The Outsider* (New York: Dell Publishing Company, 1956), p. 281.

Afterword

There is no doubt that healthy-mindedness is inadequate as a philosophical doctrine, because the evil facts which it positively refuses to account for are a genuine portion of reality; and they may after all be the best key to life's significance, and possibly, the only openers of our eyes to the deepest levels of truth.[1]

William James

What does it take to turn a "have not" into a "have" nation? Does it simply require imitating economic techniques, or does it involve such intangibles as culture, social structure, and attitudes toward foreign practices?[2]

Paul Kennedy

As the *Six Silent Killers* began, so it ends. The workforce has changed, but the organization has not. Most organizations don't know how to manage, motivate, or mobilize this new workforce, and so productivity figures continue to tumble. Everyone is frustrated. Workers are not aware of their power and, instead of being confrontational, are more likely to hide in the *six silent killers*. Managers are aware of their declining control, and so hang on desperately to old ways. To reconcile the situation, it requires the mind shift alluded to by psychologist William James and a cultural shift referred to by historian Paul Kennedy. Trust is at issue. Workers don't trust management. Management doesn't trust workers. And neither workers nor managers trust themselves. Consequently, trust is a word game played out by cynics. As one prominent executive put it, "Organizations don't give a damn about people. They ride and fall on economics. When times are good, people get treated fairly well. When times are bad, they get short shrift. It's the law of the jungle."

This cynicism is a luxury we can ill afford. The stakes are too high. It doesn't justify the guerrilla tactics of the *six silent killers*, nor the callous disregard of workers

265

and managers to each other. They are not adversaries but teammates. This post-industrial, post-modern age now finds it necessary to fall back on the bonding of the pre-industrial era, approximating the informal interdependence of the European guilds. Paul Kennedy sees the key issues as culture, social structure, and attitudes toward new or unfamiliar practices. Moreover, Kennedy wonders if the developing countries of the globe can keep pace with the developed nations. He writes, "what is clear is that the regions of the globe most affected by the twin impacts of technology and demography lie in the developing world. Whether they succeed in harnessing the new technologies in an environmentally prudent fashion, and at the same time go through a demographic transition, will probably affect the prospects of global peace in the next century more than any other factor."[3]

Obviously, it is difficult for an American to ponder such matters when: (1) the Dow has broken through the ceiling of 8,000; (2) both bond and equity markets are improbably rising together and holding firm to gains; (3) the rates of inflation and unemployment are both amazingly low at the same time (an unprecedented situation); and the GDP, which measures the rate of productivity in goods and services of American workers, couldn't be more impressive. Clearly, we are in unchartered territory. But is it authentic or, as William James might say, is it "inadequate...because the evil facts which it positively refuses to account for are a genuine portion of reality"?

Crises have always gotten our attention. The current situation is no different. Long overdue corrections are being made to bloated corporate staffs. Those still employed feel overworked. Despite this, the short-term gains speak for themselves. There is nothing that Americans cannot accomplish once they set their minds to the tasks at hand. For many organizations, but certainly not the majority, there have been positive breakthroughs which indicate that sustained growth, development, and new levels of productivity are possible with *soft approaches* to doing business.[4]

The Good News—Maybe: The Burgeoning Professional Class

According to the *United States Department of Labor Study of White-Collar Employment Growth*, the percentage of non-production workers has doubled since the end of World War II, going from 15 percent of total manufacturing employment to more than 30 percent. The increase is even greater in some industries, such as the chemical and allied products industry, where in 1983 the percentage of non-production workers was already 44.5 percent. The four fastest growing occupations in the next decade, according to the Bureau of Labor Statistics projections, are all white-collar. They are computer programmers, computer systems analysts, paralegals, and medical assistants. Indeed, nine out of every ten new jobs are created in such service fields as telecommunications, communications, trade, finance, insurance, real estate, and government, according to the Bureau. At the same time, the occupations which are declining precipitously are all blue-collar—machine operators in iron, steel, glass, and textile industries and tenders in shoe manufacturing.[5]

"Some observers," the report states, "are predicting that whitecollar workers could jump to 90 percent of the workforce by the year 2000." Presently, it is pressing 80 percent of the workforce. The Census Bureau reports the biggest job growth is in the executive ranks, where jobs grew by 50 percent in a 20-year period (1974–94). At the other end of the spectrum, we have a critical shortage of skilled labor. This finds U.S. firms importing as many as one million workers annually to meet their skilled labor needs, according to Richard D. Reinhold, president of the National Association of Temporary Services. "If we start running out of skilled workers," he warns, "it could cripple us as a competitive global economy."[6]

Professionals come into the labor force after years in school, but with little application experience. They can be trained, but this takes time and money. Too many college-trained people today come out of school looking for a position, not a job; for a secure lifestyle, not challenging work. What these times require is a mind shift. If professionals accept the fact that they are essentially untrained but trainable and, yes, undereducated but educable, the problem could resolve itself. Obviously, the American economy has deep problems, but there are some encouraging signs.

Reinventing the Corporation

During the 1990s, several companies have demonstrated schemes to eradicate the *six silent killers*, but they have not been widely published. Business leaders have been preoccupied with downsizing and damage control, while the press has been obsessed with what these practices have done to workers' lives. True, to improve productivity, corporations have largely come to rely on cost-cutting measures such as downsizing and outsourcing—replacing in-house labor with outside contractors or less expensive temporary workers. The result has spawned the *six silent killers* and a "new ruthless economy."[7] In a growing segment of the corporate culture, however, the interests of managers, workers, and shareholders are closely and deliberately linked. These *soft approaches* may be the best way to defeat these pesky *social termites*. First, workers are given more direct responsibility and control over their jobs. Second, they are given the training and information necessary to exercise their new responsibilities. Third, part of their compensation is linked to their performance. Workers are also given reassurances that layoffs will be used only as a last resort. Employees tend to be happier, more productive, and better paid under collaborative work arrangements.

These arrangements are not readily embraced because, first, the workforce must be re-educated, and then managers must be persuaded to accept diminished authority. This is more difficult than cost-cutting measures. Studies by the American Management Association of firms that have cut back their workforces since 1990, however, indicate that fewer than half raised profits and only a third increased production. Approximately 40 percent of executives at the companies surveyed were unhappy with the results. Instead, they found cost-cutting measures had a negative impact on company morale, that many key workers chose to leave, and that those who stayed were susceptible to "burnout from being expected to take on too much work."[8] To counter this possibility, many corporations are reinventing themselves.

United Airlines: Employee Ownership[9]

United Airlines was in dire straits when employees decided to purchase the airline. The company quickly gained a larger share of the market, and it has continued to increase productivity and profitability more rapidly than its competitors. It has also increased employment by 8,000 workers while its rivals were retrenching. These achievements have been reflected in the stock price, which has tripled since the buyout. But it has not been accidental. After the buyout, a group of pilots, ramp workers, and managers devised a simple way to use electricity instead of jet fuel when planes are idling at the gate, thus saving the airline $20 million a year. The only capital investment required was longer ladders so the ramp workers could plug in the electric cables.

United's employees acquired their shares in the company through an Employee Stock Ownership Plan (ESOP), a pension plan that requires a majority of its assets to be invested in the stock of the sponsoring company and is allowed to borrow to do so. The simple ownership of shares is not by itself sufficient to bring about the kind of "high-performance" workplace that has evolved at United. Employees directly participate in the choice of top management and the running of the company, which is rare for ESOP holders. Like other pension plans, ESOPs tend to be controlled by management, which may use them to further its own interests rather than those of the workers. The key here is worker participation in the management of the company. In addition to the fuel-saving plan, one team at United recommended hiring temporary workers at $7 an hour to help unload skis during the winter, far below the $38 an hour that ramp workers earn for overtime. Another team recommended giving pilots flexibility to swap assignments. This helped reduce sick time by 17 percent in 1995, saving the company almost $20 million annually. "We're no longer a company that operates by command and control," CEO Gerald Greenwald reflects as he reminisces about United's former rigid managerial style. He concedes that United now has a much more responsive culture, which is both worker- and customer-friendly.

Kingston Technology: Profit Sharing[10]

Kingston Technology is neither unionized nor employee-owned. This California company announced an unprecedented $100 million staff bonus in December 1996. Kingston makes memory boards for personal computers. During the last decade, its staff has grown from 5 to more than 500 employees. From the first, it has reserved some 5–10 percent of its net profits for employee bonuses, which it distributes quarterly on the basis of seniority and performance. Kingston continues to grow and profit as employees are strongly committed. The average bonus per employee for 1996 was $75,000. Most employees received from one to more than three times their annual salaries, which mean $300,000 or more for some.[11]

Lincoln Electric: Incentive Management[12]

Lincoln Electric is the country's largest manufacturer of arc welding equipment and supplies. It attributes much of its success to its incentive management plan, which was instituted early in the century. Between 1934 and 1974, productivity at Lincoln rose about twice as rapidly as that of its competitors, enabling the company to maintain its leading position in the industry, ahead of much larger companies such as General Electric and Westinghouse. It also paid its workers average annual bonuses that nearly matched their base pay. In 1974, some factory workers at Lincoln earned $45,000, approximately five times the then-current median income for manufacturing workers.

The company's labor policies are based on three key elements: production workers are still paid for "piecework," that is, solely on the basis of what they actually produce. Annual bonuses are based on profitability of the company and are granted according to the merit ratings of each employee. All jobs are guaranteed so that workers won't resist new ideas or innovations to their work stations.

Incidentally, during the recession of the early 1980s, workers were given sales jobs instead of being laid off. Loyalty to employees is part of the culture. Lincoln's incentive scheme is reinforced in a number of other ways. The company has no formal organization chart, few layers of management, and few visible distinctions between management and workers. It promotes from within and encourages communication between workers and management, both informally and through an advisory board consisting of elected representatives who meet twice a month with top management. Lincoln stock is also sold to employees. More than half of the employees are stockholders. Lincoln, similar to the Japanese "Just-In-Time" (JIT) material handling, has always had materials directed from the receiving dock to the work stations. Workers operate like independent contractors, ordering, controlling, managing, and using the supplies they need. One veteran employee remarked, "You're pretty much your own boss as long as you do your job. You're responsible for your own work and you even put your stencil on every machine you work on. That way if it breaks down in the field and they have to take it back, they know who's responsible."

About 25 percent of Lincoln's new employees quit in their first year. They are not comfortable with a merit system, nor with the emphasis on individual responsibility. They confess (at their exit interviews) that it puts too much pressure on them. But few leave after the first year. In 1993 the average earnings for production workers were $51,000, while many earned more than $100,000.

General Motors "Second Chance"—Fremont, California, Plant[13]

Do you recall the failure of teams to take hold at GM's Van Nuys plant (page 132)? Well, the Fremont plant could have been the same story. Instead, it proves every company has the employees it needs to be successful. General Motors' plant in Fremont, California provides tangible evidence. The Fremont plant was plagued by alcoholism and drug use among its workers, poor quality and low productivity, and exceptionally high levels of absenteeism. On Fridays and Mondays there were often not enough workers to run the assembly line. The plant closed in 1982.

In 1984, GM and Toyota formed a new joint venture at this closed plant. The new operation did not introduce new technology. Nor did it do away with the United

Auto Workers (UAW) union. Indeed, fully 85 percent of the company's former workers were rehired, including their union leadership. These "second chance" workers soon doubled the best levels achieved at the old Fremont plant, and levels were 40 percent higher than the average GM plant. Meanwhile, quality soon became superior to any other automobile plant in the United States.

Changes made were modest, but they did shift the relationship between management and workers into a true partnership. The company cut managers' pay and recalled outsourced work before laying off workers. Job applications were screened jointly by management and the UAW. Initially, all workers received extensive training—250 hours during their first six months compared to less than 50 hours at most other GM plants. This was followed by continuous training with an emphasis on a wide range of skills. Incredibly, the number of job classifications was cut from 50 to 2. Moreover, workers were divided into teams of five to ten people. Teams were responsible for organizing their assigned work into respective tasks and determining how frequently assignments should be rotated. In other words, they were mobilized into self-directed work teams. Team leaders were chosen in agreement between management and the union and were paid less than 50 cents more an hour than team members. Bonuses were based on the plant's efficiency and customer satisfaction.

So What!

As consistently powerful and positive as these simple approaches are, most companies still resist them. Why? Perhaps because we have not recovered, as a culture, from the euphoria of *crisis management* in World War II. Management's *wunderstat* or miraculous feat in that war still rings heady. Then, too, there seems a reluctance to use *soft approaches* to hard problems. Lee Iacocca, commenting on United Airlines' employee buyout, insisted, "Somebody's crazy. It can't work."[14] But it is working. These *soft approaches* appear to be the best return-on-the-individual (ROI) because of a set of complementary practices: (1) performance-based pay, (2) job security, (3) training, (4) worker participation in teams, (5) job rotation, (6) systematic information sharing, and (7) an appropriate and sustaining workplace culture. Conversely, the adoption of any one of these practices alone has little effect on productivity. Only a concerted commitment to this combination of *soft approaches*, difficult as they might be to orchestrate, is likely to keep the *six silent killers* at bay. That is why this is management's greatest challenge.

Endnotes

1. William James, *The Varieties of Religious Experience* (New York: Mentor, 1958), pp. 137–138.
2. Paul Kennedy, "Preparing for the 21st Century: Winners and Losers," *The New York Review*, February 11, 1993, p. 32.
3. Ibid.
4. Roger E. Alcaly, "Reinventing the Corporation," *The New York Review*, April 10, 1997, pp. 38–45.

5. David Szynanski, "Skilled Labor Shortage Ahead, Experts Say," *The Tampa Tribune*, March 25, 1990, Business/Finance section, 1.

6. Ibid.

7. Simon Head, "The New, Ruthless Economy," *The New York Review*, February 29, 1996, pp. 47–52.

8. "When Slimming Is Not Enough," *The Economist,* September 3, 1994, pp. 59–60. Article captures the limits of downsizing.

9. Alcaly, op. cit., pp. 38, 40, 42.

10. Alcaly, op. cit., p. 40.

11. "Company Gives $100 Million in Bonuses" (An Associated Press Report), *The Tampa Tribune*, December 18, 1996, Business/Finance, 1.

12. Alcaly, op. cit., pp. 42, 44.

13. Alcaly, op. cit., pp. 41–42. See also David I. Levine, *Reinventing the Workplace: How Business and Employees Can Both Win* (Washington, D.C.: The Brookings Institution, 1996).

14. "United We Own," *Business Week*, March 18, 1996, pp. 96–100.

Index

273